An Introduction to *Piers Plowman*

NEW PERSPECTIVES ON MEDIEVAL LITERATURE:
AUTHORS AND TRADITIONS

UNIVERSITY PRESS OF FLORIDA

Florida A&M University, Tallahassee
Florida Atlantic University, Boca Raton
Florida Gulf Coast University, Ft. Myers
Florida International University, Miami
Florida State University, Tallahassee
New College of Florida, Sarasota
University of Central Florida, Orlando
University of Florida, Gainesville
University of North Florida, Jacksonville
University of South Florida, Tampa
University of West Florida, Pensacola

AN INTRODUCTION TO
Piers Plowman

Michael Calabrese

Foreword by Tison Pugh and R. Barton Palmer

UNIVERSITY PRESS OF FLORIDA
Gainesville / Tallahassee / Tampa / Boca Raton
Pensacola / Orlando / Miami / Jacksonville / Ft. Myers / Sarasota

Copyright 2016 by Michael Calabrese
All rights reserved
Printed in the United States of America on acid-free paper

This book may be available in an electronic edition.

22 21 20 19 18 17   6 5 4 3 2 1

First cloth printing, 2016
First paperback printing, 2017

Library of Congress Cataloging-in-Publication Data
Names: Calabrese, Michael A., author. | Pugh, Tison, author of foreword. |
Palmer, R. Barton, 1946– author of foreword.
Title: An introduction to Piers Plowman / Michael Calabrese ; foreword by
Tison Pugh and R. Barton Palmer.
Description: Gainesville : University Press of Florida, [2016] | Includes
bibliographical references and index.
Identifiers: LCCN 2016015357 | ISBN 9780813062709 (cloth) | ISBN 9780813064574
(pbk.)
Subjects: LCSH: Langland, William, 1330?–1400? Piers Plowman. | Christian
poetry, English (Middle)—Criticism, Textual. | Mercy in literature. |
Justice in literature.
Classification: LCC PR2015 .C25 2016 | DDC 821/.1—dc23
LC record available at https://lccn.loc.gov/2016015357

The University Press of Florida is the scholarly publishing agency for the State
University System of Florida, comprising Florida A&M University, Florida Atlantic
University, Florida Gulf Coast University, Florida International University, Florida
State University, New College of Florida, University of Central Florida, University
of Florida, University of North Florida, University of South Florida,
and University of West Florida.

University Press of Florida
15 Northwest 15th Street
Gainesville, FL 32611-2079
http://upress.ufl.edu

For the parents of 95 Lincoln Place, Irvington, New Jersey, proud Italian Americans who sacrificed, labored, and fought for their families, their children, and their nation

Ann Genevieve Catapano LoRusso, my godmother, the best Italian cook, whose specialty was fried hot peppers and who kept our traditions from the Old Country alive. A woman of uncommon strength and a loving heart. Cherished mother of my cousins Susan Mary LoRusso Evans and Dr. Robert LoRusso.

Her husband, my godfather, Salvatore Daniel "Chip" LoRusso, the bravest and kindest of men, soldier and wounded combat veteran of World War II, a sergeant in the Second Armored Division under General Patton, and a man renowned for his care of his mother, Maria Incoronata Romano LoRusso.

His sister, my mother, Beatrice Anne "Zip" LoRusso Calabrese, a radiant and beatific woman, naturalist, philosopher, singer, and violinist.

And her husband, my father, Orlando Joseph Calabrese, naval gunner aboard the Liberty ship *Henry Bacon* during World War II, a gifted carpenter, and the purest, most sensitive reader of literature I have ever known.

CONTENTS

Foreword ix
Preface xi
Note on the Texts xxi
Acknowledgments xxiii
Chronology xxvii
Life of the Poet 1

NARRATIVE READING GUIDE

Preface to the Narrative Reading Guide: Overview of A, B, and C 17

1. Working and Wandering as the World Asks: The Prologues of A, B, and C 23

2. Becoming a God by the Gospel: Passus 1 of A, B, and C 34

3. Lady Mede Gets Ready for Her Close-Up: Passus 2 of A, B, and C 44

4. Lady Mede Tries Everything: Passus 3 of A, B, and C 53

5. An Illegal Interlude between Peace and Wrong: Passus 4 of A, B, and C 64

6. I Confess: Passus 5 of the A Text 71

7. And I Confess as Well: Passus 5 of the B Text and C Text Passūs 5–7 78

8. A Pilgrim and a Ploughman: Passus 6 of the A Text with the Conclusions of B5 and C7 93

9. The Hunger Artists: Passus 7 of the A Text with B6 and C8 98

10. Dreams of a Pardon: Passus 8 of the A Text with B7 and C9   109

11. On the Road in Search of Dowel: Passūs 9 and 10
of the A Text with B8–9 and C10   120

12. Dame Study Teaches a Lesson: Passus 11 of the A Text with
B10 and 11 (opening) and C11   131

13. John But Puts an End to the A Version   145

14. Farewell My Recklessness: Passus 11 of the B Text with C12–13   153

15. Just Will's Imagination: Passus 12 of the B Text and C14   167

16. The Dinner Party: Passus 13 of the B Text and C15.1–233   176

17. The After Party: Passus 14 of the B Text and C15.234–C16.155   188

18. Free Spirits: Passus B15.1–257 and C16.156–End   198

19. Anima and Free Will Try to Unite the World: Passus
B15.258–End and C17   206

20. Fighting for the Fruit of Charity: B16 and C18   220

21. A Spy, a Samaritan, and the Spirit's Flame: B17 and C19   228

22. Christ Was on Rode: B18 and C20   236

23. Last Man Plowing: B19 and C21   250

24. Anarchists and Antichrist: B20 and C22   260

Langland and His Contemporaries   270

Appendix 1. Persons, Personifications, and Allegorizings
in *Piers Plowman*   283

Appendix 2. Pronunciation Guide: Reading
Piers Plowman Aloud   309

Notes   319

Bibliography   337

Index   349

FOREWORD

A compelling and challenging poem with a complicated manuscript history, *Piers Plowman* has long perplexed, and simultaneously delighted, countless readers. With this volume, *An Introduction to "Piers Plowman,"* Michael Calabrese promises to assist those who find themselves perplexed so that they will then find themselves more readily delighted by this vibrant allegory of medieval life, death, and salvation. As with many medieval allegories, Will's journey implicates the reader in his experiences, and like Virgil to Dante in the *Divine Comedy*, Professor Calabrese guides his readers into enlightenment about this enigmatic but always enjoyable poem.

A highly regarded scholar of medieval literature, and of *Piers Plowman* in particular, Professor Calabrese is an editor of the *Piers Plowman* Electronic Archive and the author of several articles on this poem, including in the *Yearbook of Langland Studies*. He has also been awarded numerous Huntington Library Fellowships to facilitate his scholarship on *Piers Plowman*, and he has directed and performed in a production of its B text for the Chaucer Studio. Professor Calabrese teaches at California State University, Los Angeles, where he has long inspired students with his love for this poem—both for its rough alliterative elegance and for its eternal wisdom about the human condition. With knowledge derived from his extensive experience teaching *Piers Plowman*, Professor Calabrese offers a tour-de-force account of this masterpiece, detailing the unfolding story in all three versions (known as the A, B, and C texts), as he highlights significant changes and the dramatic evolutions of the text as Langland twice reimagined his work. Whereas most introductions to *Piers Plowman* pay almost exclusive attention to the B text—according to many, the poem's most polished version—Professor Calabrese explores these three complementary yet distinct traditions as an organic whole, providing a unique and much-needed new vantage point on a timeless poem.

With each volume in New Perspectives in Medieval Literature: Authors and Traditions, we hope that readers will discover the joys and wonders of medieval literature, a body of work that ages yet never dies. Professor Calabrese has made this objective his life mission, and he has succeeded wonderfully with this invigorating, lucid introduction to William Langland's *Piers Plowman*.

Tison Pugh
R. Barton Palmer
Series Editors

PREFACE

Once a reader begins to engage with the complex and brilliant poem called *Piers Plowman* (*Piers* for short), there is no turning back. This volume attempts to make the poem fundamentally accessible and comprehensible for new readers, who can then decide if, like so many others, they want to dedicate their lives, or a portion thereof, to exploring the infinite mysteries of this compelling but often murky poem. *Piers Plowman*, attributed to William Langland, is a long allegorical poem in Middle English from the late fourteenth century, extant in three discernible versions called the A, B, and C texts depicting the interior and exterior journeys of a man named Will, who seeks Truth, virtue, and salvation.[1] This protagonist, Will, may very well take his name from the poem's author, but he also represents longing and desire, the human will itself. The poem's name derives from its other main character, a plow-owning farmer named Peter, nicknamed Piers. Piers the Plowman becomes the central figure in many of Will's dreams. The plowman's virtue, noble spirit, wisdom, and ultimately his spiritual powers as pope and even as Christ himself inspire Will in his many quests.

Langland divides his poem into apparent books or chapters, called *passūs* (Latin for "steps"; the singular is *passus*) in the manuscripts. Many manuscripts also present a larger, two-part structure, sometimes explicitly dividing the poem into a *visio*, a "vision," which extends through eight chapters of the A text, and then, vastly expanded in B and C, a *vita*—that is, a "life" or biography of three allegorical concepts named Dowel (Do Well), Dobet (Do Better), and Dobest (Do Best), whom Will constantly seeks, however discouraged by the endless evidence of human depravity he witnesses. Whether the medieval scribes or Langland himself invented these designations, they nonetheless provide a global structure for the poem: the term *visio* emphasizes the importance of dreams, while the *vita* recalls the genre of a saint's life and the quest for an exemplary path that readers can follow to liberate themselves from sin.

During his endless walkabouts, Will meets a host of real and allegorical figures. His first assistance comes from Holy Church, who has guided him since birth in the Christian community; she helps him resolve his initial confusion and sets the stage for his upcoming journey through corruption and error in search of Truth. Later he enjoys the guidance of Patience and Conscience and converses with Wit and Thought, who help him to make sense of his experiences. Will learns from Study, Clergy, and Scripture; he eventually meets Faith, Hope, Charity, and many others more. The elaborate cast of virtues, vices, and aspects of the psyche and of Christian clerical life can overwhelm the reader, just as it does the Will. *Piers Plowman* lulls us into a dream, then overwhelms us with information until like Alice in Wonderland we are not quite sure whom to trust or how to proceed through the changing landscapes, confusing plot twists, and often arcane doctrine spoken by revolving players. Since Will often ends up confused, a reader who does not share his confusion must not really be paying attention.

In poetic richness, in intellectual complexity, and as a window into the medieval world, *Piers* stands with the *Canterbury Tales*, the works of the *Gawain* poet, and John Gower's *Confessio Amantis* as the greatest works of Middle English literature. In the broader European context, its peers include the *Roman de la Rose*, *Il libro de Buen Amor*, and Dante's *Commedia*. Reading *Piers Plowman* allows us to participate meaningfully in the study of European religious and social history and also in the study of world literature and culture.[2] Perhaps because the poem involves issues of faith, community, and work, and because it engages explicitly with the histories of government and popular revolt, *Piers Plowman*, always somewhat popular, has found new critical and pedagogic life in the opening decades of the twenty-first century. The New Perspectives Series on Medieval Literature seeks to create interest in, and accessibility to, medieval authors and works. This volume responds to the poem's new ubiquity and to the need for a basic introduction that will inspire readers to engage with the poem.

Reaching *Piers Plowman*

Several impediments prevent access to this poem, and many doors need opening before *Piers* can unlock its treasures. First, Langland's diction and poetics prove more difficult than Chaucer's already substantially complex verse. And though the vocabulary and dialect do not reach the arcane registers of the *Gawain* poems (read primarily in translation), individual lines and passages in *Piers* compete with the most challenging verses in Middle English literature. The poem digresses, speaks obscurely, and features too many characters, dreams, and long speeches. Most readers will find themselves, like Will the dreamer, puzzled, resentful, frustrated, or sleepy. As Dante needs Virgil in the *Divine Comedy* to guide him out of the *Inferno*, readers of *Piers* need help navigating out of the dark, savage wood that they sometimes find themselves in. Langland wrote three versions of *Piers*, none of them called *Paradiso*, so Will's spiritual journey progresses by no means as clearly as Dante's. But Langland offers an urgent message of sin, reform, and grace no less poignant or resonant than the Italian poet's. This book seeks to help readers hear that message. In addition to providing direction through the poem's many, often infernal realms, I will focus also on how Langland simply tells a good story about down-to-earth issues that still matter to modern society.

Knowing who speaks, to whom, and why in any given episode challenges students of *Piers Plowman* in any version. A new volume on *Piers* should therefore provide navigational summary, the single most important aid for new readers. Pure summary can defeat its own purpose in its tedium if one seeks to explain everything said or done in every episode. So I want less to equip readers with "all they need to know" than to inspire them to take on the text, alone and in detail. Therefore this book's Narrative Reading Guide performs an act of literary criticism for each passus of the poem. Although the commentary inherently engages the cultural milieu of fourteenth-century England and contextualizes *Piers Plowman* within the history of Christian doctrine, it does not seek to explain systematically all the poem's historical allusions to persons, places, wars, battles, laws, taxes, and political events.[3] Information, the mother of all literary study, can overwhelm and smother a nascent love of reading *Piers Plowman*, so I seek rather to generate excitement and accessibility, while only minimally entangling the reader in the infinite webs of knowledges and discourses that the poem employs.

I have been ever attentive to basic human meaning and to what I believe the poet intends for his readers to know, think, and feel about sin and salvation. *Piers* employs learning from an academic world that may seem no longer ours and thus appears esoteric, but the poet often provides practical, homey, and stunningly simple bits of wisdom. Langland saw his poetry as a form of moral instruction, teaching the theme "God is Love." If men and women practiced virtue, no author would compose moral poetry, much less 18,000 lines of it, forged and reforged in one poem by one restless man over a lifetime. All the versions of *Piers* reveal the poet's ethical understanding of the function of art: to teach people to do better and to seek spiritual fulfillment instead of material and animal pleasure. This simple but elusive goal informs everything Langland wrote.

Though Langland wrote only one poem, he wrote it three times, and this volume, unlike any other available guide, introduces and navigates through each version, A, B, and C. Study of the poem, in scholarship and in teaching, is moving toward parallel, comparative, and sequential engagement with the versions of *Piers*, especially since A.V.C. Schmidt has completed his parallel edition and commentary for classroom use. In 1990 Malcolm Godden saw the need for, if not exactly parallel, then certainly sequential understanding of the poem(s), and I subscribe as well to his premise in *The Making of "Piers Plowman"* that "one cannot hope to understand the poem without trying to comprehend the ways in which it developed and altered over many years, and still more, the ways in which the author's thinking developed" (vi). In practice I approach the task differently from Godden by moving through each passus instead of each version.[4] But we both engage with *Piers* as a comprehensive corpus at once sequential, parallel, and, paradoxically, simultaneous in its evolution. Unfortunately Godden's premise did not translate comprehensively into a change in critical practice, but now with a surge in resources that support parallel reading, we can explore Godden's contention about how to study the poem. For example, Sarah Wood, in a recent statement to which I wholeheartedly subscribe, writes: "The versions of *Piers Plowman* form a single continuous narrative, with each version in dialogue with the previous one" (*Conscience* 13). Attending to that dynamic dialogue will assist any reader in approaching any version, or set of versions, of *Piers Plowman* in Middle English or in translation.[5]

But parallel study of the poem still presents its challenges. The A text consists of eleven passūs (with a controversial twelfth in some manuscripts). The C text contains twenty-two passūs in a recasting of B's twenty, though C's final two passūs remain unrevised versions of B, perhaps because the poet died before getting to them. Sometimes the revisions proceed in parallel and sometimes they do not, rendering parallel comparison difficult and at times impossible. We can sometimes see clearly how A was revised to B and then to C simply by scanning across the page of a parallel text, or holding one version up next to another. But sometimes one must account for major deletions and additions, and for the outright relocation of blocks of text from one part of the poem to another. The poet and scribes did not carefully prepare the separate versions of the poem so that they could be studied in parallel centuries later, and so no guide can chronicle all the changes and additions.

Instead this book provides the reader with a sense of the evolving story in each version and attends as well to the grander differences among them, considering the character and personality of each text and the ever-aging poet who wrote them. This means drawing more attention to A and to C than they usually receive.[6] The neglect of A and C in the existing handbooks proves self-fulfilling: readers avoid A and C because guides tend not to focus on them, and guides tend not to focus on them because readers avoid them.

Concerning the vast seas of scholarship on the poem, the passus-by-passus "Narrative Reading Guide" does not attempt to chronicle or condense prior scholarship. Its voice and approach to *Piers*, intentionally critically independent, often draws on classroom experience and keeps the new reader in mind by focusing mainly on an internal experience of the poem. Critical summaries and footnotes could impede the fundamental access the book seeks to provide, but throughout the book I do refer readers to important critical works where they can learn more about the text and topic at hand. I have kept this apparatus to a minimum because a comprehensive compilation of *Piers* scholarship would defeat the purpose of a book that seeks to guide readers through all three versions, one parallel set of passūs at a time. The chapters on the poet's life and on Langland and his contemporaries, as well as the appendix on reading *Piers Plowman* aloud, contain robust references to important primary and secondary resources, which the reader will find in the bibliography. These references will take readers beyond a first reading and into the stormy but ever vibrant world of *Piers Plowman* studies, from which they will never want to escape.

Academic study of *Piers* evolves rapidly, enjoying a recent surge of published resources.[7] Whether this surge in publishing has translated so far into broader reading and teaching of the poem remains unclear, but one does have a sense that *Piers* is everywhere, and individual teachers who assign the poem will testify that students love it. For despite its difficulty, *Piers* charms readers with its moving poetry, its amazing wit, its chronicle of medieval life and history, and also its famed, challenging complexity. First-time readers will make the poem their own by embracing it as a daring adventure that explores the human condition, and by wondering if that condition has changed in 650 years. The poem exposes humans as curious, contentious, carnal, addictive, and appetitive, and yet in constant search of love and the divine rewards of a salvation that they can barely convince themselves they deserve. Readers must determine just how "medieval" and how "modern" such conditions are.

Specifically, this book attempts to bring *Piers* to life and show its relevance (not "make" it relevant) for a twenty-first-century reader. Relevance means simply that *Piers* confronts issues—personal, social, theological, civic—that all peoples and societies must struggle with. I am frankly amazed at how vitally the poem works in class and how students embrace it as both prescient and applicable to a range of current social issues. Readers can apply *Piers Plowman* to the real world at each moment of history in which they encounter it. *Piers*, by no means an old dead text, participates in as many contemporary social justice discourses as modern readers can conceive of, just as it did in its own time.

Piers criticizes wealth, praises the poor, and speaks truth to power in ways obviously appealing to contemporary, often politically engaged academia. The poem's potential associations with the pre-Reformation and its attack on the abuses of the Catholic Church, including greedy friars and ignorant parish priests, provide another attraction. Add to that the historical fact that Piers Plowman, the character, appears in the cryptic poems circulated among the leaders of the 1381 Peasants' Revolt, a violent uprising against taxes and wage restrictions, and the poem becomes a seductive dramatic context in which to present medieval literature to modern academia in an activist era.[8] I teach the poem in California, which has a formal holiday in honor of a modern-day Piers the Plowman, the union leader Cesar Chavez. But each local culture and reading community engaging with the poem will feel the irresistible transhistorical power of the archetype, which ought not to be resisted but must be embraced cautiously.

Readers might dangerously fetishize the poem as merely a social-activist rather than a Christian, spiritual work. Readers must balance their engagement. Langland *is* interested in laborers, fair wages, and social justice, no matter whether he would have sanctioned or condemned the actions of the literate "peasants" involved in a bloody revolt against excessive taxation and wage controls. *Piers*, as a reformist poem, takes its proper part in real social history. The archetypal nobility of working with the people and with the soil remains unmistakably powerful: back-breaking work and leadership always win a reader's—and a culture's—respect. All cultures struggle to justify the accumulation of wealth while so many suffer in need and to ensure that workers receive proper pay. The poem provides no simple responses to these issues, but that should not prevent us from applying Langland's concerns to contemporary crises. Such application sensitizes modern readers to the poet's own struggle to adapt Christianity to his own time. For *Piers* comes from a growing fourteenth-century mercantile society trying to apply philosophical and religious doctrines of love and brotherhood formulated in another climate and social system by Jesus of Nazareth, a radical Jewish preacher who, at least in his earthly incarnation, knew nothing of the place and people that would later be England. The need to adapt these doctrines, brought centuries later to "Britain" and then to "England" by Roman people who themselves adapted the Judean doctrines they once persecuted, produces a strange and exciting corpus of English medieval Christian literature. One has to wonder what "love," as both a personal and a social ideology, might mean in the first, fourteenth, or twenty-first century.

In the spirit of the New Perspectives series, this book facilitates study of *Piers Plowman* for modern times, with an eye on the realities of contemporary political life. Much of *Piers* may strike readers as arcane, so a contemporary audience needs a new perspective that permits it to embrace fully the poem's perpetual modernity. Readers perceive this in the poem's many social themes and concerns. *Piers Plowman* teaches doing well in the world, doing better, and then doing best. It shows how to care for—and how not to care for—the poor. It teaches about how to give charitably to the deserving; about which authority figures in government and church one can trust; about whether clergy are fit to accomplish their pastoral duties. And—quite related to our own experiences as students and scholars—it dramatizes the importance of going to school. *Piers* explores the possibility, or impossibility, of interfaith dialogue and religious tolerance; it studies class consciousness and class struggle. *Piers* praises the social role of healthy marriages and the nuclear family. It explores personal ethics and health, warning against eating and drinking to excess. *Piers* compels its readers to see beyond the needs of the body to spiritual truths and values. It warns against letting greed and money run one's life. It teaches how vocation and work shape the individual and the community, and it demonstrates how people can work together to accomplish tasks for the sake of common profit.

Funny, bawdy, raucous, and crowd-pleasing, while at other times contemplative, holy, sublime, and mystical, *Piers Plowman* can provide a moving experience for Christians and Catholics. But its appeal does not exclude, for members of all monotheistic religions will relate to its treatment of the history of Jewish, Muslim, and Christian relations. The poem contains as well what I would call, variously, Buddhist or Hindu moments, instances of nonattachment, of divine awareness, and the call for liberation from the imprisoning power of desire. Though Langland wrote for a Christian audience and does not refer explicitly to Eastern religions, of which he would have known little, he crafts *Piers* as a philosophical and ethical document that will appeal to readers from any religion, or none. Further, *Piers* features a man named Will acting young and immorally foolish. He makes friends with characters called "longing of the eyes" and "desire of the flesh," both women, supported by an undesirable named Recklessness. The episode of youthful "immortal" thinking will resonate with readers of all ages and genders, across religions, across cultures, and across time and place. Since Will grows from this reckless youth to old age and infirmity in the poem, seasoned readers, as it were, will relate to his frailty and the lessons he has learned in leaving youth behind. Readers can relate to *Piers* at various stages of their lives, for Langland, like any great poet, somehow seems to have known what would be perpetually important to all men and women.

An aspect of the book's new perspective concerns my engagement with these topics in teaching the poem at an HACU–designated Hispanic Serving Institution, California State University, Los Angeles. Students from the Hispanic cultures of Southern California, with roots in the religious cultures of Mexico and Central America, potentially have insight into, and direct experience with, the living history of religious institutions and doctrines. They know what friars are because of the twenty-one missions that friars built here, some of which are still the actual parishes they attend. Some scholars espouse the idea that medieval European literature, British literature, canonical literature of any kind, by definition, belongs to the "dominant" culture in that it contains the histories of race, class, and gender oppressions in Western civilization that scholars in the modern academy must unmask in the classroom and in criticism. The remedy for this misconception lies in providing access and ownership for all students to a shared medieval past. Not everyone, and in fact not anyone, has any apparent or unique point of access into medieval English literature. Teachers have the particular burden of bridging the gap between canonicity and relevance to provide for all students the coin of cultural capital—the currency of intellectual distinction in the East and West for nearly three millennia. Awareness of this past allows readers to combat the possible marginalization that comes from dividing students into dominant and minority literary cultures. As a poem inherently engaged with social politics, *Piers* can excite students as it excited Langland's original readers. Social relevance draws the reader into an alien medieval world and reveals it, finally, as not alien at all.

In the chapters that follow, this book offers a historical chronology, an exploration of the life of the poet, and the "Narrative Reading Guide," divided into twenty-four short sections, constituting the heart of the book. Then it considers some influences and analogues in "Langland and His Contemporaries," followed by a list titled "Persons, Personifications, and Allegorizings in *Piers Plowman*" in appendix 1. Appendix 2 offers a pronunciation guide called "Reading *Piers Plowman* Aloud" which exhorts readers to stop often in their studies and simply listen to the poet. Perhaps more than any other poet of his time, Langland compels readers to think deeply about the doctrines that he explores, but he also takes over the reader's mouth, ears, and gut with the sounds of his poetry. So I invite readers to give voice to the verses quoted and thus to let the body tell the mind what the poetry means. For this reason and for many reasons I have featured in this preface, readers could very well become aroused with the desire to return again and again to this most rewarding and recalcitrant of poems, which, as any longtime reader will attest, repays study and reveals ever new mysteries.

NOTE ON THE TEXTS

Since the book describes the ABC changes in parallel, I employ and cite Schmidt's parallel edition of the poem. Not all readers will have that book, but with no easy solution to the problem of presenting *Piers* in three versions for first-time readers, for utility's sake one text must be chosen for citation. I replace Schmidt's single quotation marks with double, and according to the requirements of my own syntax, I either do or do not retain his initial capitalization of each line in lieu of multiplying brackets needlessly to indicate changes. The consistency of using one edition as a base will foster clarity, transparency, and accessibility, and Schmidt's edition, a brilliantly engineered piece of textual scholarship, provides a wealth of information about the poet and the poem, so I heartily recommend its use and adoption.[1] The most authoritative, though by no means uncontroversial, editions of *Piers* are those in the Athlone Press series edited by George Kane (A), Kane and E. Talbot Donaldson (B), and George Russell and Kane (C). They permit serious, advanced study of the poem but are unfriendly to students and to general readers because they offer little or no explanatory notes and are no longer in print. Readers using the Vaughan edition of the A text, the Norton Critical Edition of the B text edited by Robertson and Shepherd, and Derek Pearsall's C text may have to adjust the line citations slightly when looking up passages cited here.

I provide modern English glosses of difficult words throughout the quotations, in brackets.[2] Readers should distinguish these translation reading aids from Schmidt's (very few) Middle English emendations, also in brackets.

When citing the texts, I provide version, passus, and line numbers, for example (C15.1–10), but when making a rapid series of quotations of the same version and passus within the same paragraph, I abbreviate subsequent references to the lines alone, so a reference to any following verses from C15 would read simply (11–20) or (45–55) for the remainder of that paragraph. When lines only are given, readers should refer to the most proximate citation above. Block quotations, however, always provide full citations, and when alternating between versions within paragraphs, I also provide only full citations, my standard being clarity and ease of reference in all cases. Often in discussing exposition identified as appearing in "all" (ABC) or in "both" (BC) versions, I quote or cite only one text as representative, adding references to or quotations of the other versions only when wanting to highlight a significant variation. When glossing Langland's quotations from the Latin scripture, I provide English translations from the Douay-Rheims Bible, an English rendering of the Latin Vulgate, which is the book that Langland and his audience used.[3] When Langland quotes other short bits of Latin such as legal maxims, aphorisms, and phrases from the Church Fathers, or when he paraphrases or merges scriptural quotations, the English glosses are mine.

ACKNOWLEDGMENTS

When I first contemplated this work, my colleagues Julia Boffey and Tony Edwards offered enthusiastic support for such an introductory guide; their words were always with me as I ventured through this project. Paul Thomas, director of the Chaucer Studio, has been a constant prop, and our work together in recording the entire B text of *Piers Plowman* has taught me so much about the poem and the dynamic possibilities of its performance. While working on this volume I have also furthered my research with the *Piers Plowman* Electronic Archive, an ever-evolving force in the future of *Piers* studies, founded by my great teacher Hoyt Duggan and now directed by the heirs apparent, Tim Stinson and Jim Knowles. I acknowledge their support as well that of my coeditors for the upcoming archive edition of Hm143 (X), Mrs. Gail Duggan and Patricia "Captain Janeway" Bart who always fights to get us home while never compromising our values. Our work in the archive has constantly catalyzed my critical study of *Piers*. The session "Teaching *Piers Plowman*" organized by Jennifer Sisk at Kalamazoo in 2014 offered wonderful support by caring colleagues, including Thomas Goodman, my *paesana* Gina Brandolino, and our spiritual advisor, Sister Mary Clemente Davlin OP, whose great wisdom and kindly benedictions nourish the minds and souls of so many. And I thank as well Míċeál Vaughan, Elizabeth Robertson and Stephen H. A. Shepherd, A.V.C. Schmidt, and Derek Pearsall for their respective editions of *Piers*, constant companions and sources of clarifying wisdom throughout my labors. If my book inspires students to return again and again to their editions, I will have accomplished my goal.

I want to thank the reader's services staff at the Huntington Library for endless support over the years, and I thank the library in particular for a fellowship in the summer of 2013, which allowed me to further work on this book in the afternoons while by day pursuing manuscript study for the archive. At the University Press of Florida, acquisitions editor Shannon McCarthy labored thoughtfully over this manuscript, shepherding it through many rounds of review and revision, always attentive and dedicated to the creation of an excellent and useful book; I thank her for her warmth and generosity. Nevil Parker sensitively oversaw the book's shaping and production, and Ann Marlowe copyedited keenly and insightfully, in a spirit of camaraderie and collaboration. The review process was the most professional and rigorous that I have ever experienced. The reviewers, later revealed to me as Sarah Wood of the University of Warwick and Tison Pugh of University of Central Florida, powerfully disciplined my wayward exposition into rhetorically sober, humane prose. Dr. Wood, true to the lineage of her hero Conscience, saved this author from untold error and discovered so many seams and fissures in need of critical carpentry. Her discernment and acumen in matters historical, textual, and comical made her reports indispensable to revision. Tison Pugh models his editorial methods after the character Terrance Fletcher in the film *Whiplash*, played by J. K. Simmons in an Oscar-winning performance. His uncompromising rigor drew from me the kind of drumming I would not have thought myself capable of. Countless hours spent with four-hundred-page stacks of notes and annotations from the reviewers taught me more about critical writing than I could have imagined possible after a quarter-century career. All remaining errors of conception and execution are mine alone. I also thank Tison, wearing his other hat as the series editor, and Barton Palmer for welcoming my book into the New Perspectives series.

All the work here is newly composed for the specific context of the series, with no reprint of previous essays. Readers may hear an occasional turn of phrase from my "Interior Visions: *Piers Plowman* and the Dream Vision Genre," in DeMaria, Chang, and Zacher's *Companion to British Literature*, from which I reworked a few paragraphs when I composed my first draft of this book. Also, while finishing this work, I was asked to contribute to a festschrift for A. C. Spearing, edited by Cristina Maria Cervone and D. Vance Smith, for which I composed "Langland's Last Words." In that essay I selected and elaborated further upon some C-text revisions that I had discussed in this book, examining what I take to be Langland's final labors in the particular context of Professor Spearing's achievements.

Readers will find both these essays independent of, and complementary to, the work in this volume.

I could not have finished this book without a sabbatical for the fall quarter of 2014 and a Creative Leave in the spring quarter of 2015, a welcome instance of support from my school, California State University, Los Angeles. I salute my brothers and sisters at CSULA, deeply dedicated to our students and our community under the leadership of our president William Covino and our dean Peter McAllister. I am proud to be a part of our august English department, chaired by James Garrett, where I can boast of the finest colleagues, ever eager to provide support and encouragement to one another. I want to thank my students Shane Ochoa, for bibliographic help, and Valarie Guerra, who labored in the initial typing of the Middle English texts. Ms. Guerra's notion of defining characters as agents who effect change in the landscape of the poem helped me to clarify the murky problem of how to determine inclusion in the list of characters in *Piers Plowman*. Jonathan Lee generously entered the project in the spring of 2015 and provided crackerjack proofreading and editorial assistance, including in the construction of the index, displaying great loyalty and dedication to his teacher. I believe Mr. Lee destined for the scholarly life and a professorship of his own, furthering the great Confucian tradition to which he is heir. No acknowledgment of my university is complete without thanking the Three Graces who administer the department and have been my kindly sisters for the past twenty-one years, Jeanne Gee, Yolanda Galvan, and the late Theresa Flores, an astute historian who often defeated me in debate.

My sister, Mary Ann Giglio, a bon vivant, offered endless support to my labors, as did my cousin Andrew LoRusso, the "Singing Chef," maintaining the traditions of his parents, my uncle Andy and aunt Ida, with his fabled ricotta cake, biscotti, and *pizzagaina*. He and his love, the metaphysical Nina, have always welcomed me to Santa Barbara for memorable celebrations *della famiglia*. My niece Samantha Duffy, her husband Sean, and their children Sean and Alexis always host a family dinner when I visit Jersey, providing a welcome respite from scholarly labors and a reminder of the importance of family tradition. And my darling Ying Zen, who never ceases to amaze me with her worldly knowledge, opened her mind and heart to my work, for which I thank her warmly. It will not surprise readers of *Piers Plowman* that an author's thoughts would turn to the themes of love, family, and community, all central to the doctrine of the poem itself. Accordingly this book is dedicated to those in my own *vita* who fulfilled the most important imperative in *Piers Plowman*, to "pay what you owe," in the practice of sacred charity to others and to God.

CHRONOLOGY

This section supplements "Life of the Poet" and "Langland and His Contemporaries" by providing important dates and events in literary, religious, cultural, and political history surrounding *Piers Plowman*. It also indicates significant occasions in the poem's publication history and scholarship.

ca. 1230: Guillaume de Lorris begins the allegorical dream vision *Romance of the Rose*, a poem that Chaucer translates and that influences many English medieval authors, including Langland.

ca. 1280: Jean de Meun's expansion and completion of the *Rose*.

1321: Dante's monumental epic poem the *Divine Comedy*.

ca. 1324: Birth of John Wyclif, Oxford theologian, whose works on simony, disendowment, and the corruption of Church institutions are associated with the Lollard movement and with the spirit of reform throughout the period.

ca. 1325: William Rokele, presumed to be the poet "William Langland," is born, presumably in Cleobury Mortimer in the county of Shropshire in the West Midlands of England.

1327–77: Reign of Edward III.

1337: Start of the series of conflicts between England and France known collectively as the Hundred Years War.

1339: William Rokele receives the tonsure, indicating possible future career in the Church.

1348–49: Black Plague wipes out more than one-third of the population of Europe.

early 1340s: Birth of Chaucer.

ca. 1350: Anonymous composition of the *Pricke of Conscience*.

1351: Statute of Laborers attempts to freeze wages at pre-plague rates in response to rising prices due to labor shortage.

1365: *Piers Plowman*, A version.

1376: Good Parliament, in which many of Edward III's ministers are impeached, along with the king's mistress, Alice Perrers, who many scholars believe is the model for Langland's character Lady Mede.

1377: Coronation of Richard II.

1377: Pope Gregory XI issues bull denouncing Wyclif's positions.

1377–79: *Piers Plowman*, B version.

1378–1418: Papal Schism, as rival popes are elected, serving in Rome and Avignon.

1381: Peasants' Revolt: In response to excessive taxation, bands of rebels declare war on educated authority. They behead Simon Sudbury, archbishop of Canterbury and lord chancellor, for his role in taxation, placing his head on London Bridge, and they march to London to confront King Richard. Their leader Wat Tyler is killed; John Ball as well is later arrested and executed. Despite Richard's strategic consent to their demands, their goal of ending serfdom and achieving what we might call equity fails as the revolt is crushed.

1382, 1395–97: Early and later versions of the Wycliffite Bibles.

1382: Led by the new archbishop of Canterbury William Courtenay, the Blackfriars Council (meeting in the house of the Dominican "black friars" in London) condemns twenty-four propositions of Wyclif, including his positions on the mass, transubstantiation, and papal authority, also accusing him of Donatism for denying that a priest can carry out his office if not in a state of grace. Many modern scholars believe the Council compelled Langland and other English writers to fear censorship and discipline.

1384: Death of John Wyclif.

1385–90: *Piers Plowman*, C version.

ca. 1385–92: Composition of four poems of the anonymous *Gawain* manuscript.

1388: The Lords Appellant, a group of nobles resistant to Richard

II's abuses and recklessness, purge his court at the Merciless Parliament, convicting a number of his advisors of treason.

1388: Second Statute of Laborers, enacted by the Cambridge Parliament, seeks to control the movement of laborers by criminalizing unauthorized movement as vagrancy.

1390–93: Gower's *Confessio Amantis*.

ca. 1390: Death of William Langland.

1395: Julian of Norwich's *Revelations of Divine Love*.

ca. 1390–1425: Proliferation of manuscripts of *Piers Plowman* in various versions and in "split" (combined) texts.

1397–98: Revenge Parliament in which Richard II avenges himself upon the Lords Appellant through seizure of land, exile, execution, and perhaps murder.

1399: Deposition of Richard II; Henry of Lancaster becomes King Henry IV.

1400: Death of Chaucer.

1401: Under Henry IV, Parliament passes De Haeretico Comburendo, which permits the burning of heretics, in an attempt to combat Lollardy.

1408: Death of John Gower.

1409: Archbishop of Canterbury Thomas Arundel issues his Constitutions, which seek to quell the spread of Lollardy through restrictions on books, preaching, the translation of scripture, and university instruction.

1414: Rebellion of followers of the Lollard knight Sir John Oldcastle, who is arrested and executed in 1417.

1415: Council of Constance condemns Wyclif posthumously as heresiarch. Two years later it ends the Great Schism and elects one pope, Martin V.

ca. 1416: Death of Julian of Norwich.

1428: Wyclif's body exhumed, burned, and thrown into the River Swift.

1436: Margery Kempe's autobiography, the *Book of Margery Kempe*, composed.

ca. 1438: Death of Margery Kempe.

1474: William Caxton begins printing books in England, including the *Canterbury Tales* and Gower's *Confessio Amantis*. He does not print *Piers Plowman*.

1550: The radical Protestant reformer Robert Crowley first "publishes" (prints) *Piers Plowman* with an inflammatory anti-Catholic preface, exalting the poem as a forerunner of the Reformation.

1813: Thomas Whitaker's edition, *The Vision of William concerning Piers Plouhman*.

1842: Thomas Wright's edition, *The Vision and the Creed of Piers Ploughman*.

1886: W. W. Skeat publishes a monumental parallel-text edition, determining the distinctions between the A, B, and C versions of *Piers Plowman* and thus beginning modern scholarly engagement with the poem.

1950: The successors of R. W. Chambers, including George Kane, receive approval for the editing project that will later become the Athlone editions.

1952: Thomas A. Knott and David C. Fowler publish their edition of the A version of *Piers Plowman*.

1960, 1975, 1997: Publication of Athlone editions of the A, B, and C texts of *Piers Plowman*.

1987: First publication of the *Yearbook of Langland Studies* (*YLS*).

2000: First text published by the *Piers Plowman* Electronic Archive.

2008: Derek Pearsall's revised edition of the C version of *Piers Plowman* published.

2008: A.V.C. Schmidt completes *Parallel-Text* edition of *Piers Plowman*.

20??: *Piers Plowman* joins Chaucer's *Canterbury Tales* as the most read and most beloved works of Middle English literature.

Life of the Poet

No one knows who wrote *Piers Plowman*, and if someone named William Langland did so, no one knows anything certain about him.[1] The only evidence for that name's association with the poem comes from three notes that readers penned into the pastedowns (the inside covers) of two medieval manuscripts. These short, spontaneous glosses, read together with the few references in the poem to the narrator as "Will," provide the only grounds for attributing the poem to a named author.

The first note, dated ca. 1400, in a manuscript of *Piers Plowman* from Gloucestershire but discovered in Ireland (Dublin, Trinity College, MS D.4.1), reads:

> Memorandum, quod Stacy de Rokayle, pater Willielmi de Langlond, qui Stacius fuit generosus et morabatur in Schiptone under Whicwode, tenens domini le Spenser in comitatu Oxon., qui praedictus Willielmus fecit librum qui vocatur Perys Ploughman. (Adams, *Rokele Family* 19)

> It was Stacy de Rokayle who was William de Langlond's father; this Stacy was of gentle birth and lived in Shipton-under-Wychwood in Oxfordshire, holding land from Lord le Spenser; the aforesaid William wrote the book called *Piers Plowman*. (Kane, *ODNB* 488)[2]

The other notes are found in a manuscript now in the Huntington Library, Hm 128. One, penned by Tudor historian John Bale, offers information similar to that of the Dublin manuscript but gives a different first name for the poet:

> Robertus Langlande natus in comitatu Salopie in villa Mortymers Clybery in the claylande, within .viij. myles of Malborne Hylles scripsit, Peers Ploughman, li. i / In somer season whan set was sunne.
>
> Robert Langland, born in the county of Shropshire in the village of Cleobury Mortimer in the claylands within 8 miles of the Malvern Hills, wrote Piers Plowman, line 1: In somer season whan set was sunne.[3]

The other, a shorter note by Ralph Coppinger (d. 1551), also expresses some confusion as to the name of the poet: "Robert or William langland made pers ploughman." Why were readers confused about the poet's name? The erroneous name "Robert" comes from a misreading of the opening of passus 8 of the B text. The narrative reads at this point, "Thus, yrobed in russet [Thus, robed in homespun woolen]," indicating how Will is coarsely dressed. But some manuscripts (one A and one B text) have the phrase "I Robert" instead of the past participle "y-robed." Thus a sonic mistake led some early readers to think that Robert was the poet's name. This situation illustrates the contingent nature of historical information about the poet.

However, a corrective about the name comes from another line in B (15.152), where the narrator calls himself Will and says he has "lived long in land." Scholars take the hint and have understood this as the poet naming himself: "Will long-land" = William Langland. Langland may be an invented name, and the poet may have really been named William Rokele, but as A.V.C. Schmidt concludes, from the existing evidence, "it is convenient" to call him "William Langland" (*Parallel-Text* 2.271).

Eminent scholars such as Robert Adams, Ralph Hanna, Kane, and Schmidt have attempted biographical profiles based on these identifications, on scattered historical documents relating to the poet's proposed family history, and on what can be ascertained from the poem. Kane has confirmed the poet's birthplace by studying "records of deeds of gift and grants of land made by various Langlands between 1399 and 1581 not actually in Cleobury Mortimer but a bare 5 miles away in the manor of Kinlet and in adjoining Highley" in the county of Shropshire in the West Midlands of England. The name Langland, says Kane, could have come from his mother's family, and the fact that he used it and not his father's may simply indicate that he was "not in line to inherit through primogeniture."

On the basis of the various gifts, deeds, and land grants associated with the Langlands from 1399 to 1581, Kane concludes: "The span of dates implies a family of substance" (*ODNB* 488).

Kane dates the poet's life from about 1325 to 1390, based on historical allusions in the A and C texts, arguing that possible references in C to the 1388 Statute of Laborers indicate the poet lived beyond that date. Kane bases the date of birth not only on allusions but also on his sense that the poet could not have been immature when he wrote even the first version of the poem, which strikes Kane as somewhat seasoned: "The mature excellence of the writing in the A text, and allusions in it to Edward III's French campaigns, and to a great storm in 1362, between them have suggested that the poet was born about 1330." Also helping to map the poet's birth is evidence that a certain "William Rokele, who might conceivably be the poet, received the first tonsure from Bishop Wolstan of Worcester not long before 1341," which indicates "a somewhat earlier date, say 1325" (*ODNB* 489). As Robert Adams explains, the tonsure is received by those "understood as merely contemplating careers in the priesthood, not as having committed irretrievably to its course" (*Rokele Family* 24). For the death date as well, Kane tries to make sense of the potential political content of the final version and argues for moving the poet's demise from 1387, as previously thought, to slightly later, as he explains, "having Langland alive after 1388 enables understanding of veiled, but unmistakably political, allusions in C. A better date for his death, taking account of fourteenth-century life expectation, would be *c.*1390" (*ODNB* 489).

Kane next writes one of the most important, cogent, and axiomatic observations that one can read in the great corpus of *Piers* scholarship, worth quoting at length:

> By its character Langland's poem encourages speculation about him. It belongs to a genre called the dream-vision, which takes the form of a report by a first-person narrator who claims to have experienced the vision he recounts. He figures as participant, encountering personages ranging from the allegorical or fantastic to the possible, even the historical. The dreamer, if he is named, is called after the poet and, where this can be checked, has some of his attributes. He is to an indeterminable extent fashioned in the image of that poet who, for his part, comes to live imaginatively in the personage of his creation.

The poet uses him as a means of engagement, obviously powerful in a time when poetry was written as if to be read aloud. (*ODNB* 489)

Readers should keep this paragraph to hand as an official passport into the world of the poet.

No one will ever know if Langland anticipated that modern readers would speculate about the real and the imaginary, and such urges may reflect the demands of modern positivist study. What Langland thought about his self-representation must remain mysterious, but all modern readers will want to judge for themselves this man's identity "in real life" and how his experiences may have influenced his writing. For example, one can wonder where he acquired his sensitivity to injustice and also his belligerence against the powerful and corrupt. Traditionally a thinker attains these traits in one of two ways, either through experience of poverty and destitution at the hands of the powerful, or from witnessing such injustice from the other side, as it were, when born into the power that maintains inequity and then rebelling against that privilege. Each reader will inevitably develop his or her own sense of "Will" based on the evidence in the poem. The art of scholarship and the work of sensitive reading compels one to distinguish the likely from the unlikely in the absence of certain historical truth. Kane puts the entire matter quite well, noting that in study of *Piers Plowman* "nothing seems to admit of absolute proof" but depends "on assessments of likelihood and relative plausibility of argument." Despite these ambiguities, continues Kane, "interest in the poem is actually growing," and is likely to continue:

> A vogue of scepticism about received opinions fails to diminish its power of engagement, and disagreements reflect possessive attitudes to its text, and indeed to its poet, who has been anything but marginalized, quite simply because of the quality of his poem as a memorable archive of human experience by which it has the power to engage notwithstanding the passage of six centuries. (*ODNB* 491)

Kane's bold assertion may very well hold true for centuries to come.

Despite the difficulties of discovering Langland, the poet has made it easier (or perhaps not) by offering in passus 5 of the C text an autobiographical portrait.[4] Kane shows a healthy skepticism about it.

The new episode in C, he says, depicts the poet as "a kind of itinerant 'beadsman-for-the-living' . . . a sketch that "fits the concept of a younger son in a family of standing, cherished by father and 'frendes' (that is, in Middle English, 'patrons' or 'kinsfolk'), who ended a promising career in the church by an impulsive marriage and could not fit into any of the various secretarial, administrative, or legal jobs open to a minor cleric." This Langland, one might say further, appears to modern eyes as a failed graduate student who married before qualifying exams and had to take a job tutoring children of the wealthy. Kane also notices the episodes in the text that seem like parts of a real biography: the encounters with Fortune and with Recklessness, the bouts of dementia and alienation, the final decline into baldness, deafness, and impotence. Kane notes that "each of these four carefully located disclosures leads up to a literally represented episode of moral insight and reorientation, of spiritual reassurance for the Dreamer" (*ODNB* 489), a fact that speaks to the craft of the poet in composing what seems like a plausible account of a real man's life. On the other hand, less skeptically, one can counter that craft may actually reflect reality, and perhaps Langland, like many young men, sowed some wild oats and, like all men, got older and faced the grim realities of aging. Medieval literature offers many depictions of aging, but Langland perhaps wrote about the stages of his life as he actually witnessed change and experienced the mental, spiritual, and physical advances (for better or worse) that mark the progress of all lives.

Kane sees aspects of the real poet in the C text autobiography but cautions that "further biographical inference from this episode can seem hazardous." For example, Langland may have invented Will's wife and child, and in fact the bookish Langland could be inventing his entire persona purely from texts and imagination. Kane explains that such deflection may go even further and that Langland may have had good reason to obscure his real person. For if Langland was in fact the tonsured and ordained cleric William Rokele mentioned in ecclesiastical records, then in light of his vicious ecclesiastical satire, perhaps he adopted his mother's name as a sort of nom de plume and wanted to "give the critic who is his speaking voice a markedly different external personality from his own." Kane continues: "Whether or not such identification is accepted, the breadth of his knowledge, and that he had leisure to write, imply either patronage or a relatively secure place, and, moreover, access to books" (*ODNB* 490). In the context of Kane's inquiry, all readers must ponder for themselves whether Langland had some reason to protect himself and did so by forging a plausible but fictive persona, or whether he boldly revealed his real self, confident that his privilege was already protection enough.

Developing Kane's work, Robert Adams traces a string of legal and ecclesiastical documents that mention the Rokele family. Adams offers the fullest account, however circumstantial, of the poet's potential profile, of what political and social world he lived in, and of how he could have composed the poems attributed to him.[5] Adams's book, like Kane's entry, challenges past understandings about the poet's social position. Broadly depicted, readers have longed to see Langland as a populist, a man who had himself struggled, wandered, and seen the world of the common man. This reaction of most readers arises from the poem's sensitive engagement with the realities of social injustice and suffering, issues as apparently critical in the late fourteenth century as in the twenty-first. Langland's direct experience of humanity would seem to belie any aristocratic status that would make him part of the ruling or privileged class.

Those who teach the poem know that readers tend to project onto Langland their own desire for his rebel stature, imagining him as a union leader or some sort of activist close to the people, laboring for the public good. But the biography that Adams posits for him reveals a member of one of the most politically connected, financially powerful families in England, a man of means, engaged at the highest echelons of landowning, money, and power in the late fourteenth century. Such a posh Langland may unsettle some, especially if one sees him as committed to the cause, whatever one considers the cause to be.

As Adams explains, Langland had a "professional level of education in theology," and "obtaining such an education in the fourteenth century would have been massively expensive," implying "disposable wealth beyond the means of all but a few people," a wealth that "almost certainly came, if not directly, from his father" (*Rokele Family* 29–30). This would argue against, and in fact disable, readings that demand a gritty, demotic writer, on the order, perhaps, of Jack Kerouac, another spiritually inquisitive Catholic wandering through life in search of answers while spontaneously chronicling his intense social, spiritual, and sexual experiences, however jarring, rambling, and misunderstood they may be.

Accordingly, Adams's work raises critical issues of how to apprehend the poet and raises questions that should guide a first experience with the poem.[6] Readers must confront the apparent tension between the historical records, which render a gentry Langland of higher social class than Chaucer, and the earthier version of the poet that emerges from the text. For if one bases a biography solely on the persona the poet puts forth, then "Langland can be seen as a clever but perpetually impoverished, itinerant clerk in lower religious orders. This version of Langland," writes Adams, teasing out the romanticism of the depiction, "may have worked a day-job as a chancery scribe in London, lived in a low-rent neighborhood and was trying to support a wife and daughter . . . while disdaining physical labour as improper for a person of his intellectual attainments. . . . By contrast," if one ignores "the autobiographical references as rhetorical ploys," one can come to the following conclusion: that "the poem's philosophical sophistication, combined with the Trinity manuscript note, suggests a considerably less seedy author than the overt references in the fiction—the younger son of a country gentleman," who may have belonged, in fact, to "one of the more conservative monastic orders" (*Rokele Family* 16). Adams's construction of a biography opposed to the poet's own in the C text adjusts any understanding of Langland and his work. First, as Adams argues, "any real poverty ever experienced by the author of *Piers Plowman*" was "self-chosen as an act of devotion"; second, "his birth status was higher than Chaucer's"; third, "he could not have survived for long (while writing such socially and religiously provocative poetry) without powerful sponsors"; and finally, "his use of the name 'Langland' (rather than his own patronym) may well have been demanded by his extended family rather than by his own whimsy" (17).

"Does this sound elitist?" asks Adams, quickly answering himself, "Yes" (*Rokele Family* 17). Adams's opposition between "low-rent" and "elitist" intentionally provokes and startles, designed to disrupt the modern academic imperative that wants a working-class poet who fulfills a progressive ideological demand for class-based activism. Such a mythos often resurfaces. In addition to Kerouac, in the 1970s John Lennon, surely no pauper, invented for himself a post-Beatle persona as a "working class hero." A similar disjunction may be at work in Langland's crafty persona. Biography fascinates because poets write from experience, and readers (fans) want to contemplate the interplay of event, place, and person with the art that emerges from it. Whether it's Shakespeare, Virginia Woolf, or the Sex Pistols, one wants to discover and trace their footsteps to see what they saw, to feel what they felt. But to create biography in the absence of reliable evidence, while seductive, brings risk. Adams compares the critical refashioning of Chaucer to what Langland now experiences, explaining that while "Chaucer now merely endures fashionable literary critics dressing him in modern garb . . . Langland's undocumented life openly invites these same critics to rework him and his poem completely, in their own ideological image" (14). These imperatives may generate any number of changing and competing Langlands.

As a general principle in dealing with the life of the poet and with any negotiation between history and poetry, one should recall Elizabeth Salter's axiom in *Piers Plowman: An Introduction* that "the most important reason for reading *Piers Plowman* is . . . that it contains a wider variety of fine poetry than any other work from the English Middle Ages" (1). Schmidt emends this statement to include "reading and writing about" the poem. He revises Salter's statement because he senses that "the main danger for our time is not of *Piers* being 'misread' as of its not being, as a poem, read at all; and this may be the worst form of misreading" (*Parallel-Text* 2.284). He fears something tangible that any teacher of the poem in the modern academy knows well, for *Piers Plowman* contains so much exciting political activity that one risks seeing it as an *event* in the history of social justice rather than as a poem with both social and spiritual aims.

With the work of Kane, Adams, and Schmidt in mind, readers must themselves "discover" the author in a first (or even in a tenth) reading and negotiate the borders of history and imagination. Initially readers should listen to the poem and permit, without fear, any number of imaginary biographies to emerge from the details in the text. One wonders what this man must have known, seen, and done to have written all he wrote. He knows about law, grammar, theology, scripture, ecclesiastical and court life, all of which reveals a high level of clerical education, befitting a man of his family profile and access to learning. One can believe that such a man lived and wrote a spiritual, scholarly, liturgical, encyclopedic, scriptural, allusive, bilingual poem like *Piers Plowman*. But when one reads Glutton's confession (A5, B5, C7), one sees that Langland also knows what transpires in bars in the morning when the regulars settle in for a long day of drinking. Was he there? one wonders. How does a member of the landed gentry learn about working stiffs and lovable lowlifes having a good-old time? From manuals on sin and sermons about drink, such as the Pardoner's performance in the *Canterbury Tales*? From peeking in on his father's wretched tenants? Or from heading to town, pulling up a stool, and pounding a few with the locals, getting hammered himself, either to log the experience as an artist or simply to slum, which would provide the same writerly benefit. After the bar, readers should move on to C5 and hear presumably the poet's own voice in his elaborate "apologia." One wonders if Langland has invented this persona or here speaks authentically as a bookish academic who loves to write about plowing but cannot do the work himself. This self-effacing, stumbling figure who receives only guarded approval from a skeptical Reason may or may not be the same man who later wanders in hostile alienation, scorning his superiors. And yet both of these personae do not seem akin to the family man who goes to church dutifully in B18 and C20; that man, in turn, appears distinct from the aging Will later abused by his hostile wife for his sexual impotence in B20 and C22. Readers meet Will in many guises, with no guarantee of a single coherent *vita* nor any assurance that that *vita* faithfully reflects the real life of the poet.

When readers have established an imaginary biography based on these episodes and on any other moments of apparent authorial revelation in the text, then they should consider the detailed, albeit provisional, portrait that emerges from Adams's genealogical work to determine if their own apprehension of the poet matches the moneyed, privileged career of Stacy Rokele's son. Throughout the process, readers should recall Kane's stark and stunning statement: "an authorial presence, elusive but inescapable, inhabits *Piers Plowman*. In a very real sense his poem is Langland; he is a factor in its meaning" (*ODNB* 492). If reading and comprehending *Piers Plowman* challenges students at all levels, discovering its elusive poet can frustrate even the most seasoned reader. And yet the search for Langland powerfully animates any reading of the poem and the tense, combative culture from which it emerges.[7]

Piers Plowman and History

The challenges of finding Langland are paralleled by the need to locate the poem itself in history, for Langland, whoever he was, witnessed great political and religious tumult in the late fourteenth century. Determining the nature of his treatment of these events has engaged and excited readers of *Piers Plowman* since the poem's early reception. If one reads selections from *Piers* in an anthology, the text may be accompanied by some historical documents, such as the two Statutes of Laborers, which prevented wages from soaring after the Black Death and targeted those perceived to be indolent who refused to work. One might also see documents from the Peasants' Revolt of 1381, a violent popular uprising incited in part by the Statutes and by excessive taxation, in which, amazingly, the very name of Piers Plowman (poem or character?) was used as a code word in revolutionary letters circulated among the "peasants," some of whom must have been learned clergy in order to make such references—a topic studied importantly by Steven Justice in his book *Writing and Rebellion*.[8]

That revolt killed many who could read and were thus a threat to the commoners whose fates they controlled with their administrative records. The archbishop of Canterbury was beheaded, and young King Richard II was himself vulnerable, before he cleverly endeared himself to the peasants, whom he would ultimately betray with his false promises of liberation from bondage. The plague, oppressive labor law, and class warfare take their part in English history as events along a continuum of religious and social change that deeply informs the world of *Piers Plowman*. One cannot determine poetry's precise power as an agent of change, but one also cannot deny that *Piers Plowman* witnesses those changes even if it did not help to enact them. The revolt itself, as an explosive single event, and the ongoing critique of a degenerate clergy that exploits the innocent, both assert individual liberty over institutional control. And both seek to empower the wretched against the indulgently wealthy and powerful in State and in Church. Revolt and religious reformers share common concerns because they both ask of power: who are you to control me? Consider a line from a sermon of John Ball, a leader of the Peasants' Revolt:

> Good people, things cannot go right in England and never will, until goods are held in common and there are no more villeins and gentlefolk, but we are all one and the same. In what way are those whom we call lords greater masters than ourselves? How have they deserved it? Why do they hold us in bondage? If we all spring from a single father and mother, Adam and Eve, how can they claim or prove that they are lords more than us, except by making us produce and grow the wealth which they spend? (Froissart, *Chronicles* 212)

The sermon looks back nostalgically to a time of radical equality, which the rebel leaders want to restore, citing a shared parenthood for all men and women through the book of Genesis.

Concerning religious doctrine, Steven Justice shows how the reformist ideas of the radical Oxford theologian John Wyclif figured in the Peasants' Revolt, and how this academic critique and also the revolt itself questioned, deconstructed, and violently opposed the institutional structures that would dictate human subordination.[9] To use a word common in Langland studies, both academic theological critique and street violence represent forms of "dissent." Justice argues that the religious reformers had concerns akin to those of the rebels and that the rebels were deeply influenced by Wycliffite doctrine on such issues as "wealth, law, authority and vernacular literacy in a scheme of theological and political reform" (75). Broadly speaking, Wyclif's attack on a sinful worldly clergy and its control of the people through false sacraments and empty ritual planted the seeds of critique that would flower in the Protestant Reformation 150 years later. Hatred of wealth and inequity informed the Peasants' Revolt as well. The rebels in their famous revolutionary letters of propaganda, Justice argues, invoke the social justice rhetoric of the Psalms which "promises the just poor that they will see the rich reduced to hunger and need" (74). Justice notes as well that contemporary chroniclers accused the rebels of being roused by Wyclif, leaving no doubt about the perceived connections between these two historical forces, revolt and reform.

Piers Plowman no doubt shares these concerns, though one struggles to distinguish clearly all the patterns of influence and effect between literature and history. Educated people of the time shared many ideas and beliefs concerning the injustices that arise from clerical power and corruption. *Piers Plowman*, a reformist text in the vernacular, serves as reflection, source, analogue, and amplifier of these contemporary doctrines of dissent. Doubtlessly, *Piers* often embraces the philosophies of primal poverty and equality that fueled both popular revolt and religious reform among the peasantry and among intellectuals. But *Piers* offers no single coherent perspective on the controversies of its time and resists all attempts to restrict and confine it, especially since Langland's thought evolves dynamically and ambiguously across the versions. Scholars have displayed a particular interest in whether the C text reveals Langland's reaction to how the B version was appropriated to support violence in the revolt. It falls to readers to contemplate, therefore, whether Langland's treatment of any particular religious or economic theme in C signals his desire to assert, retract, or clarify what he had written in B. Without any definitive evidence of Langland's intentions outside of the poem, readers must study thousands of local changes across the versions in order to detect any pattern of ideological revision.

Derek Pearsall, for example, attempting to comprehend the changes from B to C, argues that Langland, "conscious of the manner in which his poem had been misappropriated" during the Peasants' Revolt, perhaps sought to prevent such misuse or misunderstanding, in part by "relocating the expression of certain strong views on sensitive matters" to a character called Recklessness (*C-text* 26). These matters include priestly and fraternal poverty, grace, predestination, the status of the righteous who were unbaptized, and the role of learning in salvation. Attributing any doctrine to such a character may make it seem less authoritative and even possibly "reckless" to advocate. In this way Pearsall finds a coherent, historically based transition between the B and C versions, attributing to Langland a concern that his work, however well intended, had participated in a violent, disastrous upheaval.

Recklessness, however, creates more ambiguities than he resolves, and Langland never explicitly uses him to register regret for any particular pattern of thought in the B text. As Pearsall says, use of this character does not mean that Langland "reverse[d] his opinions" (*C-text* 26). Our sense that the poet becomes cautiously reactionary after seeing the language of the B text employed as a rallying cry for revolt lies in our reading of certain passages in C that preach order and obedience. Yet *Piers* frequently advocates obedience as inherent to social order, and we struggle to determine whether in such passages Langland intentionally distances himself from the revolt or from Wycliffite doctrine. One cannot easily distinguish poetic revision from maturation of thought or from changes in religious perspective, but studying the poem in parallel and discerning its relationship to the cultural histories it both witnesses and reflects requires readers to make the attempt.

Consider this moment, unique to C, from a speech by Reason on proper social hierarchies, associating dissent with Lucifer's rebellion. Reason says that the rich and the commons should both love truth, working together in accord to emulate the divine social order that God crafted in the "commune of heaven":

> "Lo, in heuene an heyh was an holy comune
> Til Lucifer þe lyare leued þat hymsulue
> Were wittiore [more ingenious] and worthiore then he þat was his maister.
> Holde ȝow in vnite, and he þat oþer wolde [would do otherwise]
> Is cause of all combraunce to confounde a reume [realm]!"
> (C5.186–90)

This call for social unity could well refer to the Peasants' Revolt and may represent Langland's, or at least Reason's, antipathy to its radical doctrines and violent actions. Schmidt's note acutely summarizes: "The implied message . . . is that everyone should keep his place, and that rebellion against the king's authority (not necessarily the same as the social status quo) is inspired by a devilish lie" (*Parallel-Text* 2.523). That lie, continues Schmidt, comes in the false doctrine of social equality, which breeds only discord. Perhaps Langland here disavows any role his work had in provoking such conflict, for the breakdown of hierarchy would have appalled Langland and any medieval Christian, for whom unity, integrity, and order are divinely sanctioned.

This example shows that studying Langland compels readers to engage in social, political, and religious history to try to determine where exactly the poet stands in relation to the extraordinary events that occurred while he composed the poems. With the poet's biography so vague and elusive, the search for history within the poem becomes all the more urgent and, in a way, more productive. History may have left little record of William Langland, presumably the poet of *Piers Plowman*, as scholars struggle to piece together the fragmentary evidence of his family and time. But Langland has left to posterity an endlessly engaging poem about his turbulent era, revealing a "life of the poet" fuller, richer, and more profound than documented history may ever render.

Narrative Reading Guide

Preface to the Narrative Reading Guide

OVERVIEW OF A, B, AND C

This narrative reading guide recounts the events of each passus, but a short overview of the three versions will help readers understand the nature of Langland's expansions and revisions. During Langland's time and as the manuscripts of *Piers* circulated, it is not clear if anyone ever read the poems in sequence, A, B, C. Certainly scribes were aware of texts that differed from one another, as they drew from available resources to construct complete texts from the various versions they could acquire, with one scribe creating a "deluxe" interwoven text of all three versions in Huntington Library MS 114. This book presupposes that one can read the poems meaningfully in sequence and experience Langland's literary life as it evolves through his work.

The A Text

Few readers read A first; in fact, few read A at all. New readers of *Piers* and those raised on B often perceive A as relatively clean, tight, and economical. Some provocative scholars, gaining much attention but little agreement, see A as the last of the poems, a condensed, *Reader's Digest* version, simplified for an eager readership who wanted access to the poem.[1] Unlike its expansive siblings, A maintains its focus on sin, society, and grace, as displayed by the field of folk that Will imagines and follows. A, uncluttered and short, provides a great place for new readers to start their engagement with *Piers* and a haven for the veteran *Piers* warrior who wants to rediscover the story in this early, simpler incarnation. Not that A lacks controversy once one starts digging into the textual notes and manuscript data, but it offers the fewest tangents and distractions.

Langland revised A because it fails to solve anyone's questions, as the field of folk who set out on a pilgrimage to Truth, led by Piers the Plowman, never reach their destination, and Piers, variously disillusioned, disappears with the dream that summoned him. Will wanders around looking for answers, finds some provisional ones, and then the poem ends, rather unsatisfyingly in its eleventh passus, as Will ponders what a new character named Scripture has taught him. While most manuscripts end at passus 11, three add an incomplete twelfth passus, and in one of these a reader or a scribe who calls himself John But adds a personal coda, identifying himself as an intimate of Will, whom he describes as the author of the foregoing poem—and of many more writings—before he passed away. Editors print this added ending in italics in their texts or in appendices, and no one knows why or how John But appointed himself literary executor and heroic assistant, stepping in to wrap up the untidy ending. John But adds nothing substantive to the poem, but he must have felt it needed a prayerful patch to seal up the whole matter and honor King Richard, Mary, and Jesus. Yet all of passus 12 creates controversy, because no one knows if Langland wrote any or all of what precedes John But's addition, leaving readers uncertain where his work ends and But's begins. Wherever one decides he stopped, Langland left things unclear: Will converses with Scripture about salvation, but he complains that, despite all his wanderings, he has neither discovered true virtue nor understood his own fate. At this point he may or may not have woken up from this dream (the text does not specify), as he makes his final statement on the matter of salvation, alluding to St. Augustine's observation that poor and ignorant people, in the simplicity of their prayers, go to heaven while speculating scholars go to hell. However striking this moment, the entire episode feels rather in-progress and inconclusive. It never resolves the issue of the folk's pilgrimage to Truth or the mysterious document of "pardon" that Piers tears up in passus 7. And in this ambiguous passus 12, Will meets someone, or something, named Fever—that is, one presumes, he becomes fatally ill, until Fever tells him it's not his time: he must stay and do what he must in order to live well. And here But appends his report about Will, attesting that he wrote this poem and also much more (B and C?) until Death finally struck him down. Whether one finishes reading at passus 11, 12, or 12-plus, the story of the poem in the A text seems dramatically incomplete.

The B Text

If John But saw an opening for adding material in the A text, or at least saw that the existing ending would not do, then it makes sense that the poet would himself want to revise the work, and so the B text picks up with Will talking to Scripture, omits the Fever episode, and starts writing a new chapter in Will's life. He now meets Fortune, and the narrative focuses on Will's adventures as a man. From youth to old age, as an everyman, he becomes a personal chronicle of all human lives. He matures, marries, grows old, falters, and becomes feeble. The A text ended its *visio* at passus 8 and called its passus 9 the beginning of the *vita*, that is, the biography of Dowel, Dobet, and Dobest, the practice of three levels of virtue that lead men and women to salvation. Passūs 10–12 (if one includes 12) explore Dowel, and the B additions vastly expand the full *vitae* of these characters/virtues and offer a whole new set of episodes about this man's mind, body, and spirit. In A, because the field of folk seemed so stubbornly sinful, saving society as a whole by taking a communal approach has failed. So A turned inward, and B, doubling A in size, continues this inward turn until it generates answers, however provisional, that matter to Will and to his salvation.

The B text unfolds like an omnibus, akin to Jean de Meun's part of the *Romance of the Rose* in comparison to Guillaume de Lorris's elegantly shaped courtly opening, which in this comparison parallels Langland's short, tight A text. In B Langland treats A as a provocative start and builds, sometimes grotesquely, upon it, sacrificing narrative direction and artistic unity for an expanded exploration of questions of salvation that become ever more complicated and contradictory, with every aspect of the mind and every voice from history weighing in on the question of salvation. B often sounds very "academic" and draws upon medieval tools of schooling, such as grammar, and also upon law, liturgy, scripture, and the Church Fathers. So when any topic arises—justice, salvation, paganism, learning, study, saintliness, charity, the body—B expands upon it to the point of incoherence, contradiction, and circularity, for the diverse voices do not always agree on these issues. Just as Chaucer wants to offer all viewpoints, what are sometimes called "perspectives," Langland too performs as a sort of ventriloquist, and he gives Will plenty to listen to. Achieving salvation means defeating the threat of damnation and eternal death. Thus the life of Christ, intimated in A, becomes central to B's exploration of the path to eternal life. Accordingly, B also turns Piers into Christ, converting the literal laborer into God incarnate, who fights in Piers's armor (the flesh) to save fallen humanity. Knowing this, and seeing that Christ made life possible, Christians must engage as well in a brave battle against Pride and Antichrist, fighting to retain this most precious of gifts, life itself. The poem ends, however, with nothing of the kind happening. The lack of resolution signals neither failure nor flaw on Langland's part, but rather serves as a stirring testament to what the poet saw and heard in his everyday world of uncompromising, ungrateful sin. If Dante believed that God granted him a detailed tour of the perfectly crafted architectonics of justice, Langland found no such favor. Or perhaps Langland simply expresses divine favor differently from his confident Italian predecessor. Langland's form may not be Dantesque, but readers will wonder whether he too will finally find a way to leave the darkness, once again to see the stars.

The C Text

Langland evidently did not live to revise the end of B, and the C text, as it survives in manuscripts, reads identically to B in the last two passūs. Although in this sense incomplete, and unpolished as well in many rough patches, the C text generally revises in order to clarify and consolidate, merging two major confession scenes that seemed redundant in B (The Deadly Sins and the "confessions" of Haukin the Active Man). In C Langland writes more philosophically, displaying a contemplative cast of mind that might reflect the poet's personal maturity, though one should apply biography with care. Malcolm Godden, implying that age brings change, says that in the C text Langland wrote "from a position of greater equanimity and detachment," perhaps because the "poem had already achieved some fame" (205). Detachment, on the downside, may explain why C sometimes becomes prosaic and dull, though this may be because Langland experiments in trying out new ideas and images that he never polished. Having written a powerful, complete poem in B, Langland breaks it open in places and reimagines whole episodes and characters. C features, as well, passages that assert the need to obey authority and the institutional church that may reflect Langland's discomfort with the parts of B appropriated by the rebels of 1381 and with passages that espoused positions that had come to be associated with Wycliffism. Perhaps this reflects a cautious conservatism that comes with age.

The C text smooths out some confusing passages but also loses some compelling images, among them B's claim that mankind fell when Adam and Eve ate "apples vnroasted" (B5.603), replaced in C with the bland observation that they shut the gate of heaven (C7.248–9). Whether the poet did not care, or had a corrupt copy of B to work from, or was not sure which would become the favorite lines of later readers, one just does not know, but many avoid C because of its flaws and occasional colorlessness. One of the most notoriously difficult new passages in C comes when Conscience proposes a complex grammatical metaphor, which shows how greed, in the person of Lady Mede, parallels an error in modification created by a poorly declined adjective (C3.332–405a).

While such experimental material may give some readers pause, others will be drawn in by distinctive features of the C revisions, particularly the increased bitterness of an apparently cranky Langland. His increasing venom, however, comes with an increasing sense of compassion and an enhanced longing for penitential healing and divine mercy. Perhaps the bitterness results from the poet's frustration with human sin. And yet perhaps his experiences told him, as well, that the frail human heart longs poignantly for something that it cannot "will" for itself without God's grace. Readers of the C text should therefore attend to the poet's changes in tone and be on the alert for the spear that both wounds and heals.

C is most famous for its new beginning to passus 5, the poet's "confession" as he is interrogated about his social worth by Reason, providing our greatest source of information about the poet's life and work. The episode tempts readers to see "Will" as William Langland and thus to commit a biographical fallacy. A sort of failed graduate student, Will freelances, praying for his friends who hire him to sing masses for the dead, putting his college Latin to good use. In confronting himself, Langland labors to show that he too wants a meaningful life, healthful for his soul. Such introspection suggests C as the work of an older poet. David Hume says one's tastes in literature change with age: one might read (libertine) Ovid at twenty, (dutiful) Horace at forty, and (contemplative) Tacitus at fifty ("Taste" 233). Perhaps *Piers* correlates with the poet's maturation, evolving as he becomes wiser, more contemplative, crotchety, cynical, and less optimistic about social change. Reading each version can become a dramatic experience of engagement with one man's mind as he and his poem grow old together. No one knows how old Langland was when writing C, but he was older, and the chronological template of the stages of life lends itself to understanding the changes across the versions. If this method seems more fanciful than historical, it may pay more in provocation than what it costs in whimsy.

Since Langland never revised the final passūs of B, the poems share the same ending, based on the Book of Revelation in the coming of Antichrist and the intimations of the Last Judgment, though the poem never gets *there* precisely because the poet has no access to the time outside of Time, outside of history. In the middle of the war between Antichrist and the Church, with the fate of the Church, called Unity, hanging in the balance, Conscience runs off to seek help. Thus *Piers* ends with renewed history—the renewed search for Piers Plowman. And Will wakes up.

1

Working and Wandering as the World Asks

THE PROLOGUES OF A, B, AND C

Conspectus: The prologue introduces the narrator and establishes the major themes of the poem. An unnamed speaker, later called Will, decides to wander the earth in disguise as a sheep; he falls asleep and witnesses a great horde of humanity, holy and unholy, from all walks of life. The B and C versions, contemplating how this "field of folk" may best be governed, add a parliamentary debate scene based on the animal fable of mice wanting to "bell the cat," which they decide is a bad idea.

I. Introducing Will

Piers Plowman begins with lines worth committing to memory, given here in the A version:

> In a somer sesoun, whanne softe [mild] was the sonne,
> I shop me [clothed myself] into shroudes as I a shep [sheep] were;
> In abite as an ermyte [hermit], vnholy of werkis,
> Wente wyde in þis world wondris to here [to hear wondrous things].
>   (A prologue 1–4)

Few narrative poems begin as cryptically and bizarrely: in the summer morning's warmth of the sun, a man heads out on pilgrimage, throwing a covering over him like a sheep—not a shepherd but a sheep, perhaps the lost sheep of the Gospels, a sacrifice, a shaggy, self-tormenting pilgrim, an exile, or just a traveler. He then calls himself a hermit, implying asceticism and piety (if not isolation), but he also deems himself "unholy," indicating either that he sins, that he seeks inner knowledge, or that he longs to atone for guilt and impiety. He wants to hear "wonders," but we do not know if that means the marvelous or the divine, nor what instructive value wonders can have. This soon-to-be-dreaming "I" will be the narrator and the central character in the poem; he will be the readers' eyes and ears, a projection of their own individual "wills" and of their hopes, as he makes his way through the real and imagined landscapes of the human mind and of the cultures and institutions of late fourteenth-century English society. He is a guide, but he is also "us," the evolving reader, however diverse, through time.[1]

Consider him like Dante the pilgrim in the *Inferno*, a man who appears to have lost his way, inhibited by the forces of sin from achieving his goal, as yet unstated. And like Dante he needs guidance. These parallels intensify as the narrator falls asleep and finds himself in a "wildernesse" (A prologue 12). Here he sees two buildings, a tower on a high hill and a low-lying dungeon tower, spread across a valley. In between, he finds a sea of humanity "worching and wandringe" as the world demands (19). The vision appears at once Dantesque and Kafkaesque, for he sees not the dead nor the damned but those alive and still acting in the world, with their damnation and salvation, whether they know it or not, hanging in the balance. If Dante's poem goads one to virtue by showing the final fates of the just and unjust, *Piers* stays home in the world of the everyday and examines how choices in the here and now forge one's final destiny.

The Dreamer ("Will") marks in precise detail how people live and work, and his prologue invites comparison to the general prologue to the *Canterbury Tales*, which it may have influenced. But the approach here also differs from Chaucer's. Langland does not base his persona on the fiction, as in the *Tales*, of the self-effacing, sociable narrator speaking to each one of the pilgrims, mostly in a very charming way, at a tavern. Like Dante, Langland functions more as an alienated observer than as a clever reporter. Chaucer embeds himself in the social world, interviewing subjects who do not realize they are being recorded, but Langland's portraits, because they do not originate in barroom chat, are more trenchant and piercing. He approves of certain modes of work and living and condemns others for their appetite, greed, and exploitation of the innocent. Virtue, one learns quickly in *Piers*, is inseparable from the social and communal responsibility to serve others fairly and justly.

Langland will later manifest this virtuous impulse as the character Do Well (spelled Dowel) whom Will seeks in the B and C texts. Doing well to others enacts Jesus's commandment to love God and to love one's neighbor, called in Medieval Latin *caritas*, or charity, and meaning much more than giving to the poor. Every choice in business and commerce, in political, pastoral, and clerical care, every act of consumption and spending, even in the medieval entertainment industry, involves a bond of responsibility, love, and trust. To exploit these bonds by seeking personal gain and pleasure violates the commandment of *caritas* and constitutes sin. Everything in *Piers* comes down to this principle. And throughout the poem Christ's teaching, ministry, and selfless death exemplify a life of love, providing the touchstone for all human activity. Human social responsibility in the everyday, however mundane, reflects the highest form of spiritual awareness and loyalty to God.

II. Understanding Langland's Art

Readers should be aware of the poet's particular modes of expression, which Langland establishes in the prologue, so they can recognize these devices when working through the rest of the poem. Langland uses Latin frequently, sometimes translating it into English in the poem's next lines and sometimes not. Latin quotations and partial quotations may constitute a macaronic line, that is, a bilingual line mixing Latin and English, that conforms to the alliterative patterns. The quoted Latin texts are either from scripture, from the Church Fathers' commentary on scripture, or from any number of classical and medieval collections of information and wisdom—handbooks and encyclopedias, the various compendia of knowledge available to the educated poet.

The poem's bilingualism is often obscured or lost in translations that dutifully translate the Latin and thus render the poem as monolingual. This diminishes the tension between languages and distorts Langland's mediation of the authoritative Latin documents in his culture for an English-speaking audience who may or may not know that Latin. Some readers—and listeners if the poem is read aloud—need explanatory gloss and some do not, but Langland builds a bridge of understanding and contemplation for all.² For him, poetry itself constitutes a commentary on his culture's inherited documents, an imaginative elaboration on the fragments of wisdom from Christian history and from Revelation. Langland's characters witness the bookish processes of learning, exploring its power but also confronting the difficulty of putting doctrine, in any language, into practice.

Piers excites modern academic readers because it so frequently involves learning, school, texts, and composition—the art of "writing a paper," which is, in fact, the most widespread genre in medieval literature. Such a paper, called a "commentary," offers exposition on a biblical, doctrinal, or legal text. *Piers*, though a poem, reads as an extended commentary on the texts and topics that dominate medieval Christian thought. Morton Bloomfield playfully describes *Piers* as a "commentary on an unknown text" ("Apocalypse" 32), but it is really a commentary on many texts. Accordingly, Langland uses Latin authority, translated and then commented upon, to advance the learning of Will and of the reader. One finds a similar use of Latin and English in another Middle English poem, the *Pricke of Conscience*, a work that sometimes appears in manuscripts with *Piers*.³ The vivid bilingualism of such texts emerges most clearly in a bilingual classroom or reading community, which can approximate a medieval experience of the poem with its dynamic shifts of language.

Another aspect of poetics that readers must notice in the prologue involves a different type of alternation, not between languages but between the a- and b-verses of the alliterative line.⁴ Langland often sets up an idea in the first half of the line and then, after the brief pause of the caesura, reverses it, ironizes it, or deflates it in the b-verse. For example, he praises good hermits and then condemns the bad ones: "Ermytes on an hep wiþ hokide staues [staffs] / Wenten to Walsyngham—and here wenchis aftir" (A prologue 50–51). Schmidt uses a dash at the second caesura to display an effect the poet achieves without punctuation. In the first line and a half, the poet lifts expectations, leads readers on, then in the b-verse of 51 he reveals, with a sting, the sin and perversion of hermits on spiritual pilgrimage to the shrine of the Virgin Mary in the village of Walsyngham—as they bring their girlfriends with them.

Readers can hear the growl of that b-verse of line 51, and speakers of any language, bilingual or not, will feel what Langland accomplishes with sound and with the tongue, for often the meaning of the poetry lies not in thought alone but in the physical reaction one feels in reading it. Consider Langland's praise of hermits and anchorites who, unlike so many other corrupt clerics, do not seek bodily pleasure. These true religious people, he says, "coueite not in cuntre [country (but with erotic pun)] to carien aboute [travel around] / For no likerous liflode [lecherous living] here likam [body] to plese" (A prologue 29–30). These liquid sounds force readers to feel the body and its physical processes: the line simply makes one salivate, which relates ironically to the topic. Langland says the holy hermits and anchorites do *not* indulge their bodies, so the line instances negation, while at once making readers feel the reality of carnal appetite. As an intellectual poet, Langland demands much thought, but he also speaks through the body, and his verses must be felt. Many passages in *Piers* provoke dry mental unraveling and many transport the soul mystically, while others work upon the senses as well. Langland purposefully adjusts his registers from high to low, from transcendental to base. He can stir the soul, but he also arouses the mouth and rumbles the stomach, because people are flesh and desire, always feeling a hunger of one kind or another. Langland's morality never dismisses appetite. Hunger, as a force and a character, has his function, for he makes people work. *Piers Plowman* at times instances mystical transcendence of the body, but it more often confronts the trials of living within the body, understanding and channeling its endless urges.

III. Winning and Wasting Our Way to Heaven

The body naturally draws one downward to the scatological and vile, as Langland takes his readers, if not through hell, at least through the carnality that marks existence in Dante's underworld. In the opening of the *Inferno* (I 8–9), Dante says that to show the "good" he finally experienced, he must describe the "other things" he endured. This understatement prepares readers for the shrieking, cursing, burning, bleeding, cleaving, and cannibalism that the body endures in the *Inferno*. Heaven cannot be understood unless one first sees the pain of the body in hell. Langland heads upward too, though not to such a concentrically ordered heaven, and on the way, like Dante, he brings the body along, charting its consumption and waste, processes that reveal its failure or success in practicing the twofold dictates of charity.

Central to the prologue in all versions, and to an understanding of the rest of the poem, are the concepts of "winning" and "wasting." As economic terms they reflect social and physical processes: to consume excessively means to waste in all senses. Langland weaves winning and wasting in their many manifestations throughout the poem as a motif. Winning most fundamentally means "earning," but it can also mean hoarding and coveting, and when one "wins" through treachery and exploitation, winning becomes covetousness. Wasting means failing to respect what others have legitimately won with their dutiful labors. The concept has appeared in various guises through history: conspicuous consumption, gluttony, greed, overindulgence, but in any form it destroys personal virtue and the common good. In a world where some have little or nothing, having too much just seems a waste.

Among the many instances of greed delineated in the prologue, Langland complains that priests go to London to make money (A prologue 80–83), shirking their pastoral duties to seek treasure and personal advantage. Readers will recall here a passage they likely know from the general prologue to the *Canterbury Tales* where the Parson, an ideal character, stays with his parishioners instead of selling his literate skills for profit in the city (507–14). Throughout his prologue, Langland praises the holy but spends most of his time targeting anyone displaying greed: the false beggars, cheap entertainers, appetitive friars, all the members of various professions, clerical and secular, who have chosen to use their art, intelligence, and learning to serve themselves instead of God and neighbor. They dedicate their work, be it preaching, law, or digging a ditch, to the self, to their own ease and pleasure. Langland wants his audience to see and understand selfishness, and one wonders how he plans to remedy these ills and what direct involvement the human "will" has in the processes of reform. In Will, Langland crafts an everyman who constantly confronts the realities of sin and the injustices it causes. Will stands in for the poet, but he also models the quest, struggles, and confusions of the evolving reader through time, and in this way the poet creates an immediacy that one feels in every new experience of the poem. For the timeless questions Langland confronts in this poem extend far beyond the particular concerns of any one moment of English Christian history.

IV. Rats, Revision, and Reflection in the B and C Prologues

A major addition that the B and C texts make to the "field of folk" comes in a bizarre and potentially unsatisfying episode for modern readers, in which a "parliament" of rats and mice plan to bell the cat that polices them. They never do it, after being advised by one mouse that, without the cat, both rats and mice will run rampant and destroy goods. The lesson appears to be a simple one: with an appetite so wild and ratlike, the commons must be harnessed by authority. But the episode also reveals the human tendency toward self-interest and living in ease, a theme throughout the prologues, for the mouse's wise counsel seems rather a justification after the event: they do not act against the cat mainly because they are afraid. The topical nature of the reference, based on the childhood reign of Richard II, depicted as a kitten, and alluding to the powerful influence of his uncle John of Gaunt, rendered as the cat, has limited immediacy and was even outdated by the time of the C text when it could no longer apply to a young Richard. The episode signals Langland as neither antiauthoritarian nor anarchist: people need authority, and their rulers must practice justice.[5]

From Langland's perspective the rodents' personal ambition for advancement corrupts an otherwise reasonable desire to live without harassment by belling the cat. They want more than simply to live in peace without being pounced upon, for they want rather to be "lordes olofte" (B prologue 157), inviting comparison to the ambition of Lucifer discussed in the next passus (B1.111–23). They display a claim not to social justice and equity but to pride and power, as they seek to live at their own ease (157), for controlling the cat means freedom and pleasure. If this were *Animal Farm*, one could say they want to be the pigs. On the surface the parliament scene appears awkwardly grafted onto A's controlled vision of the people in various walks of life, but both parts of the prologue critique pride and overindulgence, maintaining that people should seek "common profit," not individual indulgence. The C text keeps the scene, even though it has lost its political topicality, for its lessons about authority still apply. If Langland were only a topical poet, he would not be so widely read, but he offers an insight about society's need for governance, both personal and social, that applies to any readership he could have anticipated, and also to those he could not. If everyone pursues pure appetite, whether hermit, king, or hungry rat, society will fall into sin and sinners into hell.

In B and C the parliament is preceded by the arrival of a king (no particular one) led by knights and accompanied by clerks (clerics)—the intelligentsia essentially—and by Kind Wit, basically human common sense and natural, instinctual knowledge (B prologue 113–15). Here, after the field of folk and its renegades, Langland starts to formulate social and political theory: a just king rules while Kind Wit and the commons contrive crafts to serve common profit (116–22). In short, society functions best as a hierarchic mechanism creating order and general good.

The word "common" must be disassociated from the modern American concept of the "common man or woman" and the British notion of "commoners," for neither expresses the complexity of Langland's usage. On one level it means the nonroyal parliamentary representatives from the landed gentry, a forerunner of the House of Commons. But the term also simply means the people, all of whom are God's children and must serve him, whatever their stations in life. The crafts provide "common" for the people—that is, food, in another meaning of the word that Langland seems to have invented.[6] The wasters practice gluttony and consumption, but Langland is no ascetic: men and women must eat, and, as scripture dictates (Gen. 3:19), they must work for their food. An ordered society requires a commercial system to feed the people. That may seem self-evident, but the poem challenges its own doctrines when it contends that God takes care of the sparrows in the field and that one ought not to worry about sustenance and survival. Readers must get accustomed to how doctrines, however established with stout authority, contradict one another in the poem, a conflict that arises in part from a dissonance between Old Testament doctrine and Jesus's radical revisions. *Piers*, not a coherent, direct, doctrinal text, rather confronts all the texts that Langland knew and ponders what they might, or might not, be saying. Langland does not always make his meaning clear, and if that ambiguity does not inspire confidence, readers will see that Will too struggles to understand and persevere. Through this parliament scene, Langland has added in B and C a larger governmental perspective on the moderation of dangerous human freedom and the need to regulate appetite to beat it back from anarchy. Political order reflects the personal governance demanded of individuals. Human ambition, like that of Lucifer, threatens social and political order; therefore the health of society relies upon both civic and self-governance.

All revision does not necessarily improve, complete, or polish. In C Langland adds an unrevised and partially un-alliterative passage (C prologue 95–124), given to the stern character Conscience, on idolatry and the Old Testament priests Ophni and Phinees (1 Sam. 1–4), types of misbehaving clergy serving as negative exempla for those priests whom Langland exhorts to fulfill their pastoral duty. The lines indict the father of the wayward priests, Heli (in Hebrew, Eli), for his failure to discipline his children (C prologue 109–17). Through the biblical exemplum Conscience rebukes the idolatry of modern clergy and their greed as they gather up profits in "boxes . . . yset forth ybounde with yren" (97), a reference to profits made from the worship of relics, implying falseness and deception. Langland also makes a rather down-home point about the need for parental discipline. Both aspects of this draft revision in C complement the themes of order, self-governance, and discipline that inform the A and B versions. That C was so expanded and unpolished should not disconcert new readers. As Pearsall says, the addition of new material is "characteristically abrupt" (*C-text* 48), by which he means that Langland was not shy about dramatically expanding or deleting material. The ABC texts do not witness revision in the college context of "reworking an essay," or an author composing a poem or novel. Langland was not trying to refine his work, to get it right, so to speak. Rather he strove to reinvent, reimagine, rethink, and create anew. Some urgent message gripped him for all his life, and he struggled to express it. These added C lines on an obscure biblical passage (obscure even by medieval standards) show that when he had a theme—in this case the failure of authority, order, and discipline in family and clergy—he labored over it, leaving here a draft passage with half-baked alliterative lines. The sobriety and sternness of this unfinished addition may be a clue to the tone and tenor of this Langland in the C text, representing the poet at a bitter and even crotchety stage of life. A, B, and C may reflect the growth of a poet's mind through a lifetime of anger, frustration, and failure of reform. Such a broad biographical paradigm cannot be proved, but it provides a provocative frame in which to trace a life in words, which may be our only concrete access to the poet.

A, B, and C all end out on the street, in a Dickensian walk through the town, as the pie salesmen and tavern keepers hawk their wares. This return to people and the sounds of real life play out vitally and dispassionately, without moral indictment, because these people just go about their business. Readers might find Langland more at home as a poet here, portraying the real lives of people, than in the labored tale of the sons of Heli added humorlessly in C. Modern preferences notwithstanding, Langland writes both as the academic exegete, sternly glossing a biblical episode about beating children to prevent idolatry, and as the street poet wandering about the shops of the city. He anticipates a later English poet, Sir Paul McCartney, who six hundred years later at Penny Lane in Liverpool observes the sights and sounds of common life, images renewed and celebrated by bards of every generation.

Despite substantial changes across the texts, the prologue vividly establishes the genre of the dream vision and presents readers with a character who, for some reason or other, wanders, seeking something as yet unknown. Self-condemned as unholy, he looks for answers and confronts the current state of institutions and people, which is generally not good. The prologue explores how men and women in society live, work, and conduct commerce, either fairly or selfishly, working nobly to serve God and neighbor or sinfully to satisfy their own appetites. B and C add a study of appetite writ large on a governmental level in the rodents, who, like the field of folk, think only of their stomachs. Langland displays the need for good government and order, with duty and responsibility breeding trust and common profit. He addresses his nation's immediate politics in B, but at once looks for a "truth" that people can live by in any society at any time. Whether concerning a king making laws or a baker baking pies, Langland shows how one's actions resonate along a continuum of duty and must reflect love and justice.

Consider one final iconic image from the prologue, which provokes further contemplation of these themes: the C text reports that Kinde Wit and the commons "a plogh gonne þei make" (C prologue 145; B prologue 119 says similarly that they commissioned plowmen). The plow is both real, a central tool of work in an agricultural nation, and at once a symbol that anticipates the arrival of the title character, anchoring the theme of noble work demanded by the Fall from Paradise, the only means of redemption for humankind outside of Eden. This physical work serves community and God and sparks a worthy and proper hunger for the sustenance that society must labor together to provide. But also, based on many agricultural images from scripture, the plow symbolizes spiritual labor, the cultivation of virtue's fruits, and also God's cultivation of the human soul. These topics and images return again and again in the poem, particularly in B19 and C21, in which Piers Plowman tends the fruit of the human soul that God and the Devil contend for. Whether Langland knew or not that someday he would revise A and double its size, he nonetheless makes sure that the prologue, in all forms, plants the image of a plow, literal and metaphorical, that reappears throughout the rest of the poem. And readers too are here compelled to "put themselves to the plow" with a long row to hoe.

2

Becoming a God by the Gospel

PASSUS 1 OF A, B, AND C

Conspectus: Will meets a mysterious, fair woman, who comes down from the mountain to explain the meaning of the two towers and to introduce their respective overseers: God, here called Truth, and the rebellious Lucifer, the model of error, trickery, and disobedience. To guide Will she provides biblical examples of order, justice, and sin, schooling him in the all-important lesson of love.

Passus 1, unlike the prologue with its rat parliament, remains relatively consistent in the three versions, permitting collective discussion for the most part about the various versions, noting significant revisions. The passus begins promisingly, with Will pledging to tell readers what the towers and field signify. He then recounts how a woman, as yet unidentified, descends from the mountain. She identifies herself later as Holy Church, an allegorical embodiment of Latin *ecclesia*, the church on earth as established by Christ as his bride to serve as the mother of all Christians, providing the care, doctrine, and institutions that educate and guide them to divine grace. She signifies the Church as pure and ideal and must be distinguished from its flawed human members whose corruption Will witnesses. Holy Church has many literary ancestors, including Reason from the *Romance of the Rose*, Virgil from Dante's *Comedy*, Lady Philosophy from Boethius's *Consolation of Philosophy*, and Scipio from Cicero's *Dream of Scipio*, all supernatural figures who heroically appear to guide troubled men in need of allegorical intervention. The medieval reader would recognize the arrival of such a figure and would share Will's sense of awe. Help has arrived.

Holy Church explicates the vision (A1.1–9), telling Will to notice how busy people are about the maze, most of whom, as long as they have worship here in this world, do not imagine another heaven. This confirms a theme from the prologue: sin is marked by a here-and-now mentality, the urge to acquire goods and worldly status. Holy Church laments this distorted view of worship that glorifies possessions and neglects God. Accordingly, she identifies the high tower as the dwelling of Truth, a complex term and perhaps the most important in the poem. Primarily as a proper noun it means simply God, but it carries the resonances of faith, loyalty, honesty, the embrace of full reality, and a host of other meanings, so much so that the *MED* (s.v. "treuth") struggles to include them all and tells readers to remark carefully the word's multilayered uses in *Piers*. Truth created men and women and wants them to obey his word. He put the earth and its plenty at their service, not so they could acquire things greedily, but so that they could be fed, clothed, and nourished. He commanded, in fact, as Holy Church tells Will, that meat, drink, and vesture, as the only basic human needs, be held in common (A1.20). This ambiguous statement cannot mean that the government provides such necessities, a concept anachronistic to medieval theories of polity. Perhaps it anticipates the Enlightenment concept of "life, liberty, and the pursuit of happiness" from the Declaration of Independence and asserts a human right of access to everything that God had deemed needful to all. This sounds at once empowering and nurturing, but it does not answer the question of how these needs will be met and by whom. One wonders whether God himself will supply bread as in the Gospel miracle, or if society is to set up the social structures to provide for the needy. Langland offers no answers yet.

At this point the poem works associatively, as characters move suggestively from one idea to the next. Sometimes this fluidity distracts readers and reads like rambling, but sometimes the speaker darts back to the main issue without having gone too far astray. Langland offers one of his first such tangents here: the discussion of drink as a basic need leads to a warning about excessive drink, which sparks the example of Lot, who, when drunk, slept with his daughters. B and C expand the exemplum with the addition of two lines of Latin from Genesis in which the daughters plan the act. The addition allows B and C to say that "thoruȝ wyn and þoruȝ wommen" Lot was undone and offers the guttural line that he "gat in glotonie gerles [children] þat were cherles" (B1.32–33). Profane or untimely sex leads to accursed offspring. Concern for bastards and fear of improper coupling arise frequently in *Piers*, for such acts pervert a morally healthy family. If the exemplum seems a tangent, one notes that medieval sermon discourse, which influences *Piers*, can move freely from concept to exemplum to axiom. And Holy Church appends an axiomatic conclusion to her discussion of just need and excessive appetite: "Mesure is medicine, þeiȝ [though] þou muche ȝerne [desire]. / Al is not good to þe gost [soul] þat þe gut askiþ" (A1.33–34). In this lusciously liquid line, as in the prologue with "likerous liflode," Langland uses sound to rouse the salivating body and its appetites, reinforcing the sense that *Piers* is a poem best read aloud and felt viscerally.

In A, B, and C Will likes these words, presumably because they resonate with his experiences of bodily appetite, which may, one might presume, have driven him to the sheepskin-clad walkabout that begins the poem. He then asks Holy Church what seems like an odd question, though perhaps one consonant with his experiences so far: "'A, madame, mercy,' quaþ I, 'me likiþ wel ȝoure wordis. / Ac þe moné of þis molde [world] þat men so faste [tightly] holdiþ—/ Telleþ me to whom þat tresour apendiþ [belongs]'" (A1.41–43). Will wants to know who owns the money. The adverb "fast" implies the search for security and stability. Students of Old English elegy will recall how the protagonist of "The Wanderer" longs for "fæstnung"—the healing security of God's care in a turbulent world of exile and woe, a frequent theme in the Anglo-Saxon literature. Here, seven centuries later, people still seek surety, but Langland shows that they now crave the false comfort of money, the empty treasure of the world, and not the spiritual truths that bring eternal security.

Holy Church answers with a simple but important line—"'Go to þe Gospel,' quaþ heo [she], 'þat God seide himseluen [(and see) what God himself said]'" (A.1.44)—for Jesus answered Will's question when asked if one should pay taxes: "'*Reddite Cesari* [render to Caesar],' quaþ God, 'þat

Cesari befalliþ [what belongs to Caesar]'" (50). In using God and Caesar, Jesus starkly separates the material and spiritual worlds, and Langland similarly accentuates life's political necessities, such as commerce and taxes. Existing in that world does not inherently offend God, who placed Adam and Eve here when they lost Eden, but enjoying it solely without regard to God's own demands betrays God and imperils the soul. Langland does not encourage a simple, radical poverty, for Holy Church continues that Reason should rule human enterprises and Kinde Wit should help society to manage its money, for "'husbondrie [economy] and he [Wit] holden togideris [go hand in hand]'" (55). Langland does not demand poverty but rather care and moderation in management and spending. He seeks no Marxist "leveling" or breakdown of hierarchies, nor an end to private property, but he is ever watchful of excess, any immoderation that harms the self and others. In the prologue, merchants, for example, were "guiltless." Marxism strikes some thinkers as a form of Romantic utopianism that reimagines people as actually wanting to be equal. But Langland himself is not beyond a bit of Christian utopianism, and readers will have to determine how naïve such hope can be. One puzzles over what economic system, or what economic behavior, Langland would see as ideal or as attainable. Holy Church, then, continues to explain the landscape (59–68), as Will asks about that other building, the dungeon in the deep dale that she identifies as the castle of care and the home of Wrong, a wonderfully expressive name for the Devil, the father of falseness who egged Adam and Eve on to sin, counseled Cain to kill his brother, and bought off Judas as well, to highlight a few of his famous crimes.

Holy Church delays her identification until she has explained the towers and advised Will about their masters, who each demand his allegiance. Once he recognizes her sacred status, Will falls to his knees and prays for grace (A1.77). A, B, and C all have Will asking her not to teach him about "treasure" but to show him how he can save his soul, for Will senses that treasure, if it means material wealth, is useless for salvation. To respond to his question, Holy Church revalues the concept of treasure and renders it as a type of spiritual coin, forged in love and truth, as seen in her mantra "'Whanne alle tresours arn triȝed, treuþe is þe beste'" (83, repeated at 181). The lines have been drawn: is Will of God's or the Devil's party? Why should his allegiance be in question, one wonders, since the fates of Adam,

Eve, Cain, and Judas should adequately ward anyone off from Wrong. But the pleasure of earthly treasure, and in fact of all carnal delights, so powerfully tempts humanity that detachment from them in favor of some intangible good, such as love or truth, appears nearly impossible. Human instinct longs for pleasure and not for abstract virtue. But Holy Church denies that, for the urge to virtuous love comes, she later avers, from a "kynde knowyng [natural knowledge]" that nurtures in one's heart the desire to love God more than one's self (130). This extraordinary statement about ethics maintains that humans have a natural instinct to good. Wrong and Truth, Devil and God, body and soul, each have their claims over the "will," and the poem wonders which force will win and which treasure will be the most enticing.

In a jumbling of tongues that shows Langland at his most poetically muscular, Holy Church explains the authority behind her exaltation of truth: "I do it on [rely on] *Deus caritas* [God is love] to deme þe soþe [vouch for the truth]" (A1.84). Understanding what "God is love" means will occupy Will for the entirety of *Piers*, because understanding (and at once practicing) such love occupies Will perpetually. Holy Church does not remain for long, at least not as an allegorical superhero caring for Will, since she departs at the end of the next passus. But while here, she offers many axioms and ethical chestnuts that describe the treasure of truth situationally (A1.86–91): it means doing one's work with truth, which must mean displaying honor; it means doing no one ill, which means not harming; and it means being true of one's tongue, indicating the need for honesty in all oaths and promises, for words bind men and women together and make society possible. Serving Truth means fidelity to every word and honest practice of our vocation, no matter how small or simple. Serving God might seem far grander than this—and the poem will compound many conflicting messages about the ideal practice of virtue—yet the homey wisdom of Holy Church, if followed, earns the grandest reward.

A, B, and C each say quite radically that whoever follows truth becomes "a god be þe Gospel, on ground and on lofte / And ek lyk to Oure Lord, be Seint Lukis wordis" (A1.88–89). Scholars do not agree upon what Gospel source applies here,[1] but whatever scriptural authority lies behind this statement, it seems hubristic, especially since Holy Church soon discusses Lucifer, who had the same ambition to exceed his given state. Perhaps

Langland did not fully think out the theology of this concept but rather was attracted to the alliteration of "god" and "Gospel." And yet Langland makes clear that the pursuit of truth as a treasure brings humanity closer to God, while no other treasure can so elevate us. Perhaps truth allows humans to nurture the "image of God" within them, since Genesis recounts that man and woman are made in God's image, but the poet does not refer to Genesis. To "be a god," therefore, seems strange doctrinally and even frightening, but the poet says it, and readers must determine whether the half line succeeds as poetry only or whether it works as theology as well.

As Holy Church continues, Will learns that clerks should teach the power of truth to the unlearned, for both Christians and non-Christians believe in its power (A1.90–91). Langland continually explores the responsibilities of clerks, those who, like him, read Latin and study scripture. Learning will never guarantee virtue, but it obliges the learned to spread God's word. Holy Church's amazing contention that both Christian and un-Christian know the virtue of truth hints at a universalism that surfaces from time to time in the poem, for Langland often identifies core beliefs among Christian, Muslims, and Jews, holding out the hope that non-Christians will convert, based on historically shared doctrine. One may detect here again the mark of the utopian Langland (especially in our knowledge of a post-9/11 world), for such a universal conversion to Christianity seems as absurd as humanity leaving off sin for personal and social virtue, yet such hope adheres to faith and to art as well. Whether Langland becomes finally, in his work of revision, a despairing or a hopeful artist constitutes one of those unanswerable questions that make reading *Piers* in parallel so compelling.

Holy Church's ideas progress rapidly. She says knights and kings must follow Truth by capturing criminals until Truth determines their guilt or innocence; "truth" as a treasure is not just social ethics but hierarchal order and responsibility (A1.92–95). A and B caution that knights ought not to fast once "in fyue score wynter" (A1.99), which implies that some knights were hypocrites, fasting almost never and only for show. Langland was not happy with this expression and clarifies the matter in C by stating that knights should not leave "þe trewe partie" for "lordene loue" [love of a lord] (C1.95), that is, they must not pervert the law in deference to wealth or rank. The C text converts the rather bland critique of painless fasting into a class-based critique of influence peddling and the corrupt nature of power and privilege. Differences in versions do not always stand out so starkly, but changes like this highlight in C a frustration not merely with personal weakness (fasting) but with a failure of order and the triumph of influence over justice. However, in each version Holy Church builds society by assigning work and responsibilities for clerk, knight, and commoner. Everyone has a job to do, and "love" means working responsibly, according to the demands of station and vocation, to help others and to ensure justice.

Holy Church substantiates this discussion of responsibility and order, as she did the question of money, with scriptural authority: David made knights; Christ made angels to establish military order; Lucifer with legions was disobedient to this order (A1.96–116). Holy Church has identified truth as basic social ethics, being true to one's word and doing no one harm. Now she defines it more grandly as heroic action, what a knight must do for law enforcement, based on the martial models of angelology and biblical battle narrative. Invoking biblical mythology may seem like a tangent, but it returns the narrative focus to Lucifer, a disobedient knight in bold rebellion, whom every Christian in the field of folk must resist. Langland, however wide-ranging his exposition, never loses sight of his subject except when he intentionally models confusion, and he does not do so here. Whether angel, knight, clerk, merchant, or plowman, all must follow the truth of God by honoring the daily divine demands of duty and love. Love orders the entire universe, from the heavens to the cities, from the stars to the churning soil.

Langland seems to control the narrative and shape of the poem very well here in passus 1, as Holy Church provides to her polite student a saving solution to humanity's betrayal of Truth. Will then asks her another curious question that propels the narrative forward, as he challenges Holy Church to explain more about "truth" and his ability to comprehend it. Will claims he lacks the "kynde knowyng," the natural insight to understand what truth is, and wonders by "what craft [skill]" in his body he can discern it (A1.127–28). She responds harshly, calling Will a "dotide daffe [stupid idiot]" (129) in one of the poem's near slapstick moments. In A she deems his wits too dull, but in B and C—with lines that shame Will and the reader too—she adds that he studied too little Latin in his youth, appending the proverbial lament: "Heu michi, quam sterilem duxi vitam iuuenilem! [Oh what an empty young life I led!]" (B1.141α). Holy Church then schools Will about the force within that moves humankind to serve God—the force of love, which all versions call the "plante of pes" (A1.137). B and C, in one of the poem's signature images, elaborate upon the conceit by describing how the fruit of love ripened in heaven and fell to earth. Love is medicine,

> And also þe plante of pees, moost precious of vertues:
> For heuene myȝte nat holden it, so was it heuy of hymselue [heavy in itself],
> Til it hadde of þe erþe eten his fille.
> And whan it hadde of þis fold [earth] flessh and blood taken,
> Was neuere leef vpon lynde [linden tree] lighter þerafter,
> And portatif and persaunt [light and piercing] as þe point of a nedle,
> That myȝte noon armure it lette [prevent] ne none heiȝe walles.
>   (B1.152–58)

The imagery here recalls the Middle English lyric "I sing of a maiden," in which Christ comes to be born in Mary as still as dew in the meadow. B and C here witness Langland's meditative elaboration of the A text and prepare readers for the centrality of the life of Christ that B and C will feature later in the poem, well after A has ended. Truth, God, and love are one, for God, Holy Church tells Will, defined love itself perfectly in his compassion and selflessness in sending his son to save humanity from sin. God is the model, source, creator, object, and end of love. In addition to this generative image, B and C also add a civic metaphor, depicting love as a mayor, a mediator between the king and the commons, a "ledare [leader]" (C1.156) who shapes law. This political, legal metaphor shows love not only as a theological concept but also as a moral and social force. Love, as Holy Church explains in C, upon "man for his mysdedes the mercement he taxeth" (157). "Mercement" means paying a fine, but it puns cleverly on "mercy." That is, practicing charity—paying love's fine, as it were—saves us from harsher legal judgment. Langland does not hesitate to invoke any system of imagery that works to express the power of love and truth, but he returns frequently to civics and to everyday life.

All versions then cite Jesus as the prime example of love and mercy, as he pardons those who killed him. Langland often invokes the life of Christ as a paradigm for solving social issues. Therefore, people, says Holy Church, should "haue reuþe [mercy] on þe pore, . . . for þe same mesour [measure] þat 3e mete [mete out] . . . 3e shuln be wei3e [weighed] þerwiþ whanne 3e wende hennes (A1.149, 151–52). Students of Middle English literature will associate this economic theory with that of the Middle English *Pearl*, where God measures his rewards as he wishes, even though it may not make sense by human accounting.[2] Here Holy Church's words carry more warning than comfort, as they continue the indictment of greed that has marked the poem so intensely so far. To translate the allegory: the Church teaches what Christ taught and demands what He demanded; if the rich defy charity, they defy both the daily work of the church and also the word of God. One cannot serve both Truth and money.

Holy Church then approaches another major topic: the limits of chastity and the behavior of the clergy. "Chastite wiþoute charite," she asserts, will be "cheynide [chained] in helle" (A1.162), for chastity counts for nothing for those encumbered in avarice. In an uncomfortable analogy, Holy Church compares this situation to a homely young girl, chaste only by necessity because nobody wants her. "Give and it will be given to you," continues Holy Church more grandly, in Latin (quoting Luke 6:38), as she defines the charitable practices of fair exchange that unlock God's grace for those burdened with sin:

"*Date, et dabitur vobis*—for I dele 3ow alle [provide you everything]."
Þat is þe lok of loue þat letiþ [brings] out my grace,
To counforte þe carful acumbrid [encumbered] wiþ synne.
Loue is þe leueste [dearest] þing þat Oure Lord askiþ. (A1.175–78)

This allows her to return to her axiom: When all treasures are tried, truth is the best. She attempts to make her exit with that wonderful closing line, but she cannot go just yet.

Holy Church's image of the plant of peace remains one of the poem's most endearing and enduring images. Burgeoning love, growing heavy in heaven, falls to earth, becoming as light and piercing as a needle that no armor or wall can keep out. A generative image of Christ as God's love growing heavy becomes, strangely, as sharp as a linden leaf and a needle.

This contradictory and expressive imagery, at once gestational, botanical, sartorial, and martial, points not only to the dual nature of Christ as God and man but also to the dual nature of love as both a natural force and a weapon, as if in a medieval siege, piercing armor and scaling walls to enter the heart. Nothing can keep out God's love. The A text uniquely melds into this conceit another incongruent but charming image: Holy Church tells Will he can "preche" love as the plant of peace on his "harpe" when at a party and called to entertain (A1.137–38). B and C must have found this strange, and A alone will forever sing his song of love.

Concerning Langland's perspective on human behavior, if readers wonder whether love or condemnation is dominant in Holy Church's discourses, they have asked a central question. She makes clear that the uncharitable go to hell, and yet she defines love as the mediator of mercy, provoking the question whether mercy or justice dominates. That these issues seem unresolved and even in tension should not surprise, and B and C take up the conflict toward the end of their versions (B18, C20) in the debate of the Four Daughters of God: Peace and Mercy against Truth and Righteousness (Truth there signifies not God but the historical reality of human guilt). Langland cultivates the tension here in the early passūs and elaborates dramatically in his revisions. As Hamlet will later say, "Use every man after his desert, and who should 'scape whipping?" (II.ii.). Langland constantly ponders what people deserve and, more important, what God thinks they deserve, for he has the final say, and his accounts are always true.

3

Lady Mede Gets Ready for Her Close-Up

PASSUS 2 OF A, B, AND C

Conspectus: Holy Church's discourse continues as she turns her attention now to the opposite of Truth, that is, the falsehood and deception embodied in her rival, Lady Mede. Holy Church identifies Mede's father as "Wrong," "False," or "Favel [flattery, guile]" in the A, B, and C texts respectively, though Theology also calls Mede's father "False" in C. And in all versions Holy Church reports that Mede plans to marry someone named False. The King, Theology, and Conscience struggle to determine her nature and to establish whom she should wed.

With the standard of treasure established and the moral, social, and political responsibilities of each person in society set (at least in theory), Langland turns now to the forces that oppose Truth and that serve Wrong, the lord of the other tower in his vision. Still within his initial dream, Will learns about the dungeon down in the valley, as Holy Church tells him more about Wrong and about her rival, a femme fatale named Lady Mede. These women function as allegorical concepts, representing the Church and the "principle of economic exchange," but they also act as real women and engage in female competition, a conceit Langland develops in B and C. At the heart of this concept lies a deep archetype of the nurturing mother versus the seductive vamp, Penelope versus Helen, Spenser's

Una versus Duessa, the good girl versus the bad, and a host of other doublets throughout myth, literary history, and popular culture. Mede gets top billing in this passus, and she stands with Chaucer's Wife of Bath and Criseyde as one of the great female characters in Middle English literature. She's a vamp and a tramp, though she's called even worse, as she champions the armies of evil and renders both men and women incapable of resisting her infinite charms. In the B text she enters most grandly, for as Will turns around, he is startled by

> a womman wonderliche ycloped—
> Purfiled wiþ pelure [fur], þe pureste on erþe,
> Ycorouned [crowned] wiþ a coroune, þe Kyng haþ noon bettre.
> Fetisliche [elegantly] hire fyngres were fretted with gold wyr,
> And þereon rede rubies as rede as any gleede [burning coal],
> And diamaundes of derrest pris and double manere saphires,
> Orientals and ewages [aqua sapphires] enuenymes [poisons] to destroye.
> Hire robe was ful riche, of reed scarlet engreyned,
> Wiþ ribanes of reed gold and of riche stones.
> Hire array me rauysshed [ravished], swich richesse sau3 I neuere.
> (B2.8–17)

"Mede" can mean "reward," and in her most neutral sense, she simply refers to the principle of payment and exchange, including wages, and thus provides the cornerstone of society.

However neutral and even dynamically necessary, she is also easily corrupted and about to become even more corrupt by marrying False. This wedding will unite treachery and exchange, animating all elements of society, depicted here as the wedding party, with the thrill of graft and influence peddling, creating a "money talks" society with no moral or legal checks on how payments circulate. Merchants, jurists, lawyers, the police, criminals, everybody in civil society and in the Church will be able to buy and sell other people for their own purposes. Although sometimes "mede" functions neutrally and even beneficially, when she first appears allegorically she already looks lavish and corrupt, finely dressed in A, with some added jewels and scarlet in B, and only losing an accessory or two in C. In B Langland crafts her to resemble Alice Perrers, the young and greedy mistress of Edward III, and also to signify the Whore of Babylon from the Book of Revelation.[1]

Readers may be struck or even put off by the seemingly reductive gender stereotype, but the poet does not merely, or primarily, target women. One only has to regard the poet's comprehensive berating of her all-male entourage to realize that the poet shows no simple gender bias in his moral condemnation. On the other hand, Langland depicts Mede as alluring, charming, amoral, and in every way simply luscious. Like most such dangerous women in legend, myth, and history, she can accomplish anything she wants with impunity. That makes her, as an incarnation of money, central to a poem that relentlessly inspects human economic relations as the foundation of love and justice.

The sororal rivalry between the two women that arises in B and C illustrates Langland's detailed art of revision, one of thousands of many-colored threads in the fabric of *Piers*. In A, Holy Church complains that Mede has "marred" or harmed her and has been critical of her doctrine: "'þat is Mede þe maide,' quaþ heo, 'haþ noiȝede [annoyed] me ful ofte, / And lakkide [insulted] my lore [doctrine] to lordis aboute'" (A2.16-17). B reads, rather, that Mede "ylakked [blamed, attacked] my lemman [lover]," whom Holy Church then identifies as "Leautee [law, justice]" (B2.21). Holy Church and Mede compete as rivals, embroiled in a love triangle in which the pure couple Holy Church and Leautee are backbitten, slandered, and undermined by the home-wrecking, conniving Mede. In all versions Holy Church reports that Mede appears in "þe Popis paleis" and is as "preuy [intimate]" there as Holy Church herself (A2.18), indicating corruption at the highest level of church hierarchy. Though A, B, and C confirm that Holy Church comes from better stock than Mede, born of God Himself, Mede has outmaneuvered Holy Church in both their personal and professional relationships. She dominates commerce of all kinds everywhere and in the process controls everybody. Bad girls often win.

Soon thereafter, dramatically and inexplicably, Holy Church leaves, and she never returns. For modern readers, it may recall the temporary departure of Glinda, the Good Witch of the North in *The Wizard of Oz*, who will come again to take Dorothy home but who first lets her struggle with various impediments on her own. But there is no such return in *Piers*. By contrast, in Dante's *Inferno* and *Purgatory*, Virgil never leaves his charge until a better guide can lead him upward. Readers must ponder Holy Church's abrupt abandonment of Will. As a character, she never speaks again in the poem, but in a shift from personification to architecture, the poem later recounts the building of "holy church" itself, called Unity, and tells, as well, about its tragic invasion by the armies of Mede, Antichrist, and Pride, though Mede, like her rival, does not appear with the soldiering sins that carry her banner. Readers must savor the guilty pleasure of Langland's gossipy love triangle, for it ends here in passus 2. Langland often experiments in his poetic modes, offering an extended conceit of one kind and pushing it forward, with or without resolution, and then invoking completely new scenarios and images—chivalric, biblical, political, economic, and even grammatical. The poet uses all the tools he acquired in his reading, in search of what works, and despite the changes across versions, really, in a way, it all works.

Mede's wedding never actually occurs, unfortunately for her party, which contains all aspects of society, including everyone who stands to profit from the union, Simony and Civil most prominently. Simony, named for Simon Magus, a character in the Acts of the Apostles who tries to purchase powers from St. Peter, refers to the practice of clerics profiting from distributing the sacraments, such as penance, or pursuing appointment and advancement in the Church through bribery, called in the modern world "pay to play." Civil, as Andrew Galloway explains, "represents the corrupt practices of those [clergy] using civil law, that is, Roman law," to their advantage against their tenants on church lands, in apparent violation of customary English common law. "Wyclif and other Lollards," writes Galloway, "persistently condemned civil law as a tool for clerical greed" (*Penn Commentary* 252–53).[2] Also in the wedding party we find a "Sisour," a "juryman or sworn witness in a court of assize" (*MED*, s.v. "assisour"), and men in such positions are obviously ripe for hire and corruption.[3] Through Mede, anyone can be bought, so the wedding party includes all who work in court, commerce, and church, in the various realms of exchange, hoping to animate their business with the charming art of deceit, bound to turn a profit.

According to the wedding charter that Simony and Civil read out (A2.57–71, with additions in B and C), Mede is married more for her riches than for "any vertue or fairnesse" (B2.77); fairness means beauty but with the added senses, as in Modern English, of "justice, . . . good sense, sound judgment" (*MED*, s.v. "fairnesse," def. 5a). One says "it's not fair" when deceit or corruption occurs; and this edict makes it clear that what Mede practices is *absolutely* "not fair," and no one promises otherwise. The document licenses, in sober terms, all the evil in society, all the graft and corruption that can emerge from this marriage of the concept of "false" to the processes of "exchange." This marriage made in hell enables rampant sin to fester in a gross parody of the sacrament and of a public ceremony supposed to be healthful to the community. Accordingly, the couple commit their "soulis to Sathanas, to synken [sink] into pyne [torment] / Þere to wone [reside] wiþ Wrong while God is in heuene" (A2.70–71). The fruits of this anti-marriage will not be children in God's honor but boundless, deadly sin. The poem perpetually invites readers as well to join the celebration, to get caught up in the moment, as one does at weddings, for Langland makes all such moments pleasant and joyous, to seduce readers, as it were, with the pleasure of sin, cloaked here as sacrament and celebration. The charter, as Fauel reports, "is asseled" not in the year of our Lord but "in þe date of þe deuil" (A2.77)—quite a start for a young couple.

This wedding never takes place perhaps because Langland did not think society doomed and hoped that Mede could still one day marry Conscience or at least refrain from consecrating a union with False. Perhaps they are already cozy enough, for considering how much time they spend together, they might as well be married. In the wedding charter, B adds a bold and bitter line, as the document of marriage authorizes the couple to "breden [breed; grow fat] like burgh swyn [city pigs], and bedden hem esily [linger in bed] / Til Sleuþe and sleep sliken hise sydes [sleek their sides]" (B2.98–99).[4] C replaces this earthy diction with the bizarrely bland "And sue forth suche felawschipe [pursue such fellowship] til they ben falle in Slewthe" (C2.102). Perhaps "breed like city pigs," a signature Langlandian phrase, struck an older, calmer Langland as too raw when he composed C. Such biographical fallacy will be constantly tested, especially when the C text amplifies, rather than silences, such moments of bitter scorn. The Langland of C displays many moods.

The list of those invited to (or crashing) the failed wedding is revealing: Randolf the Reeve, Mond the Milner, and many others more. Readers might think that Langland targets only those in power who exploit the powerless, an idea arising from an early twenty-first century perspective on the raging issues of income inequity. Not so here, for physical laborers and small business owners stand to gain just as much from Mede as their superiors do. Mede may stride about as a courtly lady, but anyone, from beggar to king, can come to her court. And anyone who exploits anyone else for personal gain, against the dictates of God's commands of charity, faces Langland's withering, blistering condemnation—fortunate if literary damnation were all they ever must face.

The whole enterprise of this marriage provokes the scorn of Theology (A2.79), who believes that Mede deserves better than this marriage. It may seem odd and contradictory for him to defend such a person, but he fights for a pure and uncorrupted understanding of Mede, maintaining that God had planned for her to marry Truth. Truth here cannot simply be God, as Truth has been manifested so far in the poem, but much more likely simply means "honor, integrity" and "honesty in the conduct of one's business, work, etc." (*MED*, s.v. "treuth," defs. 3a, 4a). All versions call Mede a "mulier(e)" (a "legitimate" woman "born in wedlock," per the *MED*). A and B say she was engendered by Amends (B2.119), and C calls Amends her mother, adding that this entitles her to a better marriage even though, as C adds, False was her father (much like the figure she is to marry) and Fickle Tongue is her grandfather (C2.120–21). All versions attempt to redeem Mede, to save her, as a woman, from marriage and, as a practice, from corruption. The A and B texts cite Luke's Gospel to assert that "Dignus est operarius mercede sua [the laborer is worthy of his hire]" (A2.87; B2.123). Though the C text does not explicitly quote this axiom about economic justice, the doctrine nonetheless informs all versions of the Mede encounter in this and the next passus. Theology's vision of the wedding with a better groom would ensure such justice, but aggressive human intervention into the system of reward bends God's plan instead to serve human advantage alone. Mede may not marry False, but she certainly does not marry Truth, for if she had, a secure world of economic virtue and fidelity would be created for all. Experience shows that not to be the case. In C, Theology provides an example of Mede in bono to undergird his point, offering the legendary story of St. Lawrence, who, when martyred on a hot gridiron, calls out for the "heuene gates" to open because he deserves God's mercy and the "mede" of salvation (C2.129–36). Theology tries to show that "Mede may be wedded to no man bot Truethe" (36), and if this addition seems otiose, its teacherly, pastoral feel displays one of Langland's contemplative modes of expression in C. And one cannot help but cheer on the plucky Lawrence as, well roasted, he claims his heavenly reward.

As quickly as Theology makes this appeal, Civil agrees, but Simony opposes such a disruption of the marriage, pending payment of a bribe. Accordingly, Favel with the help of Gile puts a little money on the street to bribe the notaries and to enlist False-Wytnesse in an attempt to "amaistrien [win over]" Mede (A2.106–12). When the gold is distributed widely, "gret was þe þonking / To False and to Fauel for here faire ʒeftis [gifts]" (113–14).[5] The logic remains unclear: to what end are witnesses bribed; and why try to "win over" Mede when she does not actively oppose the marriage in the first place? It's all a little slippery, but the force of the episode is clear: when Theology tries to assert a better match for Mede and a more just result for society, the forces of graft and treachery, who would benefit from the marriage, use bribery to cozy up to Mede, seducing her to marry False. With Mede's exact agency unclear, Langland's depicting her as a vamp shatters her fragile neutrality, subjecting her to the social forces that want and need her to be evil. Dressed as lavishly as the Whore of Babylon, Mede makes an unlikely candidate for the wholesome marriage that Theology hopes for her, and one wonders if Langland, her creator, ever really intended her to marry well. Holy Church, seemingly unaware of the noble destiny that Theology asserts, never speaks of her except as a rival and a danger. Mede is doomed, or blessed, from the start, depending on one's perspective and allegiance.

The following scene in all versions, comic and bizarre, depicts the entourage saddled up on government officials instead of horses, heading to the King's court at Westminster to seek his blessing for the marriage, displaying the dependent and supportive relationship between Mede's troop and the corrupt officials. Literally, professions carry corruption on their backs. Mede herself rides a sheriff; False rests atop a corrupt judge; Simony and Civil mount on summoners, and Lyer picks up stragglers with a cart. In A, B, and C Will describes the size of the troop: "I haue no tom [time] to telle þe tail [train] þat hem folewiþ, / Of many maner of men þat on þis molde [world] libbeþ [live]" (A2.147–48). He has no time (some manuscripts read "tongue") to describe how many people follow Mede. Langland may not have Dante in mind, but the moment recalls the Italian poet's accounting of the numberless neutrals in canto III of the *Inferno*, who merit neither heaven nor hell. Likewise, Langland depicts Mede's minions as countless, though far from neutral.

Aware of the danger, Sothnesse (truthfulness) and Conscience tell the King about this parade, and he accordingly wants them arrested and hanged. The wedding party scatters when the King realizes that he ought to arrest False as a noted criminal. The evil figures like False and Liar run for cover and then enter into various professions in commerce and in the Church, finding shelter among merchants, pardoners, and friars (A2.169–94). The wedding allegory offers a myth of origins, or etiological tale, the story of how professions became corrupt, for Langland knew them in reality to be corrupt, and here reveals that industry and institutions will always make a home for falsehood and lies. King and authority cannot stop, and remain oblivious to, this infiltration. Only readers see it occur, and yet everyone pays the price.

A and B end dramatically with Mede captured, weeping and shaking when apprehended, here in A's version:

> Alle fledden for fer and flowen into hernis [fled into corners];
> Saue [except] Mede þe maiden no mo durste [dared] abide.
> Ac trewely to telle, heo [she] tremblide for fere,
> And ek [also] wep and wrang whan heo was atachid [arrested].
>   (A2.195–98)

Prior to this stark ending, C makes a critical addition:

> Symonye and Syuile senten to Rome,
> And putte hem thorw appeles in þe Popes grace.
> Ac Consience to þe Kyng accused hem bothe,
> And sayde, "Syre Kyng, by Crist, but clerkes amende,
> Thy kynedom thorw here [their] coueytise wol out of kynde [nature]
>   wende [stray]
> And Holy Churche thorw hem worth [become] harmed for euere."
>   (C2.243–48)

The last line in C about Holy Church looks unique, but it echoes from A2. In A, when the king sends a constable to arrest Mede's band, he adds, "Simonye and Cyuyle, I sende hem to warne / Þat Holy Chirche for hem worþ harmid for euere" (A2.165–66). C has leaped over B and back to A to retrieve a useful line, transferring it to Conscience and expanding it into a warning about the effect of this wedding on Holy Church, who has already departed. Maybe Langland fears that readers would forget her too quickly and so displays in C this concern for her safety. The wedding, no mere local affair, has widespread effects throughout Christendom. C's recouping of this line thus gives shape and unity to the poem's opening section by reminding readers of the danger faced by Will's gracious guide, even though, sadly, she has left his side. In C Langland wants Conscience to be heard and seems already both nostalgic and anxious for Holy Church. Readers too can only wonder why she vanishes, and they may start to fear for her as well. Conscience has many functions, but here he appears as the watchful voice of insight and awareness. His concern for Holy Church at the end of this passus adds to the C text a sense of dramatic urgency and reminds readers that Lady Mede, however much she may weep and wring her hands when cornered, is not the only woman in danger in the world of *Piers Plowman*.

4

Lady Mede Tries Everything

PASSUS 3 OF A, B, AND C

Conspectus: The King receives a cooperative Mede and asks her to comply with his will, for, like Holy Church and Theology, he does not want reward married to falsehood. The episode inspires some dramatic reworking and elaboration across the versions as the characters in the poem, and also the poet, struggle to define and to control this powerful, seductive Lady Mede. She finally marries no one and disappears from the poem, though this does little to diminish her influence.

I. The A Text

The role of King in the A text refers historically to Edward III, but the character functions across versions as a general manifestation of kingship, anxious to govern well and rule justly. Langland remains ever hopeful for proper leadership, and the poem longs for the unity of Reason and Conscience in social and governmental practice as a way to contain the chaotic power of Mede. But Mede has many supporters at the King's court at Westminster who "worsshipede hire" (A3.12), including corrupt justices whose graft relies upon her power. "Worship" implies both idolatry (as in today's phrase "worship the almighty dollar") and a display of social courtesy, for Mede, an attractive courtly lady, charms everyone. Among Langland's masterful allegories, Mede stands as his grandest and most theatrical creation, for her identity as courtly woman both masks and enhances her core identity as money. Langland wants readers, like her entourage, to submit to her charms as so many others have. The audience plays a part in Mede's seductions, and in Langland's as well, for Mede's appeal and Langland's art are both contingent on sin's allure. Concerned for her sensitive emotional state, the justices encourage Mede not to mourn (A3.16). Mede as a concept cannot be sad, but she laments both like a lady facing cruel justice and like a successful industry fearing its fall from dominion. The fleshly will, which seeks no treasure beyond earthly gain, despairs when it fears that corruption and profit may be impeded by the forces of law and ethics. Mede's cries thus express the despair of sin that fears reform, ignorant of charity and its calming, sacred joys.

Conscience can diminish Mede's power, for sin perpetually combats the innate knowledge of virtue that confounds the willfulness of avarice. God provides answers within human nature, but Langland knows that this guarantees nothing, for Mede then begins to work the room, making justices rich and guaranteeing ignorant clerks appointments (A3.19–33). Literally the scene depicts a crowd of men from law and clergy fawning over a lovely, disarming woman and seeking her favor. But allegorically they court their own urges for profit, seeking to secure funding for the enterprises particular to their graft and simony. Mede needs to be lovely and charming, for the processes and the rewards of sin have their appeal.

Mede then meets with the friars, who absolve her in exchange for funds for new window construction in their priory—and a plaque honoring her as a donor, making her a sister in their house (A3.34–52). Little seems wrong with this common practice, then or now, as all charity and the grateful attribution to kind patrons appears normal. But as always in *Piers*, the fault lies not in the practice but in its abuse, as Will explains in his outburst of a reaction to the offer, citing God's own warning: "Nesciat sinistra quid faciat dextera," which he follows with translation: "Let not þi left hond, late ne raþe [early], / Be war what þi riȝt hond werchiþ or deliþ [does]" (55–56). Will glosses his biblical citation by telling Christians to "preuyliche [privately] parte" (57) with their donations, to give discreetly so as to combat pride. Mede, and those like her who sponsor such windows, do so for personal acclaim, which corrupts the act. Demolishing any possibility of a charitable motive, Mede pays the friars a "noble" and they provide penance, absolving her of all her "shrewidnesse [depravity]" (43-45). Langland saturates his poem with the language of payment, reward, hire, wages, and accounts. Sinners trap themselves in human terms of measurement and the illusion of wealth they promise. At the end of history, God as employer, lord, and master will make his own accounting. Confusion between these systems of measure, earthly and divine, animates all versions of the poem and, in fact, provides one of the central conflicts throughout much of medieval literature. So seduced by earthly riches, people act, as Holy Church says in passus 1, with no regard for any "oþer heuene þanne here" (A1.9).

The King, ever hopeful throughout this affair, wants to forgive Mede for her proposed marriage to False. Unlike the friars, he does not sell absolution for profit but rather practices mercy for the cause of good government. Mede, inconsistent or perhaps just psychologically complex, appears surprisingly willing to marry Conscience. Allegorically, the neutral principle of "exchange" is not, by nature, inclined against aligning itself to instinctive virtue. But whatever her motives, Mede's intended has no desire for such a union, for in the next 47 lines of scathing, energetic verse, Conscience roundly refuses her offer. As he catalogues Mede's crimes, central among them her whoring, the language becomes harsh. He calls her as "comoun as þe cartewey to knaues and to alle," adding that even "myselis [lepers] in heggis" can have her (A3.121–22). And though his scorn invokes antifeminist clichés in depicting insatiable female sexual appetite, Mede does not stand for her sex but rather for the crimes catalogued throughout *Piers*, mainly committed by men, of exploitation and theft. Whores themselves appear often in the poem to receive rebuke, but never as viciously as Mede, for economic injustice provokes Langland's wrath more than any act of human sex, even its sale. Mede therefore remains ever a metaphorical whore.[1]

In the next complex episode Mede counters Conscience's arguments. She denies nothing but asserts, in an elaborate historical allusion to an episode in the Hundred Years War, how her ministration helped Edward III negotiate his campaign successfully against France, while Conscience would have led the King to flee because of hunger and cold (A3.176–95). Ironically she accuses Conscience of settling for a "litel siluer" in having the king accept terms to leave off his claim (194).[2] Mede contends that her principles of military adventurism and plunder powerfully motivate a king and help him to pay his army, while Conscience, in this formulation, is a pacifist and a capitulator and thus of no help to an embattled ruler who needs money and needs men "þat mekly hym seruen" (197). Mede then stunningly boasts that her arts make a king loved and "for a man holde [considered manly]" (199). Popes and prelates need Mede, as do emperors; masters need her to pay servants; entertainers take "mede" for putting on shows. In short, Mede defends herself by highlighting her role in all civic and social relations: "No wi3t, as I wene, wiþoute Mede mi3te libbe!" (214). Colloquially, one would say, "money makes the world go round." Mede's tone here, smug and matter of fact, compels readers to admit, as the King here does, that she has a point.

This sparks Conscience to explain the distinction between two kinds of "mede," in a critical passage that must have frustrated or at least failed to satisfy Langland, who expands it dramatically in C. Conscience asserts that the ties—the moneyed ties that bind society—need not be corrupt. Money itself lacks agency, but lust for it ruptures the ideal social bonds of justice and harmony, and Conscience explains that people should not see each other as exploitable sources of profit. He quotes from Psalm 14, a poem that begins "Lord, who shall dwell in thy tabernacle?" Among the qualified is "Qui pecuniam suam non dedit ad vsuram [he that hath not put out his money to usury]" (A3.221α).[3] People should love and loan to each other not for gain but "for Oure Lordis loue of heuene" (223). Practicing love in all human relations, says Conscience in playful irony, merits "Godis mede and his mercy" (224). God keeps good accounts, and those that want their "mede" here and now can surely have it, but at the price of forfeiting God's reward. Corrupt officials who take bribes and priests who take money for masses will have, continues Conscience, the "mede on þis molde [earth]" (233) that Jesus promised. He then cites a verse critical to the entire episode and to economic theory throughout *Piers*: "Amen, Amen, receperunt mercedem suam [they have received their reward]" (233α; Matt. 6:16). No one gets paid twice.

Conscience ends the passus with a biblical example of personal greed that brought on God's disfavor, the case of Saul who disobeyed God's orders to destroy the Amalec and kill their king Agag (1 Samuel 15). Saul kept the livestock not for himself but for God, as he explains in futility to Samuel, God's prophet: "for the people spared the best of the sheep and of the herds that they might be sacrificed to the Lord thy God" (15:15). This may not strike readers as the best example of a man driven by Mede, but it offers a dark tale of God's anger against the disobedient, and Langland must have assumed his readers knew the fuller biblical context, in which Samuel rejects Saul's excuse as absurd:

> And Samuel said: Doth the Lord desire holocausts and victims, and not rather that the voice of the Lord should be obeyed? For obedience is better than sacrifices: and to hearken rather than to offer the fat of rams.
>
> Because it is like the sin of witchcraft, to rebel: and like the crime of idolatry, to refuse to obey. Forasmuch therefore as thou hast rejected the word of the Lord, the Lord hath also rejected thee from being king. (15:22–23)

However much of the story Langland expects his readers to know, Conscience takes no chances with his hearers and illustrates the art of biblical literary criticism by explaining the *culorum* or the main point of this extended exemplum about King Saul whom God hated, and "alle his heires [heirs] aftir" (A3.257–58). Read the Book of Kings, says Conscience, and see how God treats those who seek Mede.

Saul's crime is merely refusing to commit genocide at God's behest, as Conscience grimly explains:

> Samuel seide to Saul, "God sendiþ þe and hotiþ [commands]
> To be buxum [obedient] and boun [ready] his bidding to fulfille.
> Wende [go] þidir with þin ost wommen to kille;
> Children and cherlis [servants], choppe hem to deþe!
> Loke þou kille þe king; coueite [covet] nouȝt hise godis;
> For any mylionis of moné, murdre hem ichone [each one];
> Bernes [men] and bestis, brenne [burn] hem to deþe!" (A3.244–50)

As a result of his neglect, Saul's sons are all killed, his daughter rendered barren, and he himself is slain (or kills himself: biblical accounts differ) in battle in this disastrous tale of how Israel's first king degenerated from glory into misery because he sought his own "mede." On the heels of this dire exemplum, Conscience looks to a future time when Reason will reign and govern realms, and, on the model of the good King David, one Christian king will rule humanity justly, and Mede will no more "be maister on erþe" (266). On that day, whenever it may be, humankind will be guided by "loue and louȝnesse [humility] and leaute [loyalty] togideris" (267)—

virtues that Saul, the archetype of both a bad ruler and a rebellious subject, tragically failed to display.

Then Conscience moves closer to home with another critique of social vanity—clothing, for in this imaginary post-Mede world no servant will seek silks and furs as payment for his loyal allegiance. Kynde Wyt will rule with Conscience and, in A's stunning last line, will "make of lawe a labourer, such loue shal arise" (A3.276). The image of law as a laborer promises that, infused with love, the processes of human justice will no longer be subject to the greed that squanders God's grace and imperils salvation itself. A few lines above, Conscience complains that Mede "of mysdoeris makiþ hem so riche" (272), a concession to Mede's power to seduce and reward her criminal minions, who grow fat with her profits. Conscience can only hope that honest work offers its own savor and allure, a sweet medicine that can purify the practices of Mede and bind human labor to the divine laws of love.

II. B and C Revisions

In a significant innovation in B and C, Mede promises to work with the friars as long as they love lecherous lords and continue to absolve them under her corrupt ministrations of bribery. She assures all those listening that lechery is the least of the seven deadly sins, as she explains:

> It is a freletee [weakness] of flessh—ye fynden it in bokes—
> And a cours of kynde [natural process], wherof we comen alle.
> Who may scape þe sclaundre [slander], þe scaþe [harm] is soone
>   [soon] amended;
> It is synne of þe seuene sonnest relessed [forgiven]. (B3.55–58)

Lechery becomes a minor transgression *if* one can escape the scandal, for public judgment and shame serve as potent forces of correction and sanction. Perhaps Langland wanted in B and C to amplify the sexual sins that Mede and the friars attempt to occlude, implying that Mede may not actually be capable of erasing the sin. Society's urge to police virtue (in the most positive sense of that term) will, at a certain point, defeat, or at least inhibit, Mede's power to cover sin with the simple cost of cheap confession. Ironically, Mede's words provide the hope for her own undoing.

In another intriguing sequence, unique to C (3.86–114), Langland expands freely upon a passage in A and B in which Mede encourages the law to excuse criminal retailers who exploit the poor, those who have to buy "piecemeal," vulnerable to being overcharged for basic goods. The unjust practice persists today in the inner cities, where the poor are routinely overcharged for staples. C details a range of such exploitations, describing how those who suffer from fire or flood are overcharged for their dire needs, resulting in the victims praying that the exploiters will themselves suffer catastrophe either here or in hell. Mede, of course, asks the mayor to excuse these practices: "'Loue hem for my loue,' quod this lady Mede, / 'And soffre [allow] hem som tyme to selle aȝeyne [against] þe lawe'" (C3.119–20). Money can make the government look the other way, as landowners and retailers control commodities and real estate and hurt the little guy, who cannot game the system and so is forced to pay exorbitant prices and rents for the profit of others.

This C passage, in Will's voice, is not the most well-known addition in the *Piers* corpus. Though not particularly eloquent, it contains key phrases and images that powerfully express Langland's evolving critique of greed. The poor get sold "vntidy" things—bad goods—and get cheated in measurement, because retailers "fillen nat ful [don't fill up the container] þat for lawe is seled [as the law requires]" (C3.88). The people are so beset by sellers and landowners, continues Will, that they cry out to God for vengeance, which comes indiscriminately, burning the houses not only of the unjust but of the just as well: "And thenne falleth ther fuyr on fals men houses, / And goode mennes for here gultes [because of evil men's crimes] gloweth on fuyr aftur [glow with fire as well]" (102–3). In this dire and frightening C addition, natural disasters may seem like vengeance from on high, but in reality they ravage the innocent as well. Prior to this, all versions have said that the rich build houses with money that should have fed the hungry, the wealth that could have provided food that the "pore peple sholde potte [put] in here wombe [stomach]." The exploiters use their tainted retail profits to provide timber to build their own lofty homes (83–84). In the C text, Langland, in the indiscriminate justice of disaster, finally burns them down.

After Will's excursus, Conscience offers more warnings about the health of the community and Mede's destructive power, pointing out that under Mede no city nor realm can endure without "werre [war] oþer wo oþer wickede lawes / And custumes of coueytise þe comune to destruye" (C3.205–6). Conscience creates in the C text a heightened sense of urgency and a fear of violence, but when Mede defends herself from these charges, she continues the violent imagery of fire and war. Mede has saved thousands of lives, she claims, while Conscience has made men cowards, too shy to burn and devastate the enemy as fate demands. She tells Conscience:

> Ac thow hast famed me foule [foully] byfore þe Kyng here;
> For kulde [killed] Y neuere no kyng, ne conseilede so to done;
> Ac Y haue saued myselue sixty thousand lyues
> Bothe here and elleswhere in alle kyne londes.
> Ac thow thysulue, sothly, ho hit segge durste [who dares to say it],
> Hast arwed [made a coward of] many hardy man þat hadde wille to fyhte,
> To berne and to bruttene [smash], to bete adoun strenghtes [strongholds].
> In contrees there the Kyng cam, Consience hym lette [prevented him]
> That he ne felde [conquered] nat his foes tho fortune hit wolde [wished it]. (C3.231–39)

Troops demand money, she continues, so that each soldier can live "as a man" (C3.249). Mede had said in the prior versions that she makes the king respected for his manliness (A3.199; B3.212), and now she also allows him to fortify the masculinity of his retinue. Her dominion, at least in the realm of violence, relies on her manipulation of what it means to be a man.

Studying the Mede episode in parallel indicates that Langland lavished much attention on this conflict, perhaps growing frustrated, like his puppet Conscience, with the power and authority of Mede's arguments. In this, his final attempt to achieve victory for Conscience, he invents one of the most daunting additions in the corpus: the great grammatical metaphor, distinguishing Mede (indirect relation) from Mercede (direct relation), based in the study of Latin grammar and the need for adjective and noun to agree (C3.332–406). Modern English uses number but not case or gender in this aspect of grammar, so readers fortunate to know an inflected language like Latin with a full declension system will better comprehend the conceit of this passage, which many readers have found pedantic and even bizarre. This sequence reveals the poem's multilingualism, and Langland interweaves Latin and English so beautifully in this episode that appreciation ought to precede understanding. He founds the grammatical conceit on a belief in the unity and harmony of the universe as God created it, and as displayed in every aspect of nature, including the precision and elegance of grammar. Readers should recite this passage slowly and bathe in the sounds of this harmony before returning to unravel it. Toward its culmination, Conscience explains how the order and harmony of syntax reflect the need for Christians to be faithful to Holy Church:

> Ac adiectyf and sustantyf [its noun] is as Y er [before] tolde—
> That is vnite, acordaunce in case, in gendre and in noumbre;
> And is to mene in oure mouth more ne mynne [no more and no less]
> But þat alle maner men, wymmen and childrene
> Sholde confourme hem to o kynde [one nature] on Holy Kyrke to bileue. (C3.393–97)

Such fidelity in earthy relations will create justice, what we call in grammatical terms "agreement," which informs human relations with God. And God's grace, in turn, leads him to become one of our "number," for he wanted to become "*Deus homo* [God as man]." God therefore

> nyme hym [took himself] into oure noumbre now and eueremore:
> *Qui in caritate manet in Deo manet et Deus in eo* [He who abides in love abides in God and God abides in him (1 John 4:16)].
> Thus is man and mankynde in maner of a sustantyf—
> As *hic et hec homo* [this male and this female human] askyng [requiring] an adiectyf
> Of thre trewe termisones [word inflections in agreement]—*Trinitas unus Deus* [the Trinity one God]!
> *Nominatiuo, Pater et Filius et Spiritus Sanctus.* (C3.402–5a)

These verses propose some challenging associations: we, as creations of God, says Conscience, on the model of good grammar, must modify each other in our earthy relations with consonance, harmony, and justice, so that God will modify us, in turn, with his love.

God's love, in fact, provoked him to take on human nature, that is, to bring himself into grammatical harmony with humankind (the Incarnation), modifying our being as "homo" with a fitting grammatical adjective, that is, with his divinity, for he became *Deus homo*. His humility allows our nature, in turn, to be sacredly modified. In the larger context of Conscience's argument, when human relationships are informed not by Mede but by Mercede, who stands for proper economic relations, humanity's corresponding reward is to live "modified" by God's grace. Conscience compresses the entirety of this majestic passage into one word, *Nominatiuo*, meaning "in the nominative" (case of Latin nouns), which we now share with God, but punning also on "in nomine," the phrase that begins prayer: "in the name of the Father and the Son and the Holy Spirit." As they pray these words and enunciate the nouns of the Trinity, Christians speak the grammatical harmony that binds words in language, binds people in society, and binds themselves to God in the commune of heaven. The compressed line 405 exemplifies the concept in well-wrought alliterative verse: three "trewe" (meaning both perfect and divine) "termisones" (word endings, but also destinies) lead in the b-verse to the properly declined metrical phrase in the nominative case: *Trinitas unus Deus!* Human language as a system, here displayed in the poet's virtuoso interweaving of Latin and English, mirrors the perfect grace and unity of the Trinity. These, perhaps Langland's most Dantesque verses, capture the oneness and the diversity of the elusive Trinitarian concept of "three in one," much as Dante sought to express.[4] This celestial harmony becomes manifest in the right relations of human language, which serve in this extended conceit as the guiding model for all social intercourse, which Mede would rather corrupt into chaos with the bad grammar of greed.

III. Mede's Battle of the Books

One of B's most delightful elaborations (kept, slightly trimmed, in C) comes at the end of the passus after Conscience, a skilled scriptural scholar, chides Mede for her ignorance of Latin. Mede, ever more bold in B and C, flashes a little scripture to defend her activities. "I kan [know] no Latyn?" she asks Conscience, determined to refute him by quoting Solomon, who said, "Honorem adquiret qui dat munera [he acquires honor who gives gifts]" (B3.332, 335α). Conscience, impressed, nonetheless compares her to a lady pleased with a certain phrase in Paul, "*omnia probate* [try everything]," found at the "leues [page's] ende" (339–40). But she neglected to turn the leaf to see the warning that follows:

> Hadde she loked þat oþer half and þe leef torned,
> She sholde haue founden fel[l]e [harsh] words folwynge þerafter:
> *Quod bonum est tenete* [hold on to what is best]—Truþe þat text made. (B3.341–43)

Mede, he contends, has tried to pull the same trick by partially quoting Solomon:

> And if ye seche [consult] Sapience eft, fynde shul ye þat folweþ
> A ful teneful [harmful] text to hem þat takeþ mede:
> And þat is *Animam autem aufert accipientium* [it takes the soul of one who accepts].
> And þat is þe tail of þe text [conclusion of the passage] of þat þat ye shewed—
> That þei3 we wynne worshipe and with mede haue victorie,
> The soule þat þe soude [payment] takeþ by so muche is bounde.
> (B3.348–53)

In this battle of the books, Conscience catches Mede using an incomplete quotation, choosing the part of the text that supports her art, while not turning the page to see the rest of the statement that reveals who really pays the price for receiving such a gift. Perhaps honor does come to the gift giver, but it harms the taker spiritually. Mede has neglected, says Conscience playfully, the "tail" of the text. The tail refers to the end of the passage, the part Mede ignores, but it also plays off his earlier description of her as "tikel of here tayl" (C3.166), that is, sexually indiscriminate with her end parts. Bodies made in the image of God, and the sacred corpus of scripture, must be used properly. Mede thinks no one will know how she misuses her tail(s), but Conscience can be very clever when he wants, and he wins this witty exchange. Yet whether, after three rounds of battle with Mede, he finally defeats her is another matter completely.

5

An Illegal Interlude between Peace and Wrong

PASSUS 4 OF A, B, AND C

Conspectus: Peace complains to the King that someone aptly named Wrong has wronged him. Mede intercedes to show how money and corruption impede justice: everyone has a price, and she mollifies Peace, despite his widespread losses, with money. The closeness of the versions in this passus enables us to discuss the episode in the A text and to notice significant B and C revisions along the way.

The King grows weary of wrangling over Lady Mede and demands that she and Conscience kiss and make up so both can serve him (A4.1–13). Conscience refuses and would rather be dismissed or die. He will do nothing without Reason, and the King agrees, sending Conscience to "fecche" Reason so they can all work together (A4.7). The allegory translates thus: the King wants peace and order in the realm and wants the practices of conscience and reward to be balanced, but his own conscience tells him that he cannot accomplish this without reason to guide his decisions. Reason asks Cato—presumably the Roman ethicist whose maxims were popular in the Middle Ages—to ready his horse called Suffre-til-I-se-my-tyme, indicating that Reason will endure patiently until he knows what to do (18). Waryn Wisdom and his friend Witty tag along because they have some nebulous business at court "to be dischargid of þinges" (26) and need Reason's guidance. One suspects, with no evidence yet, that these characters might be less aligned with Reason, per se, and more with the ingenuity designed to absolve them of some legal liability. Nonetheless, the King receives Conscience and Reason and seats them between him and his son, an act that represents how various aspects of deliberation, insight, intelligence, and justice can contribute to political order.

But Wisdom and Witty are not what they might seem, and the B and C texts expose them as frauds, as the poet in revision likely wanted their treachery made more explicit to the reader. Conscience thus warns Reason away from the covetous pair. "Ther are wiles in hire wordes" (B4.34), he says, for they dwell with Mede, and they would prefer receiving a dozen chickens, or as many capons and a big bag of oats, to serving "Oure Lord or alle hise leeue [dear] seintes!" (38–39).[1] In C, which names the first rascal Wareyn Wisman, Conscience makes the same point without the oats: "þey wolde do for a dyner oþer a doseyne capones / More then for Oure Lordes loue oþer Oure Lady his moder" (C4.38–39). The B and C additions intensify the clownish aspect of this absurd pair of attendants who are bound to advocate for Wrong in the upcoming proceedings. Conscience's evocation of a Psalm condemns them as enemies of God: "Contricio et infelicitas in viis eorum et viam pacis non cognouerunt; non est timor Dei ante oculos eorum [Destruction and unhappiness in their ways: and the way of peace they have not known: there is no fear of God before their eyes]" (C4.36α–β; Psalms 13:3 and Romans 3:16–18).

The conflict that drives the passus ensues, as Peace submits a bill in parliament, essentially a civil complaint, against someone named Wrong, not the Devil as in passus 1 but a generalized figure of crime. The offenses range from borrowing a horse and never returning it to stealing grain, sleeping with Peace's maid, sexually assaulting Peace's wife and two other woman (Rose and Margret, the latter a virgin), and murdering male members of Peace's household. All these severe violations of a household would have shocked Langland's readers. Revealing the anxiety of intimidation and his helplessness at the hands of Wrong, Peace says, "I am not hardy [brave enough] for hym vnneþe to loke [even to look at him]!" (A4.47). In C, Peace expands upon his fear and says that he is afraid to go to "Seynt Gyles doune [hill]," (51) the site of a street fair, which must have been a rough neighborhood where Peace was endangered. The effect of local detail encourages readers, through time, to imagine the most dangerous part of their own city, for such places always exist, threatening peace.

In all versions the conniving forces of Wisdom and Wit reveal the degeneracy of these aspects of mind under Mede's dominion. Accordingly they intervene by convincing her to pay Peace off. His suffering was real, as were the crimes against him, as he shows his bloody head to the King and says, in a great, compact Langlandian verse: "Wiþoute gilt, God wot [knows], gat I þis skaþe [harm]" (A4.65). Despite the severity and vividness of the crimes, once Mede does her work, injustice prevails. Wrong, supposed to serve seven years in irons, walks away scot free, for once Mede offers some pure red gold to Peace, he drops the charges and considers himself satisfied. Forms of the word "amenden" appear several times in this episode, both as nouns and verbs. Peace says that Mede has made "mendis" (A4.90) and that this is all he can ask for. Theology says that Amendes was Mede's mother (C2.120), but in this context the word means bribery, the manufacture of justice and healing, a betrayal of Mede's noble maternal line. The gift of gold will "amende" the "skaþe" that Peace suffers (A4.83), a metonymy for acts against him and for the violence that money has erased from history. Langland knew this would not be an isolated incident.

The King oversees the trial in hopes of justice and rejects Peace's recanting. He senses injustice and fears that Wrong will "laugh" at the law's impotence if he escapes unharmed. So he calls Reason, his closest councilor and only hope of appeal, to adjudicate. Reason knows no solution but rather launches into another of Langland's utopian visions of how society must change before he, Reason, can ever show pity for Wrong (A4.100–131; cf. Conscience's speech about future reform in 3.260–76, expanded in B and C). The allegory puzzles, for one wonders why any moral change should *ever* make Reason take pity on a felon. But no one can "reasonably" expect compassion until all of society undergoes reform and until vile miscarriages of justice, like the one just witnessed, no longer occur. Change does not come easily to allegorical characters, and Wrong will always be himself. But someday, in a world not ruled by corruptive forces of Mede, Wrong will be tempered, chastened, and subject to justice. Reason, like Conscience before him, understands justice but can only imagine it thriving in a futuristic vision, not in the current, fallen world, which Langland and modern readers alike would simply call "reality."

In Reason's chimerical future, lords and ladies will love truth, proud women will put away their fancy clothes, children will get properly chastised, clerks and knights will speak courteously and wisely, prelates will practice what they preach, and clerical appointments will not be bought by "Rome-rennares" (A4.111) who bribe the pope for advancement. None of this can happen until the tyranny of Mede ends. No evil, says Reason in Latin, should go unpunished and no good unrewarded. He promises that if the King agrees, then law shall become a laborer and "lede afeld donge" (130), a stunningly raw image, endemic to the matrix of this great farming poem, for if law, as a laborer, spreads dung, the land becomes fertile of justice. The next lines offer the airier notion that one day love shall rule the King's land (131), which may sound a bit vague and utopian but evokes Dantesque, Boethian, and Neoplatonic themes. For medieval authors, the domain of love lies not in the New Age dream of an academic counterculture as in the 1960s but rather in the eternal order and harmony of the created universe, wrought by a just and perfect God, finally manifested in society. But any hope for improvement fades in B, which cleverly adds a scene in which Mede winks at the Men of Law, and Waryn Wisdom winks back (B4.152, 54; not in C). Waryn tells Mede starkly, "Madame, I am youre man," and offers to say whatever it takes to make them all rich, putting his words at her disposal: "what so my mouþ ianngleþ [speaks]" (155). Two forces are at work here, as the King seeks to govern his realm with Reason, while Mede blithely administers her own realm, supported with a winking "wisdom" that seeks to outmaneuver Reason and make sure his vision of future justice never becomes a reality.

The King is pleased with Reason but worried about implementing justice fairly to all. Reason swears to work to this end "ȝif hit be so þat buxumnesse [submission] be of myn assente [agrees with me]" (A4.150). Buxomness, here possibly a personification, often informs the poem's ethics. It forms part of Piers's son's name in the B text, and pilgrims must cross a river called Beþ-buxom-of-speche (B5.566) to reach Truth. Reason knows that a comprehensive submission to proper authority—civil, royal, and rational—forms the basis of a healthy society and will combat the allure of Mede, who inspires her own brand of submission. This looks hopeful, and the passus ends with the founding of a sort of mutual admiration society with the King, Reason, and Conscience promising, cheerily, to work together (A4.151–58). This pledge inspires little confidence, for however eminent the alliance, their combined power seems puny compared to what Mede accomplished in nullifying the bill against Wrong. Leaving these conflicts unresolved, Langland offers no conclusive answers in passus 4.

Before their similar endings, B and C expand variously, revealing Langland's evolving sense of how to remedy the injustices that dominate this episode. In B, Conscience starkly tells the King that his desire for just leadership (which implies defeating Mede) will be impossible without the consent of the commons:

> Quod Conscience to þe Kyng, "But þe commune wole assente,
> It is ful hard, by myn heed, herto to brynge it,
> [And] alle youre lige leodes [loyal men] to lede þus euene."
>   (B4.182–84)

The future vision of society in B and C is long on hope and short on practical details, but the added inclusion of "the people" shows a larger civic vision than proposed in A. With the commons involved, everyone from high to low will serve, be served, and observe their place in the social order, in proper accord with Reason. Medieval social hierarchies are rigid and hegemonic but are informed by mutual interdependence and awareness. "Buxomness" does not enforce submission to power blindly but demands a form of loyal obedience founded in love. A king fails without the willing support of his people.

In C, Langland intensifies the theme, for here Conscience tells the King that he needs not the commune's consent, as in B, but their "helpe" (C4.176), indicating a greater sense of partnership, if that term is not anachronistic. A moment later Reason adds specific conditions to the justice that everyone seeks, expanding A and B's sense of buxomness:

> "By Hym þat rauhte [stretched] on þe rode!" quod Resoun to the Kynge,
> "But Y reule thus alle reumes, reueth me [deprive me of] my syhte!—
> And brynge alle men to bowe [kneel] withouten bittere wounde,
> Withouten mercement [penalty] or manslauht [murder] amende alle reumes." (C4.179–82)

Reason pledges to serve the King, as he does in B, but wants here uniquely to bring the people to obedience without coercion or violence, forms of abuse both disastrous and counterproductive. Reason continues pointedly: he wants to ensure the King listens to his aldermen and commons and that "suffraunce" (a form of bribed leniency) and *supersedeas* (a corrupt document dropping a charge) do not compromise justice and rule the realm (C4.187–90). Reason will not stop, as he continues to explain the benefits to the King of policy reforms:

> "And Y dar lege my lyf [bet my life] þat loue wol lene þe seluer [loan you silver]
> To wage [pay] thyn and helpe wynne [achieve] þat thow wilnest aftur
> More then alle thy marchauntes, or thy mytrede [mitred] bysshopes,
> Or Lumbardus of Lukes [Lucca] þat leuen by lone as Iewes."
> The Kyng comaundede Consience tho to congeye [dismiss] alle his offeceres
> And receyue tho [those] that Resoun louede; and riht with þat Y wakede. (C4.191–96)

Reason appeals to the King reasonably, explaining how love profits him, for kings will attend to an argument about money. So Reason tells him that "love" will, in fact, provide him silver to pay the troops and achieve victory, for Love can "wage" the King's realm better than merchants, bishops, and Lombard financiers, who were important moneylenders to the crown after the Jews were expelled from England.

The C addition may seem a somewhat disconnected elaboration on the Peace/Wrong conflict, the passus's apparent focus, but it relates in a fascinating way to the study of Mede's influence in law and governance. Langland's additions in C propose a new way of conducting state business of all kinds, based on love rather than on gathering funds from commerce and clergy. Reason does not say so explicitly, but he must be implying that merchants, bishops, and bankers are all agents of Mede, part of her corrupt, anti-love economy. Accordingly the King, in his need for money, faces the danger of becoming one of Mede's men. One might wonder what it means exactly, from an accounting perspective, that love instead of a banker can loan silver. Presumably, if the King rules justly and resists Mede, a more humane means of exchange and funding will emerge: the King will have the trust and love of his people, who will support him, so he will not have to borrow to pay his war debts. This may seem both utopian and Machiavellian, but Reason knows how to appeal to his audience, and a government based in love, however nebulous the details, defeats one based on bribery and corruption. Langland knows that the moral reform he seeks will never occur without good government, without leadership, without a majestic model of virtue, freed from the lust for acquisition that Mede and her master Wrong demand.

Reason's expanded role in C continues, for now that he has instructed the King, he prepares for his next target, the poet himself—this "Will" who has been dreaming and reporting everything. Therefore C ends this passus uniquely with Will waking up, setting up the first line of its passus 5, the poet's only surviving backstage interview, his "autobiography." In the A text, passus 5 begins the great "confession" scenes, which correspond to B5 and to C6–7. For before the poet's apologia, Langland traces the penitential impulses that first pricked him to dramatize the art of confession and led him to impose a form of it on himself in his final revision.[2]

A last thought, lest readers forget someone who has been so important and to whom we now have to say farewell if not goodbye: Lady Mede. She keeps silent in A throughout Reason's speech. In B, she mourns because "þe mooste commune of þat court called hire an hore" (B4.166). In the C text, Langland inflames the insult: "For þe commune calde here queynte-comune hore [a cunning, common whore]" (C4.161). We neither see nor hear of Mede again in the poem, at least as a personified character, but Langland leaves no doubt, in this final image, about her seductive power or about the scorn and disgust she provokes when she fails to seduce.

6

I Confess

PASSUS 5 OF THE A TEXT

Conspectus: Conscience begins preaching a comprehensive critique of the personal and social behavior of the laity and clergy. Repentance formalizes the process by hearing the detailed and lusciously evil confessions of the Seven Deadly Sins (with the exception of Wrath). The substantial differences in passus divisions across the versions complicate parallel discussion, especially because in the C text Langland composes new material and also imports much matter from later in B. Accordingly, this section focuses on the confession scenes in the A text, and section 7 studies the B and C revisions.

In passus 4, the King, Reason, and Conscience planned to govern together and to forge an alternative to Mede's regime, but the text never addresses the outcome of that plan. Will wakes up and regrets that the vision has ended. As if in wish fulfillment, he grows faint, mumbles his rosary, and falls asleep again, witnessing more, he says, than he had seen before (A5.1–8). Langland wants him asleep so that the unbound landscapes of imagination can appear. God does not send these dreams, so they contain no message of instruction or protection, as biblical dreams do. Rather the poem hastens to the dream world as a refuge and a source of information, however oblique, that the waking world will not render. Will recounts a sermon he hears Conscience preach with a cross, perhaps fulfilling the promise of the first dream that he would help the King rule. Conscience first, in a line unique to A, "preyede þe peple haue pite on hemselue" (12), a confusing if not shocking line, since it suggests a therapeutic sense of self-forgiveness that cannot really apply here. But "pite" can also mean "sorrow, grief; misery, distress; also, remorse" (*MED*, def. 3a) and thus functions here as a form of awareness, the pricking of conscience, as it were, that compels the folk to feel a corrective regret and thus to guard themselves from future sin.

The next lines (A5.13–20), in another way, may rattle modern readers, proposing that God uses natural disasters to punish human sin, a concept that inspires ridicule today when preachers claim that weather, disease, or other natural phenomena manifest God's anger. Conscience describes, as Will recounts, how the wind blows down pear and plum trees and turns great oaks upside down with their tails in the air, hiding in fear of further punishment at doomsday. Modern secular society often portrays Nature as beautiful, perhaps divine, but certainly as indifferent to human suffering and not as an agent of divine wrath. But Langland models his imagery on Old Testament apocalyptic stories such as the Flood and the destruction of Sodom, and Langland's culture and audience see disaster as a karmic response to sin, illustrative of a power that can rage and punish "in toknyng of drede / Þat dedly synne er domisday shal fordon [destroy] hem alle" (19–20).

Conscience then identifies individual agents in society and chastises them. Significantly, he first singles out the persistent figure of Waster, who stands for anyone who squanders food, money, or other goods earned by the "winners" who labor honorably. Now, says Conscience, Waster should work and earn properly, laboring "wiþ sum maner crafte" (A5.25) because everyone must have a legitimate job in a just society. In another uncomfortable moment for modern readers, Conscience tells husbands to beat their wives at home instead of letting the law do it and tells parents not to spare the rod lest they spoil the child. Conscience feels that "wynning" (here the acquisition of things) will "forwanye" young children (33), employing a unique verb that comes from the word "wānen," to lessen, and thus means "to weaken (someone) morally" (*MED*, s.v. "forwānien"). Comfort spoils and nurtures children into sin and self-indulgence, likely making them grow up wasters.

Conscience addresses next the priests and the prelates, or bishops, who should practice what they preach, threatening that if they fail in their pastoral duty, the King and his council will reduce their provisions (A5.38)—and, further, will "be steward of ȝoure stedes til ȝe be stewid betere" (39), a multilayered line that likely means "manage your own affairs better or the crown will do it for you," for "stouen" means to restrain (*MED*, def. 2a). But it also plays on the verb "steuen," to bathe, and the related noun "steue," which refers to the bathhouse/brothel or "stews" (*MED*, def. 2a), implying that the clergy commit lechery and maintain it in their bishoprics. The sound play of artful alliterative dynamics across the a- and b-verses on "steward" and "stewid" draws attention to these similar terms of guidance and control. With the added pun on "steuen," this strongly compressed line threatens the clergy with a takeover unless they reform and end their support—and patronage—of brothels.

Repentance runs in and makes Will weep, prompting, in one of the most well-known episodes in *Piers*, the confession of the Seven Deadly Sins, a logical result of the "will" feeling remorse after the workings of "conscience." This scene tests the limits of allegory. For if a sin repents, it loses its characterological status as sin, so the entire enterprise seems contradictory. The event of confession does nothing to change the face of society, but the richness of the detail and enduring power of the images convey great power and insight into Langland's moral world. As the ironic adage says, "Heaven for the climate, hell for the company," and like the gruesome sinful displays in Dante's *Inferno*, these spicy confession scenes keep readers coming back for more. They also recall Chaucer's best work, the prologues of the Wife of Bath and the Pardoner, which lustily celebrate the sheer delights of the sinful body.

The *Canterbury Tales* starts with a penitential impulse in pilgrimage and ends with a handbook on sin; the poem moves from morally nebulous tourism to administrative pastoral care, the institutional foundation of reform in Holy Church. By contrast, in *Piers* the pilgrimage to truth is preceded by confession as a precondition for a healthy advance to Truth, as sinners must purify their antisocial and competitive impulses. But Langland also wants to give his sinners an opportunity to show how much they enjoy their alluring vices and how much pleasure and material success they bring. Langland makes sin savory for the simple reason that pleasure in all forms—physical, emotional, mental—is absolutely *pleasurable*. Prospering effectively and seeing the misfortune of neighbors and competitors brings the sinners profound joy. Repentance, in exhorting them to the path of selfless Charity, has his hands full, for vital energy, ever active and usually triumphant, favors sin. Langland sees social change as the collective effort of each and every man and woman who should choose love over aggression. For Langland, sin involves competition, a kind of grasping, an urge to advancement, which one can understand from a Marxist perspective but also from Hindu and Buddhist moral doctrine. Many religions base reform on humility and on denial of competitive appetite and agree that "desire is the root of all evil." Change depends on an awareness of a good outside of one's self. So Langland portrays personal virtue and social justice as nearly indistinguishable. To do good means to care for others charitably. Against virtue rages humanity's animal appetite, hidden often behind a pleasant public face but ruthless when revealed. Readers can group the sins variously, designating Pride, Envy, and Covetousness as social because they thrive on friction and competition, but all the sins display a social component, with no victimless crimes. One can group Lechery, Sloth, and Gluttony as physical acts of indulgence, but they also involve neglect and, potentially, abuse of others. Throughout these portraits, Langland entangles all the sins in a web of familial, communal, and institutional relations. He often explores whether anyone can live a single day in the active world without sinning, displaying in these confession scenes very little evidence or hope that anyone can.

Pride, manifested as a woman named Pernele Proud-herte in all versions, comes first because all other sins arise from pride. She reveals a desire to elevate herself above others, to compete, to conquer, to disparage, to lord it over anyone and anything. In repenting, Pernele says she will put away her finery and wear a hair shirt, but one wonders if she is not overcompensating. She pledges that her "hei3 [haughty] herte" will no longer control her and that she will not react to slander, which would be quite a change, for as she says, "so dide I neuere" (A5.50–51). Considering how much medieval literature depicts destructive lust, readers might imagine the depiction of Lechery as a tour-de-force moment, but not here in the A text. Langland, concerned more with sins of ingenuity than of weakness, gives Lechery four colorless, perfunctory lines, as the sin promises to fast, either to stave off desire or as penance for his acts (54–57). Only the total omission of Wrath stands out more as a distinct feature of A's confession scenes. But although Langland omits a monologue for Wrath, anger infiltrates all the social sins, while no one practices lechery, not even Glutton's drunk pals and prostitutes. Lechery must not have engaged Langland's imagination or his reformist agenda in the A text, though that changes in B and C, both in the confession episodes and elsewhere, as sex and the body play intensified roles in Will's life and in the lives of the folk.

In contrast to Lechery, Langland makes Envy quite a crowd pleaser: pale, pasty, armed with a knife and with some markings of a friar's wardrobe, he resembles "a lek [leek] þat hadde leyn longe in þe sonne" (A5.64). Powerful language describes this sin's physical being and temperament: "His body was bolnid for wraþþe [swollen with anger], þat he bot [bit] his lippes, / And wroþliche he wroþ his fest [wrathfully wrenched his fist]—to wreke hym he þouȝte [as if to avenge himself]" (66–67). The line expresses the heavy, groaning pain of this sin, audible in the *o* sounds and snarling *wr* alliteration. The furious obsession with competition and resentment makes his body monstrous and violent. If Jesus commands love of neighbor, the social sins replace that love with unquenchable hatred, effacing the image of God in humanity and rendering it venomous and grotesque. Will elaborates on Envy's hypocrisy, recounting how he greets a friend lovingly in the market but really, in a shocking line unique to A, rather "wolde murdre hym" (84). He prays in church for others' misfortune and spies hatefully on someone with a new coat, wanting it and the whole cloth it came from too. "Þus I lyue loueles lyk a lyþer dogge [hateful dog]" (98), says Envy in a terse summary of his being, for he neither loves nor is loved, and he doubts that confession could purge his poisonous breast of gall. Repentance tells him to show sorrow for his sins, and without missing a beat, Envy replies that he is sorry, and in fact is "selde oþere [seldom otherwise]" (105), since he suffers so much sorrow when others succeed, apprehending the term as personal and not penitential. Such comic moments indicate either that the personifications of sins can cleverly use wit to outsmart Repentance or that they, so inextricably bound to sin, cannot display any emotion beyond their allegorical parameters, which makes their "confession" so wonderfully ridiculous.

Covetousness comes next, though Envy will not likely covet *his* coat, for so threadbare it is, says Will, that unless "a lous couþ lepe," she could never jump from thread to thread (A5.112–13). Covetousness claims various professions, abusing retail mercantile practice through false weights and measures, stretching cloth, and, along with his coconspirator wife, watering down the beer for "laboureris and lou3 folk" (135). Customers get to taste the good stuff, then buy a gallon of swill at the top-shelf prices. Covetousness cannot contain the pride he feels for his clever mate, "Rose þe Regratour [retailer]," who came up with this trick, in a half line that most editors end with an exclamation point: "þat craft my wyf vside!" (139). Middle English literature often exposes bad marriages, but here Langland portrays a happy couple working in tandem for family profit, an ironical portrait of marital harmony and bliss.

The confession ends as Covetousness swears off sin and, with alliterative fervor, promises "neuere wykkidly wei3e [to weigh] ne wykkide chaffare [commerce] make" (A5.143). In penitence, he vows to visit the shrine of the Virgin Mary in Walsingham and to bring his wife too. He hopes that the cross will bring him "out of dette" (145), a wonderful play upon the central spiritual theme of the poem, paying one's debt to neighbor and to God. B and C vastly expand this episode, reflecting Langland's growing sense that Covetousness, like Mede, most comprehensively embodies the evil that becomes the central target of his moral, reformist critique.

Glutton eagerly awaits his confession, ready to show his "coupe"—from Latin *culpa*, meaning sin, but with a pun on what he really likes, a "cup" of beer (A5.146–47). So he easily gets waylaid on the way to church by Betty the Brewer, her beer, and the promise of some bar snacks, and a daytime bar party ensues. All the regulars attend: tinkers, seamstresses, ditch diggers, rat catchers, priests, and whores, with a drinking game (an auction of a coat), singing, laughing, and lots of rounds in a Felliniesque celebration of fun that seduces both Glutton and the reader. He eventually gets drunk and irreverently "pisside a potel in a *Paternoster*-while" (191), the time it takes to say the Our Father. The confession ends just as this kind of revelry usually ends—with the drinker swearing off the cup forever. But fun has a price: Glutton pays with a hangover, and the reader with disgust at how the body avenges itself for all this abuse. The sinner then becomes lazy and sleeps the whole weekend. In A this is attributed to an "axesse [fever]" (203), but either through misunderstanding or sonic association, this word becomes *accidie*, Latin for "sloth," in B and C. Gluttony leads to sloth, and so Sloth confesses next, but not until Glutton has pledged to see his Aunt Abstinence, and not until he asks for a beer, a little hair of the dog, as the proverb says, and gets chastised by his wife, likely not for the last time.

Sloth sleeps, shockingly, until awoken by the allegorical Vigilate (Latin imperative for "keep watch"), who tells the lazy sin to guard himself from despair and gives him the confession formula to repeat: "'I am sory for my synnes,' say to þiseluen" (A5.219). He pledges to go to church and says he regrets having made illegal profit (lazy people like to cheat and steal instead of working). Another character then appears, a fellow named Robert þe robbour, not an allegorical sin but a version of all thieves. He thinks he has an inside track to forgiveness, and appeals to the mercy that Christ showed to his "broþer" Dismas, the crucified thief promised Paradise by a dying Christ for his great faith (239). Will doubts this appeal will work and explains that for redemption to occur, penance must guide his steps on the pilgrimage to truth and charity:

> Ac what befel of þis feloun I can not faire shewe [clearly demonstrate].
> Wel I woot he wep faste watir wiþ his ei3en,
> And knowelechide [acknowledged] his coupe to Crist 3et eftsones [quickly],
> Þat *Penitencia* his pik he shulde pulsshe [polish] newe. (A5.247–50)

With that the A text is just about done with this riffraff, though Will sees a thousand more such sinners crying to Christ and to his clean mother for the grace to get to Truth. "God leue [permit] þat hy moten [they may]!" (256), says Will encouragingly, and the passus ends. One wonders if the confessions have prepared the folk to reach Truth, and what Langland expected to achieve with these monologues, whether real human change or just theatrics. Allegorical sin by its nature can never complete the work of confession, and by binding sin in such allegory, Langland binds his characters perpetually to theater. Their performances must always remain spectacle, but also spectacular. The art of confession, the introspection that leads to self-knowledge and contrition, never becomes more effective, in the sacramental sense, in the B and C revisions. But what does evolve and expand is the extravaganza, the festive celebration of boundless and delicious evil.

7

And I Confess as Well

PASSUS 5 OF THE B TEXT AND C TEXT PASSŪS 5–7

Some revisions in the poem seem closely tied to the historical moment behind them, as in a C-text revision that calls for social unity and likely as well for calm after the Peasants' Revolt, representing Langland's, or at least Reason's, antipathy to that violence and its disordering effect (C5.180–90). And in fact throughout C5 Langland makes some of the most dramatic changes in the *Piers* corpus, perhaps reflecting concern about his poem's effect on readers and on his society. The B text indeed witnesses some changes and elaborations, as Langland expands Conscience's speech in A and reassigns it to the character Reason, and adds much detail to the various confession scenes from A as well. But in C the poet shatters the simplicity of presentation in the prior versions. Perhaps he feared that readers had misunderstood the kind of social change he advocated. Reason leaves no doubt in C that humanity should create on earth a model of the "holy comune" in "heuene an heyh" (186), a harmonious community that Lucifer shattered in his bold rebellion. Such changes likely reflect another motivation beyond the enforcement of social order: revision means artistic dissatisfaction, for no one revises a successful line or episode, though measuring success is not a simple matter. The B and C revisions to A5, among the boldest and most elaborate in the entire poem, reveal a struggle to capture in verse what sin, conscience, reason, and repentance mean, and how humanity can gain the self-knowledge that leads to grace. Langland must have seen that the programmatic march of sins, queued up for confession, however delightful and brilliant in detail, inadequately expressed his message of reform. Change need not mean the upheaval of social order but only of sin's dominance over the heart. Overthrowing sin, however chimerical that may seem, would constitute a successful "revolt" for Langland. Good guidance, pastoral administration, and communal responsibility—the focus of C's revisions—help maintain order, perhaps ironically, the strongest basis for positive social change. For these reasons, C5 demanded Langland's special care as, at once, his most personal and most political passus.

I. Gregory the Great to the Rescue

As a reflection of these increasing concerns, in C Langland transfers into Reason's speech a passage from A11 (expanded in B10) where Clergy praises Gregory the Great, the sixth-century pope who sent missionaries to Christianize the Anglo-Saxons and who thus exemplifies pastoral leadership (C5.146–67).[1] In its respective contexts in all versions, the passage criticizes clerics for riding out hunting as if they were lords and for making their knaves kneel to them, while they live at ease and despise the poor. Anywhere he is summoned as a paragon of clerical perfection, Gregory brings some badly needed leadership, administration, and pastoral authority to the problems of a rampantly corrupt clergy who have strayed from his ideals. But in C specifically the shift brings greater urgency to some prophetic verses that Langland had already added to Clergy's speech in the B text. So in his sermon in C5, after exposing the indulgences and ambitions of the lordly clergy, Reason promises them:

> Ac þer shal come a kyng and confesse 30w alle,
> And bete 30we, as þe Bible telleth, for brekynge [breaking] of 30ure reule,
> And amende 30we monkes, moniales [nuns] and chanons,
> And potte 30we to 30ure penaunce—*Ad pristinum statum ire,*
> And barones and here barnes [sons] blame 30w and repreue [rebuke].
> (C5.168–72)

In their new context, these words now serve as prelude to Will's apologia and to the march of the Seven Deadly Sins. They starkly intensify the meaning of the word "confess," threatening that clerical sins, once revealed to a king, will result in powerful penitential punishment—seizure of their lands and wealth by the crown. The king evoked here indicates temporal political power but implies as well that the heavenly King too may exact a price for clerical abuses. The Latin b-verse of line 171 means "to return to an undefiled state," as Langland believes that the clergy, as established by Christ, once practiced a purity of intention that they now have forgotten and corrupted.

After this extraordinary revision created by importing the homage to Gregory the Great, the C text rejoins B to bring Reason's sermon to a close. But as a coda to the Gregory material, C patches into B with two verses that expand and intensify Reason's implicit hope for clerical renewal, offering this promise of future reform: "Ac ar [before] þat kyng come, as cronicles [chronicles] me tolde, / Clerkes and Holy Kirke shal be clothed newe" (C5.178–79). In predicting new clothes for the clerics, a metonymy for comprehensive renewal, the reformist Langland planted seeds of what would become, 150 years later, the disendowment of a bloated, worldly clergy in England. The texts then proceed in parallel again for the moment, as in both versions Reason advises the King to love the commune and prays the pope to have pity on Holy Church. But then in C, Langland inserts into Reason's discourse another call for reform, now directed at monarchs, enjoining confessors not to absolve Christian kings unless they first practice peace and love:

> And sethe a [then he] preyede þe Pope haue pite on Holy Chirche,
> And no grace ne graunte til good loue were
> Amonges alle kyne [the various] kynges ouer Cristene peple:
> "Comaunde þat alle confessours þat eny kyng shryueth [absolves]
> Enioyne hem [enjoin them to] pees for [in order to receive] here
>   penaunce and perpetuel forʒeuenesse
> Of alle maner accions, and eche man loue other." (C5.191–96)

In A, Conscience's sermon targets the folk, prelates, and the King; in B, Reason expands the scope of reform to the pope and lawyers, who need to control their appetites; but in C, Reason focuses on a universal Christian political order founded in love. Langland's scope expands ever outward as he demands more and more from individuals, from institutions, and then from all the nations in Christendom. Wanting more may reflect an increased expectation of Christian triumph or perhaps, quite differently, a sense that Christendom was failing on an ever grander scale. In embracing global reform at the highest ranks of power, Langland cautions readers that change does not come only from individuals confessing and promising to treat each other well in business and daily affairs, but must also arise from a new way of understanding the role of clergy in the world, which includes crushing their worldliness and pomp. At the same time, worldly princes must display deep Christian principles of compassion and love. One wonders how this intensified engagement with global political and clerical structures—the macrocosm, as it were—relates to the other great C-text addition, the stunningly personal encounter between Reason and one lone man, the poet himself.

II. A Poet's Confessions

This unique episode (C5.1–108), often called the apologia,[2] comes during a break in the action in which a waking Will, who now has a wife named Kytte and dresses like a "lollare,"[3] encounters Reason, who interviews him about what exactly he does with his time, for he seems like a bum. Anne Middleton sees the episode as Langland's response to the strictures against idleness put forth in the 1388 Statute of Laborers, a premise influential in the dating of the C text.[4] Artists have frequently found themselves interrogated about the value of the life of the mind, perceived as so removed from the world that it breeds consternation and resentment from any "reasonable" observer, and so Reason demands that Will justify his social value.[5] Reason first asks him about clerical service, which he considers worthy labor, and then asks him whether he can perform a series of mostly agrarian jobs. Will confesses himself not built for hard physical work, which inspires Reason's wrath and suspicion:

> "Can thow seruen," he sayde, "or syngen in a churche?
> Or koke [pile hay] for my cokeres [harvesters] or to þe cart piche,
> Mowen or mywen [mow or stack] or make bond to sheues,
> Repe or been a rypereue and aryse erly,
> Or haue an horn and be hayward [fence warden] and lygge þeroute anyhtes [keep vigilant each night]
> And kepe my corn [grain] in my croft [enclosure] fro pykares [pillagers] and theues?

> Or shap shon [shoes] or cloth, or shep and kyne [cows] kepe,
> Heggen or harwen [trim or harrow], or swyn or gees dryue,
> Or eny other kynes craft þat to þe comune nedeth,
> They [ybetered be] therby [(so that) the lives are improved], þat
>   [of those who] byleue [sustenance] the fynden [find for you]?"
> (C5.12–21)

When Will pleads himself as "to wayke to worche with sykel or with sythe" (23), Reason asks if he lives off his lands or from a rich lineage. Essentially, Reason wonders if Will ever gets his hands dirty or is only a trust-fund boy, in his words "an ydel man," a "spendour þat spene mot, or a spille-tyme [time-waster]" or a beggar, which is "lollarne lyf þat lytel is preysed [praised]" (27–28, 31).

How extraordinary that in a poem about work, perhaps the premier medieval poem about work, the poet accuses himself of an off-putting idleness. Reason has carefully surveyed many positions in agriculture: hay baler, hayward (a fence warden, keeping cattle away from crops), hedge trimmer, planter, among others. Langland's own realm of work involves no hay, soil, hedges, or grain, but he must have wanted to express the reality of work in a poem that otherwise makes so much metaphorical use of it. Human sustenance depends on work that brings food. Langland produced nothing and so has become self-conscious about his pursuit of the life of the mind, perhaps at once looking back over decades of writing *Piers Plowman* and wondering what sort of worthwhile labor he has accomplished. Thus he wants to record the details of an agricultural labor history he knew, respected, and was indebted to, in order to give it proper place in the poem and history. The simple act of naming the labors, somewhat otiose in the immediate context, writes into history the workers who could never have so inscribed themselves.

Will then explains himself as an intellectual and a clerk, not an idle loafer who never worked, though he admits that he works differently. Too tall, he says, to bend over to do farm labor, he prays rather for the souls of his generous benefactors. As an educated man who knows Latin, he earns money by saying the formal prayer sequences for the dead—a valuable skill in medieval Christian England. Modern secular society has no equivalent vocation, but Will sounds like a former graduate student who never quite finished his degree or earned a proper position in academia but learned enough to tutor in Latin and thus scrapes by. He recites prayers and Psalms, wandering where needed and welcome, not making much money and certainly not saving any. He begs, he says, "Withoute bagge or botel but my wombe one [stomach only]" (C5.52), and thus humbly, and in accord with Jesus's words in the Our Father, seeks only his daily bread. He wields not farm implements but the Latin words of the prayers he recites for his patrons:

> The lomes þat Y labore with and lyflode deserue
> Is *Pater-noster* and my prymer [prayer book], *Placebo* and *Dirige*,[6]
> And my Sauter [Psalm book] som tyme and my seuene psalmes.
>   (C5.45–47)

As the poet struggles to justify himself in a world of labor and sweat, at least he can defend himself from the charge of "waster." Langland enforces this standard of virtue from the poem's beginning, and now, later in life, in the third version, he applies it rigorously to himself, as an artist struggling to justify why he does not labor to put food on anyone's table.

The next section (C5.53–81) may discomfit readers: Will quotes scripture's injunction against making clerks work, culminating in a haughty assertion of elite privilege: "Hit bycometh for clerkes Crist for to serue / And knaues vncrounede [untonsured] to carte and to worche" (61–62). This elitism offends twenty-first-century democratic readers, though very few medieval "knaves" would have read the text and experienced this insult. Will, becoming strident, continues to expatiate upon the issue of social station, berating those who attempt social climbing, warning that in both clergy and knighthood only those descended from franklins and married couples should aspire to advancement. Everyone should keep his or her place instead of aspiring to transcend station, he implies, by bribery and corruption, paying off clerical and political authorities to advance their children and secure them prominent and underserved church appointments. Will targets, in a biting line, "Bondemen and bastardus and beggares children," suited only to labor (65). These lines do not charm a modern audience, which either forgets or violently despises the notion of social station. But Langland sees upward mobility as part of a corrupt system of disorder, marked not by merit but by graft and the forces of Mede. No one mentions her at this point, but everyone feels her presence.

Conscience, who presumably has been listening, pipes up and questions Will about this begging and wonders if perhaps he ought to be part of an organized religious order, connected to "prior or to mynstre" (C5.91). Will, as if a nerve has been struck, admits that he has "ytynt [wasted] tyme, and tyme myspened [misspent]," (93) but like a merchant whose fortunes rise and fall in business, he hopes that in the end he will make a profit, a divine one:

> So hope Y to haue of Hym þat is almyghty
> A gobet [piece] of his grace, and bigynne a tyme
> That alle tymes of my tyme [moments of my lifetime] to profit shal turne. (C5.99–101)

Will prefaces his self-depiction as a merchant with monetary metaphors from the Gospels, which translate as "The kingdom of heaven is like treasure hidden in a field" and "The woman that found a silver coin" (98a).[7] Langland employs economic imagery *in malo* and *in bono* from the very beginning of the poem, and it makes sense that Will, so detached from anything close to real commerce in the competitive world around him, indulges ironically in the hope for profit, at once mocking and redeeming the practice of "winning." Langland shows that commerce may not lead to heaven but that God reveals a system of mercantile imagery that a good Christian poet can embrace and turn to advantage, professionally and personally.

Langland never admits to being a poet, but we cannot resist reading this misspent time as the activity that readers as well are currently engaged in: struggling with this way of life called *Piers Plowman*. Reason evidently understands the ingenuity of Will's mercantile conceit, since he approves, though rather guardedly, of his activities, as long as his life is "louable and leele" to Will's soul (C5.103). "Lovable" does not mean merely, as in Modern English, charming but, more sternly, "admirable, praiseworthy, excellent" (*MED*, adj. 2). Likewise "leele" for the soul means "loyal" in Will's relationship with his creator, a divinely sanctioned responsibility to honor the image of God within him (*MED*, s.v. "lēl," defs. 1a–e). Will believes that he has led such a life, and his entire justification constitutes one of the most provocative and complex episodes about the vocation of writing in medieval English literature. The personal, philosophical, emotional, and spiritual richness of this interlude drives Will to church, to the cross, and to his knees, weeping and wailing until he falls again asleep. After this extraordinary episode, with his self-confrontation unsteadily behind him, Langland can carry on with the confessions proper. The third time around, he simply could not listen to them again unless he unburdened himself and heard his own first.

III. B5 and C6–7 Stage the Seven Deadlies

In a dramatic revision, Langland imports into the confession scenes at C6 material from B13, where an unusual figure, Haukin the Active Man, offers a long confessional explanation of his everyday activities, presenting himself as a lumpish everyman who commits, however innocently, all kinds of sin, manifested charmingly in his losing battle to keep his cloak clean. Langland saw wisely that the poem did not need two major confession episodes, and so he relocated long passages of B13 to create one deluxe confession episode. Reading in parallel reveals the literary artistry in Langland's adaptation of Haukin's discourse into various other voices, dismantling a character into its constituent parts and finding the suitable characters who could speak those words consistently. But if Langland's expansion of the confessions in B reads as rather straightforward addition—more of the same sins with greater intensity and variety of imagery—then the inclusion in C of the Haukin material creates another effect. Readers see Haukin as a lumbering innocent, even a lovable everyman, who sins uncontrollably simply by acting in daily life. Merging his matter-of-fact voice with the existing monologues not only expands the range of sin but also makes the sinners ever more oblivious to their vice, as they prattle on in C in a frighteningly sociopathic elocution that never reaches self-knowledge.

Many portraits expand in this major shift. Pernele Proud-herte still confesses, but after she is told to repent, a newly crafted, apparently male figure named Pruyde asks for penance, acknowledging his disobedience to parents, God, good men, and Holy Church (C6.14–19). Further, in adapting material imported from B13, he boasts, as Haukin did, that he longs to be known not only as the cleverest clerk and the strongest horseman but also as "styuest [stiffest] vnder gyrdel, / And louelokest [loveliest] to loke vppon and lykyngest abedde [most pleasing in bed]" (C6.43–44). If Langland intended all this boasting, sexual or otherwise, as an expansion of Pernele's confession, then he did not maintain much gender consistency, though indicating, perhaps, that pride knows no such bounds. The poet then revises his portrait of Envy, trimming his friar's outfit and also A's and B's marvelous depictions of him as a lean leek that sat too long in the sun. But C adds some details from Haukin's discourse about how he becomes ill when he cannot dominate others and how he uses gossip and slander to sow hatred among his neighbors (C6.69–85). For many readers of all versions, Langland blurs the attributes of sin, particularly Wrath, Pride, and Envy, which blend into one another as antisocial sins. The Haukin material, freely distributed among the portraits, works well with almost any sin because Haukin complains how all aspects of the "active life" provoke misdeeds. Langland's revisions in C appear inventive and productive, though only modern parallel readers know where the material comes from, and original readers of C would simply have marveled at the vastness and volubility of transgression. Collecting all the details of sin together in confession, ironically, is something a Christian must do in penitential practice. So Langland, as a poet, models (at least for himself) real Christian work, attempting to control sin as best he can, as if literary order could translate into a moral one. But the more Langland seems to gain poetic control, the more the sins blithely expand their domains beyond Repentance's moral governance and perhaps beyond hope of reform.

B remedies Wrath's unexplained absence from A (B5.133–85) by creating the angry voice of a mendicant, a gardener in the priory, who conspires to "graffen impes [graft branches]" of lies onto his fellow friars, an image that anticipates in a perverted way Piers Plowman's tending of the tree of Charity. This grafting blooms into the friars' subservience to wealthy lords and into the practice of providing easy penance, which makes sinners flock to the friars instead of the parish priest (135–41). In C, Langland demurs at that image in favor of describing how Wrath incites women. In B, Wrath as a cook in a convent stirs up trouble in the kitchen by getting the nuns to gossip about scandalous pregnancies:

And maad hem ioutes [stews] of ianglyng [gossip]—þat Dame Ione
  was a bastard,
And Dame Clarice a kny3tes dou3ter—ac a cokewold [cuckold] was
  hir sire,
And Dame Pernele a preetes fyle [daughter]—Prioresse worþ [become] she neuere,
For she hadde child in chirie-tyme [cherry-time, spring], al oure
  Chapitre it wiste [knew]!
Of wikkede wordes I Wraþe hire wortes [vegetables] made,
Til "Þow lixt!" and "Þow lixt!" [you lie] lopen [lept] out at ones
And eiþer hitte ooþer vnder þe cheke. (B5.156–62)

C omits the romantically sweet and suggestive "chirie-tyme" but expands the scene by adding an episode in church, where Wrath sits among the women of the parish. "Amonges wyues and wydewes Y am woned [accustomed] to sitte," says Wrath (C6.143), manifesting as one of the women, seething in hatred of those around her, especially if someone receives the "haly-bred" (146), not the Eucharist but bread served after mass, before she does. Wrath then describes the effect of the mutual hatred he inflames:

Aftur mete aftirward, [heo] and [heo] chydde [this woman and that
  accuse each other]
And Y, Wrath, was war [ready], and wrathe on [provoked anger in]
  hem bothe,
Tyl ayþer clepede [called] oþer "hore," and on with the clawes—
Til bothe here hedes were bar and blody here chekes. (C6.147–50)

So much of *Piers* concerns everyday life and real human experience, and not all women serve as nuns, so in C Langland expands the B text with this more familiar scene from the pews, as the wives and widows spar over their perceived status and call each other whores. Wrath, proud of the trouble he causes, complains that he has to avoid monasteries because they do not tolerate his mischief but rather whip him on his "bare ers" with no britches between (B5.173). Langland often charts the body as a source of sin, but he also marks it as the spot that suffers sin's result.

As for Lechery, since B does not expand A's cursory portrait, in C Langland imports seedy detail from Haukin's discourse in which Will explains how sexual mischief has soiled his cloak (C6.176–83). In B13, Will says the Active Man has flirted and conjoined with various like-minded women. Lechers like Haukin commit such sins whenever they can, says Will, regardless of religious holidays or Lent, until they become too old to perform and so rely on exchanging ribald stories.

> Swiche werkes with hem were neuere out of seson—
> Til þei myȝte na moore [could perform no more], and þanne hadde murye tales,
> And how þat lecchours louye laughen and iapen [to play],
> And of hir harlotrye and horedom in hir elde [old age] tellen.
>   (B13.351–54)

In C Langland expands and intensifies the imagery, pushing the scene nearly into the pornographic as Lechery recounts his sexual escapades:

> Such werkes with vs were neuere out of sesoun—
> Til we myhte no more; thenne hadde we mery tales
> Of putrie [whoring] and of paramours, and preueden [achieved] thorw speche
> And handlyng and halsyng [touching and hugging], and also thorw kyssyng,
> Exited either oþer til oure old synne;
> Sotiled [composed] songes and sente oute olde baudes [go-betweens]
> To wynne to my wille wymmen with gyle.
> By sorserie sum tyme, and sum tyme by maistrie [dominance],
> Y lay by þe louelokest [loveliest] and louede here neuere aftur.
> When Y was olde and hoor, and hadde ylore [lost] þat kynde [natural ability],
> Y hadde likyng to lythe of [listen to] lecherye tales.
> Now Lord, for thy lewete [justice], on lechours haue mercy!
>   (C6.184–95)

Langland changes the meaning of B's phrase "no more" from aged impotence into temporary sexual exhaustion, remedied, says Lechery, by using "mery tales" and mutual touching to get stimulated again. In B13 Haukin capitulates to old age and takes refuge in filthy talk, much as Chaucer's aging Reeve does in the prologue to his offering in the *Canterbury Tales*. But in C, Lechery makes talk part of the *remedy* for detumescence. This erotic ingenuity fits well with his other practices, which include using sorcery and force to bed lovely women and then abandon them. These strategies must not work perpetually, however, because Lechery, like his counterpart in B, finally becomes "olde and hoor," reduced to mere aural sexual experience, once "kynde" finally fails. What started in A as an essentially empty portrait has become a dirty little scene, and it reveals, like the catfight in Wrath's confession, the sometimes underappreciated intensity of the C text.

Likewise the confession of Covetousness expands across A, B, and C, as Langland lavishes attention on his favorite topic and transfers generous selections of the Haukin material to beef up C's version, also adding a new passage about usury, spoken by Repentance:

> And there shal he wite witterely [know well] what vsure is to mene,
> And what penaunce the prest shal haue þat proud is of his [the usurer's] tithes.
> For an hore of here ers-wynnynge [ass-winnings] may hardiloker [more confidently] tythe
> Then an errant vsurer, haue God my treuthe,
> And arste [sooner] shal come to heuene, by [Hym] that me made.
>   (C6.303–7)

In this remarkable imagery, "ers" plays off "arste" (soonest) and creates the unique "ers-wynnynge," a distinctly Langlandian invention (the only listing in the *MED*). For a poet so learned in exegetical method and grammatical gloss, Langland knows how to express human experience without adornment, exposing the body's work through sin, pleasure, and commerce. Yet these so-called ass-winnings, however raw in expression, were honestly earned, in contrast to the treacherous profits of Covetousness and his usury.

In B and C the crowd-pleasing Glutton episode remains decidedly and purposefully "low." In a B and C expansion, Glutton, drinking and pissing and farting the night away, finally stumbles home, assisted by his mates, who try to carry him home in one piece. But too fat and too full, he vomits violently:

> Clement þe Cobelere kauȝte hym by the myddel
> For to liften hym olofte, and leyde him on his knowes [knees].
> Ac Gloton was a gret cherl [big guy] and a grym in þe liftyng [tough to lift],
> And kouȝed vp a cawdel [pudding] in Clementes lappe.
> Is noon so hungry hounde in Hertfordshire
> Dorste lape of þat leuynge, so vnlouely it smauȝte [foul it smelled]!
> (B5.352-57)

The sheer volume of what Glutton wastes indicates an abundance that others could have enjoyed, but after he has digested and vomited it, even a dog would not eat this mess. Mede and Glutton, though one a great lady and the other an oaf, similarly misuse the economy, as both channel resources for profit and pleasure. Glutton's grumbling stomach serves as the locus for any critical engagement with ethics and economics in *Piers Plowman*. So much of *Piers* involves the gut, the center of daily commerce, the great hub of ambition and exchange, the seat of natural hunger and of the appetite for excess. The visceral nature of Glutton's behavior recalls equally trenchant lines from Envy, whose mouth is so full of venom from indigestion that he cannot scrape it clean:

> May no sugre ne swete þyng aswage my swellyng,
> Ne no diapenidion [sweet medicine] dryue it fro myn herte,
> Ne neiþer shrifte ne shame, but whoso shrape [scrape] my mawe?
> (B5.121-23)

Langland uses the body for maximum revulsion in these scenes, manifesting sin as vomit or, here, as a glandular excretion to be skimmed physically from the membrane, as if that would stop its generation in the body of a man who cannot stomach anyone else's success.

Next B and C actively develop A's short portrait of Sloth. Wasting time with frivolous entertainment, he knows more about Robin Hood than about Christ and Mary (B5.394-97). Sloth never visits the sick; he forgets debts and misses church to linger in bed in his lover's arms; when manifested as a priest, he hunts rabbits better than he sings mass or reads a saint's life (406-29). Fascinatingly, he claims he cannot understand love or comprehend the good deeds his neighbors do for him: "If any man doþ me a bienfait or helpeþ me at nede, / I am vnkynde ayiens his curteisie and kan nauȝt vnderstonden it" (430–31). Ironically, one can admire the energy with which he assembles his sins, for if he applied himself to virtue as well as he has to the scope of his confession, he would have made a good man of himself.

Perhaps fear of committing this very sin motivates the poet to labor in expanding this portrait. One wonders if Langland still feels the sting from Reason's rebuke about his idleness in C passus 5, and perhaps in a subtle way he externalizes that fear into work as a poet. For in C, Langland, not himself lazy, imports an extended passage from Haukin to expand the portrait further with a meditation, in Will's voice, on the "braunches þat bryngeth men to sleuthe" (C7.69–118a), an elaboration of human frivolity, mindless minstrels, flattery, fools, and harlots, who waste time in chatter and lead people to sin. The Slothful, says Will, do not want to hear about God but rather about "harlotrie," "horedom, or ells of som wynnynge" (74–75). Sloth means enjoying fun, sex, and money, for any energy used for pure pleasure misdirects the will away from charity. Langland uses sinful triplets like this throughout the poem, implicitly opposing them to three more difficult but sacred duties that God demands, exemplified in the virtuous trio Dowel, Dobet, and Dobest. To this end, Will continues that patriarchs and prophets have saved many men from hell through sermons (88), but they cannot compete with the appeal men see in a flatterer or a fool. Rich men, at their meals, says Will, ought to replace these entertainers with beggars, blind men, and bedridden women (101–8), for these "thre manere [three types of] munstrals maketh a man to lauhe, / And in his deth-deynge they don hym greet confort" (109–10). In these ingenious verses, Langland converts the empty laughter and comfort of indulgent escapism into the spiritual laughter of salvation, which the wealthy can enjoy if they invite the needy and helpless to their table. Modern readers might wonder if Langland's hope would only inspire what we now call a photo op, a staged moment when a powerful person assumes a virtuous posture by posing with the suffering to attain public acclaim, the mere performance of charity and a hollow populism. Langland would no doubt maintain the hope for a true charity beyond craft and cynicism, but it must have been a difficult virtue to find, though certainly worth imagining and longing for.

The confession episode begun in A5 comes to an end when B and C merge again as Repentance, who has been absorbing and officiating, puts a hopeful spin on the whole affair by invoking the concept of *felix culpa*, the "happy fall" in which a tragic event occasions a redemptive result (C7.122–50). Sin, though a "sykenesse to vs alle" (124), nonetheless enabled God to become man. Langland recounts the life of Christ later in B and C, but he foreshadows that life in depicting Nature's reaction to Jesus's crucifixion, as Repentance describes it: "the sonne for sorwe þerof lees [lost] siht for a tyme" (131). In this meditative spirit of pathetic fallacy, Repentance begs Christ and Mary to have "reuthe of alle these rybaudes [scoundrels]" (149), and in a jaunty moment, Hope grabs a horn and starts to blow on the Psalm verses, including "Beati quorum remisse sunt iniquitates / Et quorum tecta sunt peccata [Blessed are they whose iniquities are forgiven, and whose sins are covered]" (152–52a; Psalms 31:1). Sinners must hold on to God's revealed Word and his poetic promise of protection. Readers, through time, must contemplate whether this song of Hope sounds sweeter than the sordid melodies of sin, celebrated so passionately by the Seven Deadlies. But a hero now approaches who may provide an answer.

8

A Pilgrim and a Ploughman

PASSUS 6 OF THE A TEXT
WITH THE CONCLUSIONS OF B5 AND C7

Conspectus: A5 ended with the horde of sinners crying for grace and looking for the way to truth. A6 begins with this weepy crowd hoping for a guide to take them to the next step after confession, the rigorous penitential journey to Truth. This short, tight passus of only 126 lines is closely paralleled by the continuing sections of B5 and C7.

I. The A Text

Before the folk meet the poem's hero, Piers the Plowman, they encounter a pilgrim, overloaded with souvenirs from the Holy Land, covered with badges and phials of holy water pinned to his clothes, a tourist in a T-shirt essentially, sporting some Levantine trinkets in the mere performance of sanctity, oblivious about how to find Truth (A6.1–24). This harlequin provides no help to the folk, and just as things look grim, in dramatic fashion a plowman pops into the scene and swears gently by St. Peter his namesake that he has been working for truth for forty years, sowing and hauling and digging and doing all he can to serve his lord, Truth. As he reports:

> I haue ben his folewere [follower] al þis fourty wynter—
> Boþe sowen [sown] his seed and sewide [looked after] hise bestis,
> And eek kepide his corn, and cariede it to house,

Idyked and idoluen [ditched and dug], ido þat he hiȝte [done what he demands].
Wiþinne and wiþoute waytide [attended to] his profit. (A6.30–34)

"He is þe presteste [promptest] payere þat pore men knowen," continues Piers, because he "wiþhalt non hy[w]e [withholds from no worker] his hire þat he ne haþ it at eue [by evening]" (A6.38–39). Piers describes a divinely sanctioned business relationship between the Christian and Christ, the most prompt of payers. Mundane labor relations may not practice justice and fairness, but Christ offers a pure and guaranteed contract. Piers proposes here a divine definition of labor as serving God and being justly rewarded for it, providing the poem a dominant metaphor for spiritual labor. However gritty *Piers* may seem in its realistic depiction of everyday work, it always aspires to one ultimate kind of labor, that of love. Readers will wonder what this appeal to divine justice and ultimate payment from Christ means in the here and now for those who work physically in order to eat today—one of the poem's ongoing inquiries, unanswered here.

Piers faces a difficult task. The crowd at the start of this passus bluster forth "as bestis" (A6.2). Piers claims that, among his other chores, he herded God's animals, and now he has more beasts to tend. They offer him money, because they cynically assume that everything in life must be paid for and that nobody does anything for anybody for nothing. Piers, the exemplar of virtue, wants no reward and promptly sends the would-be pilgrims on a rigorous journey. His directions to Truth advance through some bizarre allegory, including the directions to cross the brook called "Beþ-buxum-of-speche [be obedient in speech]" (53), hard to visualize topographically but expressing a theme often underestimated in *Piers*: the cultivation of humble compliance and the distaste for arrogant rebellious speech. In a poem so reformist in tenor and so often associated in the critical literature with revolt, readers may not surmise that every familial and social relationship begins with "buxomness," the enemy of Pride. This virtue does not manifest explicitly any of the Ten Commandments, several of which form stations along the path to Truth, but it may constitute Piers's version of the first, "I am the Lord thy God . . . Thou shalt not have strange gods before me" (Exodus 20:2–3). Langland here either adapts the commandment impressionistically to his core doctrine of deference or offers a general exhortation to humility. It may also represent Christ's injunctions to love God and to love one's neighbor, recounted in the preceding lines (A6.48–52), since Piers says that in order to practice charity, one must find and travel across this brook. Speaking humbly and knowing one's place means maintaining order and recognizing God as lord and sole authority—a moral foundation that prepares the folk to venture through the Commandments and to God.

The journey progresses to Truth's gatekeeper, Grace, attended by Amend-ȝow [Amend-yourself], to whom, says Piers, the folk must explain how they have accomplished the penance that their priest assigned (A6.85–90). Amend-ȝow holds the key to Truth's realm and thus to salvation. Seven sister virtues serve as porters to help pilgrims through: Abstinence, Humility, Charity, Chastity, Patience, Peace, and Largess. But virtue poses a wonderfully interesting danger, A, B, and C all contend. For one's "bienfaits [good deeds]" (101), says Piers, might foster pride. Welcoming Grace brings one closer to Truth and thus closer to God, but the folk must beware of "Wraþþe-þe-nouȝt" (98), the danger of irate provocation, who has "enuye to hym þat in þin herte sitteþ" (99), that is, he envies Truth and provokes the Pride that makes people praise themselves.[1] Considering this danger, one must do good without finding pleasure or pride in the act. Only humility can protect men and women from the blinding pride that drives sinners out of Truth's realm, as the sun drives out the dew and, in a strange mixed metaphor, shuts the door, "ikeiȝed and ycliketed [locked and latched] to kepe þe wiþout" (103). So if even the virtuous might submit to sin in the course of being good, the folk, as yet untested morally, now begin a much more difficult journey than imagined.

II. Some Particular B and C Revisions

The end of B5 and C7 remain faithful to much of A6, but with one exciting revision that typifies the differences among the versions. In A, when describing how sin came into the world, Piers tells the folk to get Amend-ȝow to open the gate that Adam and Eve shut when they "eten here bane" (A6.93). In B, Langland writes instead that Adam and Eve ate "apples vnrosted [unroasted]" (B5.603). This likely means that they existed in an innocent state of nature before the advent of cooking, and it also cleverly underlines their impulsiveness, for if they had waited to roast the apples, which sounds tasty, they could have deliberated upon their actions and thought better of them.

In C, Langland replaces this comic conceit with Piers's injunction to have Grace open the gate that "Adam and Eue a3enes vs alle shette" (C7.249), a colorless image that adds little, because the gate is already shut or Grace would not need to open it. C's reputation as inferior comes from this sort of dulling impulse. But not to be undone, Langland then makes a dramatic change that more than compensates for the blunder: he converts the key master from "Amend-3ow" to Mary herself, Christ's mother. A says that Amend-3ow has the key to the gate, even though the king is asleep—a confusing image, for when is God asleep? Perhaps this means that the door of grace stays ever open, day and night. B adds a liturgical Latin verse explaining that Mary opens the door that Eve shut, framing history with the actions wrought by two women, one gracefully undoing the former's sinful mischief (B5.603a). But the addition of Mary in B either created some pronoun confusion or otherwise provoked C's strangely inspired revision of the passage:

> A full leel [gracious] lady vnlek hit of grace [unlocked it for grace]:
> Heo hath þe keye and þe clycat [latch], thow þat kynge slepe,
> And may lede in þat heo loueth [whomever she loves] as here lef
>   lyketh [as it pleases her]. (C7.250–52)

Masculine "he," which had referred to Amend-3ow, becomes feminine "heo," since Mary now has the key. The sleeping king dramatically refers now to Christ, asleep in her womb, in a strikingly intimate maternal image. Jesus the baby, unborn and so fragile in his humanity, sleeps while his mother prepares to lead whomever she chooses through the gates of salvation. Langland masterfully makes sense of A's oblique conceit and turns it into something lovely and stirring, the tableau of a sleeping God and a gracious Mother Mary, laboring to save souls.

Despite C's addition of a prosaic passage describing a henpecked, uxorious husband babbling about how he cannot take part in the pilgrimage to Truth (C.291–303a), passūs A6, B5, and C7 end similarly, with the riffraff—ape keeper, pickpocket, and wafer seller—despairing of the journey because they have no connections to Truth. B alone adds a common woman and a pardoner who will pretend to go there as siblings (B5.639–42). C adds the meditative words of a new voice, Contemplation, perhaps emblematic of the aging poet himself, pledging endless devotion to Piers the Plowman in what reads much like a meta-narrative moment, referencing not only the title character but also the very poem he is composing:

> Quod Contemplacion, "By Crist, thow Y care soffre,
> Famyne and defaute [deprivation], folwen Y wol Peres.
> Ac þe way is wel wikked, but hoso hadde a gyde
> That myhte folowe vs vch a fote for drede of mysturnynge [fear of becoming lost]!" (C7.304–7)

Langland knows the dangers of undertaking this journey without a guide. In the guise of Contemplation, a figure with whom he must have felt a special kinship at this thoughtful age, he pledges not just to follow Piers but also implicitly to become the guide for his readers through time, bucking them up for all the bumps and bruises to come, the twists and turns ahead. And though Langland leads, his humble tone and shared sense of anxiety number him among the worried but hopeful folk.

9

The Hunger Artists

PASSUS 7 OF THE A TEXT WITH B6 AND C8

Conspectus: Piers the Plowman promises to guide the folk to Truth but has a half acre of land to plow first. In a test of community, Langland explores whether a group of bestial, wandering sinners can work effectively on one focused project. The confession scenes revealed them as sinful, bound to pride and envy. Working together means sacrifice and tempering that pride in favor of a larger goal than personal pleasure and profit, but it cannot be accomplished without the help of Hunger. The Black Plague in the fourteenth century led to significant rises in the price of labor, and the statutes of 1351 and 1388 sought to control the movement of workers and their ambition for higher wages. Langland's meditations on work, food, and justice (in all versions) may contain his response to the crises of labor shortage in his time. And yet the problem of balancing fairness, equity, productivity, and appetite points to a universal problem in human social history.

I. The A Text

As Piers tries to wrangle the folk, the women wonder how they can serve while the men do the backbreaking work of plowing. Their fingers, Piers tells them, can perform finely detailed work, sewing wheat sacks to preserve the harvest and garments for priests. With much work to go around, this gendering of labor illustrates that each person must know his or her own duty. Sewing wheat sacks and vestments precludes outfitting oneself with finery, so such work inherently combats pride.

The division of labor continues as a knight, in a fascinating exchange, wants to contribute to the plowing (A7.23–51). In the twentieth-century Cultural Revolution, Chinese communists sent city folk to the countryside to learn from the peasants. Piers Plowman has no such plan for members of other estates, and he does not want the knight to do any plowing but rather to maintain his work in law enforcement, which makes safe plowing possible. Piers does not shrink from instructing a knight who outranks him, since the plowman's authority is deeply sanctioned by the poet and since Piers becomes ever more Christlike as the poem advances. Even here he has the authority of a supervisor, transcending class and rank among all involved. Piers is in charge, and the wise will heed him. That the folk have appealed to a humble plowman to guide them bodes well, as it reveals their potential for humility, a form of "buxomness" and thus a first step in combating pride.

Piers tells the knight to treat subordinates well and not to take bribes, lest he have to repay them in purgatory (A7.38–44). Then Piers adds, in what seems odd advice to a knight, to avoid harlots, which are not prostitutes but losers and troublemakers, and not to listen to any tales from "deuelis disours [Devil's storytellers]" (49). Langland fears words that harm, as proved in several of the confessions, because words have targets and victims—the innocent whose reputations, so valued in the close communities of this culture, suffer from loose talk. Slander, the use of untruth as a weapon, impedes the way to divine Truth.

Piers tests the folk with plowing because of the deep resonances of the imagery and the action. Plowing depends on the biblical context of labor, sowing and harvesting, so prevalent in first-century Judean culture and so familiar to the Gospels' original audiences throughout the Mediterranean world, and also, since agricultural history changes slowly, to Langland's English audience. Professional farmers likely did not read *Piers Plowman*, but learned clerks in an agrarian culture can comprehend scenes of work, digging, sowing, and laboring, as both tangibly real and richly allusive.

Piers will feed everyone who "feiþfulliche libbeþ," but he excludes some people, such as "Iakke þe Iugelour and Ionete of þe Stewis [brothel]" (A7.63–64). Of these and of the foulmouthed, Piers says, quoting Psalm 68:29: "Deleantur de libro viuencium . . . Et cum iustis non scribantur [Let them be blotted out of the book of the living . . . and with the just let them not be written]" (A7.67, 68a). Piers's quotation of this Psalm may strike readers as incongruous and even bathetic. The Psalmist asks God to take vengeance on Israel's enemies and at one point says, "in my thirst they gave me vinegar to drink" (Psalm 68:22), a verse that finds its Christian prophetic fulfillment during Christ's crucifixion. The present context thus seems unworthy of this invocation, as jugglers and the other riffraff hardly reach the epic grandeur of the Psalmist's enemies, whom God will curse by deleting their names from the book of salvation. But Langland adapts it to his immediate culture and concern. In the absence of Israel's enemies, Langland wonders who in his world will be erased from the book of life. Piers seems a judgmental bore here, and readers may not be out of sympathy with the braggart who pipes up later in the passus and tells Piers to "go piss" with his plow:

> Þanne gan Wastour [to wraþen hym] [to get angry] and wolde haue yfou3te;
> To Peris þe Plou3man he profride his gloue.
> A Bretoner, a braggere, abostide hym alse [confronted him too]
> And bad hym go pisse [get lost] wiþ his plou3, pilide [hairy] shrewe!
> "Wilt þou, nilt þou, we wile haue oure wille
> Of þi flour and of þi flessh, fecche whanne [take whenever] vs likeþ,
> And make vs merye þermyd [therwith], maugre þi chekis [despite you]." (A7.139–45)

The energy of this scene distorts its meaning: no one likes a do-gooder bossing them around, and readers likely will side with the folk resisting Piers's humorless strictures and condemning voice, for Langland seduces readers into aligning themselves with the miscreants. Piers, like any supervisor, is tedious. Plowing and sowing are tedious, like any labor one must undertake in working toward salvation, as Chaucer's Monk makes clear in his refusal to study all day while he could be out hunting.[1] The venture of the folk working for common profit fails, and readers are partly responsible. If this seems bold, it attempts to capture Langland's art of drawing the audience into the conflicts of the poem, and not necessarily on the side of good. The folk resist virtue, and readers, falling into Langland's trap, resist as well, unconsciously numbering themselves among the wasters and wastrels. Langland's moral artistry wants readers to recognize and reject this identification.

In contrast to the wayward and lazy among the folk, we meet Piers's family:

> Dame Werche-whanne-tyme-is Piers wyf hatte;
> His douȝter hattiþ Do-riȝt-so-or-þi-damme-shal-þe-bete;
> His sone hattiþ Suffre-þi-souereynes-to-hauen-here-wille-:
> Deme[judge]-hem-nouȝt-for-ȝif-þou-dost-þou-shalt-it-dere-abiggen.
> (A7.70–73)

Such epithets are signature Langland devices and bear the ethic of the poem: Piers's wife, the colorless "work when it's time to work"; his daughter, "do right or your mother will beat you"; his son, "obey authority or else!" These rigorous names may jar contemporary readers, but obedience to authority establishes social order. Submission bespeaks reverence to parents, to local authorities in one's community, and, by analogy, to God. Piers's family displays all the virtues that the lazy, resistant troublemakers among the folk do not: duty, sobriety, and obedience.

Before the pilgrimage to Truth begins, Piers writes his will, as one might do before a dangerous journey. Among the details, he announces that he always returned whatever he had borrowed before going to bed (A7.78–96). An honest person pays debts before sundown. But when Piers says that his plow will now become his pikestaff, we do not know whether he speaks literally or metaphorically or both. Piers will not stop plowing, per se, but his plow will now function as a staff on the pilgrimage to Truth. But pikestaff can also mean a pickax, a tool for digging, arising from Piers's reference to picking at the roots and cleaning the furrows (96). Observing an almost Buddhist mindfulness, Piers will enact an interior, meditative pilgrimage while laboring. And as for paying debts, he does not merely mean that he returns a borrowed tool but rather that he observes *all* the debts that one has to pay, both to others and to God, merging the literal, the allegorical, and the spiritual. Langland writes human action as it ripples through eternity. While he likely saw plowing being done, it is not his calling, as he confesses in C5, but knowing its metaphorical power and sacred resonances, he imaginatively has made it into his vocation.

Piers now stops plowing and starts supervising, standing in judgment of the lazy who won't plow. Some drink at the pub and sing "Hey trolly lolly," which does not get much work done. Others claim disability and ask Piers to pull their weight, but it's a scam by the "faitours [fakers]" (A7.113), a bunch of slackers who try to live off others' labor, and Piers knows it. He may seem harsh in denying them care, but Piers tries to protect the truly needy, the crippled and bedridden, and feigned disability abuses the rights of the injured and infirm. Piers develops a ground-up system of justice that begins with the soil and the hands that work it. In this he observes both biblical command and the demands of everyday life, for plowing and growing do not change much over time. Langland's agrarian Christian culture inherits the burdens of Adam, who lived far away and long ago but still had to stoop and sweat to earn his daily bread, just like any English man or woman.

Piers will fund the anchorites and hermits who claim a legitimate reason for not working, promising to feed them once a day at noon, which ought to be enough for one who does not labor, "Lest his flessh and þe fend foulide [corrupt] his soule" (A7.136). Piers functions here not as the Church nor as the government, but rather as the collective will of the commons, the force of labor's productivity that will do its part to feed the needy, to care, as he says, for the "blynd or brokesshankid [broken-limbed] or beddrede [bedridden]," and for the "ankeris [anchorites] and heremytes þat holde hem [themselves] in here sellis" (130, 133). This commitment by labor to serve the needy and the religious exemplifies the pilgrimage to Truth. Not an abstract, mystical odyssey but a constant burden of charity, this journey starts with the individual "will" doing what Piers requires physically, ethically, and spiritually to ensure justice.

At this moment the braggart steps up and tells Piers to "piss off" with his plow, disrupting the whole affair. Although God made humans in his image, Nature, such as Langland understands it, makes them more animalistic than angelic. In response, Piers summons another allegorical character, the redoubtable Hunger, who makes wasters work and mysteriously cures the sick and disabled, for handouts tend to breed dependency, exploitation, and indolence. Waster's response is bold: "I was not wonid [accustomed] to werche... now wile I not begynne" (A7.151). Hunger acts mercilessly, quickly provoking labor, and Piers's authority increases with his harsh stance. Work earns food, and Hunger, who plays fair, accordingly retreats. Humans have deep animal longings, none greater than hunger, and here on the half acre their appetite, at least initially, effectively goads the folk to work. But Hunger does not offer his services full time or for free, and when he rests, the whole system of control breaks down. Because of the instability of human appetite, Langland fails in the A text (perhaps by design) to solve the problem of sin at the bodily level. This leads him in revision to interrogate Will's higher faculties to see whether, and how, they can help. No one can precisely calibrate the human stomach to make workers just hungry enough, just at the right time, to ensure that the body will labor virtuously for the common good.

Yet the rest of the passus attempts to do exactly this. Hunger suggests that Piers feed the false beggars rough grains (essentially horse food), and if they complain, to tell them to work and to earn the right to "soupe swettere" (A7.198–203). Hunger has plenty of scriptural support for his tough love, citing some good old "sweat of your brow" imagery from Genesis (216–17). Victims of misfortune merit charity (204–12α), including those "þat nedy ben or nakid, and nouʒt han to spende" (209), but those who shirk the biblical injunction to labor should receive nothing until they work for it. And when Piers reports many of his people as ill (237–40), Hunger identifies the problem as overeating and recommends a restrained diet. That will cure them, says Hunger, and will even put Fisik (medical doctors) out of business, making them sell their Calabrian cloaks (expensive and fur-lined), take down their shingles, and start working with their hands (252–58).

Throughout this Hunger episode, Piers struggles to fill the stomach or to empty it into submission. The complexities of dealing with this organ assert themselves at the end of the passus when Piers thanks Hunger and sends him on his way (A7.259–85). Hunger does not go easily. He wants, unsurprisingly, to eat some more, and the whole field of folk has to feed him what seems like an excess of food that reveals something of medieval English cuisine: beans, baked apples, onions, and cabbages, a generous meal for a friend who provided a service and some good advice, but allegorically it means that the folk have overeaten again. Now they become finicky and will eat no bran but only fine white bread; no light beer now but only heavy brown ale; and no leftovers either, only food *chaud* or *pluys chaud* [hot or very hot]" (295) will delight them (Langland uses French to make them sound extra fussy and arrogant). Plus they want high wages or they will curse the king for "suche lawis to loke [enact], laboureris to chaste [punish]" (299).[2] And yet when hunger masters them, they do not complain, for no one would resist Hunger's demands ("stryue aȝen his statut") when they are hungry, "so sternely he lokide!" (301). People get finicky when times are fat, but Hunger crushes prideful self-pampering and the rebellious behavior that comes when food is plentiful, which provokes the desire for ease, high wages, and luxury. The human animal reacts urgently when the primitive fear of hunger stirs, but no attack of Hunger can effectively regulate fallen humankind. The passus ends in the poet's voice with a cryptic warning that workmen should guard against Hunger, who always lurks, ready to harass wasters (302–7). Hunger has stolen the stage from Piers in passus A7, but he has not brought the folk any closer to Truth, the goal of the entire enterprise. Instead Hunger has revealed himself as a vital human reality that will alternately plague, impede, and impel the folk throughout their unfolding journey.

II. Revisions in B6 and C8

The parallel sections of B6 and C8 correspond to A7 closely, and the poet's comfort with his work attests to how well this passus defines the central difficulties of getting hungry people to work together for common good. But some local changes in B and C merit attention.

When reading in parallel, one feels a stern trebling from A to B to C in Piers's encounter with the knight. In A, Piers tells him to be good to his subordinates. B intensifies with a memento mori warning that even though someone is today your underling, one day he may be set above you in heaven, adding the scripture verse "Amice, ascende superius [Friend, go up higher]"[3] and the chilling reminder that in the charnel house no one can tell who was a somebody or a nobody: "For in a charnel at chirche cherles [commoners] ben yuel to knowe [difficult to identify], / Or a knyȝt from a knaue þere—knowe þis in þyn herte" (B6.48–49). In C, Langland takes his own cue and revises the bland b-verse of B.49 into a brilliant new line: "Or a knyhte fro a knaue or a quene fram a queene" (C8.46), punning on the meanings of "queen" as a sovereign or a strumpet (*MED*, s.v. "quene"), since death levels all conventional social status. For a poem that treasures obedience to social order, with reverence for authority and hierarchy, *Piers* evokes the most bracing imagery of transience and the grim illusion of worldly pomp, recalling God's reminder to Adam and Eve that they were wrought from and will return to dust. Perhaps related to this revision, C uniquely gives the knight who hears the mememto mori a wife (C8.55), a detail that compounds the image of female bones in the charnel house. Now the knight, forbidden to work the soil, nonetheless must contemplate his own and his wife's eventual reduction to dust. He thus escapes the plowing required by Genesis but not the final return to the soil that God commands.

In another compelling triplet, Piers excludes some sinners from the profits of his plowing. To A's jugglers, whores, and loudmouths, B adds the friars, part of the poem's ongoing evocation of anti-fraternal satire (B6.72). In C, Langland accuses the friars further, calling them "lollares" and "loseles" (C8.74). Few words in *Piers* carry more political weight than "lollares," because the word seems to include, in addition to its basic meaning of a bum, *the* Lollards, the proper noun referring to followers of John Wyclif, though Langland does not intend that direct meaning here.[4] In C he adds this word not to make any particular statement about Lollardy nor about reform but to intensify the accusation against the friars, now linking Friar Faytour and his kind to idle vagabonds, whose names should, along with the whores, be blotted out of the book of life. In light of C's apologia, and the poet's self-consciousness about his activities, this addition also allows the poet to continue the introspection that he started in that major intrusion of biography into the *Piers* corpus in C5. Langland sees himself and his own failures everywhere, even in the friars. Becoming one with the subject indicates that Langland reaches beyond the external moral condemnation inherent in the genre of medieval satire and models for his clerical audience a relentless self-confrontation.

Langland in C makes another stark addition, offering some paternal advice from Piers directly to his son, after the boy is introduced. Piers's advice extends the theme of obedience in the boy's long name to include the king, mayors, and great men:

> Consayle nat so þe comune þe Kynge to desplese,
> Ne hem þat han lawes to loke, lacke [blame] hem nat, Y hote [advise]:
> Lat God yworthe with al [care for it all], as Holy Wryt techeth:
> *Super cathedram Moysi sedent.* (C8.84–86α)

The scripture alludes to Matthew 23, when Christ indicts the scribes and the Pharisees who "sit on Moses' seat" whom his followers must obey in word but not in deed. This indicates that Piers's son should listen to the doctrines and laws of authorities but not imitate their hypocritical actions. This addition, advising civic obedience, may respond to the Peasants' Revolt and its bloody beheadings. Perhaps Langland knew that some of the men killed by the rebels were criminal in their treatment of the people, and so without outright condemning the revolt, he suggests obedience to the rule of law, based on principles of justice, however corrupt and hypocritical the agents of government may be. In the C text, considering what A and B intended in the boy's name, Langland turns obedience into a comprehensive Christian practice of civic order and virtue. The line found in all versions, "let-God-worþe-wiþal [leave-it-all-to-God]," which in the A and B texts is a formal part of the boy's name (A7.74; B6.82), may seem a generic statement about accepting God's will, but in C, with Langland's addition, it becomes a poignant disavowal of the violence that had based itself, without Langland's sanction, on the B text's poetic record of injustice and on its heroic empowerment of labor.[5] Langland seeks justice, but he knows that vengeance is God's alone to administer.

Another revision, concerning mercy, illustrates Langland's evolving thought across the versions and perhaps reveals as well the changing concerns of the older, more contemplative poet. In A, Piers feeds Hunger with a cheap horse bread:

> And wiþ a benene batte [loaf of bean bread] [bo]ȝede [dropped down] hem betwene,
> And hitte Hunger þermyd amydde hise lippes. (A7.165–66)

In B, with a shift in syntax, Piers addresses Hunger directly, asking him to permit the hungry workers to eat farm animals' fare:

> "Suffre hem lyue," he seide "and lat hem ete wiþ hogges,
> Or ellis benes and bren [bran] ybaken togideres." (B6.181–82)

But in C, rather we read:

> "Haue mercy on hem, Hunger," quod Peres, "and lat me ȝeue hem benes,
> And þat was bake for Bayard, hit may be here bote [benefit]."
> (C8.177–78)

C replaces the hogs with the horse Bayard, and the word "mercy" powerfully reveals a softening unto compassion of what started out in the A text as wordless force-feeding. After three attempts to negotiate with Hunger and to satisfy both human appetite and the imperatives of communal labor, Langland wants compassion to flourish in his final text.

And mercy, in fact, informs the story for the rest of the passus. When he asks for Hunger's parting advice about what to do if the folk slacken in resolve, Piers, in A and B, says that love will guide his response: "Treuþe tauȝte me ones to loue hem ichone / And helpe hem of alle þing aftir þat [according to what] hem nediþ" (A7.194–95). But in C Langland expands the passage with some love of his own, as Piers tells Hunger,

> "Hit is nat for loue, leue hit [believe it], thei labore thus faste [work so eagerly],
> But for fere of famyen, in fayth," sayde Peres.
> "Ther is no filial loue with this folk, for al here fayre speche;
> And hit are my blody bretherne, for God bouhte vs alle [saved us all].
> Treuthe tauhte me ones to louye hem vchone [each one]
> And to helpe hem of alle thyng, ay [always] as hem nedeth."
> (C8.214–19)

Love has many meanings here. The people, in their eagerness to work, says Piers, act not from love but from a fear of Hunger. And while in A, B, and C Piers calls the folk his bloody brethren, in C alone he laments that they do not return his affection, despite their fair speech. C's emotional urgency explains why the entire system of appetite regulation cannot work, for Hunger targets the stomach and not the heart. Piers learns as the poem evolves, as does Langland, and only in C do they each understand the failure of the folk on the half acre as a failure of love.

The last major revision in this sequence further bespeaks the evolution of tone across the versions. In A, B, and C, Hunger recommends restraint so that folk do not overeat and become slothful and picky. But in C a more learned Hunger summarizes Luke's parable about the rich man Dives and his neglect of the beggar Lazarus, who dies of hunger (C8.278–89; Luke 16:19–31). Hunger asserts himself as a character in the biblical tale, which features no such allegory, but the parable nonetheless displays his deadly power and God's harsh judgment of those who fail to care for the poor, for God condemns Dives to hell. Hunger then warns Piers not to emulate that stingy rich man but rather to share his bread with "alle þat grat [cry out] in thy gate" (284). Piers can also feed the "lyares and lach-draweres [thieves] and lollares," but must not give them a crumb until his "nedy neyhbores" have been fed (287–89). This biblical exemplar applies only obliquely to the dramatic context, for Piers is no selfish Dives, but Langland uses Luke's story to intensify his message about the need for charity and compassion for all those who seek food. B and C then adhere closely to A for the rest of the passus. In C Langland changes the tone of the episode emotionally, but he cannot change the truth of the human stomach. The great experiment in controlling labor with Hunger ends in a resounding failure—three times. Labor fails without love; the folk falter without grace; and Hunger enforces laws that no one dare disobey.

10

Dreams of a Pardon

PASSUS 8 OF THE A TEXT WITH B7 AND C9

Conspectus: With the folk's hunger for food satisfied but for salvation still unclear, A passus 8 tells the extraordinary story of how Truth, having heard tell of Piers Plowman and his activities, decides to offer him and his faithful folk a "pardon" that absolves them *a pena et a culpa*—from both punishment and guilt—and how a priest helps Piers read it. Every reader struggles with this episode, as Langland evidently did, because a pardon from Truth, offered through the pope, seems unassailably good. But appearances can deceive, for the folk's labor on the half acre loses value unless it functions penitentially, helping one to earn God's merit. The pardon threatens to provide a shortcut and exemption. God seems to be cutting through the confusion and rescuing the folk, their fluctuations of hunger and delicacy notwithstanding. Piers Plowman, mysteriously, wants no part of it.

I. The A Text

The passus begins with the nebulous origins of the pardon:

Treuþe herde telle hereof, and to Peris sente
To take his tem [team] and tilien þe erþe,

And purchacide hym a pardoun *a pena et a culpa*
For hym and for hise heires [heirs] for eueremore aftir. (A8.1–4)

Initially readers, and perhaps Piers also, perceive this promise as God's gift of grace to the poor struggling folk and to virtuous workers. But once a priest imposes himself as an authority, reads the actual pardon text aloud, and reveals its surprising contents, Piers tears up the document in one of the most famous scenes in medieval literature (A8.101). This "pardon" contains only two statements: "Et qui bona egerunt ibunt in vitam eternam. Qui vero mala, in ignem eternum" [Whoever does good enters into eternal life. Whoever does evil, into eternal fire.] (A8.95–96). These lines from the Anasthasian Creed starkly divide the saved and the damned, but they say nothing about *how* to do well or how to combat the urges of evil and sin. Before Piers rips this paper apart, Will surveys those who receive pardon, and those denied, according to their relative merit (9–88). Specifically everyone who helps Piers to labor will "part in [partake of] þat pardoun þe Pope haþ ygrauntid" (8).

The conventions of medieval estates satire, as in Chaucer's portraits in his general prologue, inform the distribution of pardon, as the traditionally greedy, like lawyers and merchants, deserve little or no indulgence, while the destitute and the virtuous, the old and the helpless, receive the most. Throughout this overview, Langland never makes clear precisely where Will gets this information, though several lines indicate the presence of written documents that accompany the pardon. For example, the merchants receive pardon "in þe margyn" (A8.20), indicating text added to a document, and Truth "sente hem [the merchants] a lettre" (25), which provides a specific medium at least for their instructions, which include using their profits for charity, hospitals, and infrastructure (26–35). And in the A text only Will receives a gift of clothing "for his writyng" (43) from the happy merchants, evidently pleased with the provisional pardon they receive. If "Will" indicates the narrator, then this strangely implies that he transcribed this letter from Truth, a confusing idea because Will observes these events but does not take part in them at this juncture. Since the pope granted the pardon, the rest of the information must come from a papal decree, since for example false beggars "ben not in þe bulle" (67). So at least two lengthy documents delineate the distribution of pardon, inspiring a sense of justice and moral order. But when Piers unfolds and opens the bull, "in two lynes it lay, and nouȝt o [not one] lettre more" (93), offering none of the detail that Piers, Will, and all readers were led to believe it contained. This bull, as it turns out, says almost nothing, and readers wonder what happened to the long list of pardon, which seemed part of the document but mysteriously now disappears. Piers's frustration with this shocking disjunction between the comprehensive promise of pardon and its final terms explains why he tears the document "for pure tene [anger]" (101), an action that Langland retains in B but omits from C, likely because, however apparent Piers's motivation, it does nothing to clarify an already murky situation.

Perhaps in all versions, but in A and B in particular, God tests Piers to see how he would react to an elusive pardon that provides no real pardon at all. If Piers and his creator Langland seek reform, they cannot rely on a single piece of paper, on any perceived indulgence, anything that smacks of potential exploitation. For as Chaucer shows in his critique of his Pardoner, no document or bull can save sinners from both the pain and the guilt of their actions. If the pardon contained the detailed, specifically worded directives Piers thought it contained, and not just an axiom about salvation and damnation, Piers would likely still reject it for the same reason. Perhaps, angry at himself for expecting some sort of indulgence, he now feels that God has tricked him, in a moment of weakness, into thinking that one document could end his search for justice. God indirectly tells Piers—and Langland too—that they have more work to do before their long labors can end.

At the same time, the list of those deserving and undeserving of pardon, though absent ultimately from the pardon text, delineates a true, humane ethic. Many readers fear that the innocent have received pardon only to have it taken away when Piers tears the document. The poem never clarifies the issue by describing the folk's reaction to the tearing—the disappointed poor who were promised much, or the lawyers who were promised little. Yet the tearing of the pardon does not diminish the doctrines that inform its proposed distribution. Nor does it lessen the relative worth of the folk in God's eyes. Neither Piers (at this point) nor Langland has the power to save or damn anyone, but the poet wants readers to witness and to remember the charitable who build hospitals, roads, and bridges, the "libbyng [living] laboureris þat lyuen be here hondis" (A8.63) and the "olde men and hore þat helpeles ben of strengþe" (82). Though they somehow disappear from the pardon, they are forever inscribed in Langland's book and, the poet clearly hopes, in God's as well, in a text that no one can tear.

In the larger movement of the poem, this episode provides a major transition that alters the plot and the imagery of everything that follows in all versions. Piers stops plowing and starts weeping, casting off the care of labor and devoting himself to penitential contemplation:

> "I shal cesse of my sowyng," quaþ Peris, "and swynke [work] not so harde,
> Ne aboute my belyue [sustenance] so besy be namore;
> Of preyours and of penaunce my plouȝ shal ben hereaftir,
> And beloure [frown on] þat I belouȝ [laughed at] er, þeiȝ liflode [food] me faile
> . . . .
> And but ȝif Luk leiȝe [Luke lies], he leriþ vs be folis [teaches us with fools]:[1]
> We shulde nouȝt be to besy [too concerned] aboute þe bely ioye [belly joy].
> *Ne soliciti sitis* [be not solicitous for your life], he seiþ in his Gospel,
> And shewiþ it vs be ensaumple vs selue to wisse [to instruct us].
> Þe foulis in þe firmament, who fynt hem [provides for them] a [during] wynter?
> Whan þe frost fresiþ foode hem behouiþ [they need food]." (A8.104–7, 111–16)

Despite the magnitude of this development, Piers's repudiation of plowing does not completely redirect his spiritual path. Physical work, always both real and also symbolic of virtuous action, already set Piers and the folk on a penitential, interior journey. On the half acre the folk learn not so much the specific craft of farming but rather the art of responsible, communal virtue, requisite to salvation. Plowing represents all work that builds society and fulfills God's injunction to Adam to labor with the sweat of his brow. With the experiment of wrangling the folk to work together only erratically successful, Piers decides that instead of breaking his back as the field manager of overeating minions, he needs to leave labor behind in favor of penance. Rather than accepting absolution "from pain and from guilt" in a pardon fraught with ambiguities, Piers prefers the cleansing pain of the Psalms in penance and weeping. He quotes the Psalter: "Fuerunt mihi lacrime mee panes die ac nocte [My tears have been my bread day and night (whilst it is said to me daily: Where is thy God?)]" (A8.110α; Psalms 41:4). Plowing, as the metaphor of virtuous sanctity, constantly animates the landscape of *Piers Plowman*, but before that image can be fully spiritualized, the poem needs to undertake a deeper, more interior journey. Piers, Will, and the folk must leave plowing behind, at least for now.

Piers's meditative tone in his farewell to farm work draws from both Old and New Testaments, including a Gospel passage from Luke where Jesus tells his followers not to be anxious about their sustenance:

> And he said to his disciples: Therefore I say to you, be not solicitous for your life, what you shall eat; nor for your body, what you shall put on. The life is more than the meat, and the body is more than the raiment. Consider the ravens, for they sow not, neither do they reap, neither have they storehouse nor barn, and God feedeth them. How much are you more valuable than they? (12:22–24)

The folk tried to store up grain against Hunger, but Piers now advocates detachment from worldly enterprise. The priest who read the pardon admires this display of learning, but Piers, suspicious of the priest's motives, confronts him in Latin: "E[j]ice derisores et iurgia cum eis ne crescant" (A.8.125α), a variant of Proverbs 22:10, "Cast out the scoffer, and contention shall go out with him, and quarrels and reproaches shall cease." Piers, scorning formal education and igniting a conflict between virtue and mere academic credentials, tells the priest that Abstinence and Conscience, and evidently not university scholars, have instructed him. As Piers moves from plowing to penance, he makes no friend of the bookish clergy, an agent of discord and scorn.

Overcome with too much to assimilate, Will wakes up, ending the second dream, which finds him "meteles and meneyles [hungry and broke]" (A8.129). Dreaming puts neither food on his table nor money in his pocket, and God's assurance of care for the otherwise careless birds provides nothing tangible for hungry Will. He wonders aloud whether to heed his dreams even though Cato the Roman philosopher deems them deceptive. However, Will opines, the Bible depicts important dreams divinely sent to Nebuchadnezzar and Pharaoh and read meaningfully by Daniel and Joseph. His dreams do not speak as clearly as those that God offers in revelation, Will avers, an observation that provokes him to probe further, with wit and imagination, into what his ambiguous, unstable visions might tell him.

At every turn Langland gives readers information to interpret, in dream or in speech, as he displays the art, either well or poorly done, of critical reading. The dream vision genre requires rigorous analysis of the dreamt text from the dreamer and the reader. Will knows that his vision carries meaning, however ambiguous, and as a faithful Christian he also believes that prayer, indulgence, and pardon effectively combat sin, with the pope as authority over these processes, based on Christ's words to Peter: "Quodcumque ligaueris super terram erit ligatum et in celis [whatsoever you shall bind upon earth, shall be bound also in heaven]" (A8.158–60a; Matt. 18:18). Will, convincing himself to believe in the powers of the Church as a human institution, struggles to reconcile authorities and to interpret the unstable dream. He resolves the issue by returning to the basic human obligations of charity, doctrines clearer, more tangible and stable than anything he encounters in dream, and more concrete than the institutional authority of the pope. Despite his required faith in papal administration, Will cautions the wealthy not to trust in pardons and memorial masses that they can purchase:

> And so I leue lelly (Lord forbede ellis!)
> Þat pardoun and penaunce and preyours do saue
> Soulis þat han ysynned seue siþes [seven times] dedly.
> Ac to triste on þis trionalis [three years of masses for the dead]—
>   trewely, me þinkeþ,
> It is not so sikir [sure] for þe soule, certis, as is Dowel.
> Forþi I rede ȝow renkes [men] þat riche ben on erþe:
> Vpon trist of ȝour tresour trienalis to haue,
> Be ȝe neuere þe baldere to breke þe ten hestis [commandments].
>   (A8.161–68)

Will struggles to make sense of the dream as it relates to the commodified processes of salvation in ritual Church practice, and he forces himself to reconcile theory and reality. The dream confuses Will, but he does understand, without struggle, its clear message about everyday virtue, and so in charity alone Will finds comfort and resolution. Having emerged from one interpretive morass, Will finds himself now in another, because virtue, however secure as a strategy for salvation, eludes easy definition. Will knows that Christians prosper more through charity than through anything they can buy, but this knowledge does not make Dowel any easier to define or to practice, and so Will's search continues, restlessly, as his soul hungers, like his stomach, for sustenance.

The passus ends not with more theory or speculation but rather with prayer. Will, having learned that salvation is not for sale, advises Christians to pray to God and his mother for mercy. They must hope that God will provide them the grace "suche werkis to werche [to do such deeds]" (A8.183) as merit salvation. Despite his anxiety about dream interpretation, Will resolves the conflicts in his vision by returning to virtuous labor and its uniquely spiritual purchasing power, a greater guarantor of salvation than the pardons, bulls, and indulgences that the wealthy and the wise accumulate.

II. B and C Revisions of A8

The A text's warning about false beggars (A8.67–81) who do not receive pardon occasions some revision in B, which argues that good people remain blameless when they give ignorantly to the unworthy, for only "in hym þat takeþ is þe trecherie" (B7.77). False beggars do not taint the virtue of the giver, but they corrupt the economic system of charity. Langland builds expansively on this theme in C and launches into a long meditation on the truly deserving (C9.71–161). The first line establishes a caring tone by indicating "oure neyhebores" as the most needy, and then follows a tour-de-force portrait of medieval English poverty. Langland must have felt that, for all its poignancy, the pardon episode needed more human detail, and so he has Will survey images of prisoners in cells, and of poor folk, specifically women, "in cotes [hovels]," spinning cloth piecemeal to pay for rent and to buy the milk and meal to make porridge for their hungry children, often going hungry themselves (C9.72–83). Perhaps this reveals why Piers does not tear up the pardon in C. Such an act may have struck Langland as finally unnecessary, given Piers's repudiation of its advertised promise and its non-pardoning language.[2] But this added passage on the poor, free of bathos and mawkishness, perhaps constitutes implicitly the text of a new "pardon." This sequence offers no specific absolution from pain and guilt, but by immortalizing in poetry the suffering and anxiety of his fellow Christians, Langland depicts a human deprivation that merits redress and cries out for justice.

Will does not forget men, who deserve care as well, the hungry and thirsty men, too proud to ask for help. Bound to duty and to appearing strong in adversity, these men would rather starve than beg and will not reveal their need to their neighbors. Charity and pardon will know what these men keep hidden (C9.84–87). Next (as the categories overlap) comes a parent with "many childrene" who has "no catel [money] but his craft [labor] to clothe hem and to fede" (90). Cheap beer, cold meat, and clams by the dozen, given as alms, may seem humble fare but "were a feste with suche folk" and for "crokede men and blynde" (95–97). Will contrasts the poor and wretched to "beggares with bagges, þe whiche brewhous [taverns] ben here [their] churches" (98), calling them "lollers," becoming one of the poet's favorite terms for the idle and undeserving. Those beggars receive no pardon, and Will absolves the rich from caring for such "lorelles [losers]."

> For alle þat haen here hele [health] and here ye-syhte [eyesight],
> And lymes [limbs] to labory with, and lollares lyf vsen [live idly],
> Lyven aȝen Goddes lawe and þe lore of Holi Churche. (C9.102–4)

The excess *l* alliteration spells doom for those who violate divine law and Church lore.

Will contrasts these to the "lunatic lollers"—the mentally infirm who cannot work but mill about the town with an innocent disregard for persons of rank. These antisocial beggars recall the Dostoyevskian underground man in their scorn of status, fulfilling the Gospel injunctions "you shall salute no one on the road" (Luke 10:4) and "if someone seems to be wise, let him become a fool so that he may be wise" (1 Cor. 3:18). God sends these idiots, his "privé disciples" (C9.118), into society to provoke charity in others. People display their worth through compassion for them, and they in turn manifest God's injunction to good Christians to defy rank and to become "fools" to the cares of the world. If such a fool were to "mete with the mayre [mayor] ameddes þe strete / A [he] reuerenseth hym ryht nauht [pays him no respect at all]" (122–23). These fools are also called "merye-mouthed men, munstrals [minstrels] of heuene" (126). Rich men, says Will, like to support traveling entertainers in order to please the lords and ladies who officially sponsor these performers,[3] but they ought rather generously to support these metaphorical minstrels, the "lunatyk lollares and lepares [jumpers] aboute," who are God's "mesagers and his mery bordiours [jesters]" (136–37). This class of the mentally disabled merits as much charity and compassion, Langland wants readers to know, as do the poor fathers and working mothers, who wake up at night to rock the cradle (79).

After the excursus on God's minstrels, Will returns to a venomous attack on the "lollers" and lewd hermits for their pretense of humility, designed to find them a place by the fire and a round of bacon before they move on to their next conquest (C9.139–52). Langland's additions in C add generous and equal amounts of compassion and condemnation, for he must have felt that A and B inadequately distinguished between the just and the false poor, and so he leaves no doubt about his scorn for the deceivers who exploit compassion and alms that should go to the deserving, to the sacrificing parents, and to the endearing madcap whose blithe disregard for welfare ironically manifests a true understanding of God's grace.

Readers at this point in C may forget about the pardon episode, as Langland's passionate intensity about the poor overrides narrative balance and coherence. Langland does not fear expanding an individual topic with uncommon urgency. But he does have a poem to write, he remembers, so after this excursus on the poor, he patches himself back into A and B. Langland replaces the tearing of the pardon, a scene so compelling to readers of the first two versions, with images of real life-struggles of men and women who meet the day with anxious care for their children's welfare. Such men and women may not have been the original (or current) readers of *Piers Plowman*, and no one knows whether the chastised rich ever read about their shameful greed directly from this poem. Nor do we know if lazy "lollers," sitting with their feet up at the fire of some generous dupe, warm and cozy, with hot food and brown ale, had their comfort shattered by Langland's exposure of their charade as they pored over their copies of *Piers* by firelight. Though medieval Christian poets wrote to reform, they did not write assured that anyone listened. But as Langland's fate would have it, readers still listen today to Langland's excurses, particularly to the intimate portraits of those who do, and those who most assuredly do not, merit God's pardon.

As C merges back into A and B, Langland infuses that transition with more anti-loller language, also denying pardon to "ouer-land strikares" a unique phrase that must mean wandering bums who "strike out" looking for undeserved handouts (C9.159). The unity of the versions lasts only briefly, as Will, audibly enraged in the C text, cannot stop himself from furthering his attack on the undeserving—and yet also advancing his defense of those who do indeed deserve pardon. Victims of fraud, fire, and flood (181–82), subject to accidental, blameless poverty, also deserve pardon *a pena et a culpa* (186), because for them life has become a de facto purgatory on earth. Langland in this passus does not merely revise or polish what he wrote before but rather crafts explosive new discourse, full of poignant images and compassionate longing for justice and pardon, in the poet's most elaborate expression of the widespread human need for both charity and grace.

To reveal, finally, how vile the fakers are, he recalls the lives of real hermits, who lived in edifying austerity, some fed by birds, some by the care of friends, living in isolation or working humbly for their own meager sustenance and forsaking "lond and lordschipe and alle lykynges [pleasures]" of their bodies (C9.202). To these he contrasts an exploitive class of former "werkmen, webbes [weavers] and taylours," (204) who realized they were wasting their time working when they could dress up as friars and hermits and get the "fatte chekes" (208) of the well fed.

Langland passionately cries out for true pardon in these C-text revisions, but he has not solved the problem of Dowel. He likely did not expect an immediate response to his charges against the corrupt, an instantaneous ignition of human virtue. He knew such change might never come, but he had no choice but to keep hoping and to keep revising. Langland, compelled to the cause of reform and to the exposure of evil, must have looked up from his pen from time to time to see that nothing had changed.

His C text reveals such frustration; one does not rewrite *Piers Plowman* out of a sense of contentment. A poet takes an odd path to social change. In his "Defence of Poetry," Shelley calls poets "the unacknowledged legislators of the world" (62), with the emphasis on the "un": poets might face perpetual anonymity or disregard, however much truth they reveal about human suffering and injustice.

The three versions conclude similarly with Will's exhortation to prayer and with the contention that without the help of Dowel, a pardon isn't worth "a pye hele" (C9.345), a chunk of piecrust, a flavorless bit of nothing. Any document or service that can be purchased cannot compete with Dowel. Truth's pardon provides no pardon at all but merely an observation about God's final judgment. Without virtue, institutional "pardon" cannot nourish the soul, as a bit of crust cannot nourish the body. The mature Langland made sure he told his readers what earning real pardon means. Those images of working mothers, victims of disaster, men too proud to show weakness, and of all the laborers struggling to feed their families, perpetually remind readers of those enduring, both then and now, a patient purgatory here on earth.

JJ

On the Road in Search of Dowel

PASSŪS 9 AND 10 OF THE A TEXT WITH B8–9 AND C10

Conspectus: Will begins a series of inquiries about the three Do's, first asking a pair of friars and then encountering Thought and Wit. These passūs in A, B, and C offer a series of definitions and characterizations of Dowel, Dobet, and Dobest, all of which seem correct, yet none of which seems complete. The sequence spans two short passūs in the A and B versions, and C10 combines them into one, sensing that the division has unnecessarily interrupted the search for Dowel.

I. A9 with Some Notes on B and C Revisions

In a rough new beginning, Will sets out to find Dowel, "yrobid in rosset [robed in homespun woolen]" (A9.1), an appropriately rugged garb for pilgrimage and a costume change from the sheepskin of the prologue. He roams, asking if anyone knows Dowel, starting with some friars who claim him as their own (14). From what Will has seen of the friars' false holiness and indulgences, he suspects that they lie. But nothing conclusive emerges from the actual exchange. The friars claim Dowel lives with them, but Will flexes some scholastic muscle and shouts "contra" in formal dispute of their claim, contending that "Dowel and Do-euele mowe not dwelle togidere" and that therefore virtue "is not alwey at hom among ʒow freris" (16–20). The friars offer Will a nautical allegory explaining how the wind and the water of worldly vanity surge against the "boot," the frail human body, with the temptations of material gain and fleshly desire (25–47). Dowel helps one combat the force of grievous sin and save the boat from foundering. That is, they explain, everyone falls down to the deck but can still rise to maintain ultimate control over the forces that would capsize the boat. Will thanks and blesses the friars without further dispute and moves on to inquire elsewhere. No one feels insulted or angry in this generally polite exchange, which remains by design tentative and inconclusive, indicating that answers abound concerning Dowel but still somehow do not ring true.

The plot developments in the A text become clearer in the manuscripts' rubrics, the headings (often in red ink) that either the poet wrote or the scribes added to introduce or conclude various passūs while copying the poem. Throughout the manuscripts from this point forward, especially in the expanded B and C texts, the rubrics designate a new section of the poem, separating the *visio*, the "vision" that Will had in the first two dreams, from a second *visio*, sometimes called a *vita*, essentially a biography that traces the lives of Dowel, Dobet, and Dobest as if they were saints. These characters remain impersonal and elusive and never appear, becoming manifest rather in people and situations, or embodied in the actions of characters like the Good Samaritan and Christ himself. The trio begin to figure variously in discussions of marriage, of the clergy and pastoral care, of daily human labors, and of higher spiritual achievement. One can *do well*, but can always imagine doing better and can also conceive of superlative behavior, simply "the best." Will hears definition upon definition but judges every depiction of the triad inadequate, leading him to keep wandering beyond every authority and every set of answers, however reasonable, in search of a more secure and complete expression of human virtue.

As he struggles with the friars' exemplum, Will claims that he lacks the "kynde knowyng" needed to understand their words, as he doubts his innate ability to unravel their allegory about sin, contending that he needs to live, observe, and "lerne betere" (A9.48–49). When doubt arises in Will, Langland gets him back to sleep to see what a dream reveals, and so Will rests by a tree and falls asleep to lovely birdsong. He then meets his first psychic projection, Thought. Surprised that Will has only now noticed him, Thought claims to have been Will's companion already for seven years, an elaborate way to say that Will decides to sit himself down and "think" about Dowel, for if the friars could not answer his questions, perhaps the answer lies in his own mind, an internal resource he has neglected.

Thought holds forth on the "þre faire vertues," depicting Dowel as one "trewe of his tunge," meek and mild of speech, who works hard with his hands, and is trusty of his "tailende," a pun on tallying (accounts) and "tail end," sexual parts (A9.69–75). Whoever does not take from others, and does not become drunk or arrogant, follows Dowel. Thought's definition features negation and restraint, focusing on what one should *not* do, recalling the old adage "be good and don't." Much of virtue, when one "thinks" about it, requires control of appetite, action, word, hand, and temper. Dobet does all that (or "doesn't," rather) and even more, for in humility "he is as louȝ [humble] as a lomb, louelich [gracious] of speche" (77). Dowel does not steal, but Dobet rips open bags of money hoarded by the Earl of Avarice and gives to others in need, a positive, active virtue. Further, he enters the religious life, translates the Bible, and dutifully teaches Paul's lesson of compassion: "*Libenter suffertis* [gladly suffer] . . . / ȝe wise, suffriþ þe vnwise with ȝow for to libbe, / And wiþ glad wil doþ hem good [treat them well], for so God himself hiȝte [commands]" (83a–85).

Dobest carries a bishop's crosier, hooked on one end to draw men and women away from sin and with a "pik" on the other to thrust down the wicked (A9.86–89). These three Do's, continues Thought, crown a king, indicating metonymically the governance and justice that society needs. But if Dowel and Dobet (laity) become "vnbuxum [disobedient]" to Dobest (the higher clergy) or do him any ill, the king imprisons them "wiþoute pite or grace" unless Dobest pleads for them (90–96). Will's "thought," struggling to identify virtue, imagines the Do's as recognizable members of society and clergy, working together under the just protection and law enforcement of good kingship, with the laity subject to punishment but also to mercy from both bishop and crown.

Will politely thanks Thought for his efforts but adds that he did not really savor his "segging [saying, words]" (A9.102). And yet the pair spend three more days disputing the subject, leaving no record of what they said, though it likely would not reveal much more progress. They then meet another fellow, Wit, whom Thought thinks the better teacher. Will seems shy around Wit, perhaps intimidated by his long lean look and his seeming tranquility, as he appears neither proud nor poor but rather sober and mild. In this awkward moment, Thought presents his student to this seemingly transcendental master in a compressed, witty line: "Here is Wil wolde wyte [would like to know] ȝif Wit couþe teche" (118), and with this tutoring session scheduled, the passus ends.

II. A Passus 10

Wit differs from Thought and can mean many things in Middle English, including "the faculty of understanding," "mental ability, intelligence; wisdom," and also "cleverness" (*MED*, defs. 2c, 3a, 3b), the last of which seems to apply best here. Wit cleverly imagines Dowel as a knight who serves a damsel named Anima (the human soul) locked away in the "castel þat Kynde made," that is, the human body (A10.2). A romance story needs a villain: enter Princeps huius mundi (Prince of this world), a French knight, a convenient villain for a fourteenth-century English audience, who wants Anima for himself. Worldly vanity seeks to steal the soul, embedded in human nature, while Nature seeks to wed her to a nice fellow like Dowel, a good catch, well suited to care for something so precious. Dobet, Sir Dowel's trusty daughter, serves the lady Anima. Dobest has no specified role in A, but in B and C rules over them all as a bishop, an instance of the higher clergy caring for the souls of the flock. The chivalric conceit becomes even more complex, but some other members of this romance ensemble include the trusty Sire Inwit, representing internal ethical awareness, and his sons the five senses, including "Sire Se-wel, and Sey-wel" (A10.16–24). Inner awareness, like a good father, raises the sensual appetites to serve and protect the soul.

Will, charmed by this romance, asks to hear more. Wit merges the creation story from Genesis with his conceit, explaining that Kynde, that is, God, created beasts, angels, and then "ymage to himselue [in his own image]" men and women, granting them bliss, and everlasting life in the castle called Caro, which houses the soul, Anima (A10.35–38). Sire Inwit emerges as protector, keeping body and soul safe as Wit explains in these sonic lines, unique to A:

> For þoru3 his connyng [intelligence] is kept *Caro* and *Anima*
> In rewele [rule] and in resoun [order], but reccheles it make [unless recklessness disrupts it].
> He eggiþ ei3e si3t [guides eyesight] and heryng to gode;
> Of good speche and going he is þe begynnere [origin].
> In manis brayn is he most and mi3tiest to knowe:
> Þere is his bour bremest [strongest] but 3if blod it make [unless blood makes it otherwise];
> For whan blood is bremere þanne brayn, þan is Inwit bounde [restrained]. (A10.50-56)

Wit explains that the young and the foolish lack Inwit, as do "sottis [drunks]" (A10.58-59), for one loses inner control for various reasons, some innocent (youth and mental disability) and others more blameworthy, such as abuse of the senses. The expedient Sire Princeps huius mundi, now identified as the Devil, gains power over those who fill their heads with ale until "Inwyt be drenchit" (60). Parents and friends ought to protect children from sin, and Holy Church too must help young indigents mature wisely and safely.

Wit's exposition strays far from his chivalric imagery, which he has all but forgotten, though he does call Dowel a "duc" that destroys vices and inspires fear of the Lord (A10.76), which fear makes men and women "meke and mylde of here speche" and compels students "in scole to lerne" (83-84). Fear not only motivates but also establishes humility as the foundation of human happiness and the source of the highest virtue. Wit explains the power of fear and of patient suffering: "Þus in dred liþ Dowel, and Dobet to suffre, / For þoro3 suffraunce [endurance] se þou mi3t how soueraynes [elevation] ariseþ," basing this paradigm on Luke's words "Qui humiliat exaltabitur [Whoever humbles himself will be raised up]" (118-19; 120α; Luke 14:11). Wit then completes the triad: "And þus of dred [from fear] and his dede [i.e., from acts of submission] Dobest arisiþ" (121). To explain better the generative relation between the Do's, Wit composes some verses that anticipate the eighteenth-century Scottish poet Robbie Burns in their beauty and elegance, depicting how Dobest, like a sweet flower, springs up from the ground of human humility:

> Ri3t as a rose, þat red is and swete,
> Out of a raggit [thorny] rote [root] and a rou3 [rough] brere

Springeþ and sprediþ, þat spiceris desiriþ,
Or as whete out of weed waxiþ [grows] out of þe erþe,
So Dobest out of Dobet and Dowel gynneþ springe
Among men of þis molde [earth] þat mek ben and kynde.
For loue of here lou3nesse [humility] Oure Lord 3iueþ [gives] hem grace
Such werkis to werche þat he is wiþ paied [paid, pleased].
    (A10.123–30)

A good life, like a rough root, grows into the sharp briars of endurance, finally becoming the flower of Dobest. Wit plays on the meaning of "molde," which signifies the earth but also the soil, recalling Adam's beginnings and his end. This reminder of death and damnation provokes a healthy fear, and unless so humbled by fear, humans cannot perform the "werkis" of virtue. But when God sees humanity humble and submissive, for love of their lowness he grants men and women the grace to act well, so that he, in another clever pun, will be both paid and pleased (*MED*, s.v. "paien").

After this compelling imagery, Wit turns to another, seemingly unrelated lexicon for the Do's, depicting Dowel as lawfully married life (A10.131–32). Most cultures see the value in stable marriage as a social foundation, but for Langland marriage has mythic and anthropological implications as well. Purposeful lawful behavior, and observing the proper times of sexual union and procreation, gives birth to "confessours [professed believers]" (135) including maidens, nuns, anchorites, kings, knights, clerks, barons, and bondmen too. Dowel as proper sexual practice produces legitimate offspring. But false faithless folk, liars, and thieves are "conseyuid in cursid tyme" (140), as illustrated by Cain, conceived in the accursed period after the eating of the apple. One wonders what choice the exiled couple had, since they could not return to Eden and engage in more timely sex, and one wonders as well if Abel was conceived properly beforehand. Genesis says nothing about such topics, but Wit tells Will to research the issue in the Psalter, providing a quick reference: "Concepit dolorem et peperit iniquitatem [he hath conceived sorrow and brought forth iniquity]" (150; Psalms 7:15; Job 15:35). Medieval readers often glossed biblical events with such generalized laments found in other, seemingly unrelated parts of scripture. No doubt such free play strikes modern readers as quite a piece of "wit" indeed.

Taking the idea further, Wit explains how Cain's descendants mated with those of Seth, Adam and Eve's third child (A10.178–81), reflecting how medieval readers interpreted the episode in Genesis 6:4 where "the sons of God" went in to the "daughters of men." It seems strange to realize that Langland believed that children conceived at the wrong time (menstruation, holy days) would become murderers like Cain or a race of accursed miscreants that God would destroy with the Flood. That all sounds quite epic, and thus rather alien to the experience of many of Langland's readers, who more likely understand the injunction to marriage as a basic call for stability and healthy unions at the simple level of everyday society. The connections between anthropology, mythic theology, and practical social policy remain unclear, and modern readers may find Wit's reading of scriptural taboos both ingenious and exotic.

Wit's next words return to daily English life, lamenting that since the plague, he has witnessed many foul marriages, generated by financial need, between old men and young girls, the revolting type of union that Chaucer depicts in his Merchant's Tale of January and May. Young men and old widows make an equally improper match, for the only offspring they produce are "manye foule wordis" since they have "no children but cheste [quarreling] and choppis hem betwene" (A10.192–93). Instead, he advises that no one should marry for economic reasons, but rather that a virgin and a virgin should marry, for only those equally clean and innocent can enjoy proper "bedbourd [bed-play]" (203–4). Biblical flood and divine damnation aside, in the real world, people had to live and to find love after the plague, and evidently they could not always "do well" in the process. Langland makes perfecting the art of marriage sound difficult, perhaps rightly, in this historically important sequence that witnesses both marriage theory and practice in medieval England.[1]

Likewise, says Wit, each man should tend to his wife and no other, for adultery would produce bastards, false heirs, vagrants, and orphans who please the Devil and one day dwell with him unless God's grace saves them. This seems as harsh as the antediluvian mischief he recounts above. The passus ends as Wit, realizing he needs a hasty summary to end this baggy discussion, redefines the Dowel triad as "to dreden," "to suffre," and to bring down the "mody [proud]" and their wicked will (A10.216–17), recalling the major themes of fear, endurance, and humility that inform the discussion, though unrelated to the immediate issue of marriage. Will says nothing in response, and one assumes he ponders what he has heard, still curious and unsatisfied. Wit, though smarter than Thought, does not have all the answers, and each of Will's psychic projections can only approximate the Do's. Will hears much more such speculation as the corpus expands in B and in C. A, in fact, moves dangerously close to its ending, a few hundred lines hence. Langland later reveals triumphantly that the greatest definition of Dowel lies in the life of Christ. But in his A text, with Wit exhausted, Will silent, and the poem grinding slowly to a halt, the poet has no way of knowing what his future self has planned in later versions. If Wit's discourse has not satisfied Will, one should note that progressing through *Piers Plowman*, as a character, a reader, or as the poem's author, does not guarantee the kind of satisfaction that comes from clarity and closure. And that may be the whole point.

III. Corresponding B and C Revisions to A10

Not all revisions create improvement, and Langland succeeds in one version through minimalism and in another through excess. For example, in A10, Wit economically describes the Creation as an act of divine majesty: "Þoru3 mi3t of þe maieste [divine power] man was ymaked: / Faciamus hominem ad ymaginem nostram [Let us make man to our image and likeness]" (A10.41–42; Gen. 1:26)—a minimalist, elegant, pregnant line of poetry, and an expressive translation of the dramatic verse in Genesis. In B, Wit takes the word *faciamus* and bursts out for twenty more lines about creation (B9.33–52), which include one of Langland's most important metaphors, depicting God as a writer:

> Right as a lord sholde make lettres, and hym [ne] lakked [even if he had] parchemyn,
> Thou3 he koude write neuer so wel, if he [wel]de [wield] no penne,
> The lettre, for all þe lordshipe [power], I leue [believe] were neuere ymakyd [written]! (B9.38–40)

In this confident passage by a poet in his prime, Langland, who knew and lived the physical work of writing every day, creates the moving image of

God as an author, wielding pen and parchment to shape humankind, the letter written in his likeness.[2]

In C, by dramatic contrast, Langland replaces most of Wit's meditation on the art of creation with the trenchant imagery of how people corrupt the beauty of creation with sin, particularly lechery, depicted as clouds that darken the bright human soul. As Wit explains:

> And as thow seest the sonne sum tyme for cloudes
> May nat shyne ne shewe on schalkes [men] on erthe,
> So let lecherye and other luther [hateful] synnes
> That god sheweth nat [does not view favorably] suche synnefole men,
>   and soffreth hem mysfare [to endure misfortune],
> And somme hangeth hemsulue and oþerwhile adrencheth [drown].
> . . . .
> Such lyther-lyuyng men lome [often] been ryche
> Of gold and of oþer goed, ac Goddes grace hem fayleth [fails in them],
> For they louyeth and bylyueth al here lyf-tyme
> On catel [goods] more then on Kynde, that alle kyne thynges wrouhte,
> The which is loue and lyf þat last withouten ende. (C10.159–63; 67–71)

Langland here excises B's fecund God for deadly images of the sinful hanging themselves or drowning, presumably because of their endless grief and guilt. But Langland makes no direct allusion to Judas or to the Flood here, as his images are starkly original.

In a similarly dark vein, Langland adds to Wit's speech in C a random attack on drinking. It is "inwit," he says,

> That many a lede [man] leseth [loses] thorw lykerous drynke,
> As Lote dede and Noe and Herodes þe daffe [goof],
> ȝaf his douhter for a daunsynge in a disch þe heued [head]
> Of þat blessed Baptist bifore alle his gestes [guests]. (C10.178–81)

Langland intensifies the sequence by adding into the poem Lot's incest, Noah's nakedness, and the decapitation of John, all instances of violation and terror. Perhaps the aging poet could no longer countenance his former depiction of God as writer, practicing his loving, creative craft.

Langland also deletes from C, though not for the same reason, a famous B-text addition about the Jews (B9.82–89), a powerful witness to contemporary Christian-Jewish relations in Langland's England. The B text develops an A-text passage about how those without inwit need care, as an aspect of communal responsibility. This makes Wit notice that a Jew would never let another Jew go hungry, which brings shame on Christians, he says, who think themselves superior but cannot compete with the Jews in basic charity. The passage breaks through the inherited theological hatred of the Jews as a people and celebrates an aspect of community that must have been true throughout Europe, though not in England from which Jews were in 1290 banished.

In C, Langland replaces this remarkable discourse with a generic rubric about love of enemies: "Ac thenne dede we alle wel, and wel bet ȝut [better yet] to louye / Oure enemyes enterely and helpe hem at here nede" (C10.189–90). Wit then launches into a loving exhortation of charity. Priests and prelates, he says in a compressed and stirring image, should "tulie [till] þe erthe with tonge" and teach people to love (C10.201). Christ himself owned almost nothing, says Wit, only three garments that were stripped from him before death. So to honor Christ's neediness and his humble sacrifice, Christians must give to others, for then God will make sure that they will not die for lack of "mete ne for myssyng [lacking] of clothes" (203). Such a sweet, nurturing line distinguishes the C text, just as do the vehement ravings that Langland added to Wit's speech, for Langland in C displays many moods. Perhaps B's comments on the Jews, simply not part of Langland's reality, somehow distracted from the focus on Christian charity that the poet expresses in the here and now. And yet Langland strangely omits from C another touching passage in which Wit discusses the responsibilities of the Christian "Godfader and godmoder," whose duties should extend to spiritual care and not just the "nempnynge [naming] of a name" (B9.75–79). Readers, following the tides and eddies of revision, cannot expect doctrinal or poetical consistency. In C, Langland shows that Wit can change over time and display a diversity of thought and emotion, though he has not provided his student with any more convincing definitions of Dowel than Will has heard before.

On the subject of marriage in C, Wit maintains A's and B's condemnation of expedient unions for money, but Langland's additions to the sequence draw attention to a particularly disturbing marital trend. These days, says Wit, because of "coueytise [desire] of catel [goods]," men seek women with money, and would reject a well-raised maid, "louelich [lovely] to loken on and lossum [delightful] abedde," simply because she is not rich (C10.259–62). Accordingly, unattractive women of means prosper in the husband market:

> Ac lat here be vnlouely and vnlossum abedde,
> A bastard, a bond oen [bondwoman], a begeneldes [beggar's] douhter,
> That no cortesye ne can, [ac] late here be knowe [known]
> For riche or yrented wel [well off], thouh heo be reueled [wrinkled] for elde,
> Ther ne is squier ne knyhte in contreye aboute
> That he ne wol bowe to þat bond to beden here [pledge to be] an hosebonde
> And wedden here for here welthe, and weschen [wish] on þe morwe
> That his wyf were wexe [expensive wax] or a walet ful of nobles!
> (C10.265–72)

The lovely girl cannot find a man, but the homely girl, less sexually appealing, has suitors who seek her wealth. Yet after the wedding the greedy husband wishes he could turn her into something to sell. In this morally ugly sequence, Langland makes no allowance for the anxieties of survival suffered after the Black Death and does not excuse the expedience behind these, as he sees them, profane marital practices. In his final incarnation of Wit, Langland speaks plainly and raw, and perhaps, at his age, he feels he has a right to.

The passus ends as each version fulfills, variously, its obligation to define the Do's. Their three sets of answers, when read side by side, recapitulate, refine, shift, and expand one other, with the overall effect that they basically say the same thing, though with different emphasis. They all include a message of endurance, fearing God, and loving others, though B and C expand to include the doctrine of giving (B9.202; C10.308). Wit can always formulate various responses to a problem, but he cannot completely master the issue and cannot resolve questions to Will's satisfaction, however much of a friendship they have established and however eagerly Will listens. In the next passus, Wit's wife, named Dame Study, breaks this male bond because she does not want her husband wasting time with riff-raff like Will. Wit offers much to contemplate concerning virtue, creation, humility, love, and marriage, but now it appears that his wit is at an end.

12

Dame Study Teaches a Lesson

PASSUS 11 OF THE A TEXT
WITH B10 AND 11 (OPENING) AND C11

Conspectus: In A10 Wit described proper marriage as Dowel, and A11 begins ironically with his wife, Dame Study, entering the scene to abuse him and his new friend, Will. As her contribution to the search for the Do's, Study offers a stinging condemnation of pompous, quasi-learned babble and of wisdom for hire, as she wonders, along with Job and Jeremiah, why the wicked prosper while the faithful suffer injustice. Study ultimately sends Will to her cousin Clergy, who offers more definitions of the Do's. With his head full, Will contemplates all he has heard and wonders how virtuous action might relate to the question of salvation, ultimately the only question worth asking, though finding an answer continues to prove difficult.

I. The A Text

Study, suspicious of Will, tells her husband not to cast pearls before swine, judging Will as unworthy to receive wisdom. She specifies that one ought not to waste time on such materialistic people, who prefer "lond and lordsshipe on erþe" or "ricchesse or rentis and reste at here wille" rather than knowledge (A11.14–15). Will has done nothing to provoke this anger, but like many of his interlocutors throughout *Piers*, Study sizes him up and thrashes him around with indictment and accusation. More than just comedy, the scene allegorically expresses Will's current state. Study's critique represents Will's sense of unworthiness, wrought by his inability to take up the rigorous and necessary "study" that can move him beyond the bounded mental universe of his own wit and thought. That Langland depicts this personal academic crisis as a wife's scorn for some freeloader that her husband has befriended reveals the poet's comic genius.

Study then recounts how the desire for profit now motivates all learning and devalues true scholarship:

> Ac he þat haþ Holy Writ ay [ever] in his mouþe
> And can telle of Tobie and of þe twelue Apostlis
> Or prechen of þe penaunce þat Pilatus wrouȝte
> To Iesu þe gentil, þat Iewis todrowe [stretched out]
> On crois vpon Caluarie, as clerkis vs techiþ—
> Litel is he louid or lete [accepted] by þat suche a lessoun shewiþ [teaches],
> Or dauncelid [honored] or drawe forþ [advanced]—þise disours [storytellers] wyte þe soþe! (A11.24–30)

Study, not merely a schoolmistress exhorting individual work habits, observes broadly how "study," like every other aspect of social and personal life in *Piers*, now lies subordinate to profit and greed. As she laments in Latin: "Quare via impiorum prosperatur, bene est omnibus qui praue agunt et inique?" (A11.23a), drawing on a passage from Jeremiah 12:1, "Why doth the way of the wicked prosper: why is it well with all them that transgress, and do wickedly?" which has overtones of Job 21:7, "Why then do the wicked live, are they advanced, and strengthened with riches?" In this money-driven world, biblical knowledge gains little cachet for anyone who, as she puts it in Langlandese, "haþ Holy Writ ay in his mouþe."

Minstrelsy she indicts as particularly degenerate, mired in lechery, rascals' tales, and cursing. And when men do speak of God, says Study, they indulge themselves in pretentious speculation, after gorging at dinner, mocking the Trinity with snarky questions like "how two slowe þe þridde" (A11.40) a bizarre idea that must refer, as David Lawton argues in studying medieval blasphemy, to stories like the Pardoner's Tale where, in a Trinitarian and Eucharistic parody, two older figures conspire to slay the younger third.¹ In the telling of such violent and profane stories, these men "gnawen [gnaw upon] God in þe gorge [throat] whanne here guttis fullen [are full]" (44). Their pseudointellectual babble continues with questioning of God's purpose in permitting the Fall from Paradise:

> Why wolde Oure Sauiour suffre such a worm [snake] in his blisse
> Þat be[w]ilide þe womman and þe wy [man] aftir,
> Þoruȝ whiche a werk and wille þei wenten to helle,
> And alle here seed for here synne þe same wo [woe] suffride?
> (A11.66–69)

Ironically, throughout her discourse, Study criticizes the learned for such speculation and praises the illiterate who cannot partake of her more bookish manifestations. But since she also teaches crafts and skills (one has to study to become a carpenter), she plays a role in many walks of life and thus knows where virtue lies and how academic learning itself can inflame pride. Her praise of the guilelessness and direct faith of the unlearned establishes an important motif throughout the *Piers* corpus. Study reveals the limits of "study."

She then quotes Paul, via Augustine, warning Will "non plus sapere quam oportet sapere [not to be more wise than it behoveth to be wise]" (A11.74a).² Anyone who wants to know, for example, why God let the serpent beguile Adam and Eve should have his head up his ass—and his foot too, she says, rather indelicately, in a phrase that has lost none of its force over time: "I wolde his eiȝe [eyes] were in his ars and his hele [foot] aftir" (81; the more delicate B text, 10.125, replaces foot with finger). Modern readers of Genesis may regard this as a viable question about the serpent, and one the authors of Genesis want to provoke, but Study does not approve of what today is called "critical thinking," at least not from the bloated and arrogant who speak only to showcase their rebellious wit in the mere performance of learning.

This onslaught from his bossy wife humiliates Wit, for Study treats him and Will like children. That Langland employs the old woes-of-marriage motif in the midst of all this exposition about salvation makes one wonder, pace Wit, whether Dowel really has anything to do with marriage, at least with this one, in which Wit, like old Socrates in the anecdote the Wife of Bath recounts, is pummeled with thundering nagging.[3] Cowed, dumb, and giggling nervously, Wit prostrates himself to his wife and signals Will to beg Study for help, in an awkward scene of emasculation that strains the allegory. On the literal level, Langland's comic use of the henpecked husband warns that married life demands subordination and woe as the uxorious man struggles for dignity and legitimacy, a deliciously ironic conclusion after Wit's naïve praise of marriage. But allegorically, Wit, the faculty of trying to figure things out in one's mind, must bow to Study, who provides a more informed and learned source of knowledge than internal debate can.

Study rewards a humbled Will by sending him to her cousin Clergy, who has married a woman named Scripture, and perhaps this allegorical couple can better teach Will the truth about Dowel. Study, as she explains, pertains to instruction of any kind in both learning and technical crafts. Clergy involves book learning of a kind that "clerks" engage in, an advancement for Will to a higher grade. So Study knows how to reach Clergy, which requires avoiding riches and taking the highway called "Suffre- / Boþe-wele-and-wo" since evidently poverty and endurance, then as now, mark the academic life (A11.114–15).

Study tells Will to greet her cousin for her and his wife Scripture too, boasting that she, Study, had a hand in her sister-in-law's work, having taught her law, logic, and music, the specific arts that biblical literature employs. Study boasts that she also instructed Plato and Aristotle and taught grammar to children, beating them with a stick to make them learn. However proud, she confesses that the subject of Theology puzzles her:

> Ac Theologie haþ tenid [troubled] me ten score tymes,
> For þe more I muse þeron, þe mistlokere [more mysterious] it semiþ,
> And þe deppere I deuynide [explored], þe derkere me þou3te [it seemed to me].
> It is no science, forsoþe, for to sotile inne [contemplate].
> Ne were þe [if it were not for] loue þat liþ þerein, a wel lewid [useless] þing it were. (A11.137–41)

When any topic generates confusion and doubt in *Piers Plowman*, the poem turns to love, for without "the love that lies within," Study cannot understand Theology. To be studious academically means nothing without comprehending in one's soul the divine force that binds the heavens and the created universe, animating all being. Study points to a transcendence that lies above her parchment and pens, as Will's journey continues to move him ever upward.

Langland toys with this passage in his revisions, ever trying to make it even more profound and ethereal as, Dante-like, he struggles to express the transcendent notion of God as love revealed in the grace of the scriptures.[4] Langland, at his most mystically suggestive, expands these verses in B:

> A ful leþi [empty] þyng it were þat loue [þerinne] nere [were not];
> Ac for it leteþ best by loue [esteems love best], I loue [praise] it þe bettre,
> For þere þat loue is ledere [chief], ne lakked neuere [was never lacking] grace.
> Loke þow loue lelly [loyally], if þee likeþ Dowel,
> For Dobet and Dobest ben of loues k[ennyng] [discipline].
>   (B10.186–90)

But he substantially weakens the passage in C:

> Ac for hit lereth [teaches] men to louie, Y beleue þeron þe bettere;
> For loue is a lykyng [pleasing] thyng and loth for to greue [hates to give grief].
> Lerne for to louie, yf þe like [if you wish to] Dowel.
> For of Dobet and Dobest here doctour [professor] is dere loue.
>   (C11.132–35)

Langland's failure could not be more apparent, as he struggles twice to improve upon the elegance, sentiment, and poetic resonances he crafted in A. But one learns more from his failure than from success, for it reveals the restless poetic mind grappling with the most recalcitrant demands of faith and art. Attempting to capture in verse love's animating power, Langland's language, prosody, and inspiration destabilize: all the renderings carry the same meaning, but in three tries the poet never betters his initial expression.

Back in the A text, Study digresses about astronomy and geometry, risky forms of study because they can lead to black magic like alchemy.

When class ends, Study sends Will on his way with her blessing, and he soon reaches Clergy. After some polite formalities, asking after the in-laws, and a kiss or two, Clergy begins a new set of definitions that B and C will excise.[5] But they are good definitions: Dowel involves humble workers, tillers on earth, tailors and "all kyne crafty men [craftsmen] þat cunne [know how] here foode wynne" (A11.185). Dobet means breaking bread with beggars and giving them clothes, and to "sike [sigh] with þe sory, singe with þe glade" (193), a wonderful line, unique to A, advising one to share empathetically in both the sorrow and joy of others. Dobest means holding clerical office like a bishop, preaching and chastening, unlike the friars who roam about selling absolution for profit. Langland often depicts Dobest thus, as a high administrative post where one accomplishes the greatest good by reaching the most people in pastoral care. Clergy then praises the sixth-century pope Gregory the Great, an important figure of leadership in church history. Gregory sent missionaries to Christianize the Anglo-Saxons, as retold by the Venerable Bede in his *History of the English Church and People*, and Gregory also authored *The Pastoral Care*, one of the central guidebooks for priests during that conversion period.[6]

Will chimes in, saying he thought rather that kings, knights, and kaisers manifest Dobest, based on Jesus's statement that the scribes and the Pharisees "super cathedram Moisi sederunt princeps [have sitten on the chair of Moses],"[7] assuming that they are worthy of such respect (A11.223). Scripture, wife of Clergy, answers Will and denies that knighthood and kingship can help one "heueneward"; nor, she adds, can riches and "realte [royalty]" (227–28). Scripture cites Paul's warning that rich men cannot enter paradise. Poor men in patience and penance, she continues, have, by contrast "eritage [inheritance] in heuene" (239). One may have thought Clergy a powerful authority, but no one can dispute Scripture's reading of scripture.

At this point, because various voices offer so many contradictory and overlapping definitions, Will may actually now know less, not more, about doing well than when he started out. A flustered Will resorts to his trademark exclamation "Contra" (A11.232), really just a way of saying "no way!" to Scripture's assertion about the poor. Anyone baptized is saved, he asserts, but Scripture rebukes him, explaining how that applies only in extreme cases, particularly to moments when Christians baptize Muslims and Jews before death. Scripture quotes herself on various bits of doctrine that one must follow to attain salvation, beginning with Christ's injunction to love God and love one's neighbor as oneself, and then ranging to the Ten Commandments, fixating for some reason on "ne sle nouȝt [do not kill]" and reminding Will that vengeance belongs to God (254–55). Will listens but confesses that he still feels no nearer to understanding Dowel than when he began.

Perplexed but aggressive, Will flexes his scholarly muscle on the topic of salvation, speaking for the rest of the passus (A11.258–313). He quotes a line from the Gospel of John, from the episode where Jesus debates obliquely with a Pharisee named Nicodemus: "Nemo ascendit ad celum nisi qui de celo descendit [no man hath ascended into heaven, but he that descended from heaven]" (263a; John 3:13). Prefacing this, Jesus says, "If I have spoken to you earthly things, and you believe not; how will you believe, if I shall speak to you heavenly things?" (3:12). Humans struggle to understand earthly matters, so heavenly wisdom remains altogether more obscure, for only the Son of Man, says Jesus, ought to be trusted on such issues; therefore one must be born again in God to reach salvation. With this biblical foundation, Will recounts how history provides confusing examples of salvation. Mary Magdalene, David, and Paul all committed grave sins and yet, says Will, reside high in heaven. Solomon, a revered biblical author, had riches and power and acted well. Aristotle also acted wisely, and yet both these two reside in hell. So if Will follows their example—if he "werke be here werkis to wynne" his way to heaven—he could still wind up damned into pain (276–77). Though the A text ends quite soon, Langland starts a wave here that flows through the entire *Piers* corpus: the question of whether anyone can control his or her salvation. Will then quotes a Latin phrase from Augustine, a scholar who scorned learning when he realized that "idiots are seizing heaven, while the pedagogues go to hell":

"*Ecce ipsi ydiote rapiunt celum vbi nos sapientes in infernum mergimur*"—
And is to mene in oure mouþ, more ne lesse,
Arn none raþere [sooner] yrauisshid [snatched away] fro þe riȝte beleue
Þanne arn þise kete [illustrious] clerkis þat conne [know] many bokis,

> Ne none sonnere ysauid, ne saddere [more sober] of consience,
> Þanne pore peple as plouȝmen, and pastours [shepherds] of bestis,
> Souteris [tailors] and seweris—suche lewide iottis [regular folk]
> Percen wiþ a *Paternoster* þe paleis of heuene
> Wiþoute penaunce at here partyng [parting, death], into þe heiȝe blisse. (A11.305–13)

"Idiots" indicates plowmen and shepherds, the humble, unlettered workmen. Oddly Langland, the gangly academic poet, deems learning, such as he practices openly in composing the poem, inferior to plowing and shepherding, which he likely himself never performed. In one of the most important verses in all of Middle English poetry, he explains how the humble pierce heaven with a Paternoster. They need not read and gloss like clerks, but only feel, believe, and recite the prayer as instructed by God and administered by the parish priest.[8] The simple beauty of such prayer reveals a true heart that accomplishes penance in the punishing rigors of physical work.

The passus ends thus, and so does the A text, though some manuscripts offer a passus 12 (see the next section). Will has heard everything. He has thought it all through, attended to Study, Clergy, and Scripture, and still can only conclude that nothing benefits a Christian more than labor in the simplicity of mind and spirit. The blessed "idiots" live the life of Dowel without worldly ambition, pride, or pomp. Having reached this Augustinian realization about the limits of learning, why write more? Langland could find no reason, at least for now.

II. B and C Revisions

The B and C revisions to this passus reflect the poet's need to rewrite not just the episode but the poem itself, which he doubles in length. Understanding why the A text ends reveals why Langland resumed writing. A12 stands alone and has no place in B nor C, so A11 provides transition to the continuations, in which Will can become a more fully actualized person, while at once moving ever closer to mystical revelation. Langland therefore makes significant changes in B and C at this critical juncture of new poetic creation.

In B, Study delineates more academic crimes, expanding her discussion of how wicked, worldly men prosper, adding some heft to the matter by citing Job and the Psalms (B10.23–29a). She also assails harlot entertainers who "spitten and spuen and speke foule wordes, / Drynken and dreuelen [drivel] and do men for to gape" (40–41). She then depicts a scene of friars preaching pridefully for profit at St. Paul's, explaining how this indulgence in prideful oratory neglects the basics of faith and charity (71–77). She turns to the practice of lords who eat while sitting apart from their households in a private chamber (96–117), an isolation that enforces social division, flaunts superiority, and rebukes charity, leading to the type of intellectual indulgence about God's permitting the serpent to deceive our first parents, as explained in A. The image of households so divided by class and power remains one of the enduring images of inequality and of the artificiality of social distinctions in all of Middle English literature. Study provides no solutions.

In B, Langland also revises Clergy's definitions of the Do's, replacing A's sequence of laborers (Dowel) leading up to church administration (Dobest), with a sequence of demonstrations of faith and belief. The rough and earthy in A becomes softer and more ethereal in B, pointing to a faith that transcends mortal reason. Dowel, says Clergy, means for both the learned and the uneducated to believe faithfully in Holy Church and to believe

> On þe grete God þat gynnyng [beginning] hadde neuere,
> And on þe sooþfast [faithful] Sone þat saued mankynde
> Fro þe dedly deeþ and þe deueles power
> Thoruȝ þe help of þe Holy Goost, þe which goost is of boþe [who comes from them both]—
> Thre propre [distinct] persones, ac noȝt in plural nombre,
> For al is but oon God and ech is God hymselue:
> *Deus Pater, Deus Filius, Deus Spiritus Sanctus*—
> God þe Fader, God þe Sone, God Holy Goost of boþe. (B10.235–41)

Dobest in this context means "to be boold to blame þe gilty" (B10.258) but not to criticize others without becoming pure oneself, as Clergy adds in this Latin slogan: "*Si culpare velis culpabilis esse cauebis; / Dogma tuum sordet cum te tua culpa remordet* [If you want to blame someone, beware that you yourself are not the guilty one; / Your teaching is tainted when your own sin bites you back]" (260α). Therefore, says Clergy in this unique B exposition, one should teach well and correct the faulty, but must remove the beam in one's own eye first (262α). Clergy expounds upon this point for approximately forty lines, finally merging back to the A text's praise of Gregory the Great and a rebuke of greed and worldliness among the clergy (B10.291–330, a passage Langland later moves to C5). In B, Clergy also looks at some bad Old Testament priests, Ophni and Phinees, which Langland in C, ever mining past versions, moves toward the beginning of the poem (C prologue 103–17) as an opening salvo against a failing clergy.

Relative to what exists in A or is retained in C, in B Langland adds around a hundred unique lines about teaching into Clergy's speech, ending with the prophecy that one day a king will come to confess, beat, and emend the fallen institution:

> Ac þer shal come a kyng and confesse yow religiouses,
> And bete yow, as þe Bible telleþ, for brekynge of youre rule,
> And amende monyals [nuns], monkes and chanons [canons],
> And puten hem to [make them do] hir penaunce—*Ad pristinum statum ire* [to return to a pure state]. (B10.316–19)

This vision of future political order may not ultimately satisfy Will's longings for justice, since B and C will look more to biblical prophecy than to earthly rule as an agent of reform, but Clergy's words recharge the poem and set up B's next ten passūs. Langland finds, as he studies the end of A, that he might have a lot more to say. "Thanne is Dowel and Dobet," asks Will, "*dominus* [lordship] and kny3thode?" (B10.330), as if trying to get a handle on Clergy's addition about political authority and the ultimate good. As Scripture responds, B merges back into A, asserting not the power but rather the limits of kingship and knighthood, which, like wealth, deceptively impede salvation. Scripture's answer disappoints a crestfallen Will, who thought the issue of reform solved in the form of an earthly ruler who will purge the clergy of corruption. At this point in the narrative, issues are being ripped open rather than sealed. Langland does not attempt here to resolve anything, nor to write a new ending for the A text, but rather to compose a new poem, and thus he turns the soil along A's outer borders, from which much will spring.

In B, then, in an elaboration that C retains, Will contemplates "witty" figures in history who display wisdom and learning that presumably did them no good. These include the carpenters who built the Ark, none of whom were saved. Will ponders this fanciful conundrum and reads it as a lesson about pastoral duty. He exhorts the "folk þat þe feiþ techeþ" (B10.404), that is, the clergy, to become "carpenters Holy Kirk to make for Cristes owene beestes" (409), the laity who need protection from sin and its costs. Will exhorts them to practice what they preach—"wercheþ ye werkes as ye sen ywrite [written],"—lest they be damned with those who built the Ark (412). Those charged with a pastoral duty must work virtuously, for the external product of labor has no value without charity. Will's transformation of clergy into carpenters of God, imagery consistent with the poem's association of physical labor with the work of love, also anticipates the building of Holy Church later in the poem. With this constructive imagery, Langland ends passus 10 of the B text, building at once his poem's future.

And at the start of B11 Langland creates that actual future, beginning his continuation with Will falling into a dream within a dream in which he finds himself in the "lond of longynge" looking into a mirror called "Middelerþe [Middle Earth]" (B11.8–9), which is to say, the created world—an image of narcissism, for Will's urge to look back upon his own desires blocks him from understanding creation.[9] Here the personal biography of Will begins. If in the A text Will was constrained as the inquiring voice of Everyman, trying to make sense of everyday life and ethics, in B he emerges as a Christian man with a body, heart, and soul.

As one often tends to do with a soul in a Christian moral poem, he begins to treat it recklessly. Accordingly, here in the land of longing, after the exhausting mutual interrogations with Thought, Wit, Study, and Clergy, an ungrateful Scripture scorns Will and drives him to take refuge again in sleep. This occurs in B and C while he remains asleep from A, and thus the first dream-within-a-dream begins. And in this inner vision Will makes dangerous friends, Concupiscencia Carnis (Desire of the Flesh) and Coueitise of Ei3es (Covetousness of the Eyes), two seductive women whom he joins for a long partnership in a sinful sexual life inspired by the pimping Pride of Perfect Living. There's plenty of time for fun, they reason, for a young fellow like Will, as they tell him to "acounten Clergie li3te [have no regard for Clergy]" (B11.16) and to enjoy life while he can:

> *Concupiscencia Carnis* colled [embraced] me aboute þe nekke
> And seide, "Thow art yong and yeep [eager] and hast yeres ynowe [enough]
> For to lyue longe and ladies to louye;
> And in þis mirour þow myȝte se myrþes [mirth, joys] ful manye
> That leden þee wole to likynge [pleasure] al þi lif tyme." (B11.17–21)

This playboy lifestyle does little to clarify the issue of salvation, but it anticipates events later in the passus when Kynde (Nature) offers Will a vision of this vast Middle Earth in which he sees that Reason rules all the natural world except for "man and his make" (B11.370). From this perspective, Will's dreamed sexual indulgence makes sense: as a human he behaves as humanity does—unreasonably. Supporting Will's devil-may-care attitude, a fellow named Recklessness makes a cameo in this passus, refuting Old Age by rejecting his warning that Pride of Perfect Living, Fortune, and his two female companions can bring Will nothing but trouble:

> "Ye? Recche þee neuere [forget about it]!" quod Rechelesnesse, stood forþ in raggede cloþes,
> "Folwe forþ þat Fortune wole—þow hast wel fer [a long way to go] to Elde.
> A man may stoupe tyme ynoȝ [long enough] whan he shal tyne þe crowne [lose his hair]!" (B11.34–36)

In one of the most significant changes in the *Piers* corpus, Langland moves this moment forward into C11, with the result of transforming Recklessness from a bit player in B into a prominent figure in C, though not an uncontroversial one.

After the line from B where Recklessness says a man has plenty of time to stoop when old and bald, Langland fleshes him out in C, explaining his background and his doctrines of fast living:

> Sir Wanhope [despair] was sib [sibling] to hym, as som men me tolde,
> For Rechelesnesse in his rybaudé [ribaldry] riht thus he seide:
> "Go Y to helle, go Y to heuene, Y shal nat go myn one [alone]!
> Were hit al soth [if it were all true] þat ȝe seyn, thow Scripture and thow Clergie,
> Y leue neuere þat lord ne lady þat lyueth her on erthe [anyone who ever lived]

Sholde sitte in Goddis sihte [sight] ne se God in his blisse."
(C11.198–203)

This major shift, among other results, renders most of Will's contemplation about salvation from A and in B now into the voice of this character, and thus subordinates Will's meditations to his sexual "recklessness." Will asked good questions about Mary Magdalene, about Solomon, and about the relations between virtue, salvation, sin—powerful thoughts when spoken by the "will," who can choose to sin or not to sin (A11.264–313; B10.377–475a). But Langland never makes clear what he intends by reassigning those discourses to Recklessness, by definition someone unlikely to deliberate thoughtfully, and this revision remains one of the more dynamic puzzles in the C text and perhaps even an inconsistency. Will was advancing well from Thought, to Wit, to Study, to Clergy and his wife Scripture, and it seemed that these progressively authoritative figures were settling the complex questions about Dowel, slowly but ever more assuredly. Yet *Piers Plowman* seldom settles anything to anyone's satisfaction, characters or readers, who will forever question Langland's revisions here. Some of what Recklessness says (what Will had said before) simply does not register as reckless. Will's poignant meditation on how humble laborers know Dowel better than academics do, making them more fit for grace than the arrogant clerks, and the lovely image of piercing heaven with a Paternoster, make no sense when attributed to Recklessness. On the other hand, the poet's moving of Will's sexual exploits to this passus makes perfect sense, for this period of debauchery reflects Will's impatience with learned discourse and Study's hectoring. Too much sprawling academic chatter can easily drive someone to postpone thinking about salvation until later—much later, as Augustine's *vita* shows. But in C, for better or worse, Will and R/recklessness become one, and Will's learned citation of Augustine in A and B now comes out of Recklessness's mouth. The words are the same words, but now with their meaning and function in the poem rendered obscure if not bizarre: "Ecce ipsi idiote rapiunt celum vbi nos sapientes in inferno mergimur [behold how the idiots seize heaven while we wise men are plunged into hell]" (C11.292). Langland attributes quite an insight here to the same fellow who had encouraged Will to follow Pride, Fortune, and party girls for forty years.

Augustine, called here "Austyn þe oelde" (C11.290), explicitly provides this bit of wisdom in *Piers* (see *Confessions* 8.8), but the larger story he recounts in this autobiography offers Langland as well a detailed model of psychosexual behavior. Augustine wrote the book, so to speak, on learning and recklessness, and so the reference to him has richer meaning, recalling not only his wisdom as a humble clerk but also the depravity he fought to liberate himself from. Perhaps Langland wanted to make Will sound "reckless" in his questioning of God's judgment in order to display how, like Augustine, Will feels both sexually and intellectually puffed up by his indulgences with Covetousness and Desire. Anything Will says in this state, in the afterglow of lust, must by definition be reckless. So Recklessness compromises much that Will spoke and yet enriches it thematically as well. Ultimately, he is a troublemaker, not just in his influence on Will's sex life but in how he provokes more questions than he answers, both critically and textually. Yet Langland may have his reasons for making such trouble, for trouble means more poetry. Recklessness can never end a poem, but he certainly can begin a new episode. Planning a long pilgrimage through another ten passūs of revision, Langland wanted to mute or even nullify Will's authority as best he could, in preparation for more doctrinal adventures to come. But before contemplating this crux any further, readers have to take some time to say farewell to an old companion, who is now, even as we speak, preparing to make an end and leave us forever.

13

John But Puts an End to the A Version

Conspectus: In a dramatic and controversial passus unique to A, and then only in three of its manuscripts, Will almost dies when he meets a character named Fever, who spares him from death for now. Then a mysterious friend of Will's, John But, concludes the poem and tells the audience about his poor mate the poet, who has passed away after a fruitful career writing about Piers the Plowman.

A12, one of the most bizarre and controversial bits of *Piers Plowman*, plays no role in the B and C continuations for the obvious reason that it provides an *ending*, and Langland needs in those versions not an ending but a new beginning to the journey. This passus appears in just three of the A manuscripts, in various forms of completeness, and it always raises questions of authenticity. One text, called U, ends at line 19a; another, J, ends at line 88. Only one manuscript, R, preserves lines 89–98 and also the more mysterious lines 99–117, which some editors, like Schmidt, consider not Langland's but rather the work of John But, who boasts that he stepped in when the poet died and, as a labor of love, wrapped up the poem now called the A text. Accordingly Schmidt prints these final lines in italics; the Knott-Fowler edition of A prints the entire passus 12 as an appendix; and Vaughan prints it as part of the actual text, because he uses manuscript R, which includes the But ending, as his base manuscript. The controversy about what exactly the poet wrote provokes critical analysis and even speculation, since the whole passus or just parts of it may be spurious. Certainly the poet did not author the final verses, 99–117, which offer homage to Langland and which John But claims to have written. Despite that apparent assurance, little else in this passus lends itself to clarity, providing an intriguing mystery for first-time readers who must distinguish the various authorial voices here and determine their possible motives. Ultimately understanding this episode may demand more of the critical detective work inherent to *Piers Plowman* studies.

Ending aside, the episode itself fascinates: Will converses with Fever, who in the Middle Ages and throughout much of human history might bring Death with him, and so Will interprets the visit. But not so today, for even though Will wishes to go with Fever, much as the protagonist resigns himself to go with Death in the fifteenth-century play *Everyman*, Fever directs him toward another destiny, telling him not to die but to "lyue as þis lyf is ordeyned" for him (A12.90). Fever encourages him to pray, to "do after Dowel," and to perform spiritually profitable works (94–98). This could make for a wonderful, encouraging ending to the A version, fully consonant with the themes of the poem about salvation and Dowel, but it also could suspensefully set up a sequel, a "Piers Plowman Returns," or the "Continuing Voyages of Long Will."

But before one can comprehend Fever's words as any sort of coda or dramatic transition, the unexpected John But intrudes upon the text and explains the circumstances of his intervention into the authorship of the poem:[1]

> Wille þurgh inwit [awareness] [þo wiste] wel þe soþe—
> Þat þis speche was spedelich [beneficial], and sped him wel faste [worked quickly],
> And wrouȝthe [composed] þat here is wryten and oþer werkes boþe
> Of Peres þe Plowman and mechel puple also.
> And whan þis werk was wrouȝt, ere Wille myȝte aspie [detect],
> Deþ delt him a dent [a blow] and drof him to þe erþe
> And is closed vnder clom [dirt]—Crist haue his soule!
> And so bad Iohan But busily wel ofte
> When he saw þes sawes [statements] busyly alegged [asserted]
> By Iames and by Ierom, by Iop and by oþere,
> And for he medleþ of makyng, he made þis ende. (A12.99–109)

In a charming bit of versifying, But, invited or not, writes himself into history. Johan But: perhaps a real name or a joke by a scribe "buttressing" the end of the poem. He speaks as if intimate with the poet but reveals nothing definitive about their relationship. When he says that Will died, he may mean William Langland (he never says Langland), and when he claims that Will wrote more works after this one, he may mean that the poet died after B and C, or he may be just generalizing.

John But also boasts that he has "meddled with making," and in fact he composes strong Langlandian alliterative verse, with his marquee moment the great line 104 with its studied *d* alliteration. Yet some of his addition puzzles, such as the word "bad" (106). This may mean "abided, waited" (from *MED* "bīden") or rather "begged, prayed" (from *MED* "bidden"). In fact, the slippery syntax and wordplay of this entire sequence elude verse translation, and so lines 106–9 may best be translated prosaically:

> So John waited, but ultimately he, busily and often, once he had seen all the learned matter here, including sayings of James, Jerome, and Job, went about the business of making an end to this poem, seeing that he himself had dabbled a bit in making poetry.

John But's artful intrusion mixes ambition, presumption, craft, and a studied, contrived posture of humility.

In context, the episode begins with Clergy, evidently exasperated, asserting that he has been struggling to teach Will about Dowel. Clergy judges Will as someone who wants to learn but neglects to study, a medieval "lazy idle loafer" as James Joyce would later say. How disappointing for student Will to hear that his teacher Clergy, and Theology also, displays no faith in him, and the episode reads like a trip to the principal's office. Clergy begins:

> "Crist wot," quod Clergie, "knowe hit ȝif þe lyke,
> I haue do my deuer [duty] þe Dowel to teche,
> And whoso coueyteþ ben [desires to be] betere þan þe Boke telleþ,
> He passeþ þe apostolis lyf, and peryth [is a peer to] to aungelys.
> But I se now as I seye, as me soþ thinkytȝ,
> Þe were lef to lerne but loþ [unwilling] for to stodie!
> Þou woldest konne þat I can and carpen [repeat] hit after—
> Presumptuowsly, parauenture, apose so manye

> That myȝthe turne me to tene [bring harm to me], and Theologie
> boþe.
> Ȝif I wiste witterly þou woldest don þerafter,
> Al þat þou askest asoylen [resolve] I wolde." (A12.1–11)

In the final, critical line, Clergy tells Will that he would assoil him if he knew confidently that Will would make good use of his lessons. "Asoylen" has a range of meanings, including to solve a riddle, answer a question, resolve a doubt, and fulfill a promise (*MED*, s.v. "assoilen"), all indicating a positive result for Will and perhaps even bringing some real resolution to his many questions. But then Will recounts how Scripture, another stern authority, enters the scene and "skornfully" raises a brow at Clergy's offer of a second chance. As Scripture sees it, Will must first be "schriuen," that is, confessed, and also christened at a font before Clergy can offer him more guidance, for teaching the unworthy and unbaptized brings "skaþe [harm] and sklaundre [slander] to al Holy Cherche" and is accordingly forbidden by Theology, the arbiter of truth (A12.12–18).[2] From what Holy Church says in passus 1, Will has already received baptism. So the puzzling and "loude" accusation that he needs the sacrament now makes him feel "shame" (16) and likely reflects Scripture's low opinion of him, in the spirit of hopelessness and dissolution, as A winds down to an uncertain conclusion. Theology then joins Clergy and Scripture in further disciplining the presumptuous, contrarian Will. The situation looks grim for our hero, as his presumed allies berate and abandon him as hopeless and unteachable.

Scripture knows Will's type and indicts him with David's Psalms: "Vidi preuaricantes et tabescebam [I beheld the transgressors, and I pined away]" (A12.19α; Psalm 118:158). She adds a verse from Paul, where he describes a fellow Christian's rapturous but mysterious visit to heaven, though she rephrases it into the first person: "Audiui archana uerba que non licet homini loqui [I heard secret words, which it is not granted to man to utter]," accusing Will of wanting to know more than he should (22α; see 2 Cor. 12:4). Scripture continues that she will follow Christ, who would not tell Pilate a thing when questioned, and she orders Clergy not to tell Will anything more either. And then she says something nearly incomprehensible: "For he cam not by cause to [cunne] [know how] to dowel, / But as he seyþ, such I am, when he with me carpeþ [spoke]" (32–33). This must mean something like "he didn't come here really to learn about Dowel, but, as he himself has made clear, just to jabber away with me" or, alternatively, "he's really not here to learn, as you can see from what he called me when we spoke earlier," reflecting resentment from their prior, feisty exchange. Clergy gives Will no chance to deny or explain and, in a nasty ironical twist, tells him to go and "do wel" or not, as he evidently doesn't care one way or the other whether he is saved or damned:

> And when Scripture þe skolde [scolder] hadde þis [skele] [doctrine] ysheued,
> Clergie into a caban [hut] crepte anon after,
> And drow þe dore to him and bad me go do wel—
> Or wycke ȝif I wolde—wheþer þat me lyked [whichever I wanted].
> (A12.34–37)

The meeting with the schoolmasters is over: Will has failed.

In a gesture of supplication, and with nowhere to turn, Will lifts his hands up to Scripture and seeks counsel, wondering where he can find Kynde Wit, identified here as Scripture's cousin, living with Lyf. A grateful Will, with throbbing heart, kisses her feet as she summons a "clerioun [young clerk]" to guide him. A schoolboy, called a "pore þing withalle," now guides Will, since Clergy wants no part of him. Unworthy of high-level instruction, he deserves only an assistant to help him find the answers. This boy, named "Omnia-probate [try-everything]," takes Will to "Quod-bonum-est-tenete [hold-on-to-the-good]" (A12.49–52; I Thess. 5:21). Try everything but stick to what's good: this phrase should sound familiar, for Langland takes these words from A12 and makes them part of the expanded treatment of the King's interrogation of Mede and Conscience in passus 3 of the B and C texts (see section 4 above). Mede defends her adventurousness with the doctrine "Try everything," and Conscience tells her to turn the page and to keep reading until she finds the next phrase, "stick to the good," which she willfully ignores. So Langland, the young poet of A, in his final moments, gives a gift to his older self, and the senior poet adapts Paul's advice to one of the showcase episodes in his new poem.

Will's adventures, strangely, appear to be starting anew, as he and this boy set out on their journey, but they do not advance very far. Whether

Langland knew he was ending the A text now or whether he decided abruptly to stop writing, no one will ever know, but readers see signs of imaginative demise all around. The pair first meet with Hunger, whom readers recall from the half-acre episode, where he heroically helped Piers control the folk. Not a friend here, or simply the onset of road-trip appetite, this manifestation of Hunger dwells with Death and threatens to kill "Lyf [life]" within "a fewe dayes" (A12.63–66). Will then sits down to "maunge" (72) and fills his belly (his allegorical sidekick does not need to eat). After all the heady conversation dominating the last few passūs, now, as in the half-acre episode, the appetite asserts itself once again. Langland perceives this and makes Will's body central to the B and C versions, as the A text, in its final throes, gives birth to B and C.

After Hunger, Will meets another force of human weakness that he needs to reckon with, "Feuere-on-þe-ferþe-day [quartan fever]," a compeer of Death, whom Fever calls his "duk [duke]." Even more formidable than Hunger, especially to a plague-ravaged fourteenth-century society, he cannot be appeased with mere food. Fever has two men with him, Cotidian and Tercian, forms of intermittent yet potentially deadly fever. These characters claim to have "letteres of Lyf" (A12.86), documents that foretell the end of life. In a strange and unexpected move, Will, evidently wanting to die, tells Fever, "ȝoure gates [paths] wolde I holden [I would like to follow]" (88), and yet Fever rebuffs him:

> "Nay, Wil!" quod þat wyȝth, "wend þou no ferther,
> But lyue as þis lyf is ordeyned for the.
> Þ[ou] tomblest wiþ a trepget [fall into a trap] ȝif þou my tras [path] folwe,
> And mannes merþe w[or]þ [pleasure becomes] no mor þan he deseruyþ here
> Whil his lyf and his lykhame [body] lesten [persist] togedere.
> And þerfore do after Dowel whil þi dayes duren [endure, last],
> Þat þi play be plentevous in paradys with aungelys.
> Þou shalt be lauȝth into lyȝth [taken into the light] with loking of an eye,
> So þat [as long as] þou werke [practice] þe word þat Holy Wryt techeþ,
> And be prest [quick] to preyeres and profitable werkes!" (A12.89–98)

The poem does not explain why Will wants to go with Fever. Dying would be one way to finish—or to avoid finishing—a poem. But Fever says no, telling Will he will fall into a "trepget" if he follows Fever's "tras."[3] From lines 89 on, only one manuscript witnesses the text, so we are at its mercy at this dramatic juncture—with no other examples to compare and possibly to clarify an ambiguity. As seen from the brackets in Schmidt's text, in order to make sense of the words recorded in the manuscript, he emends "wrouȝþ" (worked or made) to "worþ" (become) and converts the oblique pronoun "þe" (the objective case) to "þou" (the needed nominative form), so finding even basic meaning here demands editorial conjecture. And though B and C discard this wayward passus, Will indeed meets Fever and Death again at the end of B, where they chastise the raging army of sins who attack the Church, Unity. But here Fever spares Will, or rather reassigns him from Death to Life: go and "dowel," he tells him, so that one day when he dies he will "play plenty" in paradise with angels, after being "snatched up" to see the "light" of heaven,[4] as long as he prays and obeys scripture. Fever provides hope, a classic and dramatically satisfying way to end a poem.

Then comes John But, at line 99, bursting in with the name "Will" in what seems like a merging of the poem's hero, narrator, and author. Perhaps But really knew Langland and his later career, seeing that Langland never ended this version conclusively. Perhaps he only vaguely knew the *Piers* corpus through scribal or bibliophilic connections. Nonetheless, he entitles himself to provide this coda with a wish that all his fellow Christians will live as God would want them, adding also a prayer that God save King Richard and his faithful lords:

> Now alle kenne creatures þat Cristene were euere,
> God for his goudnesse gif hem swyche happes [such opportunity]
> To lyue as þat Lord lykyþ þat lyf in hem putte [gave them life]:
> Furst to rekne [acknowledge] Richard, Kyng of þis rewme,
> And alle lordes þat louyn him lely [faithfully] in herte—
> God saue hem sound by se and by land!
> Marie, moder and may [maiden], for man þou byseke [beseech]
> Þat barn [child] bring vs to blys þat bled vpon þe rode [cross]! Amen.
>   (A12.110–17)

John But echoes Fever's final words about living well, thus displaying his sense of thematic unity with the episode he inherited. John But, perhaps the first documented reader of *Piers Plowman*, read the poem well, drawing from its themes of virtue, responsibility, and prayer. At the same time he displays one of the first moments of critical frustration from a reader who wants the poem to end with an appropriate final statement, which his "God save the king and all the realm" coda, however conventional, does provide. The arrogance of his intervention has both delighted and confused readers for 650 years and will likely continue to do so.[5] But John But's ending is not really the end. Will and his loyal readers have to carry on, prepared for Hunger and watchful of Fever, with the faithful companion Omnia Probate ever there to assist.

14

Farewell My Recklessness

PASSUS 11 OF THE B TEXT WITH C12–13

Conspectus: In B and C, Langland creates new poems from the remains of A. Langland's imagination expands powerfully in this new effort, and B11 extends 439 lines long, tracing Will's sexual folly and his encounters with Scripture and Kynde, plus a bold new character, the Roman emperor Trajan. Both adding and trimming as he revises, Langland divides the material of B11 into two passūs, C12 and C13. The C text features a major addition on patient poverty and salvation, after which the versions continue together to the end of B11 and C13, advancing the process that renders twenty-two passūs for the C text compared to B's twenty.

I. B and C Begin Their New Poems

The B and C continuations inherently reflect the changes explored above, where Langland shifted matter from B11 into the narrative at C11, a move that made Will start his degenerate life with Fortune and her wenches a bit sooner in C than in B. In B11 this episode marks Will's entry into a life of pleasure, which endures for a full forty years, but which starts *after* he has openly debated and philosophized about salvation, evidently not to Scripture's satisfaction. When C12 begins, Will has already become degenerate, and therefore the character Recklessness, strangely, offers what had been Will's speculation about salvation.

These shifts can disorient readers, and the opening B11 material about Fortune, which we analyzed in its C-text setting (C11.162–97), merits close attention as well in its original place. In this passus Will begins the first of his two dreams-within-a-dream, since he is already dreaming when he falls asleep (B11.5). Langland, either not noticing this apparent disjunction while revising, or with complex artistic intentions, maintains the internal dream, however shifted in place, in the C text. This inner dream ends at B11.404 and C13.215, with its external dream ending when Will wakes at the beginning of B13 and C15.

In addition to the complexity of the dreams, the assignment of speakers in these passūs also creates confusion. Editors must commit to attribution, and one can only wonder how medieval readers would have done so without punctuation to guide them, though perhaps strict attribution matters less than the matter being discussed. In the B text, for example, at various points readers cannot determine who speaks—Will or the Roman emperor Trajan who bursts onto the scene. Similarly in C, though Recklessness speaks much of passūs 12–13, the division between narrative and dialogue does not make itself apparent. In the C text, shifts, additions, and unclear attributions produce what Schmidt calls an "enormous speech" that includes the B Trajan material (if it is Trajan), finally "ascribed to Rechelesnesse at 13.129." But much of "both versions," says Schmidt, sounds "quasi-choric in nature and tone."[1] If true, then determining who speaks what matters less than the message, though readers must contemplate the applicability to character of all statements in both versions. Much of what might be spoken by Trajan, a saved pagan, concerns the history of virtue, honor, and salvation, all appropriate to this character. The function of their attribution to Recklessness is not as apparent, as it threatens to reduce Trajan's hopeful assertions about salvation to the unreliable ramblings of the untrustworthy, reckless human will. Properly associating doctrine and speaker can make one's head spin, but the task provokes important questions about authority and belief in the B and C texts. And it might reveal a major shift from hope to doubt in the poem's apprehension of salvation, courtesy of the mysterious, redoubtable Recklessness.

To put it plainly, in B Will is "reckless" and in C he will become Recklessness. Thus C12 begins parallel to B11.44, in which Elde and Holynesse lament that Will, in his period of sexual frenzy, has fulfilled "al his wille" (C12.2) and now faces the resulting wretchedness. Careless of this, Covetousness of Eyes tells Will that he can confess to a friar and fear nothing. Such bad advice helps to make him reckless indeed, but the transformation may affect more than just the character Will. For perhaps the new prominence of R/recklessness in C allows the poet to express his frustration with the conflicting religious doctrines he grapples with and also with his own creative efforts in A and B. Langland may have come to consider himself both brave and reckless in taking up his poem again and again. In writing *Piers Plowman*, Langland also writes himself, allowing his characters to model his evolution as a poet. Few readers would balk at describing the poet as "reckless," and perhaps this helps explain the expanded, if still dubious, range and authority of this character in the C text.

II. Will Follows Fortune and Meets an Emperor

As B11 begins, Will gives in to Fortune and her deceptive promises. In both B and C he finds himself convinced by the teaching of "þis wenche" (B11.59), Covetousness of Eyes, and likes the option of bribing friars for any sins he in youth may commit, so he follows her, and in a rather time-elapsed fashion that spans a line or two, he becomes old and Fortune becomes his foe. Both B and C depict Will turning on the friar and his empty promises, associating the mendicant with crafty "woweris [wooers]" (71) who court widows for their money, since the friar looks for silver in exchange for a celebrity burial in the priory. The friar does not care about the soul, only the fee for the service, and thus one cannot trust the value and efficacy of his absolution, in which Will has placed his reckless hopes. In B Will indicts the friars for focusing on burial instead of baptism, which would prepare more Christians for salvation, and in C Will ends his speech with the sharp and strident accusation "rouhte [care] ȝe neuere / Wher my body were yberied, by so ȝe hadde my godes!" (C12.21–22).

In both versions Will's gamble with recklessness has provided him no knowledge of Dowel and no progress toward salvation. And thus, forty years older, he is back where he started. Yet just when Will has most gravely imperiled his soul, the poem intensifies its interest in salvation.

Scripture reenters, skips on her heels, and preaches on the theme that many are called but few are chosen, a topic that sparks a new anxiety for Will as he wonders whether he "were chose or noȝt chose" (B11.107–18). He scrambles for assurance. Does baptism not open salvation to everyone, he wonders, including Saracens and Jews? Are not all Christians bought with the blood of Christ? He then proposes a conceit: a Christian man renouncing his own faith (and thus his salvation) is like a "cherl" (127) trying to make a charter to sell goods that do not belong to him but rather to his lord, who would never authorize such a sale—so God's mercy functions. Scripture approves of Will's analogy and finds a passage in the Bible (Psalm 144:9) that testifies to God's caring love:

> Mercy, may al amende, and [as long as] mekenesse [humility] hir folwe;
> For þei beþ, as oure bokes telleþ, aboue Goddes werkes:
> *Misericordia eius super omnia opera eius* [his tender mercies are over all his works]. (B11.138–39a)

To exemplify this doctrine, there occurs one of those unexpected moments that make the poem so exciting, when an explosive event breaks the narrative out of murky doctrine. The Roman emperor Trajan, having "broken out of helle," now bursts into the poem, in both versions, with a curmudgeonly "Ye, baw for bokes!" (140), famously shaking the foundations of the discussion. He dismisses "books" and authority as nothing compared to living in truth, the sure source of the (otherwise inexplicable) salvation of this virtuous heathen. Boldly Trajan questions the authority of Scripture when she stands right there. Perhaps this signifies that even in the presence of quoted scripture, the "will" can feel itself overwhelmed by conflicting historical evidence, such as the legendary salvation of Trajan, which Will must have known from prior study. Will is dreaming, so his memory produces all these characters and voices, whether he knows it or not.

In C Langland trims some of Trajan's subsequent explanation of how Pope Gregory saved him, but in B and C the poet tries to crystalize the ultimate expression of the salvific forces of love that broke him out of hell and liberated him, a pagan, from the strict punishment of law. Love must animate law and every human intellectual pursuit:

"Lawe wiþouten loue," quod Troianus, "ley þer [is not worth] a bene—
Or any science vnder sonne, þe seuene artȝ and alle!
But [unless] þei ben lerned for Oure Lordes loue, lost is al þe tyme,
For no cause to cacche siluer [earn money] þerby, ne to be called a maister [scholar],
But [unless] al for loue of Oure Lord and þe bet [better] to loue þe peple." (B11.170–74)

In C Langland adds the terms "loyalty" and "truth" to show how they, combined with love, must animate human art and science:

For lawe withouten leutee [loyalty], ley þer [is not worth] a bene—
Or eny science vnder sonne, the seuene ars and alle!
Bote [unless] loue and leute hem lede, ylost is al þe tyme
Of hym þat trauaileth theron [labors in this regard] bote treuthe be his lyuynge. (C12.94–97)

Both B and C then resolve to the Gospel of John: "Qui non diligit, manet in morte [He that loveth not, abideth in death]" (3:14). B adds a translation, absent in C: "Whoso loueþ noȝt, leue [believe] me, he lyueþ in deeþ deyinge" (B11.176). In these passages, Trajan substantiates his dismissal of books by appealing to the forces of virtue and divine authority that override human ingenuity.

For the discourse that follows, which turns sharply into a discussion of "pouere peple" (B11.176–318, all transferred to Recklessness at C12.101–C13.128), the issue of speaker attribution to Will or Trajan in B threatens to imperil understanding. But the content of this excursus demands attention, whoever speaks it, for in both B and C Langland explores the critical theme of giving to the poor as a form of love. *Piers*, in any version, whenever unsure of where to go, returns to love and then expounds upon its meaning, inspired by the particular context. The B text (Will or Trajan) observes that Christ often appears in poor man's apparel, a common notion throughout Christian thought, based on Jesus's care for the poor. B also avers that God could have made everyone rich but did not do so because poverty actually enables charity. Langland never imagines a world free of destitution, for how one responds to the disparity in wealth determines virtue. B and C then both contend that God makes all of humanity brothers with his blood, unified by redemption and no longer divided by wealth. In this divine leveling, only sin, freely chosen, breaks the brotherhood. Only sin truly impoverishes, as revealed in the powerful lines, citing John 8:34,

> For at Caluarie, of Cristes blood Cristendom gan [began] sprynge,
> And blody breþeren we bicome þere, of o [one] body ywonne [redeemed],
> As *quasi modo geniti* [as newborn babes] gentil men echone—
> No beggere ne boye [knave] amonges vs but if [unless] it synne made [caused]. (B11.200–203)

God remedies class division not through redistribution of wealth but by redefining "gentility" and thus erasing it. God's humbling of himself, his presence in the poor, and his ultimate sacrifice make men and women his bloody brethren, in a passage that anticipates Henry V's famous speech at Agincourt and sounds equally heroic in timbre. As they ponder issues of poverty and wisdom for the next thirty or so lines, B and C remain close, but in C Langland then expands the speech dramatically, composing two hundred new lines for Recklessness, a character with whom he seems ever more fascinated.

III. C Goes Solo, but the Poor Are Always with Us: C12.156–13.99

This long unique intrusion, written expressly for Recklessness, makes his already confusing role more puzzling. One wonders what aspect of his supporting role in B would merit an expanded role and a featured episode for him in C. Part of the answer may lie in his citation, at the very start of C's addition, of Christ's radical injunction that a believer must abandon everything and everyone to follow God (C12.156–61). Both Judean and English culture could very well find this extreme and reckless, and few modern readers of the poem, outside of those in holy orders, could comfortably relate this injunction to any tangible course of action in the everyday world. Perhaps the clerical life of renunciation and poverty demands an inherent recklessness, if one defines the term as neglect of personal comfort and earthly luxury. Langland has featured fools and idiots and now the reckless as blessed beings, depicting the essential Christian commitment as a bold and risky move.[2]

In this context, to be reckless about suffering and death means accepting the grace and joy that transcends and finally defeats them both. Recklessness explains that many have suffered for God various "tribulaciounes" such as fear, famine, and slander, in defiance of the safety of the world and in rejection of the allure of worldly profit (C12.195–211). But the speaker then becomes rather exercised as he turns to the rich who value transient pleasures that ripen too fast and rot too soon, like sweet pears and cherries. The luscious fruit imagery adds a sense of erotic savor that Langland often applies to carnal gratification in *Piers*, bodily or monetary:

> Lo, lordes, lo! And ladyes, taketh hede,
> Hit lasteth nat longe þat is lycour swete [gives sweet juice]—
> As pesecoddes [peapods], pere-ionettes [young pears], plommes and cheries.
> That lihtlich launseth vp, litel while dureth,
> And þat rathest [soonest] rypeth, rotieth most sonnest. (C12.221–25)

And, at once, the deceitful pleasures of wealth provide anyone, including "bischopes, / Erles and erchedekenes and oþere riche clerkes" plenty of related vicious opportunity, because from "rychesse ope [piled upon] rychesse ariste alle vices," and from "fat lond ful of donge [dung] foulest wedes growth." In sum, says Recklessness, "Ouer-plente pruyde norischeth [nourishes pride], þer [whereas] pouerte hit distrueth [destroys it]'" (226–36). Though embracing poverty requires a reckless leap of faith, that risk ironically provides greater security than riches, which, as the earthy imagery makes clear, nourish like manure the foul weeds of vice. Langland knows that power of any kind—intellectual, political, or financial—enables more sin.

Langland's expansions here may clarify the entire "reckless" episode not only in C but in B as well, permitting readers to make greater sense of Will's period of sexual indulgence, otherwise known as youth, which he recklessly extends to forty years. Even though no character makes it explicit, readers can opine that just as Langland presents two "medes" he also offers two recklessnesses. In C Langland accordingly expands his role to distinguish subtly the reckless folly of carnal appetite from the "recklessness" inherent in trusting health and security to God and his enduring grace. Covetousness for possessions, as the text shows, creates the anxiety of having and retaining wealth, which can lead to murder and damnation. Recklessness ends the passus somewhat excitably: "Lo, how pans [wealth] purchaseth fayre places and drede [fear], / That rote is of robbares—the rychesse withynne!" (C12.248–49). These stunning verses reveal that when people purchase anything of value and beauty, they actually purchase fear. By contrast, the "reckless" poverty that brings serenity seems hardly reckless at all.

Langland here ends passus 12, continuing Recklessness's discussion of poverty in 13, which begins by remarking how Jesus and the apostles shed their wealth progressively as their ministry unfolded (C13.1–4α). Ultimately blessed figures like Abraham and Job prospered not because of poverty but through their patience in enduring it (5–24). Recklessness must account for the fact that not every holy person winds up poor and that God can grant great earthly prosperity. Thus he tells the "lewede [ignorant]," who might disagree with him, that he does not condemn riches per se but rather contends that poverty, as if in a footrace, passes purgatory more quickly than riches, "thogh they renne at ones [begin running together]" (31). Then follows a fairly tedious conceit about wealth and poverty as a merchant and a messenger traveling cross-country, in which the messenger receives expedited transit while the merchant pays fees and is thus delayed. The rich can eventually reach paradise, but only when they pay tolls, debts both real and spiritual, that the poor never incur. Langland expands the conceit for another fifty lines, including the admonition that the rich ought to

> Fynde beggares bred, bakkes [cloaks] for þe colde,
> Tythen [tithe] here goed [goods] treuliche, a tol, as hit semeth,
> That Oure Lord loketh aftur [collects], of vch a lyf þat wynneth [acquires]
> Withoute wyles or wronges or wymmen at þe stuyues [brothels];
> And ȝut more, to maken pees and quyten [repay] menne dettes,
> And spele [save] and spare to spende vppon þe nedfole [needy]
> As Crist hymsulf comaundeth alle Cristene peple:
> *Alter alterius onera portate* [bear ye one another's burdens].
> (C13.71–77α)

"Bakkes" metonymically indicates outer garments to cover the bodies of the needy, summoning an image of the poorly clad shaking with naked backs against the cold. The rich have to transport and protect a big box as they journey, but if they pay the proper tolls and "aren alle acountable to Crist and to þe Kyng of Heuene" (66), they might make it to the "Wynchestre fayre" (51). That is, they must feed the hungry and clothe the wretched before reaching salvation.

Before Langland returns to the matter of B with a workmanlike passage praising patient poverty and exhorting priests to follow it, he finishes his expansion with some complex and ethereal poetry about the conscience of the poor:

> So þe pore of puyr reuthe [pure pity] may parforme þe lawe,
> In þat a [he] wilneth and wolde [wishes and wills for] vch a wyht [each person] as hymsulue.
> For þe wil [intention to give] is as moche worthe of a wrecche beggare
> As al þat þe ryche may rayme [acquire] and rihtfuly dele [deal out],
> And as moche mede [reward] for a myte þer he offreth [small coin he offers]
> As þe ryche man for al his moné, and more, as by þe Gospell:
> *Amen dico vobis, quia hec vidua paupercula* . . . [Amen I say to you, this poor widow . . .] (C13.92–97a; Mark 12:43; Luke 21:3)

The poor act on "puyr reuthe" rather than from the drive for accumulation and earthly power that motivates the rich. And the poor man, in this formulation, longs to fulfill the dictates of charity by loving others "as hymsulue." The poor person's "will," his or her charitable impulse, though impossible to actualize, carries as much value as all that the rich can gather and distribute. Langland may have sensed that he had reached a moment of insight and distilled a lesson about the power of poverty that he never could quite express fully in the B text.[3] The Latin verses quoted from the gospels cite an episode where Jesus praises a poor old widow's humble, but relatively munificent, contribution to the treasury. The biblical authority and the poignancy of this discourse help Langland redefine recklessness as the patience to live without the comforts of material wealth and the fearlessness to give to others, no matter the cost. Creating a bold portrait of charity with this reckless revision, Langland returns dutifully then to the matter of B.

IV. Getting Back to Middle Earth

At that B juncture where Langland expands in C, Trajan speaks and will do so for around the next thirty-five lines, which C's Recklessness will parallel closely, praising poverty and encouraging proper clerical behavior. In this sequence, both B and C encourage priests to live on their proper wages from the bishop and not sing masses for silver. The C text offers a stunning local revision, telling priests to seek wages only from the pope "or þe bischop þat blessed ȝow and enbaumed [anointed] ȝoure fyngeres" (C13.106). C's intense new b-verse replaces B's statement that the bishop blesses priests that "ben worþi" (B11.291) with the concrete image of sanctified hands. Any clergyman reading this would likely look down at his blessed fingers, making and unmaking a fist, and perhaps wondering how they could, so anointed, ever grasp for silver. Even a change of a half line can transform an episode, as the poet ever refines the moral power of his art.

B and C (Trajan and Recklessness) then engage in another chivalric conceit, proposing that kings should not make knights unless those knights have the resources to support their knighthood. This means priests who have neither "connyng ne kyn [knowledge nor breeding]" but have only a title, deemed as a "tale of nauht [nothing]" (C13.112–13). The unworthy attain church titles they cannot sustain and thus defile the sacred mass "thorw here luyther [despicable] lyuynge and lewede vnderstondynge" (115).

To illustrate this effect, B and C explain discursively that a sloppy charter could not hold up in court and the fellow who made it would be called a "goky [fool]." No one wants to be a goky, but that is exactly what these "ouerskipperes" become, priests who read Latin so badly that they skip over (presumably the more complicated) parts of the liturgy (C120–22). Nothing in the discourse of B or C here strikes readers as particularly Trajanesque or "reckless," as it seems that Langland has expressed all the character-specific themes that he could and now tries to transition back to the main narrative and to conclude the attack on greedy priests in the voice of whichever character happens to be speaking.

B and C then attack bishops who permit the ignorant to flourish, and Langland here increases his use of Latin, both from scripture and from law, as if displaying the knowledge he sees lacking in others, thus demonstrating what learning, when properly employed, can do. Ignorance, each version asserts, does not exculpate bishops or idiot priests: "For *ignorancia non excusat*, as Ych haue herd in bokes" (C13.128). Then in B comes one of the many lighthearted moments in *Piers Plowman*, as Trajan realizes that he has strayed off topic and admits that the subject of ignorant priests has made him wander from the subject of poverty (B11.317–18). Perhaps readers were following along well enough but find comfort in seeing a character acknowledge that speakers sometimes recklessly go off on tangents in *Piers*. In C Recklessness makes no apology, and Will puts a coda on the episode, as if overemphasizing the need for a clear transition: "Thus Rechelesnesse in a rage aresenede [berated] Clergie" (C13.129). Reader and poet alike, it appears, try hard to follow and contain the overflowing ideas and the contending voices of the poem.

Then Langland launches rather abruptly into a new episode (but same dream), in which Kynde arrives, calls Will by name, and sets him on a mountain from which he can see all of nature. Though in C Langland replaces the mountain with a mirror that reflects Middle Earth, both versions allow Will to know and love his creator through the creatures themselves: "To knowe by vch a creature Kynde to louye" (C13.133).

Will perceives Nature as both well-ordered and beautiful, with "wilde wormes in wodes, and wonderful foweles" (B11.328). After the heady discussions of salvation and virtue, in encounters with two such boisterous fellows as Trajan and Recklessness, Will now stops to cherish something he must have taken for granted. In addition to beauty, Will also sees how Reason, as minister of natural law, rules all beasts, who somehow manage to have sex without any emotional politics or postcoital cuddling:

Reson I sei3 sooþly sewen [administered to] alle beestes
In etynge, in drynkynge and in engendrynge of kynde.
And after cours [natural course] of concepcion noon took kepe [notice] of ooþer
As whan þei hadde ryde [ridden] in rotey tyme [rutting time]; anoonri3t þerafter
Males drowen hem [draw themselves] to males amorwenynges [in the morning] by hemselue,
And in euenynges also 3ede [went] males fro femelles.

> Ther ne was cow ne cowkynde [other bovine] þat conceyued hadde
> That wolde belwe [bellow] afer boles [bulles], ne boor after sowe.
> (B11.334–41)

Birds build nests, Will opines, that would confound the best masons (C13.161), for nature, a brilliant machine, works productively without human guidance or instruction. Each creature functions reasonably and logically, Will observes, "Saue [except] man and his make [mate]," a statement he makes twice in the C text, later substituting "mankynde" for "make" (B11.370; C13.153, 181). In the first instance Will adds, rather saucily: "For out of resoun they ryde and rechelesliche [recklessly] token on [continue],⁴ / As in derne [secret] dedes, bothe drynkyng and elles [other things]" (C13.154–55). Langland exploits the themes of "recklessness" that he had uniquely expanded in C, now accusing humanity broadly of that behavior. Unlike animals, who know how to rut purposefully and be done with it, people act madly in sexual affairs and ride out of reason. Ironically, the verses at once contrast irrational humanity to detached beasts doing their natural duty and yet also associate men and women with apparently "animalistic" behavior, including "elles," that is, "other things" that Will must be too polite to mention.

Like a city boy on his first day in a national park, Will, awestruck with the order of nature, observes how birds hide their eggs, peacocks breed, and birds instinctively fly to trees for safety. Dismayed, he confronts Reason directly about his puzzling failure to govern disorderly human behavior:

> In mete [food] out of mesure and mony tymes in drynke,
> In wommen, in wedes [clothing], and in wordes bothe,
> They ouerdoen [overdo] hit day and nyhte and so doth nat oþer
>   [while others do not].
> Bestes reule hem al by resoun, ac renkes [men] ful fewe.
> And þerfore merueileth me [I marvel]—for man is moste yliche the
>   [like you], of wit and of werkes,
> Why he ne loueth thy lore [doctrine] and leueth [lives] as þou techest?
> (C13.188–93)

If in the B text Will accuses Reason of mismanagement, in C Langland adds the sordid details of human appetite, illustrative of the trenchant amplification that sometimes informs his revisions. The inclusion of clothing as an instance of human luxury artfully opposes the images of the colorfully beautiful meadows in nature, which need not labor to dress themselves up beautifully as men and woman do. Reason does not want to hear this reproach in either version and lambasts Will for questioning what he "soffre [permits] or nat soffre" (C13.195), for what he does or does not allow humanity to do is none of Will's business. And speaking of suffering, Reason adds sharply, "Who suffreþ [endures] moore þan God?" turning Will's presumptuous question into a lesson about the "souerayn vertue" of patience, based on God's infinite endurance with sinful human behavior (B11.375–81). Reason wants Will to think before throwing around accusations about who allows what to occur in the course of human life. Reason, quite fed up at this point in C, says no more, while in B he displays patience enough to explain that humanity is good because all that God made is good, though that does not prevent people from being tempted by the flesh and by the fiend to pervert lustfully God's command to multiply (B11.392–402).

Will reaches his breaking point and wakes up from the dream within a dream at B.11.404 and C13.215. But he thinks himself fully awake and laments ironically that the waking world has brought him no closer to Dowel, while the dreams by contrast have provided him with "grace / To wyte what Dowel is" (C13.217–18). A mysterious figure stands there waiting for him to wake up and tells Will that he has only himself to blame for awaking prematurely and thus forfeiting more learning—the result of his rebuking Reason for the lax governance of humanity.

If Will had kept his mouth shut, the stranger continues, Clergy and Reason would have told him more, quoting the great adage "Philosophus esses, si tacuisses [if you had remained silent, you would have been a philosopher]," to which C adds, "Locutum me aliquando penituit, tacuisse nunquam [I often regret speaking but never having stayed silent]" (B11.414a; C13.225a). Both versions mention Adam as another fool too eager to know more, meddling with knowledge of good and evil at the cost of paradise, just as Will and his "rude speche" (C13.229) mucked things up. The still unknown figure then offers a powerful conceit, comparing Will to a "dronkene daffe [idiot] in a dykke falle [fallen into a ditch]" who will not respond to the rebuke of Clergy, nor Reason, nor Natural Wit, but sits there until Need shames him into picking himself up: "and thenne woet he [he will understand] wherfore and why he is to blame" (C13.235, 241). In other words, no one can teach Will after this display of arrogance until he drags himself out of the ditch of ignorance, pride, and presumption. Will agrees and acknowledges that nothing drives a man to reform like Shame. Neither doctrine nor teacher can "reason" the sinful human will into changing, not until it takes personal responsibility and decides to reform itself.

The character Recklessness, a bit player in B and a featured speaker in C, has gone silent in both versions. Will, however, carries on his spirit. In fact, in daring to chide Reason, he acts more recklessly than Recklessness did. But Will asks a very good question, however poorly Reason receives it: Why does humanity act so unreasonably while other parts of Nature, though untaught, untrained, and bookless, work so properly and efficiently to engineer the demands of the creator? Will, still baffled, sits paralyzed like a drunk in a ditch, until Need or Shame or someone can come along to snap him out of his arrogant indulgence and its resulting stupor. This new character, our hero must wonder, seems to know so much about philosophy and about the weakness of the "will," so perhaps he can provide insight about the fallen, sinful state of humanity. As Will rises up, greets him politely, and asks his name, the passus ends, suspensefully, in both versions. Luckily, Will does not have to wait long for answers.

15

Just Will's Imagination

PASSUS 12 OF THE B TEXT AND C14

Conspectus: The mystery man who has been advising Will turns out to be Imaginatif, a complex faculty of the mind, who will remain with Will until this third dream ends passūs B12 and C14. The term comes from medieval psychology and is defined by the *MED* as 1(a), "Employing mental images" or "the faculty of combining images into composites having no correspondence in external phenomena." These relate to meaning 4(c), "the ability to form images of things not experienced, e.g. of past or future events;—also personified," which means certainly the character in *Piers*. The adjectival meanings 2(a), "Suspicious, prying, curious," and 2(b), "inventive, resourceful," may apply as well. Will has already spoken to Wit, Thought, Study, Scripture, and Clergy, and appeals now to some more agile feature of his mind that might help him comprehend all he has pondered. Perhaps Imaginatif will also help him perceive his own rebelliousness, for Will unaided cannot see it.[1]

Will's new teacher pleasantly introduces himself:

"I am Ymaginatif," quod he; "ydel [idle] was I neuere,
Thou3 I sitte by myself, in siknesse ne in helþe,

> I haue folwed þee, in feiþ [indeed], þise fyue and fourty wynter,
> And manye tymes haue meued þee to [m]yn[n]e on þyn ende [contemplate your end],
> And how fele fernyeres are faren [many years are gone], and so fewe to come;
> And of þi wilde wantownesse þo þow yong were,
> To amende it in þi myddel age, lest my3t [the power to do so] þe faille
> In þyn olde elde, þat yuele kan suffre
> Pourte or penaunce, or preyeres bidde:
> *Si non in prima vigilia nex in secunda* . . . [if not in the first watch nor in the second . . .]" (B12.1–9; see Luke 12:38)

Imaginatif, as an aspect of Will's mind, warns him that he should repent of his youthful wantonness and emend himself in middle age, before he becomes elderly and can no longer reform. Strangely, Langland omits this caution in the C text, a place where one might, tempted by the biographical fallacy, expect both poet and his persona to show such awareness of the passing of time. Langland in B sounds like the older voice at this juncture, but he may have subtle reasons for this unexpected revision. The warning in B gives Will something to consider as he ages, but characters do not age from version to version; only the poet does. In middle age one can "imagine" personal reform, but when one really gets older, one may not want to hear of it. So in C Langland makes no attempt to use Will, at least at this moment, to reflect his evolving, ripening reaction to the realization that fewer days lie ahead than behind. Perhaps Langland, having composed the introspective apologia of C5, felt he had already answered Imaginatif's warning, which he evidently took seriously.

The same motivation may be at work when Langland also omits from C Imaginatif's accusation that Will, though warned with pestilences and poverty, nonetheless went on meddling "wiþ makynge" (B12.16), fussing over his poetry, a charge that Will defends by citing the need for play to break up the rigors of duty. Everyone has a right "to solacen hym [himself]" sometime, says Will defensively, "as I do when I make [compose]" (22). He depicts writing *Piers Plowman* as solace and not only as work, which might puzzle readers who do not apprehend Langland's labors, so grave and urgent, as a form of play. But medieval poets distinguished creative art from prayer and charitable work. And just as readers delight in the rigors of reading and writing about *Piers*, Langland saw his labors as a deeply satisfying form of solace that he proudly defends, for even holy men, Will has heard, sometimes "pleyden [played] þe parfiter [more perfect] to ben" (23–24). These silences in the C text, when seen in relation to Will's apologia, reveal that Langland did indeed negotiate the past and attended to warnings that he sent to himself, through Imaginatif, across time.

In B, after Will defends his play with poetry, he tells Imaginatif that in fact he would be happy to stop his literary work and to spend all his waking time in church once he finds Dowel (B12.25–28). He reveals here the ethical poetic of the Middle Ages: writing demands labor, provides solace, and also expresses devotion to God and to his law of *caritas*. But it can be abandoned once it serves its purpose of discovering Dowel. Langland imagines a place and a point beyond the need for solace and for work, a place of peace and meditation, where he can "bidde" his "bedes" (pray his prayers),[2] which is all the labor a Christian needs (28). Readers of C may lament the absence of this compelling sequence about aging and writing, and though Langland addresses the issues distinctly in C5, he never matches B's sedate vision of a life beyond poetry and beyond struggle, for perhaps Langland never attained such a life. Piers himself, perhaps as an alter ego of the poet, seeks such peace, after the pardon disaster, when he puts away the plow and turns to tears and prayers. No one knows how that ambition unfolds. Or perhaps just not yet, for Piers will return to this poem as a spiritual tender of the Tree of Charity. But if Langland plans to give his character arc of spiritual evolution over to Piers, one wonders what changes the poet will afford to Will, his most immediate persona, and whether these changes will fulfill the poet's dream of reaching a place of peace, such as he imagines for himself in this majestic passage in the B text. The poet has planted something and will later harvest the fruit it bears.

In B Imaginatif then fulfills Will's request for information about Dowel. He says nothing that Will has not already heard in some form, but immersion in definitions helps to develop Will's awareness of virtue, and it never hurts to be reminded of "feith, hope and charitee" from Paul's epistles

(B12.29; 1 Cor. 13:13). And yet many attempts at defining the Do's specify what they are *not* and list the forces that prevent Will from fulfilling their injunctions. Imaginatif, adopting this negative way as well, discusses the agents that corrupt virtue in both clerical and lay vocations, leading to the chestnut that "catel [possessions] and kynde wit [natural intelligence] was combraunce" to virtue (45). These encumbrances corrupted no less a pantheon of figures than Lucifer, Solomon, Samson, Aristotle, Hippocrates, and Virgil, as well as Felice and Rosamunde, who must have been a couple of local girls whose good looks got them into trouble, leading to "sclaundre [slander]" and "baddenesse" (46, 48).[3] Their beauty, though not a material possession, undoes them, for one's "catel," variously manifested,[4] and one's "kynde wit," instead of benefiting the owner, can actually lead to disaster. Readers (and Langland) would know these dangers from Augustine's *Confessions* and Paul's warning: "Knowledge puffeth up; but charity edifieth. And if any man think that he knoweth any thing, he hath not yet known as he ought to know. But if any man love God, the same is known by him" (1 Cor. 8:1–3). In this context, "kynde wit" means the pretense to knowledge that deludes, just as wealth and status delude with their allure, posing as elements of real power. Therefore both "clergie and kynde wit," says Imaginatif in B, come from "si3te and techyng" (64), that is, from observation and from learning, and must be distinguished from the greater power of grace, a "gifte of God, and of greet loue spryngeþ" (68). Clerks, he concludes, never knew how grace came forth, and "kynde wit" never understood its ways. Without the power of divine love, humanity cannot comprehend, much less attain, salvation.

Not to reject the very nature of learning, which might confuse an audience that relies on reading and writing in its quest for salvation, Imaginatif hastens to add in B that clergy must not be rejected outright (B12.70). God composed the Ten Commandments, and Christ wrote a mystical text in the sand to confound the crowd eager to stone the woman taken in adultery (John 8:6–8), Imaginatif explains. No one knows what Jesus wrote, but he explained his actions, B and C agree, with the injunction that those without sin should cast the first stone, artfully combating the scribes and the Pharisees who try to confound him with an assertion of the law against the accused woman. In B, in a homey, homiletic image, Imaginatif explains how "clergie is confort to creatures þat repenten" (83). In C Langland cuts the episode in half, simply asserting that Moses and Christ both affirm clergy, ending the passage starkly but effectively with strong words from Christ:

> "That seth [He who sees] hymsulue synnelees, sese nat, Y hote [command],
> To strike with stoen or with staf this strompet to dethe!"
> *Qui vestrum sine peccato est* [He that is without sin among you] . . .
> (C14.41–43)

With lean poetic economy, Langland cuts the episode to the bone, letting Christ's mordant words bear the weight of meaning, much as they must have when first spoken to disarm that hateful mob, bent on vulgar street justice.

From this point to the end of the passus (and thus to the end of the external dream and the end of Imaginatif's speech), the B and C texts remain rather close. Imaginatif has painted learning as a cumbrance, but now he clarifies by asserting that "kynde wit" can be molded into a beneficial force, employing books as tools, or even weapons, in the battle for salvation. He compares a man trying to learn without clerical instruction to a blind warrior, swinging his axe haphazardly:

> And as a blynd man in bataille bereþ wepne to fiȝte,
> And haþ noon hap [chance] wiþ his ax his enemy to hitte,
> Na moore kan a kynde-witted [naturally intelligent] man, but [unless] clerkes hym teche. (B 12.105–7)

These wavering and diverse perspectives on learning arise because Will's "imagination" is considering the issue of clergy, both *in malo* and *in bono*, which seems a sensible debate to have, especially for a scholarly poet who wonders if his academic knowledge benefits his soul. In so many of these allegorical dialogues, and in the poem at large, speakers ponder salvation and the forces that enable or encumber it. Clergy, like wealth, poverty, wit, and all attributes of life and action, can serve "the will" well or badly, dependent upon Will's pride and whether he ensures that love guides his desires and actions. Seen this way, Imaginatif's rolling discourse about the benefits of learning (when carefully applied) makes sense as productive speculation about salvation and a useful way for Will to rebound from the awkward reprimand he received from challenging Reason. Will develops both within and across versions as he assimilates new knowledge and deepens his understanding of nature, mind, and grace. His creator learns as well, for *Piers Plowman*, like Wordsworth's *Prelude*, records the growth of a poet's mind and thus needs to be rewritten over a lifetime.

Imaginatif scans through the history of pre-Christian science, which, for all its efforts, had no salvific power (B12.121–39a). He praises the Magi who came from the East to honor Christ, as perhaps a moment of transition from ancient learning to the greater truths of Christianity. Wise men bend a knee to Christ, but no friars attended that blessed event—a comic barb, since friars did not exist at the time, indicating that those who pass for being learned now fail to meet the majestic standard of the Magi in their respect for Christ. Venturing into the past may seem a tangent, but since Imaginatif explores salvation and the forces that enable and impede it throughout history, each detail in his discussion, however disjointed (as imagination so often is), makes its own sense.

Imaginatif then launches into the strange assertion in B and C that Christ was not born in some low-life slum but in a "burgeis place, of Bethlem the beste" (B12.147). A religious culture that values the poor and associates Christ with poverty strangely reimagines his origins as posh elegance, which includes not only shepherds but "clerkes," those Magi, who came with their presents "and diden hir homage honorably to hym þat was almiȝty" (152–54).[5] He then explains why he tells Will all this, and readers want to know as well. Will misbehaved when he contradicted Clergy by maintaining that ignorant and lowly men were sooner saved than the learned. This occurred at the end of B10 and C11 (in C Recklessness speaks), in the discussion of the dangers of inflated learning, culminating in the dramatic citation of Augustine's warning that the ignorant reach heaven while the learned descend to hell (see section 12 above). Evidently Will underestimated and disparaged the power of clergy, and it seems that every time Will thinks he comprehends an idea, someone or some aspect of his mind inverts or deconstructs the doctrine, compelling him to start building knowledge again with humility. Paradoxically, he now needs to rethink the benefits of clergy while realizing that knowledge, or the pretense thereof, far from enabling his quest, brings down upon him rather a continuing series of reprimands.

To help Will understand, Imaginatif offers a simple analogy that the learned and the unlearned can both understand: If one were to hurl two chaps into the River Thames, who would survive, the one who knows how to swim, or the one who cannot? Learning, a useful a tool, can help men and women "sonner [sooner] arise / Out of synne" (B12.171–72). Among other lessons, clergy teaches that contrition can heal sin, winning God's blessing and protection, as Paul says in Romans 4:7, "Beati quorum remisse sunt iniquitates [Blessed are they whose iniquities are forgiven]" (C14.117a).[6] This means for Imaginatif that "contricion withoute confessioun conforteth þe soule" (C14.115), that sincere remorse heals the sinful soul without an intermediary. As potentially an attack on the power of institutional confession, supporting a Lollard position,[7] the concept of direct contrition anticipates the later doctrine of the Protestant reformers that a Christian does not need a priest as mediator to God. The text also says that a knowledgeable clerk "knoweþ what is synne" (B12.174), a simple but powerful statement that not only redeems the idea of clergy but also puts a burden on the learned, such as the friars, who thus have no excuse for not swimming to safety from the flood of sin where "þe fend fondeþ [tempts] a man hardest" (179). In contrast, the unlearned, not taught to focus on contrition alone, must wait for institutional penance during Lent. And if their parish priest is ignorant, then, in Luke's words, "cecus ducit cecum [the blind lead the blind]" (184a). Exposing the vulnerability of the uneducated, Imaginatif mounts a strong defense of learning.

He so continues, in both B and C, to distinguish the learned from the ignorant with a contemporary reference to the practice of hanging thieves at Tyburn, where a thief could save himself by reciting some Latin to prove himself a clerk and thus under Church, not state, jurisdiction (B12.185–90). Those who escaped this fate must be grateful, we imagine, for their bookish learning. While on the subject of thieves, Imaginatif says Will misspoke when he asserted the salvation of the thief whom Christ saved on the cross. The thief was in fact saved, says Imaginatif, but not granted "hey [high] blisse" (C14.135) and thus was not *up there*, as it were, with St. John and with martyrs, maidens, and widows. Trajan too, whom the poem celebrates so triumphantly, came from "noȝt depe" in hell and so is now "in þe loweste of heuene," Imaginatif asserts, citing Psalms 61:13: "he gives to each according to their merits" (B12.209–12a).

These celestial class distinctions in heaven agree with other medieval descriptions, as in Dante's *Paradise* and in the *Gawain* Poet's *Pearl*, where elaborate divisions seem contrived for the benefit of mortal readers, who cannot abandon expectations of relative merit and cannot comprehend divine equity.

However, as if arguing back and forth against himself, Imaginatif then once again criticizes clergy and wit for their limits, since they cannot determine why the birds behave as they do, nor explain how Adam and Eve recognized their nakedness, for only Kynde (Nature) knows about such matters (B12.224-30). The C text omits these details about Adam and Eve, also deleting B's energetic attack on those who wonder why Adam did not cover his mouth instead of his privates, since the mouth, not the other parts, sinned. In C Langland rushes through B in haste, as if not interested in B's "college dorm questions," the kinds of speculations that the young and excitable ponder. These seemingly mature revisions by the poet notwithstanding, right at this moment Will comprehends nothing clearly, and in B and C Langland remains content with the tension and the ambiguity.

The poem's imagery becomes even more elaborate as Imaginatif summons another conceit to illustrate his point that various forces aid or hinder the quest for salvation: a contrast between the peacock, a pretty bird with ugly feet and foul flesh, and the lark, a lesser bird but "swettore of sauour [taste] and swyftore of wenge" (C14.186)—no doubt cold comfort for the tasty lark. The peacock stands for the rich encumbered with wealth, which, like the birds' decorative feathers, carries only surface value, for unless the rich distribute their money in acts of charity, wealth impedes their flight upward. Imaginatif then tucks back into the issues of academic learning, explaining that even though Aristotle (B) and Plato (C) invented this very bird analogy, clergy does not know if these philosophers are saved. Yet he adds generously the hope that God will give their souls rest, considering the beneficial effect their works have had on Christian readers. Skeptical of this, Will contends that these famously learned pagans, like Saracens and Jews, cannot be saved without Christian baptism. Contemplating Aristotle's salvation remains an intellectual puzzle, while Jews and Muslims exist as a real, if remote, part of Langland's world, lending urgency to the question of their status. Will's imaginative ramblings have thus led him to a serious question about the very nature of divine justice and human virtue, contemplating the inclusions and exclusions not only from history but also among the contemporary world's great monotheistic religions.

Imaginatif leaps on Will's words with a loud "Contra!" playing upon 1 Peter 4:18, "Saluabitur vix iustus in die iudicii; / Ergo saluabitur! [The just man shall barely be saved on Judgment Day; therefore, he is saved!]" (B12.278–79). The rest of the passus ponders the question of salvation, summoning for the last time Trajan as a model of the just man who must be saved according to the virtue of his "truth." That is to say, he embraced the best that his historical moment could provide, and he would have believed something better if he had had access to it. This passage extends the definition of baptism to include water, blood, and fire, which the text associates with the inspired practice of truth that Trajan exemplifies, and then explains that God rewards pure fidelity, however erroneous:

> Ne wolde neuere trewe God but trewe truþe were allowed [approved of].
> And wher it worþ or worþ noȝt [was or was not true], þe bileue is gret of truþe,
> And an hope hangynge þerinne to haue a mede [reward] for his truþe.
> (B12.287–89)

"And wit and wisdom," continues Imaginatif in lines unique to B, "was som tyme tresor / To kepe wiþ a commune [uphold society]—no catel was holde bettre—/ And muche murþe [joy] and manhod [integrity]."[8] And then, says Will, "riȝt myd [with] þat he vanysshed" (293–95). After explaining how the true treasures of wisdom, upon which society ought to be founded, have now been perverted with personal greed and ignorance, "the imagination" has nothing more to say, and so it/he vanishes. Will has no recourse but to wake up, which he does. But disoriented from waking suddenly, he needs time to recover from this most turbulent of dreams, which included an interior vision. The text never reveals whether Will knows about that second layer of dreaming, but he is shaken this time, very shaken.

16

The Dinner Party

PASSUS 13 OF THE B TEXT AND C15.1–233

Conspectus: Will's bout with imagination has overwhelmed him, and as regularly happens in the poem when returns diminish, he wakes up, this time feeling "fay" (enchanted) and wandering like a mendicant in what appears a new beginning, a new search for answers. In an Alice in Wonderland sort of way, he winds up at a dinner party with Patience, Conscience, Clergy, Scripture, and a gluttonous "maister." In C Reason receives an invitation too, and in both versions it becomes the event of the season. As the party breaks up, Will takes to the road again as a pilgrim and meets Haukin the Active Man, in C named Activa Vita (Active Life), beginning a long encounter exploring the inherently sinful nature of human activity and the nagging difficulties of maintaining purity, as manifested in the Active Man's filthy cloak.

I. Foodstuffs

In the opening of passus 13, in a burst of innocent exuberance, Will summarizes the events and effects of the last dream. In a series of urgent paratactic constructions, he explains how Fortune has failed him in need and continues on about Elde and the greedy friars, with an excited series of "and hows":

> And how þat Elde manaced [menaced] me, my3te we euere mete;
> And how þat freres folwede folk þat was riche,
> And [people] þat was pouere at litel pris þei sette [prized them little],
> And no corps in hir kirk3erd [churchyard] ne in hir kirk was buryed
> But quik [unless when alive] he biqueþe hem au3t or sholde helpe quyte [cover] hir dettes. (B13.6–10)

The summary culminates in his remembering the mildly reassuring promise of Imaginatif that "Vix iustus saluabitur" (B13.19), which C expands into two macaronic lines, playing with grammar and doctrine across languages:

> And Y merueyled in herte how Ymaginatyf saide
> That *iustus* [the just man] bifore Iesu *in die iudicii* [the day of judgment]
> *Non saluabitur* [would not be saved] bote if *vix* [barely] helpe.
> (C15.21–23)

Such wit from Langland: he turns the word *vix*, a humble Latin adverb meaning "barely," into a character who helps the just person achieve salvation. Langland gives the small word both stress and alliteration and makes it a personified, heroic character who saves the day—barely.

This summary prepares Will for the most charming, yet charmless, episodes in the poem, a dinner party that anticipates the tea-party scene in Lewis Carroll's *Alice's Adventures in Wonderland*. Will partners with Patience, who dresses as a pilgrim and sits with him at a side board, a sort of kids' table. Conscience hosts and Clergy attends as an invited guest, as does a "maister" of divinity (B13.25), a pompous and gluttonous character likely representing, as Pearsall notes (*C-text* 251), a Dominican friar, who becomes the focus and target of critique at the meal. C alone invites Reason to the party, and Will reverences him, evidently to make up for having offended him earlier. Langland sees this as an opportunity for Will to return to Reason's good graces, and though the invitation comes late, it comes in time, and Reason appears to have forgotten the snub in B.

Conscience orders the meal, and Scripture serves hearty portions of Augustine, Ambrose, and the Gospels, but the friar gluts himself on real food, "mortrews and potages," types of thick stews with meat and beans, purchased with what "men myswonne" (B13.41–42), which means that the friar feeds off of ill-gotten gains, such as when he, or one of his kind, enlisted Mede to contribute funds for a window in passus 3. All luxury comes from injustice and exploitation, and the friars do not care where they, or their benefactors, get the money for their rib-sticking fare. But the sauce on them, called "*Post mortem*" (B13.44) and described as sour and distasteful, indicates the suffering that comes to such gluttons when the bill for the meal comes at God's reckoning, after death. B and C then follow with a Latin sentence that translates as "If you feast on sin, unless you weep and pray, you will vomit up the delicacies in torment" (B13.45a), an ugly image that recalls Glutton's debauchery from the earlier confession scenes. The stomach hungers in ignorance of the price that the soul will pay.

Will and his dinner partner must eat too, and so Conscience has Scripture bring Will and Patience some bread and meat, a sour loaf called "Agite penitenciam [do penance]" and a drink called "Dia perseuerans [a potion of endurance]" (B13.48–49)—not hearty fare but no doubt good for the soul and conducive to patience and the tempering of desire.[1] Will behaves politely and offends no one except the proper target, that greedy friar, with whom, evidently, one is permitted to display poor manners at dinner.

The friar's food in B and C sounds luscious, depending on whether one savors "wombe cloutes [fatty intestine or tripe]" (B13.63), plus goose blood (C15.68), and bacon and eggs. Langland wants readers to feel the savor of human appetite and to salivate over these rich dishes. One cannot really know what "Agite penitenciam" or "Dia perseuerans," taste like, but they sound less luscious than fried fat. Those craving lighter fare can dine with Will and Patience (in B) on "Beati quorum [blessed are those]" and "Miserere mei, Deus [have mercy on me, O God]" (B13.51–53a) or in C on the rather bland, Psalm-flavored "Pro hac orabit / Omnis sanctus in tempore oportuno [For this shall every one that is holy pray in a seasonable time]" (C15.61–61a; Psalm 31:6). C alone offers a stunning half-line describing Will and Patience as "bytyng apartye" (C14.54), meaning "eating separately," but the verse itself makes a chomping sound, as if tucking into something real. They bite, rather, into sorrow, a nutritious sorrow that feeds wisdom and reform, something the friar's rich and meaty meal will never earn him. In B and C Will says to himself (but so Patience can hear) that a few days ago he heard this friar preaching penance and fasting (B13.64–70).

In B Will becomes agitated at the friar and wishes he could pour hot molten lead down his throat, an image a bit too dire for C, which replaces it with Will's wish that he could shove the food—and the plates as well—down his throat (B13.78–83; C15.86–92). Will wants to confront the friar about his immoral indulgence, but Patience tells him to wait for the friar to undo himself, which he does, once he has eaten and drunk to excess and tries absurdly to justify his diet as simple and penitential. When the friar coughs, Conscience gives Will a look indicating he should begin an interrogation, and so he asks the "maister": "What is Dowel?" However predictable the question, readers, like Will, always attend to the answers. "Do noon yuel to þyn euencristen [fellow Christians], nouȝt by þi power" says the friar in B, while in C he adds "ne thysulue [nor to yourself] nother'" (B13.105; C15.114). Will cannot dispute these answers, but the friar's appetite and hypocrisy have undermined his credibility, and his "do no harm" doctrine sounds more like justification of his personal indulgences. Perhaps the C addition recognizes the harm he does to himself by feeding his belly. However futile the attempt to reform him, Will tells the friar that his appetite does indeed injure his fellow Christians by depriving the hungry poor. In allegory one can feast on verses from the Psalms, but Langland knows that real people must eat.

Conscience, sharing the dinner conversation around, asks Clergy to chime in, which he does, boasting of his seven sons, the liberal arts. But then Clergy quickly notes that Piers the Plowman has impugned them all, that is, has repudiated all sciences, all crafts, every system of knowledge and learning "saue loue one [alone]" (B13.124–25). "Dilige Deum [love God]" says Clergy (B13.127), "et proximum [and your neighbor]" (C15.136). Evidently the stuffed friar, in defining Dowel in negation, forgets this simple doctrine of active charity. Clergy continues that Piers describes Dowel and Dobet as two infinites, a mystical term (which C omits) indicating something unlimited that "wiþ a feiþ fynden out [discovers] Dobest, / Which shal saue mannes soule."[2] "[Þ]us seiþ Piers þe Plowman," concludes Clergy ceremoniously, proud to attribute these unique definitions of the Do's to the poem's popular hero (B13.128–30). And by defining them as "infinites" rather than personal practices, clerical ranks, or political actions, Piers impugns not only the seven liberal arts but also the very quest to find Dowel through interrogation. Accordingly, Will needs to attain a higher, more mystical awareness of love in order to ascend to superior virtue and to salvation itself.

In B Conscience adds that he too trusts only Piers Plowman, and that he will wait for him to prove the power of love, adding in Latin that "*pacientes vincunt* [the patient overcome]" (B13.135a). In C quite dramatically Langland brings in Piers himself to speak this Latin and also the first part of Patience's speech that follows, about learning, teaching, loving God, and loving one's enemies as well:

> Quod Peres the Ploughman: "*Pacientes vincunt.*
> Byfore perpetuel pees Y shal preue [prove] þat Y saide,
> And avowe byfore God, and forsaken hit neuere,
> That *Disce, doce, dilige Deum* [learn, teach, love God]
> And thyn enemy helpe emforth [with all] thy myhte.
> Caste hote coles on his heued [head] of alle kynde speche;
> Fond thorw wit and with word his loue to wynne;
> 3ef hym eft and eft [again and again], euere at his nede;
> Conforte hym with thy catel and with thy kynde speche,
> And ley on hym thus with loue til he lauhe on [smile at] þe;
> And bote he bowe [submit] for this betynge [barrage], blynde mote he worthen [become]!" (C15.139–49)

The notion, from Paul's epistles, of piling hot coals on the head of an enemy indicates to "kill them with kindness," as we would say, and with the heat of charity (Romans 12:20).[3] But after this stunning cameo, just as quickly as he arrives Piers disappears again, off on another pilgrimage with Reason as his companion (C15.150–53).

In B and C, after Patience finishes his meditation on loving one's enemies, the friar, disdainful of that doctrine and of *Pacientes vincunt*, pushes the dinner table away dismissively. The party evidently over, the group begins to dissolve as Conscience tells Clergy he wants to go on pilgrimage with Patience until, he says ambiguously, he has "preued [tried out] moore" (B13.183). Read allegorically as Will's conscience speaking, this desire indicates that in order to understand the dictates of love, Will needs to see and experience more, to contemplate his desires more deeply and more "patiently." Whatever he learned in exposing the boorish friar and from the insights of his virtuous dinner companions has not satisfied Will's longing for knowledge. Clergy tries to stop Conscience and make him read the Bible:

> "What!" quod Clergie to Conscience, "are ye coueitous nouþe [now]
> After yeres3eues [annual payments] or 3iftes, or yernen to rede redels [solve riddles]?
> I shal brynge yow a Bible, a book of þe olde lawe,
> And lere [teach] yow, if yow like, þe leeste point to knowe,
> That [what] Pacience þe pilgrym parfitly knew neuere." (B13.184–88).

Conscience refuses, preferring to follow Patience and indicating that Scripture alone cannot purify the human will:

> "Nay, by Crist!" quod Conscience to Clergie, "God þee foryelde [repay].
> For al þat Pacience me profreþ [offers], proud am I litel [I am not very proud];
> Ac þe wil of þe wye [man, Will?] and þe wil of folk here
> Haþ meued my mood to moorne for my synnes.
> The goode wil of a wight [man] was neuere bou3t to þe fulle [fully bought]:
> For þer nys no tresour þerto [comparable] to a trewe wille."
> (B13.189–94)

That is to say, unraveling the allegory further, that unless patience guides Will's conscience in a "mood of mourning," then the mere reading of scripture, however powerful the revelation, means nothing. Langland explores here the inner, contemplative processes of coming to a "true will" (with pun intended), the highest treasure humanity can possess, but one that cannot be accomplished simply by picking up the book and reading.

In C Langland gently condenses this contemplative and plaintive sequence, maintaining Conscience's caution about Clergy and his quiet resolve for the patient trials to come:

> "By Crist," quod Consience, "Clergie, Y wol nat lye,
> Me were leuere [I would rather], by Oure Lorde, and Y leue sholde [by my life],
> Haue pacience parfitlyche [perfectly] then half thy pak of bokes!
> Lettrure and longe studie letteth [prevents] fol monye [very many],
> That they knoweth nat," quod Conscience, "what is kynde Pacience.
> Forthy [therefore]," quod Concience, "Crist Y the byteche [commend];
> With Pacience wol Y passe [journey], parfitnesse to fynde."
> (C15.179–85)

In the midst of these revisions in C, Langland deletes Patience's claim that he and Conscience together can bring about universal peace and the conversion of the Jews and Muslims (B13.206–11), an event Clergy says he will happily wait for as well. One might think Langland older and less hopeful in omitting this quest for universalism from C, judging it pointless and jejune. But despite his silence here, Langland returns to these themes in B15 and C17, where he depicts universal conversion as one of the Christian clergy's prime obligations.

With B's glorious expectations for conversion tempered for the moment, Langland nonetheless in both versions sees the urgency of the journey for Patience and Conscience and sends them on a quest "parfitnesse to fynde" (C15.185), the second pair of characters in C to set out on a private venture, since in that version Piers has already departed with Reason. The urge for pilgrimage indicates that the friar, his gluttonous appetite, and his perverse rendering of Dowel prove useless in the quest for salvation. Will must seek answers elsewhere. The struggles and debates at this dinner party predictably expose the weakness of the friar, but they also expose the limits of Clergy and reveal Conscience's dependency on Patience, whose doctrines of quiet endurance and love provide the party with its only hope. And although only the C text features an appearance by Piers, both versions nonetheless appeal to him as the ultimate authority on virtue and love, signaling that one way or another Will must finally reunite with the elusive Plowman, whose spiritual authority grows ever more powerful and Christlike.

In the meantime, Will takes to the road again as a pilgrim, and pilgrims must eat. So Patience packs some allegorical snacks, perhaps leftovers from the dinner party: "Sobretee [sobriety] and symple speche and sooþfast [trusty] bileue" (B13.218). As Will perceives it, Patience and Conscience then meet a "mynstral," later identified as the lovable character Haukin the Active Man in B, or simply Activa Vita (Active Life) in C. Not much of a minstrel, Haukin cannot sing, dance, or play music, and he cannot fart so well, evidently an important part of any comic's repertoire (B13.231–34). Not only a minstrel but a wafer seller and perhaps also a maker of cakes, this common man, a medieval Willy Loman, works hard at his craft to serve others and to scrape by.[4]

Haukin/Active Life hates idleness, and in B he employs an extended conceit about baking the bread for the faithful who pray for Piers the Plowman (B13.238). That is, he provides physical bread to feed the working class as they labor, but his bread also signifies the Eucharist, and thus spiritual sustenance for the community he proudly serves. Such work qualifies him to observe that nothing reforms people quite so well as a simple lack of bread. No papal blessing on paper can benefit humanity, he says, and no mass service can make peace among Christian peoples until pride is overthrown through "payn defaute [bread scarcity]" (B13.256–60). Haukin here recapitulates themes Langland explored earlier in the Hunger and half-acre episodes. Then, sounding like any proud workingman, he says he gets up quite early in the cold to make bread (B13.261–71), showing that he knows about honest labor, free from the desire for luxury that might enlarge pride. If Haukin appears very down-to-earth in B, in C by contrast, Active Life applies his theory about pride and bread to the story of Sodom and Gomorrah—a strange subject for a baker to preach about—an example of a people who fell into sin because of too much bread: "Plente of payn the peple of Sodoume / And reste and ryche metes rebaudes [lechers] hem made" (C15.232–33). Readers may accuse C of converting an engaging regular guy into a dry biblical exegete. But C's diminishment of the character results from Langland's transporting most of what follows in the B text into C's confession scenes in passūs 6 and 7, distributing Haukin's various weaknesses and crimes to the appropriate sins (stitching them rhetorically into their new contexts), and thus consolidating the two confession episodes into one—an efficient and judicious decision by the poet.[5]

II. Haukin the Active Man (B13.264–end)

If Langland's decision to consolidate the confessions tightens the poem, one can also argue that his portrait of Haukin in B, the apparent redundancy aside, constitutes one of the most successful character sketches in medieval vernacular literature. His self-depiction as a small business owner, trying to bake well and please his customers, who sometimes frown upon his wafers, seems quotidian, but Will then explains the allegorical levels of the "active life":

> I took greet kepe [care], by Crist, and Conscience boþe,
> Of Haukyn þe Actif Man, and how he was ycloþed.
> He hadde a cote of Cristendom as Holy Kirke bileueþ;
> Ac it was moled [moldy] in many places wiþ manye sondry plottes [stains]—
> Of pride here a plot, and þere a plot of vnbuxom [rebellious] speche,
> Of scornyng and of scoffyng and of vnskilful berynge [unwise behavior]. (B13.272–77)

Much more than just a working man trying to make a living, Haukin represents "activity," all socioeconomic identities and practices, everything distinct from the contemplative life, the withdrawal from the world. Activity inherently assumes sin, as manifested in stains on his cloak. Marking him a sinner just for living life strikes some readers as a harsh indictment of such a lovable fellow, but that is precisely the point: everyone sins simply by existing and acting in the fallen world. Haukin reflects the human condition, every possible manifestation of what goes wrong once we simply "do" anything. So pride, scorn, arrogance, self-glorification, pretense, sanctimoniousness, religious pretension, and sexual boasting—he calls himself "styuest [stiffest] vnder girdel [belt]" (B13.294)[6]—inform all his activities. His list of human frailties could go on forever, as human sin knows no bounds.

Conscience marvels at this dirty cloak of Haukin, who tells him to take a look at his back, turning around to reveal even more blotches and stains, as he simply cannot keep his "cote of Cristendom" clean (B13.274; 314–18). Haukin then recounts (319–42) his backbiting, jealousy, provocation of violence, slander, and all the features of Envy, to whose portrait Langland accordingly relocates this passage in C. In a delightful moment, Haukin says that when he cannot get the upper hand on someone, he almost has a heart attack, or he falls into a twelve-month-long fever of envy. Though so afflicted, he nonetheless despises the "lechecraft [medicine] of Oure Lord" and instead visits a witch, refusing the spiritual remedies that can cure his burning sin and preferring a magical "charme" to the power of "Goddes word," which, he laments, has never brought him "boote [relief, advantage]" (334–42). Next follows more of his lecherous practices (343–54), lines Langland appropriately moves in C to Lechery's monologue. Will sees the stain of lechery and explains how Haukin has made certain signs to maids, picking up like-minded, lecherous women for sport:

> For ech a maide þat he mette, he made hire a signe
> Semynge to synneward [suggestive of sin], and somtyme he gan taste
> Aboute þe mouþ or byneþe [beneath] bigynneþ to grope,
> Til eiþeres will wexeþ kene [sharpened], and to þe werke yeden [went to work]. (B13.345–48)

In C Langland converts this discourse into a boastful first-person confession for Lechery. The change of speaker and of context by necessity nullify the disgust Will feels when he observes what Haukin does with his mouth and how he is later reduced, like Chaucer's Reeve, to mere talk in old age (B13.351–54). One can almost see Will shaking his head at Haukin's folly, but considering his adventure with Recklessness and his female entourage, Will can claim little right to sit in judgment of the "active life." The C-text revisions productively unify Langland's sprawling confessions, but they sometimes sacrifice such imaginative moments of ironic play.

Haukin's next confession concerns mercantile practice and competition, such as stealing a good servant from a neighbor, gathering goods with guile, and mourning in church, not for the sins committed but for the loss of chattel or loan. Also, when he plows, he impinges on his neighbor's field (B13.355–99α). Appropriately, Langland transports this material to Covetousness in C6, as he continues to find new homes for most of Haukin's speech. Acts of gluttony and sloth likewise follow, in C6 and C7, to Gluttony and Sloth.[7] In B Will describes Haukin's appetite for cursing and eating in terms befitting the hungry sinner from the confession scenes:

> Yet þat glotoun wiþ grete oþes [curses] his garnement hadde soiled
> And foule beflobered [slobbered on] it, as wiþ fals speche,
> As, þere no nede ne was, Goddes name an idel [in vain]—
> Swoor þerby swiþe [very] ofte and al biswatte [sweated] his cote;
> And moore mete eet and dronk þan kynde [nature] myȝte defie [digest]. (B13.400–404)

Accordingly, in C, Langland adapts this final statement about consuming more than the body can possibly process to Gluttony's first-person account of his overindulgence (C6.429). With such a record of behavior in each vice, Haukin, the humble baker, finds his way into every sin, both literally and allegorically.

Will, having learned the evil ways of minstrels like the fun, farting Haukin, and after describing Haukin's descent into despairing sloth, indicts lords and ladies for neglecting the poor and honoring instead such "fool-sages, flatereris and lieris," the fiend's disciples, enticing men and women to hell (B13.422–27α).[8] He exhorts "patriarkes and prophetes, and prechours of Goddes wordes" to reprove humanity through their sermons and save them from hell (428–29). Will then urges "clerkes and knyȝtes" (437) to welcome those in need instead of supporting minstrels. He concludes that these humble wretches, the poor, the blind, and the bedridden, and also the learned will help the wealthy earn their way to heaven. When having a party, says Will in apostrophe to whoever among the wealthy might hear his words, and seeking to "solace youre soules," with entertainment, make sure to invite,

> The pouere for [instead of] a fool sage sittynge at þ[i] table,
> And a lered [learned] man to lere þee what Oure Lord suffred
> For to saue þi soule fram Sathan þyn enemy,
> And fiþele þee [fiddle for you], wiþoute flaterynge, of Good Friday þe storye,
> And a blynd man for a bourdeour [jester], or a bedrede [bedridden] womman
> To crie a largesse [reward] tofore [before] Oure Lord, your good loos [worthy merit] to shewe.
> Thise þre maner minstrales makeþ a man to lauȝe [laugh],
> And in his deeþ deyinge þei don hym [provide him with] gret confort.
> (B13. 444–51)

Will's words reflect Langland's art of spiritually transforming the earthly and carnal into the divine and salvific. Langland remakes minstrelsy, mere pleasure that soothes the soul in the most casual sense of the term, into destitute men and women who bring spiritual "comfort" to the rich who, in acts of charity, welcome these poor and disabled into their homes. With this dramatic metamorphosis, and with three lines from Will that wrap up the current action, B13 ends:

> Thus Haukyn þe actif man hadde ysoiled his cote,
> Til Conscience acouped [blamed] hym þerof in a curteis manere,
> Why he ne hadde wasshen it or wiped it wiþ a brusshe. (B13.458–60)

Conscience asks a compelling question of the very human, fallible Haukin, which we can translate in the spirit of Conscience's studied courtesy: "So, sir, if I may inquire, why have you not washed the garment, or at least given it a good brushing?" Call this the charm or perhaps simply the innocence of Conscience in the B text, in which Langland still wonders why human will alone cannot restrain sin. By the time he composed C and apportioned Haukin's activities among the Seven Deadlies, he was forced to concede that *being* human means *being* sin.

17

The After Party

PASSUS 14 OF THE B TEXT AND C15.234–C16.155

Conspectus: The interrogation of Haukin/Activa Vita continues, as Patience and Conscience offer solutions to the problem of constant sin, resulting in a study of confession and culminating in praise of "patient poverty," which the poem often sees as humanity's safest path, morally, to salvation.

I. B 14.1–131a; C 15.234–310a

After Conscience's question at the end of B13, Haukin defends himself and his filthy coat with flimsy excuses: with only one coat, he has to live and to sleep in it; married, he must care for wife, children, and household. Keeping things clean with kids seems understandably exhausting, but Langland then comments in the background in Latin (he often works in asides that only readers hear): "Vxorem duxi, et ideo non possum venire [I have married a wife, and therefore I cannot come]" (B14.3a; Luke 14:20). In the Gospel, a series of men offer excuses for not accepting the invitation to the supper offered by the wealthy lord in Jesus's parable, a metaphor for salvation in the kingdom of heaven, a great feast indeed. Attachments to the world, even to wife and family, imperil salvation if they consume one's attention to the exclusion of God. Haukin's poignant account of trying, but failing, to keep his coat clean remains one of the most familiar, seemingly humane passages in the poem. Though he washes the cloak, he reports, with the "sope [soap] of siknesse" and "þe losse of catel [possessions]" (6–7), both humbling traumas that combat sin, and though the priest has assigned him "penaunce, pacience, and pouere men to fede [to feed the poor]" (10), he cannot keep that cloak spotless:

> And kouþe I neuere, by Crist! kepen it clene an houre,
> That I ne soiled it wiþ siȝte [a look] or som ydel [sinful] speche,
> Or þoruȝ werk or þoruȝ word, or wille of myn herte,
> That I ne flobre [slobber] it foule fro morwe [morning] til euen.
> (B14.12–15)

Have no fear, says the very comprehending Conscience, who instructs him to keep it clean with the three components of penance: *cordis contricio, oris confessio, satisfactio* (contrition of the heart, confession of the mouth, and reparation). Conscience does not reject the "active" life but rather teaches Haukin how God accommodates its seemingly endless perils with the gift of his cleansing sacrament.

Patience speaks next. He supports what Conscience said, adding that he will provide Haukin, and by extension all the "active" people, with food even if no plow were to dig the earth and no grain were to grow, since, says Patience, "We sholde noȝt be to bisy [anxious] abouten oure liflode [livelihood]" (B14.34). This extraordinary promise of support avers that God will provide for his people, just as he feeds the sparrows, affirming the poem's mantra "*Pacientes vincunt* [the patient conquer]" (34α). In C, however, the context differs. Activa Vita contends that too much bread led Sodom to indulgence and lust. So Patience offers this dark twist on his promise in B to provide food without the anxiety of labor:

> "Pees!" quod Pacience, "Y preye ȝow, Sire Actyf!
> For þoȝ nere [though neither] payn [bread] ne plouh ne potage [stew] were,
> Pruyde wolde potte hymsulf forth thogh no plough erye [ever plowed].
> Hit am Y þat fynde [provide for] alle folke and fram hunger saue
> Thorw the helpe of hym þat me hyder [hither] sente." (C15.234–38)

In B, Patience promises that, human plowing aside, God will provide for his creatures, but in C he recontextualizes the idea of an idle plow to say that even if men and woman never ate bread, they would still be subject to the sin of Pride, a catalytic sin that finds a way to "put himself forth" in both dearth and abundance. Patience's tone marks the distinct character of the C version, replacing the hopeful, nurturing partnership of Patience and Conscience from B with a stern warning that without Patience humanity cannot control its raging pride. After this, in B and C Patience reveals to Will the food he brought for the pilgrimage, in a hearty, homey image, breaking out a piece of the "Paternoster—Fiat voluntas tua [thy will be done]" (B14.49). He offers this nourishment to Activa, giving the wafer seller a sacred scrap of prayerful bread, in a gesture both warm and humane despite the allegory: "'Haue, Haukyn,' quod Pacience, 'and et þis whan þe hungreþ, / Or whan þow clomsest for [feel numb from] cold or clyngest for [wither from] drouȝte'" (50–51).

In B and C Patience explains then *how* the patient conquer with illustrations from scripture of God caring for the inactive who did no earthly labor (B14.60–67), including Moses bringing forth water from the rock (Exodus 17:1–7), and the episode when ravens feed Elijah and God provides him with water despite the drought (1 Kings 17:1–7). Then Activa asks Patience a simple question in each version. In B Haukin wonders, "Where wonyeþ Charite?" (B14.97) while in C Activa asks, "What is parfit pacience?" (C15.276). He follows these good questions with another, shared by B and C: "'Wheiþer paciente pouerte,' quod Haukyn, 'be moore plesaunt to Oure Driȝte / Than richesse riȝtfulliche wonne [acquired] and resonably yspended [spent]?'" (B14.101–2). Patience answers in both versions with reference to Solomon: "'Ye—*quis est ille*?' quod Patience, 'quik—*laudabimus eum*! [Yeah? Who is he? Quick, let's praise him!]'" (103). Patience's sarcasm condemns the search for such a man as chimerical, for very few can escape the seductive power of riches, as the poem illustrated in the Lady Mede episode, so long ago.[1]

Riches, no matter how obtained and employed, make it harder to attain salvation. And while the rich enjoy their wealth, the poor, likely meaning their tenants, fall behind and suffer "in arrerage [arrears]" (C15.288). The poor man complains that even humble birds and beasts rely on the coming of summer, an expectation that allows them to endure the harshness of winter. Accordingly the poor, says Patience, should also be blessed with the expectation of joy to temper their periods of misery:

> Thenne may beggares, as bestes, aftur a blisse aske,
> That al here lyf haen lyued in languor and defaute [deprivation].
> Bote God sende hem somtyme sum manere ioye
> Other here or elliswher, elles were hit reuthe [a shame];
> For to wroþerhele [destruction] was he wrouht [made] þat [that one for whom] neuere was ioye yschape [joy was never designed]!
> (C15.297–301)

Beggars should claim the same rights as beasts, hoping for "sum manere ioye" to relieve their wintry sorrow, unless condemned never to experience any happiness, which must refer to those damned by God to the perpetual suffering that no endurance can remedy. As in Dante's hell, at a certain point patience fails and sinners must abandon even hope.

In C Patience intensifies the issue into a climax about divine justice for the rich. In B he warns, rather prosaically, that many people, materially successful, receive their heavenly reward on earth: "For þei han hir hire [hire, payment] heer, and heuene, as it were / (And is greet likynge [pleasure] to lyue wiþouten labour of bodye)" (B14.128–29). By contrast, C's lines bring the passus to a close, and passus endings ought to pack some dramatic punch. Patience delivers, telling the Gospel story of Dives, the rich man (Luke 16:19):

> Angeles þat in helle now ben hadden somtyme ioye,
> And Dyues in his deyntees [delights] lyuede and in *douce vie* [a sweet life],
> And now he buyth [pays for] hit bittere—he is a beggare of helle!
> Many man hath his ioye here for al here wel dedes,
> And lordes and ladyes ben cald [called] for ledes [because of the attendants] þat they haue,
> And slepeth, as hit semeth, and somur euere [endless summer] hem folleweth.
> Ac when deth awaketh hem of here wele [luxury] þat were er [before] so ryche,
> Then aren hit puyre pore [simply poor] thynges in purgatorie or in helle. (C15.302–9)

Langland here expands Patience's lament about finding heaven on earth into a dire, haunting threat of damnation, knowing that he must end the episode with a stout coda about the "active" pursuit of money. Activa asked if proper spending would please God more than poverty. Patience does not believe such reasonable spending possible and imagines rather that the rich will wake one day to find themselves in hell, like those angels who once lived in joy, and like Dives, who enjoyed his heaven on earth. Patience condemns sternly and impatiently, and the poem offers no solutions to these problems. Rather, Langland leaves readers in C with the harsh image of the blithely rich, living like angels, in an eternal summer of dreamlike oblivion until death awakens them in purgatory or, worse, in hell. The "active life" at this point offers Will little more than failure and deadly danger. Yet however dire, Patience's words leave some glimmer of hope in "purgatorie," implying that patient suffering, under God's watchful ministrations, can still purify the willful souls of sinners not yet banished eternally from grace.

II. B14.132–end and C16.1–155

As C begins a new passus and B14 continues, both versions advance the previous discussions. Patience goes on about how wealth impedes salvation and how working people get a raw deal in life and "selden deyeþ out of dette" (B14.135), a chestnut that may compel modern readers to shake their heads in a some-things-never-change sort of way. In B he gives the rich a chance at redemption: they can receive a double reward if they "haue ruþe, and reward wel þe poore," which, however, rarely occurs (145–56). In C Langland omits Patience's equivocation, likely judging it too contingent and pondering, in favor of expanding B's imagery about how the poor suffer most in winter:

> Muche murthe is in May amonge wilde bestes,
> And so forth whiles somur laste here solace duyreth [pleasure endures];
> And moche murthe among ryche men is þat han meble ynow and hele [enough movable goods and health].
> Ac beggares aboute myssomur bredles [breadless] they soupe,
> And ȝut is wynter for hem worse, for weetshoed þey gangen [they go with wet shoes],

Afurste and afyngered [thirsty and hungry], and foule [foully] rebuked
Of this world-ryche men, þat reuthe is [it is a pity] to here.
(C16.10–16)

Instead of exhorting the rich to show pity for the poor, in C Langland moves them emotionally, as he tightens B's passage and forges more trenchant patterns of imagery for Patience. Accordingly, the following parallel sections provide stark contrasts in development. Patience in B prays for the rich, who show pity neither to the poor nor to prisoners, asking grace that they amend their ways. He then asks for comfort for the destitute and offers this hopeful reflection upon Christ's most inclusive ministry:

Thus *in genere* [according to the nature] of his gentries [nobility] Iesu Crist seide
To robberis, to reueris [thieves], to riche and to poore,
To hores, to harlots, to alle maner peple.
Thou [i.e., Christ] tauȝtest hem in þe Trinite to taken bapteme
And be clene þoruȝ þat cristnyng of alle kynnes synnes. (B14.181–85)

Patience bases his doctrine on the scriptural verse "Conuertimini ad me et salui eritis [Be converted to me, and you shall be saved]" (B14.180α; Isaiah 45:22), and he adds that grace and confession provide contrite sinners with a patent that even the Devil himself must honor when he comes to claim the human soul.

In C Langland dramatically replaces Patience's prayer for the rich with an appeal to Christ at once more dire, more disciplinary, and yet more directed to a sacramental solution:

Riht so haue reuthe on vs alle, þat on þe rode deydest [you who died on the cross],
And amende vs of thy mercy and make vs alle meke,
Lowe and lele [loyal] and louynge, and of herte pore.
And sende vs contricion to clanse with oure soules,
And confessioun to kulle alle kyne synnes
And satisfaccioun þe whiche folfilleth þe Fader wille [will of the Father] of heuene. (C16.22–27)

This revision does more than just tighten, for, like the other changes in C, it continues to mute any hope for the rich. Langland looks at his younger self and wonders how he ever was so naïve. Perhaps the poet got tired of praying for something that would never come true. In B Patience says that confession can cleanse "as manye siþes [times] as man wolde desire" (B14.188), always holding out hope for penance. In C Langland omits that comfort, just as he omits B's prayer for the rich and the promises of inclusion. For here a more caustic Langland, preferring the rhetoric of exclusion, neither expects mercy from, nor wants mercy for, the rich unless they repent. In the C text Patience takes shelter, rather, in recalling the framework of confession, his version of the three Do's, and prays to God for the contrition that comes from "sorowe of herte," for the confession that comes from "shrifte of mouthe," and for the "*Satisfaccio*" that pays for the soul and requites sin's debts (C16.29–31). The poor inherently "tholieth [endure, suffer]" (32) all three by virtue of their humility and deprivations, and in so doing teach the ignorant and the learned, the high and the low, to undertake the ultimate duties of Dowel, Dobet, and Dobest, without whose support at Domesday "is al an ydel [in vain], al our lyuynge here" (37).[2]

In B and C, Patience at this point launches into one of the wittiest passages in the *Piers* corpus, an animated exposition on how Poverty, now personified, proves invulnerable to the Seven Deadlies. The episode reads as almost cartoonish, as Poverty, like Charlie Chaplin's endearing Tramp in *City Lights*, squares off and defeats the Goliath-like sins, such as Covetousness. Patience celebrates an age-old truth: sins cost money or arise from having and protecting money, and the poor prosper because they cannot afford to get themselves into the kind of trouble that money brings. This "virtue" may seem one of necessity, for once the poor acquire wealth, they might become susceptible to pride. No one in the poem mentions this, but the safety of the poor registers more as an accidental than an active virtue. Yet since the poem has shown the difficulty of keeping one's coat clean, and since the half-acre episode proves that natural forces like Hunger provide only temporary morality, then perhaps this virtue of necessity, though imperfect, at least defeats its vicious alternative. In a comic wrestling conceit, for example, Patience displays how Poverty eludes the grasp of the giant Covetousness:

And þei3 Coueitise wolde cacche þe poore, þei may no3t come togideres,
And by þe nekke, namely, hir noon may hente ooþer [cannot grab each other].
For men knowen wel þat Coueitise is of a kene wille,
And haþ hondes and armes of a long lengþe,
And Pouerte nys [is not] but a petit þyng, apereþ no3t [does not reach] to his nauele—
And louely layk [an exciting bout] was it neuere bitwene þe longe and þe shorte. (B14.239–44)

Covetousness will soon tire of this folly and give up trying to get hold of the poor. Lechery hates the poor as well, says Patience, because he "3yueþ but litel siluer," and brothels would fall into ill repair if they relied on his patronage: "A straw for þe stuwes [damn the brothel]! It stoode no3t, I trowe, / Hadde þei noon [no patronage] but of poore men—hir houses were vntyled!" (B.14.250–53). C strangely loses the image of a whorehouse with an untiled roof, reporting rather that "hit stoed nat, hadde they noen haunt bote of pore!" (C16.92), basically the same idea, with emphasis on the foundation rather than the roof, but it pales next to B's comic metonymy. The survey of Poverty's power culminates in Patience's reminder that Jesus was poor and "in þat secte [bodily form] Oure Saueour saued al mankynde" (B14.259). Patience ends his speech in both versions with a poignant conceit in which "marriage" to patient poverty is compared to wedding a loving maid, with full consent of her will, who leaves her family to follow her mate. Such a consensual marriage beats a union motived by advantage, necessity, or greed, and since poverty is "sib [kin] to God hymself," this spiritual marriage draws the soul closer to God's loving family (B14.262–73).

In B Haukin and in C Activa Vita inquire further about the nature of poverty. C describes Activa as "al angryliche and arguinge as hit were" (C16.113), reflecting his frustration with the complexity and fluidity of these doctrines and demands. In response, Patience holds forth, citing a long set of sometimes paradoxical maxims in Latin describing the ironical benefits of poverty, depicting it as a "hateful good," a "removal of care," a "gift of God." Haukin and Activa ask for a translation, since neither knows

Latin, so busy they are about worldly cares. Patience glosses each element from his list in an expressive sequence, though nowhere as clever as his animated description of Poverty's invulnerability. The ninth and final definition, "Absque sollicitudine felicitas," he explains thus:

> The nynþe it is swete to þe soule, no sugre is swetter;
> For pacience is payn [bread] for Pouerte hymselue,
> And sobretee [sobriety] swete drynke and good leche [doctor] in siknesse.
> Thus lered [taught] me a lered [learned] man for Oure Lordes loue, Seint Austyn—
> A blessed lif wiþouten bisynesse [anxiety] for a body and for soule:
> *Absque sollicitudine felicitas* [happiness without anxiety].
> (B14.313–17α)

Patience, true to his name, reveals here and in his other expanded definitions that enduring the lack of material goods means eventually attaining spiritual treasure, a transformative promise of justice essential to Langland's ethics and theology. To be poor requires a struggle for health, bread, and drink. But to endure poverty wisely, says Patience, means receiving those mortal necessities in the form of peaceful spiritual consolation. Poverty frees people from the anxious care, the "bisynesse" that the business of wealth and grasping inevitably bring. Poverty enables the virtues of the poor just as riches provoke the vices of the wealthy.

In B, Langland nears the end of his passus and the conclusion of what has been an extended adventure with Haukin. In the next passus he introduces a new character for Will to question, Anima, the complex properties of the soul, shifting away from the sins of the active life and their remedies in patient poverty. In C, however, still early in his passus, Langland completes his own version of the "active/patient poverty" drama and prepares to introduce his rendering of Anima, whom he converts into Liberum Arbitrium [Free Will]. In B Langland thus has to provide a coda to the Haukin episode. "Allas," the Active Man cries, wishing he had died and been buried right after being christened, in the one moment of freedom from blemish (B14.320–21). Now he can only weep and regret that he displeased his "deere God," swooning, sobbing and sighing that he ever sought "lond and lordshipe" and to have "maistrie ouer any man mo than of hymselue" (324–28), seeking power over others instead of governing his own appetites. He then pledges to dress himself henceforth only in shame:

> "I were noȝt worþi, woot God," quod Haukyn, "to werien any cloþes,
> Ne neiþer sherte ne shoon [shoes], saue for shame one [only]
> To couere my careyne [body]," quod he, and cride mercy faste [eagerly],
> And wepte and wailed—and þerwiþ I awakede. (B14.329–32)

Langland coherently concludes the Haukin episode, a manifestation of the "will" inevitably "active" in the world. And so through abject tears, Will wakes from dream number four. Because the C text so alters the passus structure and the status of Haukin, Langland offers no such lament or pledge from Activa and no wake-up call for Will. He simply pushes forward with the next episode.

The revisions in the C text add moments of despair, critique, and poignancy, but as so often in revision, something must be lost. Here Langland loses nothing less than this stunning image of a penitent Haukin, reduced to shame, or perhaps rather emboldened and fortified by it, in a poignant and fitting climax to Patience's discourse. This scene allows Langland to continue a pattern of imagery he established earlier, for Haukin's remorse recalls Imaginatif's picture of the drunk in the ditch whom neither Reason nor Clergy can help. Only Need can pick him up and only shame "shrapeþ [cleans off] hise cloþes and hise shynes [shins] wassheþ," teaching the drunk that he alone "is to blame" for his sin and disgrace (B11.431–32). The C text's diminishment of Haukin undoes this linkage between episodes, although both versions still have much to say about need, shame, remorse, and contrition. But those issues must wait until Will learns more about himself, about the responsible use of knowledge, and most of all about charity and its effect on the global human community, from his next encounter, with Anima and Liberum Arbitrium. For charity, like shame, can also wash away pride, bleaching it and beating it clean like a dirty cloak.

18

Free Spirits

PASSUS B15.1–257 AND C16.156–END

Conspectus: Both the B and the C text introduce their respective characters, Anima (the Soul) in B and Liberum Arbitrium (Free Will) in C. This new figure's wide-ranging discourse explores the human experience of physical reality, the ways people act in the world, the dangers of pride and learning, the failings and responsibilities of clergy, and the many demands of charity.

At the end of the previous passus in B, Will is awoken by Haukin's tears, so for anything productive to happen, the poem must put him back to sleep. But he wanders around at the opening of B15 in an "underground man" moment, prowling about the city like Dostoyevsky's jumpy, irreverent character, raving and disgruntled, refusing to show respect to people of rank who pass him on the street, becoming a "fool," despised by some and evidently misunderstood by many, as he explains:[1]

> Ac after my wakynge it was wonder [extraordinarily] longe
> Er I koude kyndely [naturally] knowe what was Dowel.
> And so my wit weex and wanyed [waxed and waned] til I a fool weere;
> And some lakkede [blamed] my lif—allowed [approved] it fewe—
> And leten [considered] me for a lorel [a rogue] and looþ [loathe] to reuerencen
> Lordes or ladies or any lif ellis—
> As persons in pelure [fur] wiþ pendaunt3 of siluer. (B15.1–7)

This period of existential alienation ends when Reason pities Will and rocks him to sleep, where he dreams that an immaterial being "wiþouten tonge and teeþ" (B15.13) begins to question him, prompting Will to wonder about the nature of such a creature.

The C text, mid-passus, omits Will's transformation into a fool and introduces Liberum Arbitrium, described as a "ledare [leader]" of Active (C16.156). In this way Langland transitions in C from the Activa Vita episode to this new figure, in lieu of the new passus and new dream from the B text. Liberum Arbitrium's self-introduction matches that of Anima in asserting his intimacy with God and boasting of how neither Peter nor Paul could keep him out of heaven, a claim that may fit better with "the soul" than with "free will" (165–70). To highlight his unique differences from his prior manifestation in B, Liberum Arbitrium expounds upon the function of human choice as an agent distinct from the physical body, though dependent upon it. When Will thinks the body therefore superior to the "free will" that needs it, Liberum Arbitrium offers the vibrant analogy of flame on a log:

> "Thenne is þat body bettere þen [than] þou?" quod Y. "Nay, no bettere," quod he;
> "Bote as wode were afuyre: thenne worcheth bothe [both work],
> And ayther is otheres hete [heat], and also of o wille;
> And so is man þat hath his mynde myd [with] *Liberum Arbitrium*."
> (C16.177–80)

In B and C, these new characters then explain the various aspects of their being. Both go by many names—Anima, Animus, Mens, Memoria, Racio, Sensus, or Amor, plus their English equivalents—and also Conscience (B15.23–36), though one ought not to conflate these figures with the independent character of the same name. Langland depicts Anima and Liberum Arbitrium as partially interchangeable, while peppering C with added references to the notion of individual will. After thousands of lines of inquiry, critiquing the behavior of clerks, beggars, friars, lords, and all manner of sinners, Langland here produces another version of "will" with a particular emphasis on personal choice, symphonically recapitulating a theme from earlier movements but with new richness and complexity.[2] As he advances through his visions, the character Will discovers his nature, one faculty at a time, and now confronts the part of himself responsible for choice and action. One wonders if perhaps this aspect of "the will" can best teach him about Dowel and charity.

Then something unexpected happens. Anima/Liberum Arbitrium quotes several definitions from Isidore of Seville's *Etymologies* explaining in Latin how Anima takes different names according to his various actions (C16.197–99a). Impressed, Will compares these various titles to those of a bishop, in a casual enough, sort of chatty comment, but the question offends Anima, who rebukes Will for wanting to know so much about his names. Anima has set a trap, and Will, innocent and curious, as if politely conversing with a stranger on a train, now realizes that his companion is a bit loopy. The apparent madcap turns on Will in accusation: "'Thenne artow inparfit,' quod he, 'and oen of Pruydes knyhtes! / For such a lust and lykynge Lucifer ful [fell] fram heuene'" (210–11). This blooms into an attack on the pretense of knowledge, which gums up grace just as honey does the mouth. Adam and Eve sought to know too much, and their "coueytyse to conne [desire to know]" put them out of paradise (222). As Paul warns, "Non plus sapere . . . quam oportet sapere [do not seek to be more wise than it behoveth to be wise]" (227; Romans 12:3). Anima/Liberum Arbitrium then turns on the Friars who mislead people with speculation about the Trinity, when they ought to stick to tangible practical instruction focusing on sin and the Ten Commandments (228–39a). An evil priesthood infects the Church like a blight spreading through a tree (240–53). The learned must give up their finery, the "lecherye of clothyng," leave off Pride, share with the poor, and be virtuous with their tongue and tail (254–57). Their hypocrisy reflects their pride, and hypocrisy, says Anima/Liberum Arbitrium in a nasty bit of imagery, "is yliknned in Latyn to a lothly dong-hep [dung heap] / That were bysnewed al with snowe [covered with snow], and snakes withynne'" (264–65). Will's innocent questions have ignited a firestorm of anticlerical satire from the complex, free-willed "soul."

Anima/Liberum Arbitrium then quotes at length a Latin passage from John Chrysostomos on the need for a dedicated, pure clergy. B adds (and C drops) an aside that if the ignorant had access to this kind of information in Latin, they would expose the pride and ostentation of the clergy who gird themselves in silver and with gilded weapons, decorative adornments for pretentious knights and not bookish, pastoral clergy (B15.119–27). B calls these posers "Sire Iohan and Sire Geffrey"—snooty high-class names (123), and C loses some colorful imagery in omitting this attack on the dandies with daggers. C also omits Anima's animated description of how a bishop, overseeing the estate of a deceased cleric who hoarded money, savors the chance to seize and spend it: "He was a nygard," says the bishop, "þat no good myȝte aspare [share] / To frend ne to fremmed [stranger]—þe fend haue his soule!" (140–42). One might expect the prelate to distribute this treasure to the poor, especially after he condemns the cleric for his stinginess, but he has another plan. What the clerk hoarded, continues the cheerful bishop, "spene [spende] we in murþe!" (143). Despite this loss in C, in both versions Will interrupts the clerical satire when he hears the critical term "charity" and asks what it means (B15.149) and where he can find it (C16.285). Perhaps he hopes that this question will return Anima/Liberum Arbitrium to topic and temper his blistering tangent on clerical corruption, which does not advance Will's learning. Langland either cannot control his characters or cannot control himself, and sometimes Will functions to keep everybody, including his creator, focused. In controlled chaos, with the artful pretense of disorder, the poet manages the progress of his poem while allowing for organic ruptures of anger and condemnation.

Then something stunning happens in B. First Will laments (in both versions) that he never saw real charity practiced as Paul describes it: "Non inflator, non est ambiciosa, non querit que sua sunt" (B15.156a; 1 Cor. 13:4–5). Consider those Pauline verses, translated and in broader context:

> Charity is patient, is kind: charity envieth not, dealeth not perversely; is not puffed up; Is not ambitious, seeketh not her own, is not provoked to anger, thinketh no evil; Rejoiceth not in iniquity, but rejoiceth with the truth; Beareth all things, believeth all things, hopeth all things, endureth all things (1 Cor. 13:4–7.)

The B passage that follows, which C omits, offers nothing less extraordinary than the poet, William Langland, revealing his name:

> "I haue lyued in londe," quod I, "my name is Longe Wille—
> And fond I neuere ful charite, bifore ne bihynde.

> Men beþ merciable to mendinaunt3 [mendicants] and to poore,
> And wollen lene [loan] þer þei [where they] leue lelly [believe truly]
>   to ben paied." (B15.152–55)

With these oblique words, the poet provides readers the only hint about his identity, yet he deletes them from his final version, displaying even less desire to reveal himself to history.

And in B, having introduced himself, Long Will reports that the search for charity so far brings him only confusion and distortion, as he quotes Paul:

> Clerkes kenne [teach] me þat Crist is in alle places;
> Ac I sei3 hym neuere sooþly but as myself in a mirour:
> *Hic in enigmate, tunc facie ad faciem* [now in a dark manner; but then face to face].
> And so I trowe [believe] trewely, by þat men telleþ of [say about] charite,
> It is no3t chaumpions fight, ne chaffare [a business matter], as I trowe.
>   (B15.161–64; 1 Cor. 13:12)

However enigmatic Charity may be, Will knows (and Anima agrees) that he does not bargain, challenge, or crave and does not dress himself in pomp (B15.165–68). In C, Liberum Arbitrium adds that Charity shows compassion and kinship with others, displaying empathy just as a child does in laughing when others laugh and frowning when others frown (C16.300–302). Langland may have weakened the whole passage by deleting the personal revelation of Will, but here he adds great poignancy in depicting what a "mirror" means, revealing beautifully how charity in its ideal manifestation displays childlike empathy with the other, reflecting the simplicity of Jesus's words: "Quodcunque vultis vt faciant vobis homines, facite eis [And as you would that men should do to you, do you also to them in like manner]" (C16.307; Luke 6:31). In another C addition, Liberum Arbitrium boasts that Charity defies even mortality: "Of deth ne of derthe dradde [feared] he neuere" (311). As his third revision continues apace, an older, more contemplative Langland looks further up the path than he had in B.

Anima and Liberum Arbitrium then elaborate on the role of charitable compassion, and both aver that Charity sometimes labors "in a lauendrye [laundry]" (B15.187), cleansing pride of the stain of sin, an image more powerful in B because of Haukin's dirty cloak. Both versions cite Psalms: "Laboraui in gemitu meo [I have laboured in my groanings]," a verse Langland uses allegorically to depict the beating of the garment in B and the name of the laundry in C (B15.191; C16.331; Psalms 6:7). Both speakers then arrive elegantly at "Cor contritum et humiliatum, Deus non despicies [A contrite and humbled heart, O God, thou wilt not despise]" (B15.194; C16.334a; Psalm 50:19). Such moments of unity, when B and C together summon the Psalms, reveal a truth that Langland would never shake nor lose in revision, for without this assurance of God's mercy on the penitent heart, he would have, and could impart, no hope.

Will wants "to know" Charity and, in C, "to be with" him. Not without the help of Piers Plowman, says Anima, for Piers knows him perfectly, adds Liberum Arbitrium (B15.195–96; C16.335–38). B alone provides the charming image of prideful men, enemies of Charity, who kowtow to lords but have "pepir in þe nose" around the poor (B16.203). Then in B Anima, telling Will how to recognize Charity, makes one of the corpus's most dramatic and controversial assertions:

> Therfore by colour ne by clergie knowe shaltow hym neuere,
> Neiþer þoruȝ wordes ne werkes, but þoruȝ wil oone [only],
> And þat knoweþ no clerk ne creature on erþe
> But Piers þe Plowman—*Petrus, id est, Christus.*
> For he nys noȝt in [not found in] lolleris ne in londleperis [wandering] heremytes. (B15.209–13)

Piers is Christ. For unknown reasons, Langland omits from the C text this simple but extraordinary identification, for many readers the key to understanding the evolving role of the Plowman in this poem.[3] If Piers is Christ, then the search for him becomes a search for God among the humble figures from daily life. Honest work ennobles humanity, and now the noble worker becomes the divine, just as the divine became a humble man, a carpenter's son.

Both versions continue to explore Charity and his many traits, Anima calling him "Goddes champion" and a courteous child, delightful at dinner, and "liȝt [joyful]" in speech (B15.216–18), implicitly contrasting him to the hypocrites in Matthew who make a sad spectacle of themselves: "Nolite tristes fieri sicut ypocrite [(And when you fast) be not as the hypocrites, sad]" (219α; Matthew 6:16). Anima and Liberum Arbitrium agree that Charity can appear dressed in homespun woolens, in gray robes (austere dress), in fur, and in rich knightly armor, and that in all those guises he gives to those in need (221–22). Both texts praise the sainted kings Edmund and Edward as exemplars of charity but argue they find charity sometimes as well among priests "in raggede wedes [clothes]," though never among beggars, and "raþest [most readily]" among those in rich robes (223–29). Such fine dress, says Schmidt, indicates a bishop or abbot, in lines warning "against judging outward austerity as a reliable sign of inner character" (*Parallel-Text* 2.650). B and C identify Francis as the soul of charity, while sadly, in his modern descendants, charity "to selde [seldom] haþ . . . ben knowen" (232). Charity commends the rich and, evidently imagined here as a liveried servant of an affluent household, receives the robes of those wealthy who "wiþouten wiles [deceit] ledeþ hir lyues," an idea based on the biblical verse "'Beatus est diues qui [Blessed is the rich man that (is found without blemish)]" (234–34α; Ecclesiasticus 31:8). Charity can be found at the royal court if "þer þe counseil [advice] is trewe [honest]" (235) and uncorrupted by greed, but not so easily at the consistory (ecclesiastical) courts. And in contradiction to comments above about charity being soonest found among those in rich robes, Anima/Liberum Arbitrium laments that though Charity at one time dwelled among the high prelates of the Church, avarice now prevents them from distributing their wealth to the poor (244–48). Will's quest for the elusive Charity, like the pilgrimage to Truth and the search for Dowel, so far proves frustrating and chaotic.

In B Anima offers a prayer that God will provide humanity the grace to follow charity, offering this rhetorical homage to Charity's virtues:

> Neiþer he blameþ ne banneþ [curses], bosteþ [boasts] ne preiseþ,
> Lakkeþ [blames], ne loseþ [lauds], ne lokeþ vp sterne [sternly],
> Craueþ, ne coueiteþ, ne crieþ after moore:
> *In pace in idipsum dormiam.* (B15.252–54α)

The Latin Bible verse alluded to comes from Psalm 4, which praises the comforting power of God's radiant countenance: "In peace in the selfsame I will sleep, and I will rest: for thou, O Lord, singularly hast settled me in hope" (Psalms 4:9–10), an inventive allusion associating Charity with peaceful quietude and security in the Lord. Passus B15 continues for another 350 lines, but C16 ends soon, so in C Langland devises a stunning, contemplative conclusion, as Liberum Arbitrium advises anyone "hoso coueyteth to knowe" (C16. 368) this marvelous figure named Charity first to understand his nature:

> For noþer he ne beggeth, ne biddeth [asks alms], ne borweth to ȝelde [borrows to pay elsewhere].
> He halt hit for [considers it] a vyce and a foule shame
> To begge or to borwe, but of God one [only]:
> *Panem nostrum cotidianum* . . . [our daily bread]. (C16.370–72a)

Liberum Arbitrium playfully uses "covet" to express the opposite of covetousness, the very urge for charity, which one must ardently desire. Liberum Arbitrium contends that Charity neither begs nor borrows, which he condemns as shameful vices—except from God alone. As seen in the Middle English *Pearl* and the Parable of the Vineyard it retells, God purifies an economic system with his own accounting of justice, and no one faces shame in asking God, the source of all charity and grace, for proper payment. Latin lines can sometimes be read as distinct from the voices speaking around them, so either Liberum or perhaps Langland ends the passus with "Panem nostrum cotidianum" from the Paternoster. In this humble evocation of the only prayer Jesus ever wrote, Will perceives the true foundation of all charity. Critical of beggars, the poem now makes beggars of us all.

19

Anima and Free Will Try to Unite the World

PASSUS B15.258–END AND C17

Conspectus: In the previous section, Anima (in B) was exploring Charity in his various guises. Here Anima continues that discussion by focusing on how Christ's suffering provides a model for all that one must endure in the course of daily life. He then references the Desert Fathers and the uncommon rigors of their sacrifice. The recounting of how St. Egredius (Giles) was fed with wild deer's milk sparks a long discussion in B and C about how God provides for his faithful in miraculous ways. Those who believe only in the quest for wealth, shows Anima, have never imagined or comprehended the sustaining power of God. The C text opens a new passus after its contemplative coda about Charity in passus 16, so Langland creates for Will and Liberum Arbitrium a bit of dialogue as an engine to the new passus, permitting a transition back to the B-text material about God's sustaining power. Throughout this sequence, Anima and Liberum Arbitrium both constantly return to Charity and also to the enchaining power of acquisitiveness that militates against it. Somehow they both arrive at the theme of the Universal Church and the conversion of the Jews and Muslims.

As B progresses, Anima, in a complex sequence, describes how in various Christian legends God sent birds to feed his holy people. Wild beasts did not feed them, Anima notes, though they licked and bowed down to God's faithful, while the birds brought food. St. Anthony, for example, was fed once a day by a bird and Egredius by a hind. Modern readers, and perhaps medieval ones too, might question the reliability of such methods of sustenance. Perhaps Anima does not want everyday Christians milking deer or waiting for birds to deliver dinner but rather seeks to dampen the fire of acquisition that so drives humanity to compile wealth and goods. The fact of such gentle animals instead of fierce lions and leopards feeding the worthy represents, Anima argues, how "meke þyng mylde þyng sholde fede" (B15.306), that is, virtuous and lawful folk should support the holy members of religious orders today. This mutually mild, humble model of charity, as Anima applies it, purifies religious donations, ensuring that "lords and ladies" will not use unearned profits to support friars, who in turn will not accept such gifts, demanding rather that they be returned to the exploited tenants who overpaid their lords (B15.298–312). Though oblique and puzzling, this conceit leads Anima to another extraordinary image, unique to B:

> For we ben Goddes foweles [birds] and abiden [wait] alwey,
> Til briddes brynge vs þat we sholde [by lyue].
> For hadde ye potage and payn ynogh, and peny-ale [cheap beer] to drynke,
> And a mees [dish of food] þermyd [with it] of o maner kynde [some kind],
> Ye hadde riȝt ynoȝ [plenty], ye religiouse—and so youre rule [religious code] me tolde. (B15. 313–17)[1]

The poem often engages implicitly with Jesus's comforting words in Matthew that men and women ought not to be anxious about survival:

> Therefore I say to you, be not solicitous for your life, what you shall eat, nor for your body, what you shall put on. Is not the life more than the meat: and the body more than the raiment? Behold the birds of the air, for they neither sow, nor do they reap, nor gather into barns: and your heavenly Father feedeth them. Are not you of much more value than they? (Matt. 6:25–26).

But Anima fancifully complicates the Gospel imagery, depicting birds as feeding the virtuous but also showing the virtuous, "Goddes foweles," waiting patiently until "briddes brynge" them sustenance.

God's people, fed by birds and yet birds themselves in this dynamic pattern of imagery, nonetheless receive God's care. Schmidt hears a play on "fowls" and "fools" echoing a theme of God's special love for the mentally infirm who need clerical care, and he wonders if the "whimsicality" of this lexical play led to the line's omission in the C text (*Parallel-Text* 2.651; and see C11.251). Yet from this challenging, swirling whimsy Anima draws a clear, tangible conclusion: religious orders, by implication the greedy friars, must content themselves with simple food and drink, as long as they have "payn ynogh" to live. Jesus's words in Matthew guarantee such sufficiency, but as Anima (and Langland) remakes the imagery, the lords and ladies, the modern birds who feed the "lif-holy men" as in the legends, must not acquire the money they intend to use as alms by taking from "hir tenaunt3 moore þan trouþe wolde [more rent than is proper]" (B15.310). Despite the baroque complexity and the free play of signification in his imagery, Anima finally brings the issue back to the basics of injustice and exploitation, returning to the ethical core of the poem, the dictates of Christian charity. Money wrongly taken from the poor must play no part in religious charity, the earthy manifestation of God's care for his holy, innocent birds.

In C Liberum Arbitrium offers a version of Anima's discourse about the fowls feeding the holy, omitting the complexities of birds feeding birds and the powerful image of living on "bread enough," but maintaining the lines on treating tenants fairly and the overall theme of how ill-gotten gains pollute the divine pattern of almsgiving, established by God in his feeding of the holy hermits and recluses (C17.25–50). But Liberum Arbitrium expands B's material curiously, referring to the biblical episode in which the blind Tobit shows suspicion at his wife's receiving a kid as a gift. The possibility of corruption and the fear that the gift might really be a theft send Tobit into a fit of self-loathing and make him exclaim, in Langland's version of the quotation, "Melius est mori quam male viuere [It is better to die than to live sinfully]" (C17.40α).[2] Presumably Liberum Arbitrium tells the story to contrast a grasping clergy and the cautious Tobit, and the biblical text explains his thinking: "And when her husband heard it bleating, he said: Take heed, lest perhaps it be stolen: restore ye it to its owners, for it is not lawful for us either to eat or to touch any thing that cometh by theft" (Tob. 2:21). He then trenchantly glosses the episode as an indictment of the clergy:

> This is no more to mene bote men of Holy Churche
> Sholde reseue [receive] riht nauht but þat riht wolde [what justice requires]
> And refuse reuerences [gifts] and raueners [criminals'] offrynges.
> (C17.41–43)

One sees the logic of C's allusion and exposition upon Tobit, for it develops B's critique of the profits that "lords and ladies" accumulate through exploitation to fund an appetitive, grasping clergy that never considers itself to have "bread enough."

Accordingly, in what follows, both versions expose the appetites of a corrupt clergy whose worldliness militates against charity and whose appetites misdirect wealth away from those who need it most and to those who need it least. Anima notices the irony of giving "to swiche as ben riche" (B15.323), offering an extended conceit about how giving to the wealthy religious is like planting trees in a dense forest or carrying water to the Thames (331–40), making the timeless observation that the rich always get richer. Instead, says Anima, the rich should be feasting beggars who are really in need. Liberum Arbitrium bypasses this and, preferring a good exemplum to an imagistic conceit, instead injects an exposition on the generous St. Lawrence, a third-century martyr who distributed church funds to the poor (C17.65–72). The larger context here (one can be led down paths in *Piers Plowman* and forget the view from the mountaintop) concerns how the clergy, variously manifested, fail in their main function to care for those in need; rather, they win, gain, and take, increasing inequity and injustice. Liberum Arbitrium's unexpected ode to Lawrence glorifies how clerks in the old days knew how to distribute rather than accumulate wealth, however inapplicable the Roman martyr's story may be for contemporary English clergy, who do not face execution. Use of such a remote example may point to Liberum Arbitrium's, and Langland's, frustration with corruption, compelling them to dig into the legendary past for material that can inspire reform. With his analysis of wealth's tendency to accumulate, Langland points to a larger phenomenon central to his critique: if the clergy did not accept ill-gotten gains, the rich would behave less rapaciously; if the rich did not give to the already wealthy clergy, the clergy would reform and the poor would benefit. Langland's exposure of this corrupt system, which benefits both the rich laity and the (equally rich) clergy, anticipates the action at poem's end when sin triumphs over Contrition and everyone, except Conscience and Will, profits from a system that substitutes cash for moral action.

Both versions shortly launch into a critique of human learning, starting with astronomers, shipmen, and shepherds (B15.358–75; C17.94–110). In either text the discussion ventures deep into the particular failings of the various disciplines, but overall this critique of learning exposes the frailty and fickleness of human planning in commerce and agriculture, professions that attempt to predict the weather to ensure prosperity. One might object that people must use ingenuity to fortify themselves against bad weather and other adversities and also to labor, as demanded by Genesis. But Anima and Liberum Arbitrium neither critique work nor dispute the Bible; rather they expose the hubristic human pretense of controlling the environment. God condemns humanity to labor, but when we become too busy about the world, we succumb to dangerous ambition. No one mentions Adam, Eve, and Lucifer here, but their stories of failed rebellion always lurk.

From here both B and C return to the critique of an ignorant and therefore corrupt clergy, though Liberum Arbitrium offers a few more details than Anima about the sad state of academia:

> "Go we now to [consider today] eny degre, and bote Gyle be holde a maister [held up as a master],
> And Flaterere for his vscher [teacher's aide], a ferly [marvel] me thynketh!
> Doctours of decre [decrees, law] and of diuinite maistres,
> That sholde þe seuene ars conne [know] and assoile a *quodlibet* [resolve a point of debate],
> Bote they fayle in philosophie—and [if] philosoferes lyuede
> And wolde wel examene hem—wonder me thynketh!
> Lord leue [permit] þat this prestes lelly seien [faithfully say] here masse,
> That they ouerhippe nat [not skip over] for hastite, as Y hope they do nat,

Thogh hit suffice for oure sauacioun soethfaste [true] byleue,
As clerkes in Corpus Cristi feste syngen and reden
That *sola fides sufficit* [faith alone is enough] to saue with lewede [ignorant] peple." (C 17. 111–21)

This passage is packed with difficult and potentially contradictory ideas: Guile and Flattery have become professors, who "fail in philosophy" if real philosophers were to examine them. They neglect the seven liberal arts, and Liberum Arbitrium hopes they will not, in haste and ignorance, skip over parts of the mass, even though "faith alone" guarantees salvation. Anima and Liberum Arbitrium have been critiquing the pretense of human learning in opposition to God's natural care of his people—the sparrows alluded to earlier in the episode. But now they indict ignorance because it imperils Christians who need to be taught well by an educated clergy. A worried Anima describes himself as "afered of folk [afraid for the clergy] of Holy Kirke" because of the gaps in their learning (B15.384). Will has previously been told that inflated learning harms by provoking ambition, and now he hears that clerical ignorance harms as well. This may seem like a contradiction, but the perspectives elide quite well: sciences and planning reflect human anxiety about survival but potentially also empower human greed; yet competent, faithful, charitable learning provides the foundation of the clergy, who must serve a flock that needs good guidance, without the priest "skipping over" parts of devotional prayers. We may have traveled far from the initial idea in this sequence about the Desert Fathers living in the wild, but we can detect an oblique link back to those exemplary lives, assured of God's care. Those holy men and women of legend lived in humble faith without ambition, the ambition that today goads an ignorant clergy into profane neglect of their flocks. Both speakers mention that faith alone suffices for salvation, a complex theological issue but not an assertion that invalidates the need for learned, compassionate pastoral care, without which the "lewede peple"(C17.121) would remain helpless.[3] Langland persistently critiques and even vilifies the clergy, but he never abandons them.

Unexpectedly then Anima and especially Liberum Arbitrium, who expands the argument by thirty lines, launch into a topic apparently unrelated to the discussion so far in this sequence: the conversion of the Saracens (Muslims) and Jews. "What is Holy Churche?" asks Will. "Charite," says Liberum Arbitrium, calling it a "loue-knotte of leutee [fidelity] and of lele [loyal] byleue" (C17.125, 127) with

> Alle kyne Cristene [Christian peoples] cleuynge on [cleaving to] o wille [one desire],
> Withoute gyle and gabbyng [lying] gyue and sulle and lene [sell and loan].
> Loue-lawe [law of love] withoute leutee, allouable was hit neuere;
> God lereth no lyf to louye [instructs no one to love][4] withouten lele [trustworthy] cause! (C17.128–31)

All actions and, by analogy, all forms of religious doctrine (signified by "love-law") must display not only ardor but also truth. This complex formulation helps to make sense of the sprawling discourse of Anima and Liberum Arbitrium, which we can unravel thus: Christians must be free of greed and must give freely to those in need, a duty the clergy and the wealthy (often the same) neglect. Christians and their clergy have betrayed scripture and profaned their sacred exemplars—the Desert Fathers, and the saints. The clergy, instead of repairing this waywardness, exploit it by courting worldly advancement and by living fat, not content merely with their daily bread. We have lost, says Liberum Arbitrium, our fidelity to a unifying doctrine that can guide us: "lief [life] and loue and leutee, in o byleue [one belief] a [in] lawe" (126). Christians have severed these ties and broken these laws of love in their infidelity to one another, to duty, to God, and, in a word, to "charity." While on the topic of law, Liberum Arbitrium makes a slippery transition to peoples who believe in "a love-law" but whose religions are erroneous, however similar they may be to Christianity in their reliance on principles of fidelity. So a critique of Christian behavior leads in both versions to a consideration of Christianity's relations with other faiths. Langland's audience can interpret this flow of argument in various ways. They can conclude that Christians, in their sinfulness, have become like the Jews and Saracens. Or they can surmise that Christians can learn from practitioners of these religions because they display fidelity to "law" itself, although believing in a law that lacks Truth. They might conclude as well that a faithful Christian clergy should be less busy about its prosperity and pleasure and more concerned with the proper teaching of doctrine that will convert the non-Christians, welcoming them into the one true religion.

Anima and Liberum Arbitrium weave these themes and motifs throughout the rest of these sequences in B and C, guided by the central hope that if the clergy were to reform, universal conversion would ensue: "Ac ȝif prestes doen here deuer [duty] wel, we shal do þe bettre, / For Sarrasynes may be saued so yf thay so byleued— / In þe letynge [leaving] of here lyf to leue on [believe in] Holy Churche" (C17.122–24). An ideal society has each Christian man and woman, taught well by a dutiful clergy, serving God's law and abiding in charity, so that one day everyone will come home to Holy Church and error will fall away into God's love and mercy. Langland elaborates on this theme in inspired poetry, savoring the liquid alliteration, as Liberum Arbitrium spins his tale of love, law, loyalty, and lechery. "Iewes and gentel Sarresines" believe that they "lelyche [truthfully]," follow their faith, loving and believing in "o [one] Lord almyhty" (132–35), but Liberum Arbitrium contends, in an extraordinary statement, that love alone guarantees nothing:

> Ac Oure Lord aloueth [accepts] no loue but lawe be þe cause:
> For lechours louyen aȝen þe lawe and at þe laste ben dampned,
> And theues louyen and leute hatien [hate honesty], and þe laste ben hanged;
> And lele [loyal] men lyue as lawe techeth, and loue þerof aryseth,
> The whiche is þe heued [head] of charite and hele [health] of mannes soule. (C17.136–40)

Love, however ardent, and law, however loyal, do not necessarily follow truth, as illustrated in one way by the Saracens, who love their (erroneous) law, and by lechers and thieves, who love *against* the law and get damned or hanged. Liberum Arbitrium continues with Dantesque lines echoing the anaphora of Francesca in *Inferno* V but more worthy of Beatrice herself:

> Loue God for he is goed, and grounde of alle treuthe;
> Loue thyn enemye entierely, Goddes heste [behest] to fulfille;
> Loue thy frende þat followeth thy wille, that is thy fayre soule.
> (C17.141–43)

Loving God and neighbor, as God demands, purifies error, maintains the true faith, and allows Christians to care for the soul, depicted intimately as a friend. "And þat is charite, leue chield, to be cher ouer [to cherish] thy soule," concludes Liberum Arbitrium: "Contrarie [oppose] her nat, as in consience, yf thow wolt come to heuene" (148-49). B has more than 200 and C 150 more lines of elaboration of what today is called interfaith dialogue but really for Langland's readers serves as a rousing, apocalyptic call for universal religion and a new world order.

In C15 Langland eliminates some similar urging for universal religion from the B text (see section 16 above), so the resurgence of those musings in both versions here may surprise. Readers will question whether *Piers Plowman* primarily concerns itself with a new world order or rather with particular acts of charity in English towns, farms, and cities. *Piers* does not, in fact, confine itself in any way or on any scale. It wants to convert non-Christians globally and also to inspire simpler, humane virtues like not watering down the beer in the pub and not cheating customers when selling wool and dry goods. The poem associates all these acts, and its central ethical message varies only slightly, for love, truth, charity are one and the same, each manifested along various continua of human action by the everyday Christian in social relations, and by the clergy at the level of pastoral care, both locally and universally. A properly devoted clergy, committed to love and truth and resistant to greed, will draw all peoples, including Jews and Muslim, to the one true faith, for a new world order starts at home. Langland tempers expectations of modern tolerance, however, when B and C then tell the traditional story of how Muhammad (Mahomet) tricked his followers into believing that God spoke to him by putting grain in his ear so a dove would pick at it and seem to be whispering to him (B15.398-410; C17.165-82). This cartoonish tale may disappoint modern readers excited by Langland's ostensible openness to interfaith dialogue and the respect he often shows for both Muslims and Jews, praising their religious rigor and fidelity, elsewhere in this sequence and in the poem.

Anima and Liberum Arbitrium each elaborate on the Muhammad scenario, and both do so purposefully by drawing moral lessons for the English clergy. Anima, in exposition unique to B, cleverly explains how "Englisshe clerkes a coluere [dove] fede þat Coueitise hiȝte [is called] / And ben manered [model themselves] after Makometh, þat [so that now] no man vseþ trouþe" (B15.414-15). Throughout medieval literature, especially travel literature like Mandeville's or Marco Polo's *Travels*, Christians notice a purity of faith in the "other" that shames the Christians back home. *Piers* reverses that model: Christians, in the idolatry of their greed, bring themselves to the level of Muhammad, here mocked as a base trickster, the enemy of Truth.

Liberum Arbitrium omits the next 75 or so lines of B, in which Anima ventures on an elaborate tangent into church history, offering exemplars of charity and proper fidelity, in contrast to the failing, greedy clergy of today (B15.416–90α). Highlights include the observation that "Elleuene holy men al þe world tornede [turned] / Into lele [faithful] bileue" (437–38), an homage to the Apostles and an incitement to contemporary clerical reform. The experience of reading in parallel reveals Langland passing over this material and only rejoining B at "Allas, þat men so longe on Macometh bileueth!" (C17.187). Both B and C aver that Saracens and Jews "han a lippe [a mouthful, a bit] of oure bileue" (B15.501). This "little bit" makes it likelier that they would "turne" to the true belief, if clergy were to "trauaile" and "teche hem of þe Trinite" (502). Langland nears interfaith awareness, though one should not confuse the issue with modern "nonjudgmentalness" or tolerance. Langland wants Christians to win, and he cannot accept religious difference, but he can appreciate how a commonality enables conversion if the Christian clergy, his immediate subject, can reform and apply itself to the task. All pagans, here indicating Muslims, pray and perfectly believe in the great, holy God "and his grace asken," though they err in praying to Muhammad, a "fals mene [intermediary]," a corrupt belief that imperils the soul of the papacy and the bishops whom the pope appoints, futilely, in Muslim lands (B15.503–9; moved to C17.255–61).[5]

But unsure of modern clergy's potential, in both versions Anima and Liberum Arbitrium reminisce about how saints and holy men of yesteryear "deffouled here flesche," "forsoke here owne wille," traveled far "fro kuthe [kith] and fro kyn" and were "baddeliche ybedded [poorly housed]" (C17.195–97), in a nostalgic lament about the degenerate present and the idealized past. Whether concerning spiritual warriors or the courtly knights of old, medieval literature often sees the past as a time of epic greatness and superstar heroism. Now, the "rede noble," a coin, is reverenced over the "rode," Christ's cross, a perversion of priorities that sparks idolatrous "werre and wo" over money (200–204). Yet greed will not prosper, for the "riche and religious" (206) who worship the cross stamped on coins more than the cross of salvation will "ouerturne [come to ruin]," (209), just as the wealthy

Crusaders, the rapacious Knights Templar did. And indeed, warns Liberum Arbitrium hauntingly, the time of recompense "approcheth faste" (209).

The two texts continue with more "if only" reveries: if only clergy would surrender their lordship of lands; if only knighthood, Kind Wit, the commons, and Conscience could "togederes louyen lelelyche" (C17.217). These desires anticipate what historians call disendowment, the stripping of temporal property and wealth from a bloated clergy, which would occur some 150 years hence in the English Reformation under Henry VIII. Accordingly, Anima and Liberum Arbitrium launch into the familiar medieval discourse on the "Donation of Constantine," the false fourth-century document (but not in Langland's time known to be so) with which the emperor granted an endowment to Pope Sylvester for curing him of illness. As Langland and other reformers perceive it, this "donation," giving the church temporal power, laid the foundation for clerical worldliness and addictive corruption, because institutions hold onto temporal power fiercely at the expense of charity and pastoral care. And so both texts affirm a Lollard doctrine that the secular nobility should strip the church of its lands and flush out the poison of corruption. Liberum Arbitrium explains:

> Taketh here londes, 3e lordes, and lat hem lyue by dymes [on tithes],
> Yf 3e kynges coueyte [desire] in Cristes pees to lyuene.
> For if possession be poysen, and inparfit hem make,
> The heuedes [heads] of Holy Churche and tho that ben vnder hem,
> Hit were charite to deschargen hem for Holy Churche sake,
> And purge hem of þe olde poysen, ar [before] more perel falle.
> (C17.227–32)

C had added lines 228 and 230 and continues with around fifty more lines on the subject. Some readers detect a softening of radical religious and political thought in C, as Langland draws back from the unrest of 1381 that recklessly misapplied his poem, but the C text contains much unapologetic Lollard, reformist doctrine, or perhaps Lollardy asserts much Langlandian reformist doctrine: one cannot easily distinguish the two. But C's added lines, charging the king to heal a Holy Church infected with poison, emphasize the urgency and authority for such a purge as a precondition for kings to enact "Cristes pees." A reformed clergy, in this ideal paradigm, could not fund the internecine wars among Christians, which defies God's injunction "Mihi vindicta [revenge is mine]" (C17.235α; Romans 12:19; Deuteronomy 32:35). Like much of the discourse from Liberum Arbitrium and from Anima, this doctrine sounds less specific to character than to poet—as assertion of authorial voice that readers can contemplate but never confirm.

Liberum Arbitrium then rails against the pope's military adventures.[6] The notion of papal armies and "antipopes" may shock modern readers as the stuff of fiction, and with difficulty we gauge how even medieval Christians, trusting in leadership and believing in "Holy Church," reacted to the reality of popes in battle with one another. Langland documents here in the C text one powerful response: anger and disdain, using the moment to lament clerical failure and to hope for the new world religious order he has been cultivating in both versions. So in C he reprises the Muhammad-and-the-dove imagery from B and gives it artful new meaning. Muhammad, says Liberum Arbitrium, did not gain the "maistrie" over his flock with "manslaght" or force of arms but rather with the dove in "pacience and priué gyle" (C17.241–42), and Christian prelates should do the same, asking Christ to send *his* dove (as it were, the real one), the Holy Ghost:

> In such manere, me thynketh, moste [must] þe Pope,
> Prelates and prestis preye and biseche
> Deuouteliche day and nyhte and withdrawe hem fro synne,
> And crie to Crist a wolde [so that he would] his coluer sende,
> The whiche is þe hy Holy Gost þat out of heuene descendet
> To make a perpetual pees bitwene þe prince of heuene
> And alle maner men þat on this molde libbeth [live on this earth].
>   (C17.243–49)

Anima spoke of Christians feeding the dove called covetousness (B15.414), and in C Liberum Arbitrium spiritualizes the image, exploiting scriptural references linking doves to mercy, to the Holy Spirit, and to salvation.[7] Langland gives focus, shape, and direction to the Liberum Arbitrium episode by specifying what work the clergy must perform and what effect it will achieve globally: mastering their free will, they should focus not on winning wealth, consolidation of power, and institutional bloat, but rather on pastoral care, teaching, and the bringing of spiritual truth and inspiration to Christian and non-Christian alike. Langland often takes the long and winding path, both within and across versions, as voices wander and rage in Will's head. But the poet always reaches a place of doctrinal clarity, however momentary and contingent, that distills his hope for simple yet radical change in the institutions that can bring humanity into peace with one other and with God.

The B and C texts rejoin to address the pastoral duties of a bishop who should supply to his flock spiritual and bodily sustenance (B15.569–76a; C17.283–92). Liberum Arbitrium adds some striking chivalric imagery comparing the bishop to a knight or king, committed by nature to fight and be killed "amonges here enemyes in mortel batayles" in order "the comune to defende" (C17.288–89). Liberum Arbitrium does not exhort actual crusade, for reconquest of the Holy Land, with bishops' swords shining, plays no part in Langland's global theology. The analogy incites the clergy to battle not against Muslims but "to destruye dedly synne" (291), the ultimate enemy that threatens the ultimate prize, the human soul. Perhaps this chivalric imagery anticipates the coming events in B and C when Jesus jousts for the human soul. Or perhaps it expresses a sort of redirected "crusade," not against earthly armies but against error, as a clever way of expressing the goal of religious unity achieved not by armies but by the heroics of a fiercely committed clergy in a crusade of pastoral care. Langland must have believed that if Christians themselves fail, how could they expect Jews and Muslims to convert? Conquer ourselves, so his argument goes, and the "others" will follow.

Accordingly, Anima and Liberum Arbitrium then meditate once again, somewhat uneasily, on religious division and the hope for reunification: Moses taught the Law to sustain a people until the Messiah, Christ, would come to fulfill it, as displayed in his miraculous power such as the raising of Lazarus, even though the Jews saw him as a sorcerer (B15.595) and Jews *and* Saracens called him a "iogelour [a hack magician]" (C17.308). B and C end almost identically with hopeful macaronic verses about how to build on Jewish and Muslim faith in God, extending it to the Son and Spirit, illustrated with lines from the Credo:

And sethe þat this Sarresynes and also þe Iewes
Conne [know] þe furste clause of oure bileue, *Credo in Deum patrem*
  [I believe in God the father],
Prelates and prestes sholde preue [try], yf they myhte,

> Lere hem littelum and littelum [little by little] *Et in Iesum Christum filium* [and in Jesus Christ the son],
> Til they couthe speke and spele *Et in Spiritum sanctum* [And in the holy Spirit],
> Recorden hit and rendren hit with *remissionem peccatorum* [the forgiveness of sins],
> *Carnis resurrectionem* [resurrection of the body] *et vitam eternam* [life everlasting]. Amen. (C17.315–20a)

Why characters named Anima and Liberum Arbitrium discuss such topics will continue to baffle readers. In B's long passus 15 and the corresponding C sections the topics have ranged freely from learning (*in bono* and *in malo*) to charity, exemplary figures in history, the ongoing degeneracy of the clergy, and God's care for his faithful. Perhaps the final theme of universal religion, based on the notion that Jews and Muslims "have a suspectioun [expectation] to be saef [saved]" (C17.313), unifies the sprawling themes of this episode, which always returns to the responsibilities of the clergy to teach well and to occupy themselves with a pastoral duty that combats their poisonous greed and draws the world together in one Christian faith. This constitutes more mono-faith monologue than interfaith dialogue, but how Langland envisions communication and understanding among the faiths, and to what ends, provokes contemplation in a post-Holocaust, post-9/11 world. Langland's hopes strike modern readers as vague, chimerical, and hegemonic, for it seems strange that he could have believed that Jews and Muslims really would be so awed by Christian virtue that they would submit to Christian law, without which they remain excluded from redemption. But as an English Christian of his time, he could see the world in no other way, however noninclusive this seems from a modern perspective. Ultimately for Langland the only exclusions and inclusions of any consequence are from heaven, and no one locked in error and sin, regardless of the kind of law they follow and which doves they cherish, will be saved. Simply being Christian instead of Muslim or Jew provides no inherent privilege. Seemingly aware of this, Will soon asks a question that seeks to unravel the mysteries of salvation once and for all, or at least until more questions arise. In the next passus, then, he learns even more about charity, the active virtue that animates the one true law.

20

Fighting for the Fruit of Charity

B16 AND C18

Conspectus: As B and C match up again in parallel, Anima and Liberum Arbitrium continue to answer Will's question "What is charity?"—an issue that one might imagine ought to be settled by now. But *Piers* concerns itself less with settling issues through definitions than with the ongoing experience of creatively expressing divine truth in human terms, so charity can be defined and redefined endlessly. There follows, with some significant differences in B and C, the description of the Tree of Charity and the return of Piers Plowman, who tends the tree while menaced by the Devil. As the life of Christ begins to unfold, Will begins his next major encounter, with the three Theological Virtues, Faith, Hope, and Charity, embodied by Abraham, Moses, and the Good Samaritan. The first of these dialogues, with Abraham, completes this passus.

Perhaps the excursus on the clergy's global mission in the previous passus struck too grand and futuristic a posture to define adequately something so simply beautiful as charity. So Langland tries another approach to capture its essence, a return to natural imagery. In B Anima describes the virtues that form the parts of this excellent Tree of Charity:

"It is a ful trie [excellent] tree," quod he, "trewely to telle.
Mercy is þe more [root] þerof; þe myddul stok [trunk] is ruþe;
The leues [leaves] ben lele wordes, þe lawe of Holy Chirche;
The blosmes beþ buxom [humble] speche and benigne lokynge;
Pacience hatte [is the name of] þe pure tree, and pore symple of herte,
And so þoru3 God and goode men groweþ þe fruyt Charite."
  (B16.4–9)

In the B version Piers the Plowman lords over this land, with Liberum Arbitrium tending it for him. In C, by contrast, Liberum Arbitrium tells Will about the tree, with no reference to Piers, a remarkable difference that informs the rest of the poem. In B the mere mention of Piers sends Will into another swooning dream within a dream, specifically a "loue-dreem" but not a sexual one, as before, full of Recklessness and lust (B/C11). Now, rather, he longs for Piers, burning with a higher, spiritual urgency. And Piers, no longer the cranky plowman trying to manage the lazy field of folk on the half acre, becomes here rather a type of Christ. Will describes his desire:

"Piers þe Plowman!" quod I þo, and al for pure ioye
That I herde nempne [named] his name anoon I swowned after,
And lay longe in a loue-dreem. . . . (B16.18–20)

Both love dreams further Will's search for truth, while at once they anticipate Nature's dramatic injunction to Will to "lerne to loue" (B20.208), with "love" evolving meaningfully from one dream to the other, from the carnal to the spiritual. This edifying dream of a Christlike Piers spiritually purifies Will and prepares him to meet with Faith, Hope, and Charity. Langland has been preparing for this reentrance of Piers throughout the B text, and its emotional power strikes readers as much as it does Will. We cannot know why Langland excises Piers from C, though perhaps he intended another, later and even more glorious return of the Plowman, which he never executed because he never completed the revision. That speculation aside, one can ponder productively his absence in C as it stands, for it may indicate that C has lost faith in his own creation, and to lose faith in the hero of the B text would be dire indeed. If Langland compensates for this loss in any way in the remainder of the C text, he has very little time in which to accomplish it. So for the moment Liberum Arbitrium instructs Will in the C text, playing the role crafted in B for Piers.

Piers and Liberum Arbitrium describe the "Flessh" as "a fel [fierce] wynd" (B16.31) that rages against the Tree of Charity, while the three posts of the Trinity hold it steady against sin. In C Liberum Arbitrium expands significantly (C18.58–80), depicting the varieties of fruit that spring from this tree as analogous to the moral diversity in humanity: "Ac somme ar swettore [sweeter] then somme and sonnere wollen rotye [rot]" (60) and "somme of vs soethfaste [faithful] and some variable" (69). He expands this imagery to include widows and widowers, virgins, monastic clergy, and all those who live in chastity, describing them as apples of various sizes: "Summe litel, somme large, ylik apples of o kynde" (70). Surprisingly, he expounds further on the purity of virginity, not a major concern in the *Piers* corpus:

> Thenne is Virginite, more vertuous and fayrest, as in heuene,
> For þat is euene with angelis, and angeles pere [peer].
> Hit was þe furste fruyte þat þe Fader of heuene blessed,
> And bad hit be [bade that it exist], of a bat [clod] of erthe, a man and
>   a maide. (C18.89–92)

This new fixation on purity makes sense in the context of what happens next in C, after Will asks (in B and C) to taste an apple. In B, the Devil tries to grab the fruit that falls off the tree of Charity, seizing the lost souls of the dead. Piers Plowman beats him back. But in C Langland creates an entirely different scene, where the character Elde [Old Age], at Liberum Arbitrium's prompting, climbs the tree and shakes the fruit loose. The addition of Elde may reflect the poet's awareness of the passing of time, as for Prospero in Shakespeare's *Tempest*. C's emphasis on both virginity and old age reflects just such a temporal urgency, an awareness both of death and of the means of defeating death by preserving purity and Edenic innocence. Whether or not he knows his time is running short, Langland is contemplating the end of things and the world grown old.[1] In C he has only two passūs left to thwart the fiend as he scampers for the fruit that Elde shakes to the ground.

Further dramatic differences between B and C in this episode arise from the absence of Piers in the latter version. The B text describes how Piers pounds the Devil with the metaphorical stakes of the Trinity that hold up the tree:

> And Piers, for pure tene [anger], þat a pil [pile] he lauȝte [seized],
> And hitte after hym, happe how it myȝte,
> *Filius* [son] by þe Faderes wille and frenesse [grace] of *Spiritus Sancti* [the Holy Spirit],
> To go robbe þat rageman [devil] and reue [snatch back] þe fruyt fro hym. (B16.86–89)

Piers, becoming ever more Christlike, nonetheless remains a plowman, and the literal image of a tough farm worker defending his crops against disaster remains stirring and powerful. Without Piers Plowman in C, much more nebulously the "majesty of God" moves the "will of God" to take up the second prop (the second person of the Trinity) to pound on the Devil. Will describes the drama: "Thenne moued hym moed in *magestate Dei* [the mood stirred in the majesty of God] / That [so that] *Libera Voluntas Dei* [the Free Will of God] lauhte þe myddel shoriare [seized the middle prop]," explained above by Liberum Arbitrium as the "*Sapiencia Dei Patris* [Wisdom of the Father]" (C18.118–19, 40). Though much less concrete and visceral than having the Plowman beat down the Devil, the C-text version draws its scenario from the higher forces of divine energy that moved God to send his son in the Incarnation as a weapon against the Devil. A Christlike Piers in B gives way to Christ himself, who flies with the Spirit "to go ransake þat ragman [devil] and reue hym [strip him] of his apples" (122). Despite this ethereal recasting, B and C agree about what happens next in a dramatic sequence that begins with the retelling of the Incarnation, as Will sees it unfold: "And þanne spak *Spiritus Sanctus* in Gabrielis mouþe / To a maide þat hiȝte [was called] Marie, a meke þyng wiþalle" (B16.90–91). With the Incarnation, God formally intervenes in human history, providing the foundation of all hope, and so the Nativity story follows logically from the Devil's attempt to steal the fallen fruit of the human soul. The poem moves toward the life of Christ, the ultimate *vita*, the ultimate exemplar of charity, and the story of the greatest chivalric hero in arms, for Christ plans to joust with the Devil to determine "who sholde fecche this fruyt—the fende or Iesus suluen [himself]" (C18.130).

The events of Christ's life and ministry follow. B attributes his learning and development to the tutelage of Piers the Plowman, who teaches Jesus "lechecraft" (B16.104), the healing arts, while C cites Liberum Arbitrium as his instructor. One wonders whether Christ, God himself, can be taught anything by anyone. But the passage imagines the Incarnation as a transition in both divine and human history: God learns to become human and how to conduct his ministry from within the human will.[2] Christ's miraculous healing powers provoke suspicion among the Jews, who tell him "Demonium habes [you have a daemon]" (B16.120a; John 7:20).[3] Christ condemns the Jews, and his struggle with the Jewish community culminates in Judas's betrayal (B16.121–66; C152–78). Doctrinally, in the recounting of the *vita Christi*, the ultimate version of Dowel, both versions appear to have reached a well-earned spiritual place, where Will's inquiry into human action yields to the story of God's perfect selflessness in sacrificing himself to an ungrateful people who scorn and plot against him. Here the acts of Judas and the Jews represent the betrayals Christians commit every day against God in their selfish disregard for his commandments to love and in the sins the poem has been tracing since the prologue. But the compelling story of Jesus's death and resurrection comes to an abrupt halt as Will awakes, provoked by "moche noyse" in C (18.179), but in B by a stunning vision of Christ on the cross:

> In a Þursday in þesternesse [darkness] þus was he taken
> Thoruȝ Iudas and Iewes—Iesus was his name
> That on þe Friday folwynge for mankynde sake
> Iusted [jousted] in Ierusalem, a ioye to vs alle.
> On cros vpon Caluarie Crist took þe bataille
> Ayeins [against] deeþ and þe deuel, destruyed hir boþeres [both their] myȝtes—
> Deide, and deeþ fordide [undid death], and day of nyȝt made.
> (B16.160–66)

On the verge of recounting the ultimate defeat of sin and death, Langland dramatically disperses the dream, perhaps because Will, and readers too, need to experience and to learn more before proving themselves worthy of such rapture. Whatever his pedagogical motivation, Langland disrupts the thrilling drama of Christ's battle, creating tremendous suspense in the reader and frantic longing in Will, who wipes his eyes and, "as an ydiot" (B16.170), goes searching for Piers (and in C for Liberum Arbitrium), trying to return to the dream world for answers.

Will awakens into an even more complex situation than he thinks, structurally speaking. In B he wakes up, unknowingly, from an inner dream, the specific love dream of Piers. Though not having a dream within a dream in C, Will wakes again later in the C version when the exterior dream in B ends. If a dream within a dream in B provides an exciting and provocative device for Will's interior journey, waking up twice from the same dream in C creates a less coherent narrative scenario. Readers may want to find some intentionality or device in Langland's permitting Will to wake twice in C, and Schmidt believes that the Tree of Charity episode does in fact occur during an "effectively" inner dream, "despite the lack of a 'swoon' at [C18] 4 like that at B[16] 19" (*Parallel-Text* 2.666). However, perhaps Langland, faced with the narrative complexities of the long poem he was revising, simply nodded.

Will's waking nonetheless provides a transition in both B and C to the next episode: his encounter with Faith, Hope, and Charity, embodied by Abraham, Moses, and the Good Samaritan. These figures bridge the Old and New Testaments and reveal the consistency and integrity of salvation history. They provide personal immediacy to the poem, for readers experience the story of grace unfolding in the lives of these biblical icons as they take their proper places in God's plan and enact their sacred duties. Abraham/Faith appropriately explains the Trinity to Will, since Abraham recognized, served, and fed the Trinity during its divine visit to him and Sarah. Christianity relies—however ahistorical and ingenious it may seem to the modern scholarly mind—on the devices of prefiguration from the Old Testament, so from Christianity's perspective, Abraham hosted the Trinity. But before he tells that proud personal anecdote, Abraham explains the complexities and unity of three persons of God in one, which in C confuses Will, who thinks the whole thing "myrke" (C18.197). This sparks Abraham, in lines also unique to C, to tell Will not to think too much until he knows more, but to believe loyally in the Trinity, however paradoxical it may be.

The following expositions in B and C (16.181–224; 18.188–239) challenge readers with their ingenuity and complexity, as Abraham explains the Trinity in an associative, almost deconstructive free play, comparing it to the triad of wedlock, widowhood, and virginity. Alternatively, he sees the Trinity as the trio of Adam, Eve, and their children. Relating these various triads to one another is challenging: the implied correlation of the Son of God to a widow, formed by the might of marriage (the Father), is strained at best and in any case bizarre, a form of fancy that pours forth various tangible but unrelated images to express something mystical and arcane. Abraham does not have to make rational sense and likely intends his words to be read as impressionistically as they are rendered. Marriage has ethical meaning, and in C Langland focuses on the related theme of procreation, expanding B's commentary on the apocryphal biblical verse "Maledictus sit homo qui non reliquit semen in Israel [cursed is the man who does not leave his seed in Israel]" (C18.223).[4] Perhaps this betrays an older poet now looking ahead, cherishing the thought of the next generation with hope for a future—the musings of a sentimental, grandfatherly Langland. He certainly courts that cliché at moments in C, as here when he talks about love, marriage and children: "And man withoute a make [mate] myhte nat wel of kynde [his progeny] / Multiplie, ne moreouer withoute a make louye, / Ne withoute a soware [sower] be [could there be] suche seed—this we seen alle" (224–26). In this way Langland adapts the imperatives of Genesis to the poem's hopes for social reform. The Trinity, as family, emblemizes ideal human activity, the divinely sanctioned procreation that creates personal and social stability. Soon Will introduces readers to his wife and daughter, in a moment that warmly personalizes Abraham's Trinitarian imagery and his faith.

B and C recount the biblical scene in which Abraham tends to God as three persons, confirming his authority on this issue of the Trinity (Gen. 18:1–15). Here too we perceive the evolving sensibility of Langland as the older poet, again concerning procreation, in lines unique to C about the unlikely birth of Isaac: "And what Y thouhte and my wyf he vs wel tolde. / He bihihte [promised] vs issue and ayr [heir] in oure olde age" (C18.245–46).[5] The increasing emphasis on the role of Elde prompts Langland to add this bit of wonderment about how God can defy a mortal sense of physical time, revealing a divine power that, like the Trinity, roams beyond rational understanding.

Abraham continues to recount his adventures, such as circumcising

Isaac, and in both B and C Will then sees a "la3ar," or a leper, so named for the biblical Lazarus, playing among prophets and patriarchs in the so-called "bosom of Abraham," an image of caretaking, of parental nurturing, and of Paradise itself (B16.255; Luke 16:19–31). The tableau reminds readers, as well, of a lesson not forgotten but nearly lost in all the dreams, dreams within dreams, and related hubbub: God cares for the poor and diseased, who earn their way into heaven because they have expressly *not* earned the prosperity valued by society but worthless in God's final judgment. Will marvels at the leper, whom he calls a "present of muche pris" (B16.260) that the fiend wants to fetch but that Abraham protects until Christ comes to defeat the Devil. Abraham believes in faith and lives in hope, and Hope, accordingly, is on the way.

21

A Spy, a Samaritan, and the Spirit's Flame

B17 AND C19

Conspectus: Meeting Abraham as Faith provided only the first component in this new triad, a superior version of the Dowel, Dobet, and Dobest template. So next comes Hope, depicted as Moses, but he too proves insufficient in the quest for ultimate virtue without the final component, Charity, depicted as the Good Samaritan. In this and the next passus, B and C remain close. The poems start to dovetail as they progress to B19 where Langland stopped revising, either because the poet was content with these passūs or because he died before rewriting them.

Moses names himself "Spes" (Latin for Hope) and also calls himself a "spie" (B17.1). The *Middle English Dictionary* struggles to make sense of this line under the definition "one who searches for someone or something" (s.v. "spie," def. 1e), surely the blandest and least spy-like definition it can muster. Yet Moses does not seem like any kind of secret agent, as in the main definition: "One who spies on the activities of another; one sent out to make secret observations in a foreign land" (1a). Still, he seeks, and Langland never shies away from employing bold words, here provoking readers to contemplate the meaning of this patriarch in salvation history. This ancient lawgiver, like Abraham, knows secret information and knows, as well, about Christ's new law of love, "Dilige Deum et proximum tuum [Love God and love your neighbor]" (B17.11α). Such Old Testament figures reveal a marvelous simultaneity of the divine, for God observes no division of historical time, as temporal mortals perceive it. These patriarchs, though placed in an epic national history and destined to wait for redemption, know that God created only one unified law. Thus Moses has a "hard roche" cut not with the Ten Commandments but only with the laws of love, upon which depend, as Jesus said, "tota lex et prophetia [the whole law and the prophets]" (9–14; cf. Matt. 22:40).

In B and C this befuddles Will, who struggles to process Abraham's explanations of the Trinity and now must assimilate a whole new concept of "law." Will prefers cumulative learning and cannot always see the dynamic interrelations of the seemingly discrete doctrines taught to him. In a homey metaphor Will tells Spes that a man who walks with one staff appears healthier than a man who uses two, and so he hesitates to take up a second staff by adopting this newfangled lesson that advises something ridiculous, to love not only the good but also a "sherewe," "lorels" (B17.37–47), and "lyares" (C19.45). Angry and frustrated, Will tells Spes to hit the road: "Go þi gate" (B17.46). Too much complex information overloads Will, who cannot simultaneously comprehend the sum of salvation history in the abstract virtues that carry it and also in the personae that labored in history to realize God's salvific grace. He longs for a single answer and thus cannot trace the sequential, evolving, and yet timeless moments of history that defy logic and reason. Even though both Abraham and Moses speak of Christ and thus of the future that they themselves never witness historically, their contributions lack the Gospels and the ultimate virtue of Charity, which comes in the form of the Samaritan (see Luke 10:25–37).[1]

In this conceit, Abraham and Moses (Faith and Hope) play the role of the priest and the Levite who bypass the wounded man, whom only the Samaritan stops to care for. This paradigm may strike readers as strange because Abraham and Moses ought not be equated, one thinks, with these negligent failures. B recounts that Moses in fact ran from the man "as doke [a duck] dooþ fram þe faucon [falcon]!" (B17.63). In C Langland drops this silly, distracting image, but B and C make the same critical point: one practices true charity in the acts of caring physically and financially for someone in need, which faith and hope simply cannot perform. Langland adapts the parable to trumpet the virtues that animate the poem from the beginning. Now Will knows the whole story of virtuous charity from the calling of Abraham, to Moses on Mount Sinai, and finally to the dangerous road between Jerusalem and Jericho. Metaphorically this road, for Langland and for all readers through time, represents not only human vulnerability to actual violence but also the trials of life itself, a road perpetually fraught with thieves (sin) ready to rob and beat us until we are "semyvif [half alive]," "naked as a nedle," and at the mercy of whoever happens along (B17.56–57). Will perceives how the frailty of the human condition, the inherent vulnerability of living in a world of violence and terror, leaves us physically at each other's mercy and spiritually dependent upon God's.

When Will tells the gentle Samaritan about the failure of Faith and Hope, he, acting as charitably as one would expect, excuses his fellow Virtues, revealing that they could not have helped the wounded man even if they had tried. He decodes the allegorical meaning of his parable, surpassing the apparent meaning that Jesus as storyteller must have intended:

> "Haue hem excused," quod he, "hir help may litel auaille:
> May no medicyne vnder molde [on earth] þe man to heele [health] brynge—
> Neiþer Feiþ ne fyn Hope, so festred be hise woundes,
> Wiþouten þe blood of a barn [child] born of a mayde.
> And be he baþed in þat blood, baptised as it were,
> And þanne plastred wiþ penaunce and passion of þat baby."
> (B17.91–96)

No one inflicted with sin can ever become "stalworþe ... Til he haue eten al þe barn [child] and his blood ydronke" (B17.97–98). In this powerful poetry the Samaritan, more than just a character representing charity in Jesus's parable, becomes Christ's own minister or perhaps Christ himself as healer whose blood and whose sacraments cure the wounded, all who have fallen prey to sin. Faith and Hope wait in joyful anticipation of this history-changing divine intervention, powerless against sin and death without the Incarnation and the Passion. Bound by their historical moment, a moment that longs for final fulfillment, they could not but fail where Charity succeeds.

In B alone the Samaritan, intensifying his Christological identity, describes how he rides the horse called Caro, that is, how he himself took on human flesh, leading the cowardly Devil to hide in hell. He boasts that in three days the "feloun" will be "fettred" in the ultimate triumph, as it is written: "O Mors, ero mors tua [O death, I will be your death]" (B17.111–12α; Hosea 13:14). At that time, Faith will be a forester, searching the road for the wounded, and Hope will heal their injuries, as these virtues take their new, proper places in history, guarding humanity from the "outlawe" in the woods, which they could not do before the coming of Christ and his Passion (113–24, 103). This unique B exposition foreshadows the scene of the Harrowing of Hell that comes later in both poems, yet Langland omits the Samaritan's exposition from C, skipping ahead to Will's burning question (C19.96–102), essentially, "Sir, since you know so much about Faith and Hope, can you help me understand the Trinity and the law of love?" In C's striking addition, Will reports that Hope told him to love everyone and further that he should

> Noþer lacke ne alose [neither blame nor praise], ne leue [believe] þat þer were
> Eny [anyone] wikkedere in þe worlde than Y were mysulue,
> And moest inparfyt of alle persones, and pacientliche soffre [tolerate]
> Alle manere men, and thogh Y myhte venge [avenge myself],
> Y sholde tholye [endure], and thonken [thank] hem þat me euel wolden [wish me evil]. (C19.103–7)

These lines reveal the unique mood of Langland in the C text, close to the end of his work. Will strangely recounts something Moses never really said: that Will should see no one in the world as more wretched than himself, should see himself as the most imperfect of all persons, and should endure his sinful failures with gratitude and without seeking vengeance against the evil of others. This self-abnegation may speak to Langland's increasing despair or to his increasing wisdom and self-knowledge as he composes C. "A saide soeth [he said the truth]" (C19.108), replies the Samaritan approvingly, confirming Will's wretchedness, as Will, and his poet too, continue to prepare themselves for the end, for all the ends that are going to occur too soon and yet right on time.

Then with Langland doing some tinkering between the versions, the

Samaritan launches into one of the poem's most intriguing conceits: the metaphor of the Trinity as a hand, with God the fist, the son the fingers, the spirit the palm, working together without losing unity. C drops from B one cosmic image describing how the Trinity, as a hand, holds the universe, "wolkne [sky] and þe wynd, water and erþe, / Heuene and helle and al þat þer is inne" (B17.151–62). But nonetheless the playful trope continues in both versions, exploring creation wrought by the "werkmanshipe of fyngres" (175), with special emphasis on how the Holy Spirit (sometimes neglected) is just as much God, "neiþer gretter ne lasse [lesser]" (180). To offend the spirit means offending God, the Samaritan continues, as he switches metaphors and calls the Trinity a torch, with wax, wick, and flame as the three components. We must fear, he warns, the afterglow of the extinguished flame, which signifies the withdrawal of God's mercy from those who destroy love. Without the flame of the Spirit, God will "graunte no grace ne forgifnesse of synnes" (222). But when God's love rages, his might melts into mercy, in yet another rich metaphor of fire and ice:

> þe Holy Goost gloweþ but [only] as a glede [ember]
> Til þat lele loue ligge [lays] on hym and blowe.
> And þanne flawmeþ [flames] he as fir on Fader and on *Filius*
> And melteþ hire my3t into mercy, as men may se in wyntre
> Ysekeles [icicles] in euesynges [eaves] þoru3 hete of þe sonne
> Melteþ in a mynut while [minute's time] to myst and to watre.
> (B17.224–29)

This provides for Will and for every Christian struggling in despair the assurance that the "Fader" will "for3yue folk of mylde hertes / That rufully repenten and restitucion make, / In as muche as þei mowen amenden and paien [pay]" (B17.235–37). This last line, not the most imagistic or poetic of Langland's verses, stands among his most human, as it contemplates how much repentance humanity must contribute to the economy of grace. Sinners do the best they can and believe that God will recognize the sincerity of their effort and supply the "remenaunt [remainder]" (239). In this contractual pattern of imagery, sinners pay what they can, and God covers the rest of the debt, unless, the Samaritan implies, something has been withheld.

The Samaritan offers a final caution to Will: do not expect the flaming grace of the Holy Spirit if you are unkind to your fellow Christians; not all the pardon and indulgences in the world will help you then, for "vnkyndenesse quencheþ" the fire of the Holy Spirit (B18.256). Readers detect here the reformist spirit of the poem, critical of the pardon industry, displaying a distrust of any shortcut to salvation, any attempt to reduce the demands of virtue to a transaction, something one can buy—unless God sets the terms of the exchange. *Piers Plowman*, for all its complexity, offers a direct and constant ethic: love as Christ commanded to love. If obeying that law were easy, no poet would write 3,000 lines, expand them to 7,000, and rewrite them again. *Piers* studies how an animal desire to defeat and abuse others brings men and women more pleasure than any injunction to love them. According to Genesis, Cain quickly proved his primitive hatred for Abel, and Langland knows that nothing has changed from that moment of easy violence and snickering scorn for so-called brotherly love. *Piers Plowman* never depicts its ethic, however simple, as simple to accomplish. From all Will has seen of human appetite, imitating the Samaritan's behavior and keeping the Spirit's flame raging is more difficult than it seems.

The rich draw a singular warning in B and C because the accumulation of wealth inherently militates against the demands of loving kindness. Every society asks what, if anything, should be done about inequity: seize and redistribute wealth, or encourage the rich to share it willingly and charitably. Reading *Piers Plowman* compels one to understand the question, though perhaps not to answer it. To this point, in C Langland expands the Samaritan's speech explicitly to remind readers how Dives, the rich man in Jesus's parable, is not only "dampned for his vnkyndnesse" (C19.232) but also "dwelleth with þe deuel in helle" (241). But then the Samaritan quotes in Latin from the parable of the unjust steward: "Facite vobis amicos de mammona iniquitatis [Make unto you friends of the mammon of iniquity]" (248α; Luke 16:9). In this notoriously recalcitrant parable, Jesus praises a seemingly corrupt steward for the generosity he displays to his lord's debtors, accepting partial payment of what they owe. Even though he does so in order to make influential friends for himself, the steward's display of wise caution shows him to be economically thoughtful and thus deserving of divine treasure in heaven. The Samaritan invokes the story to encourage the rich to behave generously, and accordingly the forgiving lord in the parable models God's forgiveness of those who, like the steward, have acted wisely in their master's affairs. The Samaritan adds a coda in both versions:

> Vch a riche, Y rede, reward herof take
> And gyueth 30ure goed to þat God þat grace of aryseth [from whom grace arises].
> For þat ben [those that are] vnhynde to hise, hope 3e noen oþer [expect no less]
> Bote they [except that they will] dwelle there Diues is dayes withouten ende. (C19.249–52)

God, like the lord in the parable, closely watches all his stewards and how they conduct their business, which is ultimately his as well, with salvation or damnation as the final reckoning.

The Samaritan continues closely to recount crimes against the Spirit, acts of violation against the godly virtue of innocence. These violations arise from "coueitise of any kynnes þyng" (B17.285), a general phrase that covers all kinds of exploitive, sinful acts without any specific historical referent. Will, calmly alarmed about his chances for salvation, wonders, hypothetically, if God would accept his appeal for mercy if he were guilty of sins against the Spirit. The Samaritan responds to Will that repentance can transform God's justice into mercy, which, from a righteous legal perspective, no one deserves, a point that anticipates the debate of the Four Daughters of God to come in the next passus. Sinners have no recourse but to throw themselves on the mercy of God, for they cannot demand it by right. He seals the notion with "Misericordia eius super omnia opera eius," an echo of Psalm 144:9: "the Lord is sweet to all: and his tender mercies are over all his works" (B17.314α). So Will can hope.

Before the Samaritan departs, in both poems he invokes an anecdote familiar to readers of Chaucer's Wife of Bath's Prologue, the old adage that three things make a man run out of his own house: smoke, a leaky roof, and a nagging wife—one of the sexist clichés the Wife attributes to her drunk, beleaguered husband (B17.317–50; *Canterbury Tales* III.278–81). Here, however, these three elements (wife, rain, and smoke) drive humanity from the house of salvation, and are explained as the wicked flesh that cannot adequately be controlled, the rain of sorrow and suffering that try one's patience, and the smoke that obscures charity: "þe smoke and þe smolder þat smyt in oure eiȝen, / That is coueitise and vnkyndenesse, þat quencheþ Goddes mercy" (B17.343–44).[2] With this sonic flourish, which smites the reader's senses with the acrid sounds of sin, the Samaritan pricks his horse and vanishes like the wind. B and C end the passus as the Samaritan leaves and Will, as seems appropriate after this intense encounter and dramatic exit, wakes up from his external dream in B and for a second time in C. He offers no reaction to what he has witnessed, nor any indication of what happens next, after Faith, Hope, and Charity, like the mystically unified Trinity itself, have offered such rich and complex manifestations of virtue. Will has learned about the unity of God, of history, and of love, established among men and women through charity. This may be the "treasure" of truth he has been seeking since his encounter with Holy Church, but hearing a long lesson does not constitute personal, internal reform and does not mean that Will now can stop dreaming and return to the world ready to love. That Langland did not revise so extensively in this sequence indicates that B's dramatic flair and moral doctrine struck the right tone for what the poet plans in the next passus, the visionary culmination of Will's quest, wrought with some of the most meditative and ethereal religious poetry ever composed in English.

22

Christ Was on Rode

B18 AND C20

Conspectus: In a spiritually compelling episode, Will attains his greatest comfort and insight before the catastrophic events in the final two passūs shatter his peace. Cheered on by Faith, Will receives a vision of the crucifixion, with the Samaritan and Piers the Plowman merging into Jesus, who fights Death and the Devil for the human soul.

B and C open with Will once again as the underground man, feeling alienated, wandering about the countryside, poor, tired, ragged, and miserable, until sleep transports him through the penitential season of Lent to the moment of Christ's entry into Jerusalem on Palm Sunday:

> Wolleward [wool-shirted] and weetshoed [with wet shoes] wente I forþ after
> As a recchelees renk [reckless man] þat of no wo [woe] reccheþ [cares about],
> And yede forþ lik a lorel [beggar] al my lif tyme,
> Til I weex wery of þe world and wilned eft [desired again] to slepe,
> And lened me to [rested until] a Lenten—and longe tyme I slepte;
> Reste me þere and rutte faste [snored hard] til *Ramis palmarum* [Palm Sunday].
> Of gerlis [children] and of *Gloria, laus* [praise] gretly me dremed
> And how *Osanna* by orgene [organ] olde folk songen,

And of Cristes passion and penaunce, þe peple þat ofrauȝte [that he offered to the people]. (B18.1-9)

These seemingly dejected verses are among the most assertive in the poem, robust with hope and Hosanna, as the poem's mode and Will's tenor change. His reference to Palm Sunday and Christ's passion indicate the upcoming salvific events of Holy Week. In relation to Dante's poem, Langland begins here the "commedia" movement of the epic. Scenes of gory torture notwithstanding, Will has traveled, metaphorically, to hell and back. Yet someone else must suffer, and survive that actual journey, for Will's sake.

B and C begin this tour-de-force passus with numerous coalescences. A figure appears described as similar to the Samaritan and also to Piers the Plowman—revealed as Jesus himself, riding into Jerusalem like a knight, but without spear or spurs (B18.9-14). Langland here revisits the chivalric imagery he periodically employs, but infuses it with the humility that marks the biblical episode, which recounts not a military but a spiritual triumph. For in this combat, Jesus will joust not with another knight but with the Devil, fighting for the "Piers fruyt þe Plowman," the human soul (B18.20). So explains Faith, who reappears in this dream, from a window, to hail Jesus as the son of David and to help Will interpret the vision. Getting the ensemble cast from the previous dream back on stage reveals that Langland knows how to put on a spectacle. But some of the associations remain slippery: Jesus—simultaneously knight, Samaritan, and Piers—fights for the fruit *of* Piers. Langland blends together biblical parable, Passion drama, chivalric imagery, and plowman iconography into an impressionistic whole, as the central event of human history, itself an adroit blending of literary modes, unfolds before Will's eyes. This battle between life and death, provoked by the Incarnation, enables the salvation that has been, and will continue to be, all that matters to Will, to Langland, and to any Christian.

Will's line "Is Piers in þis place?" (B18.21; C20.19), a traditionally endearing moment, betrays a childlike innocence and sense of recognition, as Piers's return brings together all the aspects of that character: virtue, prayerfulness, dedication, leadership, brotherhood. In answer, Faith, winking at Will knowingly, explains the polyvalent Piers as Christ, humanity, and as the intersection of the two:

> This Iesus of his gentries [as a nobleman] wol iuste [joust] in Piers armes,
> In his helm and in his haubergeon [mail coat], *humana natura*.
> That Crist be noȝt biknowe [not recognized] here for *consummatus Deus* [fully God],
> In Piers paltok [Piers's jacket] þe Plowman þis prikiere [horseman] shal ryde;
> For no dynt [blow] shal hym dere [harm him] as *in deitate Patris* [in the divinity of his Father]. (B18.22–26)

Faith sets the stage for the upcoming contest, with all the popcorn-chomping excitement of a fan about to watch an epic match, as Death has been bragging about killing all the living, and Life says he's a liar—fighting words in any century (B18.27–35a).

Immediately Will finds himself at the scene of the trial and crucifixion. He hears the cries against Christ of "crucifige" and "tolle, tolle," and "ave raby!" inserted in macaronic verses that merge the biblical text with a rough-and-ready English street chatter, in which a "cachepol" (bailiff) and "ribaud" (scoundrel) play the parts of the ruffian Jews who harass the radical Nazarene preacher in the Gospels (B18.46–56). The chaos resolves into the uncommon poise and elegance of the verses on Christ's death, here in C's version, which adds two lines expanding the description of the earthquake that marks the cosmic moment:

> "*Consummatum est*," quod Crist, and comsede [began] for to swoene,
> Pitousliche and pale as a prisoun [prisoner] þat deyeth;
> The lord of lyf and of liht tho leyde his eyes togederes.
> The daye for drede [dread] þerof withdrouh [withdrew] and derke bicam þe sonne.
> The wal of the temple to-cleyef euene [split evenly] al in two peces,
> The hard roch al to-roef [broke], and riht derk nyht hit semede.
> The erthe to-quasche [shook] and quoek [quaked] as hit quyk [alive] were. (C20.57–63)

He who made the light in Genesis now shuts his eyes in the darkness of death, with the light of the sun withdrawing in response. Langland preserves every word from B but also, in line 63, animates another heavenly body from Genesis, the earth itself, which "shakes as if it were alive" and "shatters to pieces." C's addition borrows an image that B and C both employ later as a fellow named Book describes the earthquake again. When Jesus was born, says Book, "þer blased a sterre," showing all the world that a child was born "that mannes soule sholde saue and synne distruye [destroy]" (C20.241–44). When Christ dies, Nature again reacts:

> And lo! how þe sonne gan louke here lihte [lock her light up] in heresulue
> When heo sye hym soffre, þat [he who] sonne and se made.
> Lo! þe erthe for heuynesse þat he wolde soffre
> Quakid as a quyk thyng and al to-quasch [split apart] þe roches.
>   (C20.254–57)

Langland, in his final revisions, thinks upon last things, shaking the ground twice in reverence to God's battle with Death. Perhaps the older poet feels closer both to the calamity and to the redemption that follows hard upon.

The macabre drama continues as a Dead Body rises from these fissures and foretells the battle to be fought, averring that no one knows who will win but that an answer will come Sunday, in about three days. Despite the absence of any real suspense, as a Christian would read it, the poem makes the known and inevitable exciting and suspenseful. Action continues as a "cachepol" breaks the thieves' legs but "was no boy so boold Goddes body to touche; / For he was knyʒt and kynges sone" (B18.73–76). The chivalric conceit continues as a "knyʒt," actually the Jew Longinus, in an ungentlemanly act of cowardice attacks the helpless body of the Lord.[1] Appropriately, the blind Jew is un-blinded by Christ's blood, as he weeps, begs for mercy, and is converted. But not striving to forge a moment of Judeo-Christian unity, B and C both amplify the curse against the Jews from Matthew 27:25, "His blood be upon us and our children":

> For youre champion chiualer, chief knyʒt of yow alle,
> ʒilt hym recreaunt [admits defeat] rennyng [galloping (in the joust)], riʒt at Iesus wille.
> For be þis [when this] derknesse ydo [is done], Deeþ worþ [will be] yvenquisshed;
> And ye, lurdaynes [villains], han ylost, for Lif shal haue þe maistrye.
> And youre fraunchyse, þat fre was, fallen is in þraldom [slavery]
> And ye, cherles, and youre children, cheue [prosper] shulle ye neuere,

Ne haue lordshipe in londe, ne no lond tilye,
  But al barayne be and vsurie vsen [practice usury]. (B18.99–106)

This imaginative conceit spun from the short and unique Gospel verse depicts the Jews as treacherous knights, violating the chivalric code. It then morphs into a contemporary European depiction of the Jews as thralls, churls who cannot own land and who resort to usury, which, if not a reality in Langland's England during the long Jewish banishment, always serves as a convenient mode of anti-Judaic rhetoric.

Readers cannot easily correlate this passage with the longing for the conversion of the Jews and Saracens explored above (in B15, C16–17). Three forces concurrently influence the poem at this juncture, revealing the complex ironies inherent in Christian treatment of the Jews in medieval literature. First, the poet immerses himself in the fervor of historical recreation as he generates the emotion that drives this Passion play. Second, Langland discriminates, as medieval authors often do, between the "good Jews" and the bad ones, for Faith, the revered Abraham, paradoxically condemns his own race. Third, with no real Jewish usurers to target in fourteenth-century England, Langland uses the Christ-killing usurious Jew as a symbol for un-Christian practices that provoke his ethical critique throughout *Piers Plowman*. Will himself, in fear from this vision and also of the "false Iewes" (B18.110), falls into a sort of interior vision, though not a formal interior dream, as he descends, with Jesus, "ad inferna" (111), where another drama must play itself out before Christ will vanquish Death and Devil and save humanity. Maybe Will fears that the Jews will condemn him too, and the issue is never resolved; like many aspects of Jewish-Christian relations in medieval texts, these questions remain suspended and unintegrated in the meaning of the poem as a whole. But the poet makes his reformist target nonetheless clear: not merely the absent Jews, but every person within the sound of his voice.

Langland next presents in both versions (B18.110–end; C20.113–end) one of the great set pieces in medieval literature, the Debate of the Four Daughters of God, a scene featured in the late medieval morality play *The Castle of Perseverance*, based on the source text from Psalm 84.11: "Mercy and truth have met each other: justice and peace have kissed." Medieval writers expand this verse into a formal debate between the allegorical characters who hold the fate of humankind in their hands. The straightforward conflict pits two sisters, Righteousness and Truth, who believe that people should be legally condemned for what Adam and Eve did, against two other sisters, Mercy and Peace, who believe redemption possible, since a heroic new adventure, soon to occur, will undo the initial terms of judgment. Lively, at times poignant and at times playful, the debate features both gentle and stern barbs among the sisters. Mercy, who always keeps calm, offers an unsettling but effective explanation of how the scorpion's sting can only be cured with dead scorpion venom. Therefore, since Adam and Eve were tricked, another beguiler must trick the trickster and win life back for humanity. Peace's lover, Love, sends letters authorizing the sisters to ransom humanity, and the exchange continues rather legalistically, as Langland supplements the chivalric imagery of the episode (Peace notes that Jesus jousted well) with some dry legalistic language of documents and "patents" (B18.181–86). After all, in legal matters everything must be done by the book. The entire scene asks readers to ponder the nature of law, which Langland has been doing somewhat despairingly throughout the poem, as for example in the miscarriage of justice in passus 4 when Wrong violates Peace with impunity. The poem now labors in this "debate" to ensure that a grander and more secure justice will forever prevail.[2]

Righteousness rejects this line of argument outright, calling Peace either crazy or drunk. She agrees with Truth that humanity's pain should "be perpetuel and no preiere hem helpe" (B18.199). Readers know who will win this debate and may even feel compassion for the two mean sisters who are "right" but who will lose the argument. Victory in the debate, however, will not guarantee anyone's personal salvation, so neither Will nor his audience can claim safety until they become, as individuals, faithful and penitent. For this reason Will senses the urgency of the moment, aware of himself now in a special place, a redemptive, holy space where divine forces settle cosmic matters. The scene recalls those moments in classical epic when we listen in on happenings on Olympus, as the gods debate the fates of the suffering, ignorant men and women below. Langland offers a glimpse as well of what Chaucer calls "godes privitee," the secret workings of grace that are not recounted in the Gospels but must have occurred behind the scenes during Holy Week in order to permit human salvation. The question of the

Do's, which so long obsessed Will, is at once answered and also replaced by the majesty of God's heroic quest and the redemption it enables.

Peace explains the reasons for this conflict. Humanity had to know damnation in order to comprehend salvation, as she proves with a series of homey and conventional tropes: If there were no night, she asks, how would we know the day? Without woe, how would we know joy? What is peace itself without knowledge of war? (B18.202–16). In C she wonders as well, how would we know color if "alle þe world were whit or swan-whit alle thynges?" (C20.213).

There next arrives, in both B and C, a character called Book, who might be described in sports broadcasting terms as a "color commentator," an expert called on to analyze the action on the field. Embodying all of scripture, Book recounts the history of Christ's birth, the star of Bethlehem, his ministry, and the miracle of Peter walking on water. After reporting the earthquakes that mark Christ's suffering and rip hell open, like all good commentators, Book offers a prediction about today's contest: Jesus wins, and wins big, against Lucifer and breaks the patriarchs out of prison. Confident in this forecast of victory, Book offers to be burned if wrong, acknowledging his authority as worthless unless Jesus comforts humanity, makes his mother proud, and defies the Jews so long as they don't convert (B18.254–59). Truth takes over the commentary from Book as the action begins, and readers return anxiously to watch the epic battle unfold, however foregone the result.

Satan sighs as he sees the onslaught coming, since he has seen "swich [such] a light" before when forced to give up the soul of Lazarus, so now "care and combraunce," he concludes, "is comen to vs alle!" (B18.265–67). Langland in C has been reproducing B almost verbatim, yet here he rallies and adds fourteen lines of Devil details, at once Miltonic and Dantesque:

> Ac arise vp, Ragamoffyn, and areche [fetch] me alle þe barres [sticks]
> That Belial thy beelsyre [grandfather] beet with thy dame [mother],
> And Y shal lette [prevent] this loerd and his liht stoppe.
> Ar [before] we thorw brihtnesse be blente [blinded], go barre we þe ȝates!
> Cheke [fortify] we and cheyne [chain] we and vch a chine [hole] stoppe,

That no liht lepe in at louer [louver] ne at loupe [loophole].
Astarot, hoet [shout] out, and haue out [summon] oure knaues
    [servants],
Coltyng and al his kyn, the ca[rn]el [crenel] to saue.
Brumstoen boylaunt [brimstone boiling] brennyng out cast hit
Al hoet on here hedes þat entrith ney [near] þe walles.
Setteth bowes of brake [crossbows] and brasene gonnes [brass guns],
And sheteth out shot ynow [shoot enough shots] his sheltrom [army]
    to blende [blind].
Set Mahond at þe mangonel [catapult] and mullestones [millstones]
    throweth
[And with] crokes [grappling irons] and kalketrappes [spiked
    balls] encloye [disable their horses] we hem vchone [each one]!
(C20.281–94)

The names of the devils, and the muscular, explosive language of weaponry make this a tour de force of alliterative poetry, on a par with the great battle scenes of *Cleanness* and the *Wars of Alexander*.[3] Langland may be getting to the end of the line in this, C's last revised passus, but he rages here dramatically with this surge of mock epic satire that recalls cantos 21–22 of the *Inferno*, where the playful devils scurry about to harass Dante and Virgil. One cannot imagine Milton's Pandemonium without this scene, one of the sonic and visual gems in *Piers*. The futile energy of heroic failure always excites an audience. And yes, for this moment, as in any proper Miltonic scene, one roots for the devils as the scrappy underdogs.

Lucifer recognizes Christ and warns his mates that no "deueles queyntise [cleverness]" can defeat this lord and his light (B18.274), but he finds comfort in the same a-deal-is-a-deal argument that Truth made: these souls are his, he contends, as per the law, and God will not deprive him of his rights (276–79). Langland amplifies the legal argument in C:

Thus this lord of liht such a lawe made;
And sethe [since] he is so lele a lord, Y leue þat he wol nat
Reuen [deprive] vs of oure riht, sethe resoun hem dampnede
    [damned them].
And sethen we haen ben sesed [have had legal possession] seuene
    thousand wynter,

> And neuere was þera3eyne [any complaint against it] and now wolde
> bigynne,
> Thenne were he vnwrast [untruthful] of his word, þat [he who] wit-
> nesse is of treuthe. (C20.306–11)

The devils' argument, both "true" and "righteous," recalls that made by the stern sisters in the debate, but a purely legalistic claim will not grant anyone victory, because God's will transcends judicial reasoning. Langland has added the devils' special pleading here in C so that readers will perceive just one more time how God's mercy defies logic and law. And perhaps, like all great religious poets, he just wanted to give the Devil his due.

But the spirit of courtesy does not last long, as the devils squander their last remaining bits of credibility and become absurd. Satan wheels around at Lucifer and blames him for using guile to trick Adam and Eve, because that trickery disables the legal argument entitling the devils to the human soul. Their treason, with guile at the root, vitiates their claim (B18.285–91). C expands, explaining exactly what Adam and Eve attained at the Fall. One often hears what the first couple lost, but they gained something as well—the power of knowledge, as Satan, accusing Lucifer, explains: "And byhihtest [you promised] here and hym aftur to knowe / As two godes, with God, bothe goed and ille" (C20.317–18). Many nonreligious readers who study Genesis as epic myth interpret the Fall as no fall at all but rather as a heroic refusal to remain subservient and infantile in Eden, with no labor except picking fruit that someone else has grown and giving names to lions, tigers, and bears, in a state of arrested development, a false, infantilized paradise. In this reading, Eve becomes Prometheus, defying the control of the gods. Langland would never have taken this radical stance, but he recognizes the human ambition to know. And, as Langland sees it, that quest for knowledge, which animates so many aspects of *Piers Plowman*, creates the primal disaster. Since *Piers* rebukes ambition for higher status and any failure to obey the proper chain of command, what modern readers might see as a bold challenge to patriarchal authority in Genesis can never be anything of the sort for Langland. His C-text addition entices readers into thinking him of the Devil's party, but he is not. For as Langland apprehends the story, Knowledge, a seductress, misled Eve and her naïvely obedient husband. They should have resisted her.

Langland, clearly having fun with these devils, expands in C the role of another diabolic figure, Goblin, who takes over some lines from B's character "the Devil." Devil/Goblin saw displays of Jesus's power while he lived, which bodes ill for the devils now that Jesus confronts Death itself. Langland makes a striking revision here concerning Jesus's ministry. God's "body," says this fiend in B, was always busy "to saue men from synne if hemself wolde" (B18.305), while in C Goblin calls God busy, rather, "To lere [teach] men to be lele [loyal] and vch man to louye oþer; / The which lyf and lawe, be hit longe y-vsed [consistently practiced], / Hit shal vndo vs deueles and down bryngen vs alle" (C20.338–40). This stunning emotional intensification highlights the active virtue of loyal love, a warm, sacred force of compassion that Langland evokes whenever he can in the C text. One ought not seek knowledge, like our ambitious first parents and (the poet implies) like every worldly clerk in the English Church, but rather should practice love, the power that the devils fear most. If this mock epic scene anticipates Milton, so too does Langland's moral, psychological understanding of how the incarnation, ministry, death, and resurrection of Christ reverse the human failures of the Fall. This humbling act of divine sacrifice animates the law of human love that spells the devils' doom, however well armed and fortified their realm.

In C Langland makes a strange addition, as Will, sounding much like the poet, comments on Lucifer's lies and the devils' infighting:

> Sethe þat Satan myssaide [berated] thus foule [foully]
> Lucifer for his lesynges [lies], leue Y noen oþer
> Bote [but that] Oure Lord at þe laste [in the final judgment] lyares
>   here rebuke [may rebuke],
> And wyte hem [blame them for] al þe wrechednesse that wrouhte is
>   here on erthe. (C20.350–53)

He then quotes a verse from David's Psalms (5:7) that chastises liars and predicts God will punish them: "Odisti omnes qui operantur iniquitatem; perdes omnes qui loquuntur mendacium [Thou hatest all the workers of iniquity: Thou wilt destroy all that speak a lie]" (C20.356a). Will notices that he has gotten too excited in protecting his readers against lying and has wandered off topic: "(A litel Y ouerleep [digress] for lesynges sake, / That Y ne sygge [say] nat as Y syhe [saw], suynde [in pursuing] my teme!)" (357–58).[4] He adopts here an intimate tone that may clash with the epic strains of the Harrowing story itself. If we allow this conflation of Will and his creator, then we detect here a poignant moment for Langland, who is two-hundred-odd lines away from the end of his life's labor and thus indulges himself in the direct counsel that he must have imagined he earned the right to give. George Economou, in his translation of the C text, renders these verses convincingly into folksy idiom, conveying just this sense of entitlement wrought from life experience: "(I've digressed a bit for the sake of lies, / To call them as I saw them, pursing my theme!" (191).

Back to the action, the breath of Christ (the Son alone but with the force of the Spirit) accomplishes its military mission, in lines that burst with *b* alliteration, then open wide with *w* sounds in a stroke of onomatopoetic triumph for the poet and his God: "And wiþ þat breeþ helle brak wiþ Belialles barres— / For [despite] any wye [soldier] or warde [guard], wide open þe yates" (B18.322–23). Christ now speaks, in B more energetic and muscular, in C more quiet and contemplative:

> So leue it noȝt, Lucifer, ayein þe lawe I fecche hem,
> But by right and by reson raunsone here my liges [ransom my faithful]:
> *Non veni soluere legem set adimplere* [I have not come to destroy the law but to fulfill it; cf. Matt. 5:17)].
> Thow fettest [took] myne in my place ayeins alle reson—
> Falsliche and felonliche [feloniously]; good feiþ me it tauȝte,
> To recouere hem þoruȝ raunsoun, and by no reson ellis,
> So þat [that which] wiþ gile [guile] þow gete, þoruȝ grace it is ywonne [won].
> Thow, Lucifer, in liknesse of a luþer [hateful] addere
> Gete bi gile þyng þat God louede;
> And I, in liknesse of a leode [man], þat Lord am of heuene,
> Graciousliche þi gile haue quyt [repaid]—go gile ayein [against] gile!
> (B18.349–58)

Readers find much to admire here including the feisty *f* alliteration of 352, the oxymoron of gracious guile in the a-verse of 358, and the clipped, tight parallelism of its b-verse, "go gile ayein gyle."

> Christ in C, by contrast, displays much less energy:
> So leue hit nat, Lucifer, aȝeyne þe lawe Y feche here

Eny synfole soule souereynliche by maistrie [simply by absolute
power],
Bote [but rather] thorw riht and thorw resoun raunsome here my
lege:
Non veni soluere legem set adimplere.
So þat with gyle was gete, thorw grace is now ywonne. (C20.393–96)

Though quieter here, in C Langland adds for Christ an exciting new attack on "clergyse," during what Pearsall calls a "magnificent elaboration" of the imagery of wine and drinking of the grapes of wrath.[5] So after Christ in B and C calls the Devil the "doctor of death," in C he continues:

For Y þat am lord of lyf, loue is my drynke,
And for þat drynke today Y deyede, as hit semede.
Ac Y wol drynke of no dische ne of deep clergyse [deep academic
learning],
Bote of comune coppes [common cups], alle Cristene soules;
Ac thy drynke worth [will be] deth and depe helle thy bolle [bowl].
(C20.403–7)

Jesus's preference for drinking from common cups instead of from deep clergy suggests that he comes not to save friars and glamorous prelates, who take the elite path of book learning, but rather the everyday Christian. Clerical readers can only hope their actions will somehow appease God, lest they drink deep hell down with the devils. But if common men and women ever read this passage or had it read to them, their hearts would be comforted by Christ's kingly rhetoric. He sounds much like Shakespeare's Henry V here, who defines the common soldiers as his bloody brothers and promises them eternal life through eternal fame. Shakespeare likely read the following, in fact, in crafting his miraculous king:

For we beþ breþeren of blood, but noȝt in baptisme alle.
Ac alle þat beþ myne hole [whole] breþeren, in blood and in baptisme,
Shul noȝt be dampned to þe deeþ þat is wiþouten ende. (B18.377–79)

All good kings win hearts when they become one in body and blood with their people.

Jesus overrides the prior legal arguments and asserts that he can do as he wishes: "it liþ in my grace [lies in my power of grace] / Wheiþer þei deye or deye noȝt for þat [because] þei diden ille'" (B18.387–88). As in Milton, the show battle yields to its predetermined outcome, defined by God, as Jesus enacts a new legal principle (though a standard medieval maxim) to replace the devils' outdated doctrine of lawful possession. Jesus asserts, "nullum malum impunitum, et nullum bonum irremuneratum [no evil is unpunished and no good unrewarded]," promising that he, unbound by the devils' narrow understanding of legal rights, will temper justice with mercy (C20.433; see also A4.126 and the parallel text in B and C). In both poems God binds Lucifer in chains, and the coward devils, their cause lost, scatter into the nooks and crannies of hell in disgrace, powerless as Jesus leads forth from damnation "which hym luste [whomever he wanted]" and leaves behind to suffer "which hym likede" (C20.449). Peace begins piping, and general joy ensues, with a few clichés about how one appreciates the sun more after rain and how peace feels sweeter after war. The former opponents among the debating sisters then kiss in a glorious moment of sororal bonding (B18.422).

By all narrative and artistic standards, the poem comes to its best possible ending, which Langland preserves unchanged in C:

> Til þe day dawed þise damyseles carolden [sang and danced],
> That men rongen [rang bells] to þe resurexion—and riȝt wiþ þat I wakede,
> And callede Kytte my wif and Calote my doghter:
> "Ariseþ and go reuerenceþ Goddes resurexion,
> And crepeþ [crawl] to þe cros on knees, and kisseþ it for [as] a iuwel!
> For Goddes blissede body it bar [bore] for oure boote [good],
> And it afereþ [frightens] þe fend—for swich is þe myȝte,
> May no grisly goost glide þere it shadweþ [where it (the cross) casts its shadow]!" (B18.426–33)

In this intimate domestic portrait, Will, as he wakes from his dream, perhaps again becomes the poet, William Langland, who wakes from the dream of poetry, calls his wife and daughter (here first mentioned), and leads them to church as a family to worship the cross and take refuge in its protective power. This puts a lovely coda on the chaos and conflict of Will's dream, as husband, wife, and daughter, a triad reflecting all the triads in the poem, but also simply a real family, humble themselves to revere the cross, the jewel that surpasses all the treasures that have lured men and women to sin for thousands of years of history and thousands of lines of poetry. Calm, unity, peace, clarity: all the anxiety of struggling through *Piers Plowman*, as a poet or as a reader, falls away in deference to the quietude of the cross and the comfort of the Christian community.

And then he loses it all.

23

Last Man Plowing

B19 AND C21

Conspectus: The final two passūs of "Piers Plowman" were left untouched by the poet either intentionally or because revision was forestalled by sickness or death. In the manuscripts that witness the C text, these two passūs are almost identical to the ones that end B, differing only in the way that manuscripts, not versions, differ.[1] Thus B and C share but one ending, however much one can speculate about how the poet would have revised.[2] One might contend that the poem should have ended with the family in church in peaceful prayer, just a moment ago in B18, but it does not, and Will and his audience must again return to work. So in the aftermath of the Crucifixion, Conscience tells Will the meaning of Christ's heroic actions, describing him as knight, king, and conqueror. Conscience then expounds upon the events that follow in early Christian history, including the establishment of the Church and the Pentecost. He teaches Will, in a homiletic and teacherly way, the significance of what he has just witnessed, the death, harrowing, and resurrection of the incarnated God, who fought Death in Piers's arms.

After emerging from the vision of Christ's death and resurrection, Will reports that he has written down his dream, in one of the poem's several references to the self-conscious processes of composition and another moment where Langland erases the division between narrator and poet:

> Thus Y wakede and wrot what Y hadde ydremed,
> And dihte me derely [dressed myself well], and dede me to kyrke [took myself to church],
> To here holly [fully] þe masse and to be hoseled [receive communion] aftur. (C21.1–3)

If the last passus ends in peaceful, communal calm with Will's family on the way to church, his next two dreams shatter that serenity. They do not undo God's assurance of grace, the fruit of Christ's victory over Death and Devil, but cosmic justice does not serve Will in the here and now, and over the course of the poem's two concluding passūs he loses much of what he labored for. Perhaps that is why the poet begins, in this moment of personal urgency, by reporting that he wrote down what he dreamed, as if afraid that some unknown, silencing disaster were about to strike, perhaps in fear that he might not dream again. This apparent anxiety compels him to concretize his marvelous experiences as a written chronicle gifted to an unknown future. He has no guarantee that his words will outlast him or ever be heard, and he wants to draw our attention to that contingency while he can. For during mass, as if with no control over events, and with no mention of wife or daughter, Will falls asleep. As his dream begins, he observes a bloody figure, fresh from jousting, and wonders, as readers do as well, whether he sees Jesus or Piers Plowman and who so bloodied him. He questions Conscience, fortunately still nearby, though Will has not seen him since B14/C15:

> In myddes of þe masse, tho men ȝede [went] to offrynge,
> Y ful eftesones aslepe—and sodeynliche me mette
> That Peres þe Plouhman was peynted al blody,
> And cam in with a cros bifore þe comune peple,
> And riht lyke in alle lymes [limbs] to Oure Lord Iesu.
> And thenne calde Y Consience to kenne [teach] me þe sothe:
> "Is this Iesus the ioustare [jouster]," quod Y, "þat Iewes dede to dethe?
> Or hit is Peres þe Plouhman! Who paynted hym so rede?" (C21.4–11)

Conscience says that Christ wore Piers's arms (became man), which prompts Will to wonder about Jesus's various names and ranks, beginning a new quest for knowledge. Evidently, despite the magnificence of Christ's victory in the Harrowing of Hell and the resulting celebration, Will still finds himself puzzled by the traumas of salvation history and so dreams of confronting his conscience for answers.

The terms "knight, king, and conquerour," indicate the various roles that Jesus plays in salvation history, and Will finds himself in another triad discussion, another version of the Do's. As Conscience recounts God's various military exploits, he explains that Christ first vanquished the Jews, and readers cannot escape the tone of religious hatred in the exposition. Their rejection of Jesus, as the Christian poet understood it, leads to a form of slavery for the Jews, who will be "lowe cherles" (C21.35), while the Christians "aren frankeleynes and fre men" (39). But as the rest of the poem will expose in detail, this divide guarantees nothing for Christians, muting any sense of Christian triumphalism. Christ, as king, makes his people "free," but Langland gives these fortunate Christians nothing to gloat about and quickly undermines them in these two final passūs. For the surging armies of Christian sinners that soon swarm the stage will squander their freedom in betraying Christ and so bloodying him over and again. History, as the medieval poet saw it, demands that Langland report the Christian triumph over the Jews, but observation of daily life compels the poet to turn his pen to condemn as well, just as virulently, an ungrateful people who refuse Christ, however they may bear the name of Christians.

Before this disaster occurs, Will needs to know more about Christ and his dutiful accomplishments, and so Conscience trumpets his heroic act in binding Lucifer in irons, in verses that sound more like Hesiod or Shelley, at once classically heroic and Romantic:

> And toek Lucifer the loethliche [hateful], þat lord was of helle,
> And bonde him as he is bounde, with bondes of yre [iron].
> Ho was hardior then he? His herte bloed he shedde
> To make alle folk fre þat folweth his lawe. (C21.56–59)

Conscience reminds Christians that they cannot savor Christ's conquest without conquering sin by putting themselves "to penaunce and to pouerte" and also by allowing themselves to "wilnen and soffren" much woe in the world (C21.67–68). This last complex phrase demands that one must not only suffer but also "desire" and "await expectantly" the suffering, and even "be full of keen desire, yearn" for it (*MED*, s.v. "wilnen," defs. 1a(a), 1b(c), 1a(c)). To display willingly such desire allows Christians to imitate Christ in his longing to joust against Death and Devil. Conscience not only comforts Will with the epic story of salvation but also tacitly rallies him for the personal battles ahead: Death and the Devil succumbed to the powerful Christ, but the frail and incautious human "will" must fight an ongoing battle against them for the entirety of each human life. God enables but does not guarantee salvation, and Christ's heroics exemplify the fortitude that each Christian must marshal against sin.

Conscience then retells the story of the birth of Christ, the three gifts of the Magi (allegorized variously as truth, righteousness, loyalty, and mercy), and recounts his political and military career, his rise, almost Alexander-like, to the status of conqueror, which he attained through "wyles and wyt," for he knew "to conne mony sleythes [how to accomplish many tricks]" (C21.99–100). Jesus, properly for a conqueror, took care of military business through any means possible, fleeing, hiding (from Herod's slaughter presumably), fighting, suffering, and healing until he gathered into his domain, "alle hem þat he fore bledde [everyone for whom he had bled]" (107). Conscience turns to Jesus's further ministry, such as his turning water to wine, allegorized as providing "lawe and lyf-holinesse" (111) to a people who lacked law and were not apt to love their enemies. Such an act proved his divine lineage to his mother and to those around him, and through these means "comsede he Dowel [he undertook to do-well]" (123). Feeding the five thousand, in turn, portrays Dobet.

In this sequence, one might imagine Dobest as the Passion itself, but Conscience depicts it rather as the forgiveness of sin, the act of imagination that Christ devises after he finishes His Father's work. Accordingly, Christ accomplishes Dobest after his ministry, death, and resurrection when he establishes the papacy, the Church on earth, which will bind and unbind God's judgment and administer the pardon of Piers the Plowman:

And when this dede was doen, Dobest he thouhte,
And 3af Peres power, and pardoun he graunted:
To alle manere men, mercy and for3euenesse;

> [To] hym, myhte men to assoyle [wash] of alle manere synnes,
> In couenaunt þat they come and knoleched [acknowledged] to paye
> To Peres pardoun þe Plouhman—*Redde quod debes* [pay what you
>   owe]. (C21.183–88)

The appearance of Will's old friend Dowel may surprise here, if readers have forgotten about that endless search for the ultimate set of definitions, but the return of the triad helps the final two passūs reaffirm the experiential world and details of human social duty. The labor, ministry, and sacrifice of Christ mean nothing to the sinner who cannot find and imitate Dowel. And to "do-well" successfully, when in doubt, one must imitate Christ. Such a suggestion seems conventional and obvious, but this poem has earned the axiom rigorously. Conscience's final words laconically summarize the poem's ethical imperative: *Redde quod debes*, a stark, cold, and simple formulation—simple to say and remember but difficult to actualize. And as it turns out, when the accounts are reviewed, much is owed, perhaps even too much to repay.

The real-time action of salvation history takes over as Will witnesses the Pentecost, during which Conscience commands him to kneel (C21.210). The strange scene that follows recounts the origins of various walks of life, as Will sees Grace, working with Piers and with Conscience, summon the people to distribute skills for their various professions (C21.214–52). Grace gives art to preachers, priests, lawyers, merchants, laborers, masons, painters, astronomers, philosophers, and more in a survey akin to that in the field of folk, a reminder of how all abilities come from God, who provides these treasures, as Grace describes them, as "wepne to fihte with þat wol neuere fayle" (219) in battle against Antichrist. God gives humanity a lot, more perhaps than what *he* owes, increasing the amount that humanity must repay. Grace promotes Piers Plowman to his "procuratour" and his reeve (259), which may seem a demotion for Piers, already identified as Christ himself, but Piers, ever a flexible characterological tool for Langland, plays many roles throughout the poem. Here, being Grace's minister of the doctrine *Redde quod debes* defines the role of the pope, Christ's vicar on earth. Grace finds Piers Plowman, with his vast experience with work and justice, to be just the right person for the job.

Grace supports this new post with some accoutrements, four great oxen to pull Piers's plow (the four Evangelists), and horses as well (the Church Fathers), and two harrows (the Old and New Testaments), as the allegory of the poem returns to the hearty and familiar imagery of the fields (C21.263-74). Piers plants grain, the Cardinal Virtues (Prudence, Temperance, Fortitude, and Justice), into the human soul. Grace explains these virtues as active, social, and communal; all ranks of society must practice forethought, restraint, and patience, fighting for the right, firmly and fearlessly (275-310). Sin soon ravages God's gracious plan, but the poem establishes that God did his job and planted virtuously, with no flaw in design. God gives the farming tools needed, all the inspired books of revelation. Only the depraved human will would refuse these tools and fail to plow the virtuous life. As the farming metaphor continues, the fruits of the fields, when ripe, need to be housed, so Grace instructs Piers to build such a house, the Church itself, called Unity, mortared with Christ's sacrificial blood, roofed with Holy Writ, and administered by the priesthood designated as the haywards (fence wardens, keeping cattle away from crops) in this agrarian conceit (C21.319-36). Langland here redefines work as the spiritual chore of building the Church, which, established on earth after the Incarnation, becomes God's second attempt, a Paradise potentially regained to give humanity another chance. Unity, however, faces the danger that another clever devil in disguise will infiltrate and destroy it. Never naïve about real moral danger, Langland knows the limits of allegory and the frailty of the will.

Jesus the jouster has dispatched the devils, rendering them impotent, so evil finds reinforcements, and this time Jesus will not joust. For humanity, so Will learns, must pay its own debt and fight this battle against sin, fortified with grace, a very good weapon, but in the current military context not overwhelming firepower. If Will thought the Harrowing of Hell and the Debate of the Four Daughters provided the final word about humanity's fate, he, and by extension the human "will" he represents, faces a rude awakening, for an epic battle takes shape, with the outcome this time by no means secure. The *Piers Plowman* universe prepares for war with disaster looming. But no clever devil from hell brings a downfall this time. For the new "fall" is wrought by human agents, as Pride espies Piers's noble labors and gathers a great host to assail Unity (C21.337-57). He has enlisted into this army some unsavory figures, including one Surquidours, the allegorical representation of human arrogance (*MED*, s.v. "surquidrie"); Spille-Loue, a killer of love and presumably enemy of Charity; and Speke-euele-bihynde, a manifestation of gossip, slander, and the terrorizing forces of envy that pit men and women in society against one another. As in the confession of the Seven Deadlies, sin mainly takes the form of social hostility, animal competition, and vicious machination to destroy the happiness of others. No devil is needed this time to bring men and women to ruin. Driven by pride, humanity undoes itself.

The sins enact a plan of intrigue and evil that corrupts the processes of Contrition and Confession and pollutes the purity of penance, without which no one can reform, find forgiveness, or summon the virtue to undo the vicious damage of sin, as Spille-Loue and Speke-euele-bihynde chillingly threaten:

> And Peres berne [barn] worth broke [broken open], and þei þat ben in Vnite
> Shall come oute, and Conscience; and ȝoure [caples tweyne] [two cart horses]
> Confessioun and Contricioun, and ȝoure carte the Bileue [cart of Faith]
> Shal be coloured so queyntly and keuered vnder [perverted with] oure sophistrie,
> That Consience shal nat knowe [be able to distinguish] be Contricioun
> Ne bi Confessioun ho is Cristene or hethene;
> Ne no manere marchaunt þat with moneye deleth [deals in finances]
> Where he wynne with riht, with wrong or with vsure. (C21.346–53)

Sophistry blurs Christian identity, coloring confession "so quaintly" that no one can distinguish Christian from pagan, and merchants will practice usury, the domain of the Jews, undermining the potential for virtuous profit. *Piers* has spoken of universal conversion before, but less as an actual ambition for interfaith dialogue than as an indictment of Christian failings. Here, in a related trope, when Christians fail they essentially become non-Christians—"hethene" or Jews. Conscience knows the strength of Pride's army, senses dire disaster looming, and suggests the Christians retreat into Unity, as the imagery ranges freely from agricultural to military

(C21.358–83). Christians dig a moat, but some sinners defect, since prostitutes do not repent, and assessors (jurymen) and summoners take bribes to join the armies of Pride. Others, however, for fear of evil, weep tears of penance, which, along with the "clannesse [cleanness] of þe comune and clerkes clene lyuynge [pure living]" (C21.382), will sustain the Church in this time of crisis. The battle rages, and the outcome hangs in the balance in this suspenseful episode, with the climactic season finale still to come.

Conscience feels a surge of optimism and starts a communion service for those who have completed the penitential work of *Redde quod debes* (C21.384–98). But pride and sin, not merely allegorical warriors besieging Unity from without, still reside within the hearts of the men and women who have fled into the Church, ostensibly (and ironically) to escape from Pride. With this infiltration, proper order and liturgical sanctity break down, and the hostility Piers faced earlier when trying to get the lazy loafers to plow the half acre now rages again. When a random brewer hears that communion comes with a price, penance and the practice of social justice, he vows that as long as he can sell cheap beer from the same hole as fine ale, he's not going to "hacky [hack around] aftur holiness," telling Conscience to shut up (309–405). Conscience panics to hear this and warns the brewer that he better seek the assistance of the Cardinal Virtues, which prompts another character, an ignorant vicar, to pop up in despair because, as far as he knows, no one cares for the Virtues nor for what Conscience has to say (412–61). The Church, "Unity" itself, does not break down (secure in allegory), but people cannot resist the impulse to defeat rather than to love one another, as was proved in the Confession scenes. Sin satisfies too well and erupts too naturally to be abandoned in favor of some stern virtues and the imaginary profits they promise in some abstract afterlife. Immediate gratification of personal desire easily overwhelms the "will."

As for "cardinals," continues the vicar, punning on the Cardinal Virtues, the only ones he knows are in Rome, dressed in fur and lecherous, and he expects no virtue or sanctity from them (C21.416–30). The pope, for his part, has even made war against fellow Christians, slaying instead of saving people.[3] In contrast to the disastrous pope, says the vicar, Piers the Plowman pains himself to till for all men and women, travailing "for a tretour [criminal] also sore [as arduously] / As for a trewe tydy [upright] man, alle tymes ylyke [equally]" (441–42). "And worschiped be," he continues, "He þat wrouhte [made] all, bothe gode and wicke, / And soffreth [endures] þat synnefole be [exist] til som tyme þat þei repente" (443–44). Piers, as a variable entity, denotes not simply Christ or Peter the first pope but also a merger of the divine and human realms wrought by the Incarnation. His charitable labor on behalf of both the vicious and the virtuous parallels God's patient tolerance of the wicked. While the worldly pope "pileth [pillages] Holi Churche" (445), and "fynde folke to fihte and Cristene bloed to spille" (448), Piers does God's work and serves his community. In the heroic, complex figure of Piers, who has borne much weight in the poem that bears his name, lies the only hope of human reform.

Virtue suffers further perversion as a lord steps up and praises the Spiritus Intellectus, one of the seven gifts of the Holy Spirit sent by God, as Isaiah describes, to fortify and perfect the human will (C21.466; Isaiah 11:2–3). He likely picks up on two references to the related Cardinal Virtues: the vicar's lament that contemporary greed corrupts the Spiritus Prudencie into "gyle" (458), and the brewer's scornful mockery of the Spiritus Iusticie (400) in his defense of his corrupt business practices. The lord selfishly perverts the Spiritus Intellectus into the practical wisdom of keeping an eye on a treacherous reeve who might be stealing from him (462–67). He then comically employs another of the Holy Spirit's gifts (also one of the Cardinal Virtues), Spiritus Fortitudinis, to support his aggression in taking back the profits that the reeve has stolen, "wolle he, null he," to give the money back (467). In this climate of anxious human mistrust, true virtue depends on animal men and women practicing higher arts that temper their primitive, competitive fears and their urge for power and profit. Will took his family to church to revere the cross and to find shelter under its protective shadow. Instead, the dream he slumbers into during the mass exposes how human appetite scorns and debases the sacred gifts of the Holy Spirit and the divine virtues designed by God to inspire and sanctify his people.

Because of the virulence of carnal appetite, as revealed in this dark and bloody dream, the poem moves toward neither transcendence nor resolution but rather to warfare, and like the classical Hindu battle epic the *Bhagavad Gita*, *Piers Plowman* provides powerful if only nebulous answers to its inquisitive warriors. Witnessing Christ's battle with Death inspires a meditative, familial peace that Will enjoys for a mere moment in B18/C20. Now, as human chaos rages, a king appears out of nowhere, promising to rule the commons and to defend Holy Church and the clergy from "cursed men" (C21.470). He promises that as their head, he will also be their "hele [health, prosperity]" (474), vowing also to obey the Spiritus Iusticie in ruling over his people, invoking the final of the Cardinal Virtues mentioned in this passus (477). He pledges finally not to "craue" of his people anything except what his "kynde [his natural right]" requires (479). A cautious Conscience appears to accept the king's rule, but on the condition that he govern "in resoun, riht wel and in treuthe" (481), for in *Piers Plowman* all assertions of authority, however benevolent, meet with healthy skepticism. Conscience stands ever ready to enforce the dictates of virtue and the allegiance to "truth" that must guide all claims to rank and rights of governance. At this precarious moment, without resolution or further debate, the vicar politely departs, beginning his long journey home, and Will does the only thing he really can: he awakens and writes down what he dreamt.

24

Anarchists and Antichrist

B20 AND C22

Conspectus: After that glorious dream of Christ's epic heroism and the militant rebellion of Pride, Will, now awake, confusingly encounters a figure named Need. When Need leaves (though need itself never does), the siege resumes as the forces of Pride and Antichrist lead a dramatic assault against the Church, Unity. In this final passus, and in Will's last opportunity to understand virtue and salvation, Langland provides much anxiety but few answers, as he sets his characters on a new pilgrimage.

Will has written down his last dream, and, having written, he gets hungry, as the stomach, throughout the poem the seat of both appetite and economy, asserts its undeniable power. Will does not know where to eat, but Langland, never at a loss for allegory, turns this moment of hunger into a meeting with a nasty fellow named Need, who greets Will foully and calls him "faytour [deceiver]" (C22.5). Need both asserts his power, for no one can deny essential appetites, and also accuses Will of failing to act in accordance with Spiritus Temperancie (8) as the king and others did in the previous passus, to justify the satisfaction of the basic human need for food and clothing. This accusation puzzles Will and readers as well, all the more so, as Pearsall explains, because neither the king nor anyone justified himself according to the spirit of temperance in that episode.[1] The king's pledge to observe the spirit of justice in not craving anything beyond what his nature demands (C21.479) implies temperance but does not assert the virtue proper as an excuse or justification for his claim to power. But, as Schmidt indicates, Need means here to assert the superiority of temperance over the other three Cardinal Virtues that Piers sows in C21, which too often invite perversion and abuse, as that dream proves (*Parallel-Text* 2.715). So at this moment of confusion for both Will and his readers, Need's references remain nebulous but purposefully provocative. For they blindside and disorient Will, compelling him to study his recent dream and to understand his "needs" in relation to the virtues that Piers plants while establishing the Church. He must determine how to reconcile need with the Virtues while comprehending the primacy of *Spiritus Temperancie*, which Need calls the greatest among them "be ver [by far]" (C22.23). Addressing this topic now appears to have little bearing on the martial epic poised to resume in the next dream, with the armies of Antichrist about to assail Unity. But Holy Church long asserted the basic human need for food, drink, and clothing (A1.12–26), and Langland wants here to revisit those imperatives and to contemplate the frailty of the will one more time, while the enemies gather at the gates and before he rejoins the urgent final battle.

Whatever Will did or did not learn about temperance, Need commences to teach him the truth now. Vulnerability brings no shame, as long as one moderates need with the *Spiritus Temperancie*, superior among the Cardinal Virtues, says Need, because it strengthens the humility of those who suffer want (C22.20–39). Need's compressed alliterative line puts it well: Need "meekens" men, he says, "For Nede maketh needé [the needy] fele nedes louh-herted [need to feel low-hearted]" (C21.37). The stark repetition prods Will, and the readers too, with "need." Will can excuse himself for his animal urges, or at least understand their nature, as long as he does not use "need" as an excuse to justify reckless appetite. Doctrine helps, but examples persuade. Christ displayed vulnerability, Need then explains, and intentionally humbled himself to a wretched level to turn abjection and sorrow into joy. Need concludes by comforting Will that submission to need, according to this divine exemplar, brings no disgrace:

> Forthy be nat abasched to byde [wait patiently; beg][2] and to be nedy,
> Sethe he þat wrouhte [made] al þe worlde was willefolliche [willfully] nedy,

>   Ne neuere [never was there] noen so nedy ne porore [poorer] deyede.
>   (C22.48–50)

This episode, both intensely primal and deeply spiritual, plays a complex and puzzling role in what follows, as the poem nears its conclusion. As the vices assail Unity, Will's awareness of his own frailty and of Christ's willing self-abasement implicitly inform the search for Piers Plowman that begins just as the poem ends. Without this knowledge of the power of need to humble human pretense, Will could never find answers to his questions about virtue and salvation. Langland never states this explicitly, but he certainly depicts "need" as a precondition to whatever knowledge Will attains in his final dream, which now begins (C22.51–52). And, as well, the Need episode reasserts the fragility of the "will" and proves its vulnerability to the upcoming attack.

Will never specifies if he ever found anything to eat, and an empty stomach would compromise the authority of a dream.[3] It seems rather late for us to start cataloging dreams according to Macrobius, but the causality of need and hunger as prelude to the final dream cannot be ignored. Such dreams cannot be interpreted as prophetic, says Macrobius, because they arise from physical and mental events during the day. But such an explanation and dismissal cannot apply to Will's dream of Antichrist, based firmly on an authoritative vision of St. John in the Book of Revelation. So for this final dream Langland brings together the best and the worst of causes, with the bizarre effect of simultaneously authorizing and de-authorizing what he sees. Langland likely intended to create this interpretive tension. For the poet now integrates Will, as a fleshly man bound to Need, into the registers of divine revelation, giving this final dream a dual origin: from God himself in scripture and also from the grumbling human stomach, the poet's two favorite and most authoritative muses.

The dream returns Will dramatically into the epic action, as Antichrist "in mannes fourme" (C22.52) leads Pride and the Sins in battle, ravaging the crop of Truth, assisted by friars whom Antichrist rewards with expensive robes. In the preceding passus Grace prepared humanity for this onslaught by distributing the treasures of wit, craft, scripture, and virtue, but now faithful Christians are outmanned and outgunned, and Antichrist seizes power over everyone except "foles" (74) whom Conscience leads into the safety of Unity, so named because they look foolish from a worldly perspective in refusing the glories offered by Antichrist.[4] Throughout this episode Will remains a witness, while remaining free of the power and allure of the enemy. Langland crafts the scene in this way for dramatic narrative effect, but the poet also implies that the "will," however besieged, must resist this prideful assault and remain detached from it. Otherwise Will could cherish no hope, and nowhere in *Piers Plowman*, except in hell among the devils, does Langland deny his characters hope.

As the armies of evil approach from all sides, a *resistance* movement rallies to the cause of Unity, made up of those

> þat were mylde men and holy, þat no meschief dradden [feared no evil],
> Defyede [defied] alle falsenesse and folke þat hit vsede [practiced it];
> And what kyng þat hem [the sinful folk] confortede, knowynge here gyle [aware of their deceit],
> Thei corsede [cursed], and here consail [council]—were hit [whether it be] clerk or lewed [uneducated]. (C22.65–68)

The good, either educated or uneducated, unite in their resistance to false kings. These mild and holy men, like Noah, often animate sites of destruction. Figures who preserve the integrity of justice, these few virtuous flee, as did Noah's family, into the protective covering of the Church, Unity, as Conscience, chief military strategist here, summons his secret weapon, Kynde, who "cam oute of the planetes" (C22.80) to send forth fevers, coughs, "cardiacles [heart attacks]," cramps, and toothaches (82). Against Pride, Kynde (Nature) wields the weapons of frailty and mortality that bring human presumption to its knees, here embodied in one of Antichrist's prize warriors, "the lord þat lyuede aftur lust" (90), a metonymy for acts of carnal pleasure. In response to Kynde, he futilely summons a knight, Comfort, and then he panics: "'Alarme! Alarme!' quod þat lord, 'vch lyf kepe his owene [every man for himself]!'" (92). In real battle when ranks break, each soldier must secure his own safety. But the comment carries an extra-military aspect, as it highlights the utter weakness of these forces of Antichrist in the face of Kynde, who soundly routs the proud and the seemingly invulnerable.

Emboldened by the tide of battle, Elde and Death, the heaviest artillery, join Kynde and romp over Pride's armies, leveling kings, knights, kaisers, and popes, plus many lovely ladies and their lovers (C22.93–106). This allegorical upheaval reveals sin as the essential human condition, for with no price to pay, one can revel in pleasure, careless of death until Death nears. Death, the most powerful weapon against Pride and Antichrist, can only be defeated by repentance and humility, and so a merciful Conscience ends the assault of Kynde, hoping its violence is sufficient to shock men and women into rejecting pride and becoming "parfyt Cristene" (C22.108). His hopeful act echoes the scene in which Piers calls off Hunger after he sufficiently chastises the laboring folk plowing the half acre. But the mercy backfires as Fortune responds by giving some people long life, which Lechery further graces with the pleasure of Idleness. As Covetousness, armed with Avarice, enters the fray against Conscience, it becomes clear that enlisting Kynde to control Pride has proved as unreliable as employing Hunger to regulate work. The rebellious human will never remains chastised for long.

As Fortune bestows his lecherous longevity among the married and unmarried, a great host gathers against Conscience (C22.110–20). Covetousness, as well, ponders how he can undo Conscience and the Cardinal Virtues, so he rouses pope, prelates, the king's court, justices—essentially everyone who can buy or be bought with temporal power or material goods—to join with Antichrist in the battle (121–39). This strikes readers as an ideal moment for Langland to bring Lady Mede back into the poem, and perhaps she would have appeared in the C text revisions. But here in spirit only, she nonetheless dominates (or corrupts) human relations with greed and self-interest. As the evil forces conquer, Life grows comfortable and goes shopping, dressing in the latest fashions, riding with Pride and praising no virtue (143–51). Life and Fortune then join together, as it were, and give birth to Sloth, who grows up (quickly) to marry Wanhope, daughter of a corrupt juror named Tomme Two-tonge (162). Sloth, however lazy his name might make him, nonetheless actively slings "drede of dispayr [horror of despair]" (164) throughout the battlefield. Elde, stirred by Conscience, steps up as the next champion against Life, who, outmatched, turns and runs to a doctor who "lette [prevent] sholde Elde / And dryue awey Deth with dyaes [remedies] and drogges [drugs]" (173–74). Elde goes straight for the doctor and kills him in three days, an inversion of Christ's three-day triumph over Death. In response, Life decides to eat, drink, and be merry, and so runs to Revel, who displays one very viable response to mortality, however fruitless pure pleasure may be. The poet's unknown personal history aside, Langland may have left this thrilling, heart-pounding passus unrevised simply because he could not possibly improve upon it.

Then a tragedy occurs, though a comic one, as Elde, chasing Life, takes a shortcut over poor Will's head, reducing him to poor *old* Will. Indignant at this assault, Will reproaches Elde for trampling him and receives this response:

> "3e—leue [yeah, I need permission], lordeyne [chump]?" quod he,
>   and leide on me [set upon me] with age,
> And hitte me vnder þe ere—vnnethe [barely] may Ich here.
> He boffeded [buffeted] me aboute þe mouthe and beet out my wang-
>   teeth [back teeth],
> And gyued [crippled] me in gowtes—Y may nat go at large.
> And of þe wo þat Y was ynne my wyf hadde reuthe [pity],
> And wesched wel witterly [wished indeed] þat Y were in heuene.
> For þe lyme [limb] þat she loued me fore, and leef [pleased] was to
>   fele—
> A nyhtes, nameliche, when we naked were—
> Y ne myhte in none manere maken hit at here wille [make it do as she
>   wished],
> So Elde and heo hit hadde forbete [beaten it]. (C22.189–98)

Will has been growing old with *Piers Plowman*; it just hits him now, and neither he nor we can escape. So he becomes desperate and seeks the help of Kynde, who says to run into Unity and there learn to love, a sentiment moderns know from its assertion by another English poet, this time from Liverpool, John Lennon, who six centuries years later claims that "all you need is love." What about clothing and food? asks Will. Forget that, says Kynde: learn to love and lack nothing (210–11). The poem has asserted this transcendental carelessness before: God feeds the birds of the field, so one ought not be overly concerned with life. Will obeys by venturing through Contrition and Confession until he comes to Unity, but he offers no verbal response to Kynde's promise that loyal love alone will clothe and feed him. One of the great unanswered questions in *Piers Plowman* is simply how to eat and be saved at the same time. Will's silence might indicate that he cannot accept what Kynde says about love without relating it to what he has learned about food from Hunger, from Need, and from every other manifestation of the body's frail animality. Convinced or not by Kynde's assurances, he comes into Unity (213), driven either by faith, fear, or the helplessness of sudden old age.

 Meanwhile the battle continues, as Sloth and sixty drunk Irish priests join the fray against Conscience (C22.217–27). So besieged, Unity teeters near collapse. Conscience cries out to Clergy for help, which reveals a great irony: the imperfect priests and prelates themselves have contributed to this disaster, yet only Clergy can come to the rescue. In the final disaster in the poem, the friars exploit this opportunity to enter Unity to administer confession. Everyone knows, or should know at this point, that they will flatter the rich and seek only personal profit, with no intention of providing the heroic succor of spiritual care needed at this critical moment of battle. Dramatically the character Need, who accosted Will earlier in this passus, returns to indict the friars and expose their avarice. He tells Conscience that the friars ought not to be trusted as agents of spiritual healing until they faithfully follow the austerity and poverty they have chosen. Having no guaranteed endowment, the friars will abuse the practice of begging, flattering the riche, says Need, and lying for their own profit, unlike those who labor honestly for their sustenance and then share it with those who beg from true need. Since these friars, continues Need in ironical scorn, supposedly "forsoke the felicite [pleasures] of erthe, / Lat hem be as beggares, or lyue by angeles fode" (240–41), that is, let them be true mendicants, not greedy flatterers, or let them live on angel food, which one imagines is very little, or as Pearsall glosses, "nothing" (*C-text* 372). Conscience nonetheless welcomes them on the condition that they act according to the ideals of their founders, Francis and Dominick, and beg only for necessities while healing the people, learned and "lewed" equally (242–52). Conscience (or Langland) gambles on the restoration of the original intentions of the fraternal orders, however perverted now. But the text never clarifies whether hope for reformation or simply hapless naïveté permits their entry. Conscience, revealing his doubt about the friars' sincerity, berates them by recounting how most everything in creation—heaven, the stars in the sky, even military and religious chains of command—follows definitive structure and numerical count. Everything except the friars. He bases this concept on the Psalm verse praising God as the one "Qui numerat multitudinem stellarum [Who telleth the number of the stars]" (256α; Psalm 146:4). Heaven "haeth euene nombre," and all creation takes part in the divine order, except the mendicants, whose ranks, like those of hell itself, increase "out of nombre!" (269–70), for whatever cannot be counted brings danger and disorder. Envy hears this (273–76) and sends friars to school to study logic, Plato, and Seneca, who teach the doctrine that all goods must be shared in common. The friars, evidently fearing a hellish branding, here shore up their academic authorities to prove that they, as mendicants, can rightly claim the possessions of others. Will calls these doctrines lies, knowing they will license a comprehensive system of greed and exploitation where money changes hands and friars enjoy their profits, but Christian sinners will never "be aschamed in here shryft [confession]" (284) and will never feel the sting of self-confrontation. Accordingly, all who fear such shame can "fle to þe freres" (285) and pay cheaply for absolution. Everybody lies, everybody cheats, and everybody wins.

In the poem's final dramatic sequence that follows, Peace, appointed by Conscience as porter to Unity, tries to keep out Hypocrisy. Too powerful to contain, Hypocrisy wounds many who (only seemed to) follow Conscience and the Cardinal Virtues and thus will now need medical care. Conscience calls an honest doctor, who justly applies remedies and accordingly enacts *Redde quod debes* as his doctrine of penance:

> Consience calde a leche [doctor], þat couthe wel shryue [take confessions],
> Go salue [relieve] tho [those] þat syke [sick] were and thorw synne ywounded.
> Shrift schop scharp salue [crafted a sharp remedy], and made men do penaunse
> For here mysdedes that thei wrouht hadde,
> And þat [made sure that] Peres pardon were ypayd, *redde quod debes*.
> (C22.305-9)

Sir Lyf-to-lyue-in-lecherye, faced with the trauma of needing to fast on a Friday, groans in fear that such penance will kill him, preferring one "frere Flatrere" with his softer remedies (C22.312–16). The friar identifies himself as Sire Penetrans-domos (Penetrate-the-houses) (341), a nasty phrase from St. Paul, who was speaking not of friars, who would not be created for twelve hundred years, but rather of seedy forces of evil that medieval satirical poets apprehend as anticipating the licentious friars.[5] Paul's letter forebodingly predicts dark things to come in the wake of these penetrators:

> Know also this, that, in the last days, shall come dangerous times. Men shall be lovers of themselves, covetous, haughty, proud, blasphemers, disobedient to parents, ungrateful, wicked, without affection, without peace, slanderers, incontinent, unmerciful, without kindness, traitors, stubborn, puffed up, and lovers of pleasures more than of God: Having an appearance indeed of godliness, but denying the power thereof. Now these avoid. For of these sort are they who creep into houses, and lead captive silly women laden with sins, who are led away with divers desires. (2 Timothy 3:1–6)

Just such a man then tries to talk his way into Unity. Peace says no, but Hende-Speche (349), the friar's rhetorical charm, wins him admission, where he applies to his sick patient, Contrition, a healing plaster called "a priué payement" (365).[6]

Without moral self-inspection, and without paying what they really owe to God, sinners pay for the illusion of contrition, confession, and reparation, and the friar's business thrives:

> Thus he goeth and gedereth [gathers], and gloseth [glosses over
>   things] þer he shryueth [where he confesses]—
> Til Contricioun hadde clene forȝete [forgot] to crye and to wepe,
> And wake for his wikkede werkes as he was woned [used to doing]
>   bifore. (C22.369–71)

Sloth and Pride follow the friar into Unity, with the result, as Peace explains, that the folk, so "enchaunted" with the Flatterer's remedies, now "drat [dread] no synne" (C22.379–80). Without fear, that natural prick of the conscience, moral order collapses both in the microcosm of the will and in the larger Christian community, rendering Conscience impotent and Unity useless.

Conscience leaves to become a pilgrim and seek Piers Plowman, who might help the friars to attain a "fyndynge [founding]" (C22.384), an endowment or means of proper support and sustenance, so they can stop flattering sinners and stop opposing him, Conscience, the essential victim of their confession-for-profit enterprise. And he commands Kynde to avenge him against those sinners who enjoy the friar's false medicines, flouting their internal moral urgings. Knowing the rigors of the journey ahead, Conscience asks Kynde for good fortune and health until he finds the elusive Piers Plowman who "Pryude myhte destruye" (381–83), bringing victory to the forces that today were routed in tragic defeat. Will then speaks the last line of the poem, reporting Conscience's final longing: "And sethe [then] he gradde aftur [cried out for] Grace tyl Y gan awake" (387). And the poem ends. No summary, commentary, resolution, nor comfort, and no further report about Will's writing—only the dream of the beginning of a new pilgrimage for Conscience, traveling alone in the hope of finding Piers. Langland fails magnificently, in three versions, to overcome the appetites of sin. So as the cry for Grace echoes in Will's brain, waking him from his final vision, the poet brings his work to a dark, uncertain end and leaves Contrition, the will's capacity for self-knowledge, wounded, sick, and unwilling to labor in healing repentance.

Thus ends the corpus of *Piers Plowman*, and here begins the continued pilgrimage of all readers who remain spellbound by its intensity, by its complexity, by its poetic grace, and by its undaunted exposure of human weakness and sin. Hope alone remains. Continue the journey.

Langland and His Contemporaries

Work with poetic manuscripts and with legal records has revolutionized the study of medieval English literature by identifying some of the scribes who copied major works from the Age of Chaucer and Langland. Ever since Linne Mooney identified Chaucer's scribe as a man named Adam Pinkhurst, thus discovering the "Adam" in the short poem "Chaucer's Wordes unto Adam, His Owne Scriveyn," scholars have learned more about Pinkhurst and a number of other scribes who worked day jobs in the London Guildhall copying legal records.[1] Being so skilled at writing and educated in Latin, these men moonlighted and copied many important manuscripts that contain the canonical vernacular literature of the period. Despite these advances in scribal identification, scholars have very little corresponding knowledge of any sense of community among the poets. And since "Langland" remains a particularly elusive mystery man, one can only hope that more knowledge of scribes and their world may lead back to that poet and to the community of creative artists, if there was one, who composed the major poetry of the late fourteenth century.

Scholars often call Chaucer, John Gower, the *Gawain* Poet, and Langland "Ricardian poets," as being active during Richard II's reign, but besides Chaucer's two references to Gower—one earnest and one playful—in the *Troilus* and in the Man of Law's Introduction in the *Canterbury Tales*, these writers left little evidence of a school of poets sharing work or even displaying awareness of one other's art.[2] The *Gawain* poems, of uncertain dating, are removed in place and language from the work of the London poets. Langland started writing before Chaucer and Gower, but they do not specify if they knew him or his *Piers Plowman*. Unlike the Romantics, the Beats, the Dharma Bums, or even the Elizabethan poets, Middle English authors have left little trace of a community and even less of what they knew, thought, and felt about their contemporaries.

Until History unlocks her secrets on this matter, another way to approach Langland as a medieval author involves taking a less archeological approach and exploring instead the topics and themes that he shares with his contemporaries, near contemporaries, and related writers, both English and Continental. One can productively bring *Piers Plowman* into dynamic dialogue with the major writers and texts that a modern reader would likely encounter or can now seek out after reading *Piers*. Medieval writers across genres, and even oceans away from each other, often recapitulate religious and philosophical themes from a long shared tradition of texts extending back to early Christian and classical authors, including works in the dream vision genre. Further, the English poets, however unaware of one another, respond to the same spiritual, cultural, and political events of fourteenth-century England. So even if the major authors wrote independently, they do not practice complete independence really, and one can read *Piers Plowman* productively in the context of both medieval English and Continental literature. The following brief overview surveys works in the dream vision genre and then comments on the major medieval writers who might be brought into dialogue with *Piers Plowman*, suggesting some strategies for engaging with these authors.

The Dream Vision Genre

Piers Plowman instances one of the most popular literary forms in the Middle Ages, the dream vision. Works in this tradition include the Middle English *Pearl* (ca. 1380s), the *Romance of the Rose*, and the early dream visions of Chaucer (late 1370s to early 1380s) all of which are indebted to an early Christian work and a classical text, Boethius's *Consolation of Philosophy* and Cicero's *Dream of Scipio*. Medieval authors were fascinated with dreams and with dream theory and used the device to transport their narrators into other worlds of imagination.[3] Dreaming, in this medieval genre, is akin to creating literature, for dreams, like poems, cry out for analysis. Thus poets, by having their character sleep and dream, create landscapes, journeys, and dialogues that challenge the understanding of both the dreamer and the audience, who must "read" along together to interpret the dream text. From his schooling Langland would have known well the several categories of dreams from Macrobius's very influential *Commentary on the Dream of Scipio*. In Cicero's work, part of his *De Republica*, the younger Roman general Scipio receives a dream-visit from his famous war-hero grandfather Scipio Africanus, who instructs him in virtue and immortality. Macrobius's detailed commentary on the dream served as a popular school text and offered a model for dream classification and interpretation that later writers adapted, helping them distinguish authoritative dreams, such as Scipio's, from false ones. Langland would have also known Boethius's *Consolation of Philosophy*, a work that Chaucer translated. The *Consolation*, not a dream vision per se, nonetheless offers another central model for the genre because though Boethius appears to be awake, he might as well be dreaming when he gets a visit from his teacher, Lady Philosophy, who, like Africanus in Cicero's work, comes to instruct and guide her troubled charge. The dream vision genre often features such a visit from a dead or divine authority figure, and in *Piers* this visit comes first from Holy Church. These authoritative dream visions in Cicero and Boethius—and many in scripture, both Old and New Testament, and also in classical texts such as the *Aeneid*—supply nothing short of lifesaving or life-changing information.

Protagonists in medieval vernacular poetry, however, seldom receive reliable warnings or divinely sanctioned information. Chaucer, for example, explores this problem in the *Parliament of Fowles* (ca. 1380) and in the *House of Fame* (ca. 1379–80). In these visions, featuring the poet himself as the dreamer, Chaucer ponders the complicated nature of dreams and seems to mock the notion of interpreting them accurately, while realizing the desire that drives them. Langland, perhaps no more confident about unraveling dreams, would certainly agree with Chaucer that dreams reflect the anxious desire for some sort of fulfillment. Each dream in *Piers Plowman* reflects a new psychic outpouring from the "will" as it seeks its object, salvation. For Langland, dreams serve as ongoing and serious attempts to learn how to love and to serve God and neighbor, the very definition of charity. That Holy Church visits him only briefly and leaves him to other less reliable guides for the remainder of the poem in every version illustrates how Langland adapts the genre to reflect doubt about making progress toward knowledge and salvation through dreams. By invoking the genre and then having Will's teacher abandon him, Langland both summons a traditional literary form and undermines it purposefully in the spirit of skepticism, pessimism, and perhaps even occasional despair, as religious and social institutions crumble around Will in both the waking and the dreamt world. Readers will have to determine further to what purposes Langland employs the dream vision genre, for Will dreams almost all the time and even dreams sometimes when dreaming. His visions often create confusion and anger, but they also enrich his faith and bring him hope.

Continental Authors

Guillaume de Lorris (active ca. 1230) and Jean de Meun (1240–1305): *The Romance of the Rose*

The Old French poem *Roman de la Rose* was begun in the mid-thirteenth century by Guillaume de Lorris, who wrote 4,058 lines of an unfinished courtly romance, telling the story of a young allegorical lover appropriately named Amant (the Lover, essentially a man trapped in the participial state of "loving"), as he seeks through impediments, trials, and confrontations to attain the "rose," a young girl whom he falls in love with in the Garden of Delight after being led in by Leisure.[4] Approximately forty years later (1276–80) Jean de Meun expanded the poem into a sprawling, encyclopedic 21,780 lines of further adventure and discourse, including encounters with characters such as Faux Semblant (False Seeming) and La Vieille (the Old Woman), whom Chaucer would transform into his Pardoner and Wife of Bath respectively. Despite great differences in topic and style, Jean's poem ends much like *Piers Plowman* with a violent medieval siege, as the forces of the Lover infiltrate the Castle of Jealousy and Amant seizes the rose in a deeply uncomfortable scene of sexual conquest. Chaucer translated the poem, which is too little studied as a source and influence on Langland. The two poets' adaptation of the dream vision genre, the dreamers' engagements with scores of confusing and conflicting authorities, and their personal traumas as they struggle with the powerful forces of "will" and "reason," link *Piers Plowman* to the *Roman* as complex studies of human appetite and desire. *Piers*, though not a conventional "courtly" love poem, explores love, both human and divine, as one of the most powerful forces in both the human heart and throughout the created universe.

Dante Alighieri (1265–1321)

Not long before Langland's probable date of birth, Dante, the supreme poet of the European Middle Ages, composed the *Divine Comedy*, another major source and influence on Langland. Though not technically a dream vision, the *Comedy* employs the central narrative paradigm that Langland enacts in *Piers*: a man, wandering and confused, receives the gift of divine intervention that sets him on a path of personal, social, and spiritual discovery, as he tries to understand the workings of the universe and fulfill his hopes for salvation. Scholars debate whether English poets outside of Chaucer, who visited Italy, knew Dante's work, and Langland makes no reference or explicit allusion to him. Whether the associations are broad and cultural, wrought from Langland's and Dante's shared sources, or whether *Piers* reveals a debt to the Italian poet is unclear. Influence can be direct and specific or indirect and yet capacious. Both poems feature rigorous trials, combative dialogues, vicious critiques of clerical abuse, and traumatic experiences of alienation. And though Will visits hell only in a theatrical vision of Christ's Harrowing, he nonetheless undergoes the same type of infernal crises of confusion and despair that animate Dante's journey. Both poets master the earthly and the sublime poetic realms like no other writers in the whole of medieval literature, as they summon from deep within themselves, and from deep within the sounds of English and Italian, a new and unique language of divine truth, as best the mortal voice can make and the fleshly ear can hear. In the process they invent patterns of sound and thought neither heard nor imagined before in human language.[5]

English Contemporaries

The Pricke of Conscience, Anonymous (mid-fourteenth century)

The *Pricke of Conscience,* likely the most popular poem of the English Middle Ages, considering its many extant manuscripts, offers a long apocalyptic meditation on the wretchedness of human life, judgment day, the pains of purgatory and hell, and the joys of heaven, designed to *pricke* (incite, awaken, goad) the human conscience by detailing the inherent emptiness of the pleasures of the flesh, the transitory nature of all mundane joys, and the utter frailty of illusory human power. Will's aging and increasing frailty in *Piers* develop similar themes. The *Pricke* even sometimes appears anthologized in the same manuscripts as *Piers Plowman*, indicating that medieval readers associated the two works and copied them together. Like *Piers*, the *Pricke* educates the ignorant who know little Latin by translating passages from Scripture, the Church Fathers, and other authorities so that they may reform in the hope of receiving mercy and grace. But readers will want to compare the poems' styles and teacherly methods, since the *Pricke* is direct, harsh, and brutal in its depiction of human filth and decay, and just as rhetorically enflamed in its depiction of the joys of heaven. Because of its length and the surface simplicity of its four-beat rhyming couplets, the *Pricke* will never rival *Pearl* nor *Piers* as poetry, but it cannot be rivalled as a witness to the authentic experience of piety, psychology, doctrine, and literary production in the English Middle Ages.[6]

Geoffrey Chaucer (ca. 1345–1400)

Chaucer, the premier English poet of the age, stands as the most likely author to be compared to Langland in class, in scholarship, and in any community of readers of medieval literature. Chaucer may have read Langland, but he makes no explicit reference to him beyond his portrait of the humble, virtuous plowman in the General Prologue, which might be an homage to *Piers Plowman* or could just as well be a conventional image. As a courtier, a diplomat, a servant to the two kings, a prominent London citizen, and a Customs official, Chaucer lived at the center of both poetry and politics in fourteenth-century England. History leaves a record of his life that is, to date, lacking for Langland. And yet we can deduce from their poetry that both were men of profound learning and keen insight into human behavior who shared a great concern for the moral decay and institutional failures they witnessed in the world around them. One sees these shared concerns when comparing the *Prologue* of *Piers* to the General Prologue of the *Canterbury Tales*. On the surface it appears that Langland viciously indicts the criminal sinners of his world, whereas, by contrast, a kindly, curious, and seemingly tolerant Chaucer draws less critical portraits of the various members of his society. Chaucer's methods of critique and even condemnation work less directly though no less trenchantly than Langland's. Chaucer depicts himself as a gentle reporter, a listener, to whom the various pilgrims reveal themselves. Langland's Will, rather, roams as an alienated, usually rough-clad, often bitter, rambler. Despite this dramatic difference in self-characterization, both poets betray the reformist spirit of their age as deeply moral Christian writers committed to religious and social change. In the opinion of many readers, Chaucer does not explicitly engage with contemporary events such as the Peasants' Revolt, the Statutes of Laborers, and with Wycliffite doctrine to the extent that Langland does. But this distinction may be overstated, and readers can discern in Chaucer, particularly in his ecclesiastical satire, a serious engagement with fourteenth-century political and religious history throughout the *Canterbury Tales*, however starkly his persona differs from Langland's. Beyond the *Tales* and the early Dream Visions, Chaucer also composed Classical epic in his *Troilus and Criseyde*, a mode and genre seemingly alien to the world of *Piers Plowman*. Langland crafts his own form of epic, with plenty of warfare and love as well, as he recounts the many battles waged over the fate of the human soul and explores the heroic power of love, both human and divine, in the epic struggle for salvation. And in their respective "epics" both poets explore virtue and the struggle for human self-governance. For these and for many other reasons, including the poets' shared propensity for bawdiness and theatrical comedy, comparative study of Chaucer and Langland continues to deepen our appreciation and understanding of both writers and of their age.[7]

John Gower (ca. 1330–1408)

If *Piers Plowman*, as poem and character, was appropriated by forces in the Peasants' Revolt as a populist rallying cry and as a heroic, imaginary leader of the forces of equity, then John Gower's Latin work, the *Visio Anglie* (a dream vision like *Piers*), occupies an opposite historical position, for it condemns the Revolt as a disgusting instance of animalistic disorder by an unruly mob that did not know its rightful place. Gower's work thus provides what is best described as the royalist or aristocratic perspective on events, offering a fascinating antithesis to *Piers Plowman*. The *Visio* serves as the first chapter, retroactively added, of Gower's long

Latin poem on the state of fallen humanity, the *Vox Clamantis* (1377–1381: the "voice of one crying"). Gower bookended his poem with another historical study of the fall of Richard II, the *Cronica triperitta*. As John Carlson explains in his edition of these two Latin texts, Gower considered his entire work as a study of the "varied misfortunes that befell England in the reign of Richard II" (7). Carlson characterizes the *Vox* as a study of the "failings and, concomitantly, the ideal" behavior that should be practiced by "clergy, commons, king and lords" (4). In his *Troilus*, Chaucer famously christens his friend "moral Gower" (Book V, 1856), no doubt because of the comprehensive understanding of human sin displayed throughout Gower's works. But the term may keep the understudied Gower in Chaucer's shadow, rendering him to modern minds as somewhat "establishment," both religiously and politically in comparison to a radical Langland or a playfully anti-authoritarian Chaucer. Gower's major English work, the *Confessio Amantis*, (1386–1393) a vast collection of tales—classical, ancient, folkloric, and romance—appears, in its elegant manners, royal dedications (first to Richard and then to Henry of Lancaster), and its literary self-consciousness as quite remote from the "real world" of *Piers Plowman*, but first impressions can mislead. The *Confessio*, a dream vision like *Piers*, depicts an allegorical everyman, not "Will" but "Amant," the "Lover," who receives instruction not from Holy Church but from Venus, in a series of narrative illustrations of each of the Seven Deadly Sins, designed to cure him of his lovesickness. The *Confessio* provides a marvelous foil for *Piers*, as it approaches the same problems of human self-governance and the persistence of willfulness but does so by constructing a narrative architectonics that demands complex critical unraveling. Gower's voices and narrative discourses, rendered in "tales," inspire comparison to Langland's many interlocutors and their endless speeches and tangents. "Will," as struggling student and dreamer trapped in desire, can be compared to Gower's "Amans," also bound allegorically to his appetites. One might think that Gower's literary saturation in the classical and folkloric, and his personal role as a prince-pleaser, might render him forever alien to the (supposedly) gritty and demotic Langland and his poem of social justice. More comparative study will likely animate a greater critical understanding of these seemingly disparate figures in Ricardian Literature.[8]

The *Gawain* Poet (active ca. 1380–1400)

Four marvelously elegant, mostly alliterative Northwest Midland poems have come down to history in a unique English manuscript (Cotton Nerto Ax), likely originating in Cheshire, in diverse genres and in a dialect that Chaucer mocks as obscure with the Parson's dismissive assertion that as a Southern man, he cannot "rum, ram, ruf by lettre" (*CT* X 43).[9] Little is known of the poet outside of what might be deduced from the poems, so we have even less documented evidence for him than for a proposed William Langland. John Bowers, noting that establishing a "Life of the Author" is bound to be "highly speculative," deduces from the poems a potential career and background that reflect his culture, learning, and possible positions in courtly society (*Gawain Poet*, 1–13). The poems of the *Gawain* manuscript reveal an aristocratic sophistication and courtly ethos that seem, on the surface, removed from the street world of *Piers*. Transcending this deceptive impression reveals that each poem merits complex comparison to Langland's poem. *Pearl* is written in iambic tetrameter, in complex stanza form, heavily alliterated but not actually in alliterative lines. Like *Piers* a dream vision, though unlike *Piers* tightly crafted, this elegant gem of a poem, reflects in shape its editorial name and central imagery of matchless, flawless perfection. It shares with *Piers* the theme of education, as the Pearl Dreamer, a man quite like Will, struggles to understand the theological discourses and the personal story of the "Pearl Maiden." This figure, likely the dreamer's dead daughter, appears to him in his sleep and, like Holy Church, provides consoling doctrine to her grieving, distraught father, whom she never treats, however, with filial piety or affection. The finely wrought *Pearl* invites comparison to the sprawling, explosive *Piers* and reveals Langland's complex adaptation of the dream vision paradigm. Both poems ask what humanity can grasp about grace and mercy while still struggling, trapped in flesh and fallen in ignorance.

Cleanness, sometimes called Purity, offers an assortment of Biblical exempla, with homiletic exposition, including stories of the Flood, Sodom and Gomorrah, Nebuchadnezzar's assault on Jerusalem, and Balthazar's Feast, though it also recounts the "Parable of the Wedding Feast" from Matthew and a sanitary version of the birth of Christ. The poem revels in violence and like *Piers* explores the themes of justice and mercy. Both texts wonder what prevents God from simply destroying and damning humanity for sin, and in Cleanness readers struggle to discern evidence of grace in the blood and rubble of divinely marshalled slaughter. *Patience* retells the biblical book of Jonah, a complex study of the difficult virtue of "patience" and of the pride that impedes it, themes again central to Piers. The Arthurian chivalric romance *Sir Gawain and the Green Knight*, the best known poem of the four, seems in genre most remote from *Piers*. However, *Piers* often employs chivalric imagery, such as in its depiction of the human soul, Anima, as a courtly lady living in the Castle of Caro, and also in its elaborate depiction of Jesus as a knight, king, and conqueror, jousting against Death. *Piers* also explores knighthood, kingly responsibility, and the stubborn frailty of human flesh with its tendency to sin. Langland's poem thus parallels the themes of *Gawain*, in which an innocent, idealistic young man learns the weakness of his impulses to virtue and the strength of his weaknesses to sin. Perhaps most dramatically, both poems explore the concept of "truth," as both a human responsibility and divine force of love and justice—easy to talk about but difficult to attain.[10]

Julian of Norwich (ca. 1342–ca. 1416)

Julian of Norwich, a fourteenth-century anchorite and the first attested woman writer in English, famously experienced miraculous divine visitations, leading her to compose her elaborate meditations upon Christ, *A Vision Showed to a Devout Woman*, and *A Revelation of Love*. Her works, like *Piers*, explore the power of God's love in mystical visions, full of scenes and images emerging from scripture, but also arising from the intimate experience of the presence of God in her mind and heart. Her mode of expressing theology not systematically but impressionistically compares to that of Langland, for he too scatters, and perhaps even hides, his beliefs in various conflicting discourses throughout the poem. Both authors work for their revelations and make their readers work as well. Reading Julian and seeing how she engages the divine presence can help readers to appreciate the mystical aspects of *Piers*, serving as a counter balance to the tendency to read the poem primarily as a reformist document and an exhortation to social justice.[11]

Wycliffite Writings (late fourteenth–early fifteenth century)

Tracing the relationships among Langland's poem, the so-called Lollard movement of religious reform, and the body of Pre-Reformation texts often called "Wycliffite writings" after the Oxford theologian John Wyclif (ca. 1324–1384), provides one of the great challenges in *Piers Plowman* studies. The complex question of how poem and history relate confounds audiences, new and old, but in an initial inquiry, readers can try, as they work through the poem, to determine how *Piers Plowman* relates to the various doctrinal, satirical, sermonic, theological and institutional movements of the late fourteenth and early fifteenth centuries.[12] To confront this issue means seeking Langland in his own time and locating him in the vast continuum of European religious history leading to the Protestant Reformation. *Piers* inevitably reflects its time, a period yeasty with critique and conflict over the proper manifestation of God's church on earth. Like Chaucer, Langland wrote satire and composed some of the most virulent anti-clerical material in English, and in this way *Piers Plowman* participates in the historical and religious reform movements contemporary to it. But poetry does not function like the doctrinal and theological texts produced by the Wycliffites and Lollards, documents that often propose particular institutional reforms and challenge orthodox Catholic beliefs. David Lawton poses a provocative question that encapsulates the issue, wondering whether Langland had Lollard sympathies or the "Lollards had Langlandian sympathies" ("Lollardy and the *Piers Plowman* Tradition" 793). That is, did the poet express the doctrines of the reformers, or did they learn about injustice and corruption from the work of the poet? The answer lies likely in a complex combination of the two, too complex to be unraveled definitively but significant enough to demand a reader's vigilant engagement. *Piers Plowman* also inspired a series of religious and political satires, poems grouped conveniently as the "*Piers Plowman* Tradition," employing the imagery and iconography of the poem to expose clerical evil.[13]

Margery Kempe (ca. 1373–ca. 1438)

The Book of Margery Kempe is the extraordinary autobiography of a late fourteenth-century woman, mother of fourteen children, who either composed or narrated an account of her frequent, passionate, and intimate visitations from Jesus, guiding her to become chaste and to experience the humanity of Christ. Unlike Julian, whom she visited, Margery never adopts an anchoritic life but rather travels, journeying to Rome and to the Holy Land, appearing in inquisitions before church leaders, including the Archbishop of York, and venturing widely through the landscape of medieval Europe, both strengthened and tortured by her frequent visions and by her endless tears. Her real-life experiences are akin to Will's encounters in his dreams, as he too confronts various authorities and also receives mystical visions of the incarnated Christ, sometimes manifested in the person of Piers Plowman. Scholars ponder the barriers between literary craft and personal emotion in Margery's story, a window into medieval Christian piety and the life a woman, wife, and mother, who seeks, like Will, to discover what it means to love and serve God.[14]

Appendix 1

PERSONS, PERSONIFICATIONS, AND ALLEGORIZINGS IN *PIERS PLOWMAN*

Originally this appendix was to be titled "Characters in *Piers Plowman*," which intriguingly entailed determining who or what qualified as a *character* as opposed to a *concept*. Although the list ultimately expanded, even encompassing comestibles, the character-versus-concept question remains central to an understanding of *Piers Plowman*, for Langland often maintains an uneasy border between the two. Not every mention of "reason" or "conscience" evidences a dramatic character per se, and the convenience of capitalization in modern editions (which is itself by no means consistent or uniform) does not necessarily reflect how Langland and the poem's medieval audiences conceived of these references. Nor do such uppercase initials reflect the medieval transmission of the poem, for manuscripts occasionally spelled names with capitals, but not consistently or according to any standard. And although we cannot always determine the status of each iteration of a concept or character, the struggle to do so becomes a dynamic part of the complex act of reading. One learns much, in fact, when contemplating the gray areas between abstract idea and fully actualized allegorical character.

Further, on the grand stage of *Piers Plowman*, characters come and go. Some are unique; some are added in B, yet not retained in C; and since B and C are double the size of A, they present many characters inherently new to the poem. Accordingly, these listings provide a line reference to each character's first appearance in each version, indicate if Langland does not retain that character in B and/or C, and draw attention to glaring absences. The short expositions sketch for each figure the dramatic roles they play in the poem and their function in Will's journey, and note if they undergo major transformation from version to version, such as Haukin the Active Man being reduced in the C text to Activa Vita and Anima in B becoming Liberum Arbitrium. Readers will want to pursue the characters' names further in the *Middle English Dictionary* (*MED*) throughout their reading of *Piers*. Definitions of such entities as Conscience and Truth demand involved linguistic and literary study with the *MED* definitions as a guide. Not every figure here receives critical discussion in the Narrative Reading Guide, for this list is not designed to correspond to the book's text but rather to serve as a tool for students of the poem itself, as they encounter complex, strange, and often ambiguous entities in Langland's landscape. Readers also can use this appendix in conjunction with the book's index to find page references and learn more about the characters that receive critical analysis in the Narrative Reading Guide.

The entries here use the spelling of the first instance in the first version—which may be only the first variant of many—and then offer a Modern English translation in brackets for assured clarity. The exposition sections, when making a cross-reference, use modern spellings for characters who obviously have clear Modern English associations and still exist in common language, such as Reason, Envy, Gluttony, and Simony. In both heading and exposition, for characters unique either to the historical culture or to the poem, the name is presented as the ingenious Langland has adapted or created it, as printed in Schmidt's edition. This applies especially to the exotic, epithetic, sentence-long names that Langland invents, for example, for Piers's wife and children.[1]

Concerning the standards of inclusion, the listings omit common nouns referring to the occasional brewer, baker, lawyer, or vicar who might appear or pipe up in the visionary landscape, unless that entity expands into a full-fledged character or constitutes a personification. So the list includes only those with an extended speaking part, whose actions effect change in the actual narrative. This makes the appendix more a dramatis personae than a "persons and places" list, because many editions already identify historical and biblical figures (see Schmidt's "List of Proper Names," *Parallel-Text* 2.916–22). So figures mentioned in the poem such as Adam and Eve, Job, Mary Magdalene, St. Paul, Solomon, Saul, Dominick, Anthony, and doubtless dozens more, do not appear here when they are alluded to or, as authors, quoted. However, for example, when Abraham as Faith and Moses as Hope physically enter the stage, they become characters in the poem rather than distant biblical exemplars and therefore appear in the list.

If a concept plays an active part in the allegorical landscape unique to the poem, such a "character" appears here as well, though such entities do not speak. For example, Matrimony, Continence, and Maidenhood as three fruits on the Tree of Charity are included (B16.67–72), and so too the spiritual foods that Langland makes out of Psalm verses, such as a dish called "Beati quorum" in the Dinner Party scene (B13, C15). And when the Spiritus Sanctus speaks in Gabriel's mouth in a vision (B16.90), both Spirit and Gabriel function as actual characters in the poem and not just as biblical allusions.

Some characters appear and then reappear under a new identity. Truth—certainly God and the object of the folk's pilgrimage in the *visio*—later becomes a female figure, one of the Four Daughters of God in the debate over the human soul in B18 and C20. False, likewise, who appears as part of the armies of Pride and Antichrist, may or may not be the same character poised to marry Mede in passus 1. Life engages in battle with Death in the episode of Christ's crucifixion and resurrection, but Life appears again at the end of the poem as a happy-go-lucky fellow and the lover of Fortune. In general, Langland makes no effort to maintain any formal consistency but rather summons whichever allegorical figure best serves the local events. He does not craft a tightly bound dramatic universe as in a play, and yet he always performs theater. Because of these complexities, readers may differ in imagining how to construe the concept of "character" in *Piers Plowman*. This list should provoke debate about what actually constitutes a character and should facilitate study of the sometimes mystifying personae that, in various guises, cross the stage of this fantastical poem.[2]

Abraham (B16.173; C18.183). The biblical patriarch Abraham, here appearing as an embodiment of faith, beginning Will's education in the three Theological Virtues, Faith, Hope, and Charity, and explaining the mysteries of the Trinity.

Actiua Vita [Activa Vita; Active Life] (B13.225; C15.195). A character, specifically named Haukin the Active Man in B, who represents the inherent difficulties of living without sin in an "active" life. His role is drastically reduced in the C text as his "confession" is parceled out to the various sinners in the formal confessions of the Seven Deadly Sins in C6–7.

Agite penitenciam [Do penance] (B13.48; C15.56). Name of the sour bread that Scripture serves Will and Patience in the Dinner Party scene. See Matthew 3:2.

Ambrose (B19.271; C21.270). St. Ambrose, here specifically manifested as one of the four horses that harrow the land the oxen (Evangelists) plow.

Anima [Soul] (B15.23; not in C). The personification of the soul, transformed in C into the character Liberum Arbitrium. While "soul" and "free will" appear to be different entities, these characters share many self-descriptions as manifestations of human sense and will, including desire (Animus) and knowledge (Mens), plus Memoria, Racio, Sensus, Conscience, Amor, and Spiritus. C adds the component of free will when the character "does or does not do God's will" (C16.191–92).

Antecrist [Antichrist] (B19.220; C21.220). The biblical character from the book of Revelation and leader of the armies of Pride that besiege the Church, Unity, with uncertain results in the finale of the poem.

Astarot [Astaroth] (B18.405; C20.447). A diabolic character, one of several in a pandemonium, in Will's vision of the Harrowing of Hell, depicted as hiding with other devils in a corner when Christ comes.

Austyn [Augustine] (B19.271; C21.270). St. Augustine of Hippo, revered doctor of the Church and model in his *Confessions* of a degenerate life redeemed; here specifically manifested as one of the four horses that harrow the land the oxen (Evangelists) plow.

Beati quorum [Blessed are those] (B13.52; not in C). Food made metaphorically from bits of Psalm 31:1, served at the Dinner Party.

Beatus virres [Blessed is the man] (B13.52; not in C). A cook who prepares a dish of "Beati quorum," served at the Dinner Party. Langland draws the name from Psalm 31:2 and has put an English possessive ending upon *vir*.

Beleue-so-oþer-þou-best-not-sauid [Believe-so-otherwise-you-will-not-be-saved] (A6.76; B5.589; C7.235). Apparently an adaptation of the First Commandment, allegorized as the buttresses of the Tower of Truth by Piers Plowman as he directs the folk on their pilgrimage.

Belial (B18.322; C20.282). A diabolic character, one of several in a pandemonium, in Will's vision of the Harrowing of Hell. He is mentioned as keeper of the gates of hell, "Belialles barres" (C20.364).

Bere-no-fals-wytnesse [Bear-no-false-witness] (A6.67; B5.580; C7.226). The Ninth Commandment allegorized as a hill, mound, or barrow that the folk must turn at on the road to Truth as instructed by Piers Plowman.

Beþ-buxum-of-speche [Be-obedient-in-speech] (A6.53; B5.566; not in C). Though not explicitly one of the Ten Commandments, an allegorical brook that may obliquely represent the First Commandment as it takes its place among several depicted as physical markers on the road to Truth. It may also represent Christ's injunctions to love God and to love one's neighbor, recounted in the preceding lines.

Boke [Book] (B18.230; C20.239). Personification of the books of scripture, who appears between the Debate of the Four Daughters of God and the Harrowing of Hell to guarantee Christ's victory over Death and Devil, adding condemnation of the Jews if they fail to believe.

Byde-wel-þe-bet-may-þou-spede [Pray-well-the-better-you-may-fare] (A6.83; B5.592; C7.239). An allegorized bridge over the moat of Mercy that the folk must cross on the road to Truth as instructed by Piers Plowman.

Calote (B18.428; C20.472). Will's daughter, mentioned along with his wife Kytte, accompanying him to church to revere the cross after Will wakes from his vision of the Harrowing of Hell.

Caro [Flesh] (A10.38; B9.49; not in C). Name of the castle that Nature (Kynde) makes to house the soul in Wit's chivalric conceit.

Catoun [Cato] (A4.17; B4.17; C4.17). The Roman philosopher Cato the Elder, here specifically manifested as a loyal knave of the character Reason.

Charite (1) [Charity] (B14.100; not in C). The virtue personified as God's chamberlain in a conceit offered by Patience in answer to Haukin's question about where charity dwells.

Charity (2). See **Samaritan**.

Clergie [Clergy] (A11.105; B10.150; C11.93). Cousin of Study and husband of Scripture, a representation of both the clergy and their art of learning. Clergy's castle, housing his sons, the seven liberal arts, is tended by the "lord of lif" (B13.121; not in C). Un-personified, clergy also functions throughout *Piers* as the practice, vocation, and art of academic learning. While his role in salvation is often questioned if not accompanied by virtue, he is also the embodiment of religious authority, active in the king's council and significant for the strengthening of power, both spiritual and political. Later "clergy" frequently comes to mean simply "learning" and an educated class of clerics for whom academic privilege does not guarantee but rather hinders salvation.

Confort [Comfort] (B20.91; C22.91). A knight called upon for succor in the heat of battle by the "lord þat lyueþ after likyng of body."

Concupiscencia Carnis [Desire of the Flesh] (B11.13; C11.174). One of two fair damsels, along with Coueitise of Eiȝes, whom Fortune introduces to Will.

Confession (B19.334; C21.333). The sacrament of confession, here manifested with Contrition as one of two horses to draw the cart of Christianity in which Piers Plowman will bring in the sheaves, harvesting the souls of the saved.

Consience [Conscience] (A2.103; B2.139; C prologue 95). A powerful manifestation of moral rectitude throughout the poem. Often functioning as Will's inner voice, in constant dialogue with him regarding honor, duty, and labor, Conscience first appears in the C-text prologue, though not introduced until passus 2 in the A and B texts, at which juncture, in all versions, he refuses to marry Lady Mede.

Contemplacion [Contemplation] (C7.304). Added in C alone, a character who pledges endless devotion to Piers Plowman as he leads the field of folk on the pilgrimage to truth.

Continence (B16.68; as Wydwehode, C18.86). One of the three fruits on the Tree of Charity tended by Piers Plowman, signifying the chaste life of the widowed, growing higher on the tree than Matrimony but below Maidenhood/Virginity.

Contricion [Contrition] (B19.334; C21.333). With Confession, one of two horses to draw the cart of Christianity in which Piers Plowman will bring in the sheaves, harvesting the souls of the saved. Contrition appears also as a personification of one element of Confession, who is revealed to be sick and in need of healing during the siege of Unity (B20.317; C22.317).

Cotidian [Quotidian] (A12.84). Incarnation of a severe, potentially deadly fever, and one of the companions of the character Fever in the unique final passus of the A text.

Coueite-nouȝt-menis-catel-ne-here-wyues-ne-none-of-here-seruauntis-þat-noiȝe-hem-miȝte [Covet-not-men's-property-nor-their-wives-nor-any-of-their-servants-that-you-might-bring-them-harm] (A6.60–61; B5.573–74; C7.219–20). The Tenth Commandment allegorized as a croft or small farm that the folk must encounter on the road to Truth as instructed by Piers Plowman.

Coueitise of Eiȝes [Covetousness of the Eyes] (B11.14; C11.175). One of two fair damsels, along with Concupiscencia carnis, whom Fortune introduces to Will.

Coueitise [Covetousness] (A2.62; B2.86; C2.90). An important figure in all the economies of *Piers*, both as one of the Seven Deadly Sins (Greed) and as a constant manifestation of the appetite for wealth and advantage. The nemesis of those who work hard and attempt to lead a virtuous Christian life, he appears also as one of the mock cardinals who will serve Antichrist when Pride becomes pope (B19.225; C21.225). In the wedding charter of Mede and False, "Coueitise" is specified as the kingdom or county in which the couple will live and presumably hold sway (A2.62; B2.86; C2.90).

Craft (B19.258; C21.257). Ability, know-how of any kind. While Craft is used widely in the poem to indicate the professions and arts that should observe the dictates of Charity, here Grace tells Piers Plowman to make Craft his steward when he crowns Conscience king. That is, when the Church is established on earth after the Pentecost, Craft will dutifully and virtuously feed the people.

Cristendom [Christendom] (B19.333; C21.332). Christianity, metaphorized here as the cart in which Piers Plowman will bring in the sheaves.

þe cros [The Cross] (B19.324; C21.323). The metaphorized timber that Grace gives to Piers Plowman to build Unity. This figure may simply be a sacred synecdoche and not a form of personification. Grace includes with this timber Christ's crown of thorns as well. See also Holy Writ (2) and Mercy (3).

Cyvuyle [Civil Law] (A2.54; B2.63; C2.67). A character at Mede's wedding and a close companion of Simony. Named for the body of "civil law" as distinguished from canon law and common law, he here represents the clergy's ability to undermine justice by manipulating and abusing legal practices governing ecclesiastical lands and the treatment of tenants.

Dame Studie [Dame Study] (A11.1; B10.1; C11.1). Personification of book learning, including the composition of scripture but also various fields of technical study and craft such as carpentry. Wife of Wit and cousin of Clergy, Study reprimands her husband for wasting time with Will and then takes over his instruction, finally passing him off to Clergy.

Dame Werche-whanne-tyme-is [Dame Work-when-it's-time-to] (A7.70; B6.78; C8.80). Piers's wife as Langland introduces her when the plowman decides to depart on spiritual pilgrimage. Her name exemplifies laboring dutifully while honoring God by observing holy days.

dede body [Dead Body] (B18.64; C20.66). A haunting character that arises from the dead to explain Christ's impending resurrection. This moment, likely based on Matthew 27:51–53, displays Langland's art of creating characters from elements in the fictive, though ultimately scriptural, dreamscape.

Deeþ [Death] (B18.29; C20.28). Obviously a concept and human reality present throughout the poem, but here depicted as a chivalric force in combat with Life—a manifestation of Christ's battle to win the human soul. See also his role in the unique final passus 12 of the A text, where he companions Fever and Sickness (A12.64).

Deuel [Devil] (B18.294; C20.324). A diabolic character, one of several in a pandemonium, in Will's vision of the Harrowing of Hell. The phrase "þe devel" in this episode may refer either to him or to one of the prior speakers such as Satan or Lucifer.

Dia perseuerans [potion of endurance] (B13.49; C15.57). Name of the drink that Scripture serves to Will and Patience at the Dinner Party. Some manuscripts read "diu perseuerans" [long suffering], echoing Matthew 10:22.

Dixi; Confitebor tibi [I have said; I will confess to you] (B13.54; not in C). Two ingredients in a dish made metaphorically from bits of Psalm 31:5, served at the Dinner Party.

Do-riȝt-so-or-þi-damme-shal-þe-bete [Do-just-so-or-your-mother-will-beat-you] (A7.71; B6.79; C8.81). The daughter of Piers Plowman, whose name bespeaks the virtues of obedience and accountability.

Appendix 1: Persons, Personifications, and Allegorizings • 291

Dobest [Do Best] (A9.69; B8.78; C10.76). Third in a triad of elusive characters whom Will seeks throughout *Piers Plowman*: the ultimate, superlative virtue.

Dobet [Do Better] (A9.69; B8.78; C10.76). Second in a triad of elusive characters whom Will seeks throughout *Piers Plowman*: superior virtue.

Dowel [Do Well] (A8.154; B7.169; C9.318). First in a triad of elusive characters whom Will seeks throughout *Piers Plowman*: basic virtue. An endless string of speakers define him, and his superior and superlative brothers, variously throughout the poem.

drede of dispair [horror of despair] (B20.164; C22.164). The allegorized vice that Sloth spreads with his sling in the attack on the Church, Unity. It may indicate a lazy disinclination to give in to despair, that is, a slothful desire to shrug off the threat of death and damnation, or it might indicate the fear that the desperate feel, too indolent, from Sloth's influence, to act virtuously and hope for grace.

Elde [Old Age] (B11.27; C11.188). Perhaps a projection of Will's future self, who futilely warns young Will about the dangers of following Fortune and bodily pleasure. In C (18.106) alone he climbs the Tree of Charity and shakes the fruit to the ground, indicating death. He reappears (B20.154; C22:154) to engage in battle with Life in the great siege of the Church, Unity, eventually running over Will's head, besieging him with gout, and making him bald, toothless, and impotent.

Enuye [Envy] (A2.60; B2.84; C2.88). The bitterest among the embodiments of the Seven Deadly Sins. Envy confesses and claims, unconvincingly, to feel remorse for his past acts. Described as lonely, with ragged clothing, in a constant state of prideful competition, Envy speaks in a selfish, vengeful tone as he nurses his hatred of others. In the wedding charter of Mede and False, "Enuye" is specified as the "erldom" in which the couple will live and presumably hold sway (A2.60; B2.84; C2.88).

Erl Auerous [Earl Avarice] (A9.80; B8.87; C10.86). In this instance, the sin of covetousness personified as a hoarding magnate.

Faith. See **Abraham**.

Fals (1) [False] (A2.6; B2.6; C2.6). The betrothed of Lady Mede, representing the tragic unification of economics and deception. In A he is also called Falshed (A2.50), in B Fals Fikel-tonge (B2.41), and in C Fals Faythlesse (C2.42) and also Falsness (C2.70). B contends that Fals is Mede's father and had a "fikel tonge" (B2.25). C refers both to Fauel (C2.25) and to Fals as her father and makes Fikel-tonge her "belsyre," or grandfather (C2.121). It appears that Mede might marry someone of her own lineage.

Fals (2) [Falseness, Falsehood] (B20.131; C22.131). Perhaps the same fellow who was supposed to marry Mede in the *visio*, or perhaps the opposite of Good Faith, whom he supplants as Pride's forces besiege Unity.

fals doom to deye [false judgment to die] (B18.28; C20.27). Written in many B manuscripts as "false doom and death" (thus tallying three entities for this line), an example of Langland's blurring of concept and character, here with the exact meaning unclear. Pearsall (*C-text* 323) translates this unique figure as "the false judgment of death upon mankind," indicating the force of condemnation that Jesus will combat and defeat to save the human soul.

False-Wytnesse [False Witness] (A2.111; B2.147; C2160). In the debate over Lady Mede's marriage, a character whom Favel asks Guile to bribe so that he will exert control over Mede, ensuring her corrupt marriage to False and thus furthering the ambitions of Simony.

Fauel [Flattery] (A2.6; B2.6; C2.6). A charming trickster who brings Mede and False together as a couple with his "fair speche" (A2.23; B2.42; C2.43). C also refers to Fauel/Favel as Mede's father (C2.25).

Faunteltee [Youthful Folly] (B11.42; C11.314). Character who calls Will by the nickname Phippe and successfully encourages him to give in to Fortune and a life of sexual pleasure.

Feuere-on-þe-ferþe-day [Fever-on-the-fourth-day, Quartan] (A12.82). As his name implies, a seriously grave messenger of Death, appearing to Will only in the unique final passus of the A text.

Fiat voluntas tua [Thy will be done] (B14.49; C15.252). Food made from a line of the Paternoster, part of a lunch packed by Patience, offered in B to Haukin and in C to "vs alle," presumably meaning Active, Will, and Conscience.

Fisik [Medicine] (A7.253; B6.268; C8.291). Personification of the industry and craft of medicine. Hunger tells Piers that if the folk follow a moderate diet, then Fisik will lose business and become impoverished, forcing him to sell his expensive Calabrian cloak, abandon his practice, and work the land instead. Life employs him later to fend off sickness and death in the siege of Unity (B20.169; C22.169).

the Flessh (B16.31; C18.35). The human body essentially, metaphorized as a powerful wind that blows against the Tree of Charity.

Fortune (B11.7; C11.168). Embodiment of the classical goddess Fortuna, who sets Will upon a life of pleasure and recklessness for forty years. She reappears as the lover of Life in the final passus (B20.156; C22.156).

Frere Flaterere [Flattering Friar] (B20.316; C22.316). A physician and surgeon who purports to heal the spiritually sick with easy (and meaningless) penances. Tragically summoned by Contrition and Conscience to enter into Unity. Later identified as Sire Penetrans-domos.

Glotonye [Gluttony] (A2.64; B2.93; C2.97). The supersaturated version of Hunger. Here in the wedding charter of Mede and False, Gluttony represents the desire for overconsumption.

Glutoun [Glutton] (A5.146; B5.297; C6.349). Perhaps the same character as Glotonye or perhaps distinct to the confession of the Seven Deadly Sins. On his way to church, Glutton gets sidetracked by a barmaid who invites him in for a drink, in a signature scene in *Piers Plowman* that exemplifies the dangers of temptation and overconsumption. Later in the text, in B and C, during the plowing of the half acre, he attempts to satiate Hunger but rather corrupts the hardworking laborers into overeating wasters (B6.300; C8.324). At this juncture the A text (7.285) refers rather to "glotonye" and not an actual character.

Gobelyn [Goblin] (B18.292; C20.323). A diabolic character, one of several in a pandemonium, in Will's vision of the Harrowing of Hell.

Goddes grace to amende [God's grace to amend] (B14.20; not in C). An allegorical fabric dye that Conscience tells Haukin the Active Man to use to cleanse his sin-stained cloak after it is washed and scrubbed by Dowel and Dobet.

Good Feiþ [Good Faith] (B20.131; C22.131). A character representing the faith forced to flee during the attack of Simony, to be replaced by Fals, in the epic siege against the Church, Unity. Christ also cites "good feiþ" as the authority requiring that Grace destroy Guile, in his debate with the devils (B18.348).

Good Hope (B20.167; C22.167). An entity employed in battle by Elde to fight off Wanhope, as Conscience battles Pride in the siege against Unity.

Grace (A6.85; B5.595; C7.242). Truth's gatekeeper, as described by Piers Plowman, as he offers to lead the folk on pilgrimage. Also a character appearing at the Pentecost, counseling Piers Plowman and Conscience to summon the commons to receive gifts of wit, wisdom, craft, and virtue with which to combat Antichrist (B19.214; C21.214).

Gregori [Gregory] (B19.272; C21.271). Pope Gregory the Great, who Christianized the Anglo-Saxons, invoked earlier as ideal cleric and genius of pastoral care, here manifested as one of the four horses that harrow the land the oxen (Evangelists) plow.

Haukyn þe Actif Man [Haukin the Active Man] (B13.273). A common man, a wafer seller and minstrel, who represents the inherent difficulties of living without sin in an "active" life, for he cannot keep his coat clean. Transformed in C to Activa Vita.

Heele [Health] (B20.153; C22.153). The confident state of health, along with "highness of heart," that discourages virtue, fear of Death, and the need for contrition during the battle for the Church, Unity, at the end of the poem.

heighnesse of herte [highness of heart] (B20.153; C22.153). Companion of Heele, representing a general sense of confidence that makes Life indifferent to Age and Death during the battle for the Church, Unity.

Hende-Speche [Charming Speech] (B20.349; C22.349). A personification of the charm of Frere Flaterere, which he employs to persuade Peace to let him enter into Unity, presumably to heal the spiritually sick.

Hendenesse [Gentility] (B20.145; C22.145). A character scorned by a proud, well-dressed Life in his prideful indifference to Age and Death.

Holy Chirche [Holy Church] (A prologue 63; B prologue 66; C prologue 64). First introduced as a concept in the prologue, a full-fledged allegorical character in passus 1. As the institutional Church, she has instructed Will since birth and guides him all too briefly as he begins his search for Truth and salvation. Though a literary descendant of Boethius's Lady Philosophy, she also enacts a folkloric paradigm akin to the figure of Glinda the Good Witch of the North from *The Wizard of Oz*.

Holy Wryt (1) [Holy Writ] (A1.119; B1.130; C1.125). Allegorical representation of the authority of scripture. The knowledge of Holy Writ, widely manifested and cited, guides readers and characters in the text.

Holy Writ (2) (B19.330; C21.329). The Bible, here metaphorized as the roofing material Grace gives Piers Plowman to build the Church, Unity. See also þe cros and Mercy (3).

Holy Writ (3) (A12.97). A teacher whose doctrines Will must follow, invoked by Fever in this unique final passus of the A text.

Holynesse (1) [Holiness] (B11.44; C12.1). A companion of Elde, who laments that Will gives himself over to Fortune and her temptations.

Holynesse (2) (B20.145; C22.145). A character scorned by a proud, well-dressed Life in his prideful indifference to Age and Death.

Hope. See **Spes.**

Hunger (A7.157; B6.172; C8.168). A powerful character summoned by Piers to help regulate Waster and compel the lazy folk to work for their sustenance. Though initially effective, Hunger proves difficult to manage and seems always to want more food.

Ierom [Jerome] (B19.272; C21.271). St. Jerome, here specifically manifested as one of the four horses that harrow the land the oxen (Evangelists) plow.

Imaginatif [Imagination]. See **Ymaginatif.**

Iohan [John] (B19.267; C21.266). The Evangelist John as one of four great oxen given by Grace to Piers Plowman to help till the field of Truth.

Iohan But [John But] (A12.106). The mysterious figure who adds an ending to the A text's final passus and claims to have been an intimate of the poet "Will." He leads a prayer for King Richard and for the readers' souls. His status as an actual character depends on how readers judge his authenticity and origins.

Iudas (B16.144; C18.166). The biblical Judas, mentioned throughout the poem but here appearing as a character in a vision of the betrayal of Christ.

Kepe-wel-þi-tunge-Fro-lesinges-and-liþer-speche-and-likerous-drinkes [Keep-well-your-tongue-from-lies-and-hateful-speech-and-luxurious-drinks] (A11.120–21; B10.165–66; not in C). An important stop along the road to Clergy, in Study's directions to Will. Without keeping his tongue free of lying, gossiping, and drinking, Will can never advance on the road to Dowel.

King (A prologue 91; B prologue 92; C prologue 90). A generic monarch. While Langland did not labor to distinguish kings historically, specific datable references across the versions identify the king in A and B as Edward III, and in C as Richard II, though Richard as the boy king (crowned 1377) is also alluded to in B (prologue 196). But one can read the "king" whenever mentioned as a non-historically-specific figure of royal authority who should embody the ideals of social and political leadership, just governance, and love of his people. His most dramatic and extended appearance comes in overseeing the trial and failed marriage arrangements of Lady Mede.

Kny3thod [Knighthood] (B prologue 116; C prologue 142). Incarnation of the concept of knighthood, the belief in chivalry, honor, and duty. Introduced as a character in B and C as part of the king's royal court alongside other figures of virtuous behavior, such as Conscience, Kind (Natural) Wit, and Clergy.

Kynde [Nature] (A10.2; B9.2; C10.129). Nature as protector of the Lady Anima in Wit's chivalric conceit about the human soul. Later the force of Nature summoned by Conscience to chastise the forces of Pride with sickness and infirmity (B20.85; C22.85). Kynde also refers specifically to God as creator (A10.27; B9.26; C10.152), since in medieval literature Nature is often seen as a manifestation of God's will and power.

Kynde Cardinal Wit (A12.15). The character of Kind Wit manifested as a cardinal to whom Scripture says Will must confess in the unique final passus of the A text.

Kynde Wit [Natural Wit] (A1.53; B prologue 114; C prologue 141). Introduced as part of the king's council, serving as an example of rational thinking with a primary focus on duty. Kind Wit guides other characters and allegorically reflects one's innate ability to distinguish virtue from vice. But Will also refers to him generally as a coveted faculty, without actual personified status.

Kytte (B18.428; C20.472). Will's wife, mentioned, along with his daughter Calote, accompanying him to church to revere the cross after Will wakes from his vision of the Harrowing of Hell.

Lavacrum-lex-Dei [Laver-the-law-of-God] (C19.73). God's law allegorized as a washing basin or baptismal font and depicted as the grange where the Samaritan takes the wounded man to heal in Will's vision of the parable.

Lawe [Law] (A3.150; B3.161; C3.198). The concept of law personified as someone controlled and manipulated by Lady Mede for the sake of lawyers' profits. He is described as lordly and loath to work for justice without bribery.

La3ar (B16.113; C18.144). The biblical Lazarus, raised from the dead by Jesus in Will's vision of the life and ministry of Christ. The generic "la3ar" is a diseased beggar.

Leccherie [Lechery] (A2.61; B2.89; C2.93). Licentiousness or, broadly, self-indulgence. In the wedding charter of Mede and False, Lechery is specified as the "lordssshipe" or district in which the couple will live and presumably hold sway.

Lecchour [Lecher] (A5.54; B5.71; C6.170). Personification of Lust, one of the Seven Deadly Sins. His portrait in the confession scenes dramatically expands from A to B, and in C, which refers to the character as Lechery, expands further with the inclusion of material from Haukin the Active Man's discourse.

Lex Christi [Law of Christ] (B17.72; not in C). The grange where the Samaritan takes the wounded man to heal in Will's vision of the parable. Replaced in the C text by Lavacrum-lex-Dei.

Libera Voluntas Dei [Free Will of God] (C18.119). In C alone, the force that beats the Devil with the second prop that holds up the Tree of Charity. To be distinguished from Liberum Arbitrium, who narrates these events in C and in B himself wields the third prop, with Piers narrating (B16.50).

Liberum Arbitrium [Free Will] (B16.16; C16.156). In B, a personification described by Anima as working the land under Piers the Plowman as he tends the Tree of Charity. At C16.156 he takes up the much more elaborate role of replacing Anima, no longer included as Piers's assistant.

Lif [Life] (B18.31; C20.30). A concept and human reality present throughout the poem but here depicted specifically as a chivalric force in combat with Death—a manifestation of Christ's joust to win humanity's soul—with Death defeated in the end.

Longe Wille (B15.152; not in C). "Will," the allegorical manifestation of questing human desire and the hero of the poem, self-identified at this revealing moment as a persona for the poet, William Langland.

Longeus [Longinus] (B18.79; C20.81). Name traditionally attributed to the Roman soldier converted after spearing Christ's side. Here a character in Will's vision of the crucifixion.

lord þat lyueþ after likyng of body [lord that lives for the pleasures of the body] (B20.71; C22.71). A minor character who speaks at line 92, crying alarm and looking for Comfort when Kynde and Death join the battle against Pride and chasten the sinful folk with disease and fear, during the siege against Unity.

Loue [Love] (B13.140; not in C). Mentioned as a concept throughout the poem but here specifically a former lover of Patience, who taught him "love your enemies."

Lucifer (A1.109; B1.111; C1.106). The Devil, manifested here as the character Wrong, keeper of the Castle of Care in the vision of the Field of Folk. Also a diabolic character, one of several in a pandemonium, in Will's vision of the Harrowing of Hell (B18.272; C 20.295).

Luk (B19.265; C21.264). The Evangelist Luke as one of four great oxen given by Grace to Piers Plowman to help till the field of Truth.

Maidenhode [Maidenhood] (B16.71; as Virginite, C18.89). One of the three fruits on the Tree of Charity tended by Piers Plowman, signifying the virtuous life of the chaste, superior to both Matrimony and Continence/Widowhood.

maister [master (of divinity)] (B13.25; C15.30). One of many friars throughout the poem, this one specific to the Dinner Party episode with Will, Clergy, Conscience, and Scripture (with Reason attending in the C text).

Maistris of þe Menours [Masters of the Minorites] (A9.9; B8.9; C10.9). Friars whom Will meets and questions as he sets out on his search for Dowel. They claim the virtue as their companion to a skeptical Will.

mansed preest [accursed priest] (B20.221; C22.221). An unnamed Irish priest, one of a crew of sixty, who denounces Conscience and savors profit and drink in the siege against Unity.

Marie (B16.91; C18.125). Mary the Mother of Jesus, invoked throughout the poem and appearing here as a character in a vision of the Annunciation.

Mark (B19.266; C21.265). The Evangelist Mark as one of four great oxen given by Grace to Piers Plowman to help till the field of Truth.

Mathew (B19.266; C21.265). The Evangelist Matthew as one of four great oxen given by Grace to Piers Plowman to help till the field of Truth.

Matrimoyne [Matrimony] (B16.68; C18.86). One of the three fruits on the Tree of Charity tended by Piers Plowman, signifying the virtuous life of the wedded, the lowest hanging on the tree, below Continence/Widowhood and Maidenhood/Virginity.

Mede [Lady Mede] (A2.16; B2.20; C2.19). One of the most dynamic characters in *Piers Plowman*, whose name basically means "the principle of exchange." She plans to marry False, though the King wants to join her to Conscience. Charismatic and engrossing, Lady Mede charms and persuades almost everyone, while they in turn desire to please her. She disappears from the poem after her botched wedding, with no loss of influence. Scholars often associate her with Alice Perrers, the gaudy mistress of an addled King Edward III.

Mendis [Amends] (A2.83; B2.119; C2.120). A character based on the concept of healing and making amends. She engendered Lady Mede in A and B, and C specifically identifies her as Mede's mother. B and C refer to this character as Amendes.

Mercy (1) (A6.73; B5.586; C7.232). The moat that the folk must cross on the road to Truth as instructed by Piers Plowman.

Mercy (2) (B18.115; C20.118). One of the Four Daughters of God locked in debate over the fate of humankind. She and her sister Peace win the day over Truth and Righteousness.

Mercy (3) (B19.327; C21.326). The virtue of mercy, metaphorized as the mortar that Grace gives Piers Plowman to build the Church, Unity. See also **þe cros** and **Holy Writ (2)**.

Middelerþe [Middle Earth] (B11.9; C11.170). The created world, described as a "myrrour" in which Fortune shows Will the wonders of his deepest desires, leading to a long period of reckless self-indulgence.

Miserere mei, Deus, Et quorum tecta sunt peccata [Have mercy on me, O God, And on those whose sins are covered] (B13.53–53a; not in C). Food made metaphorically from mixed verses of Psalm 50:1 and 31:1, served at the Dinner Party.

Moses. See **Spes.**

mous þat muche good kouþe (B prologue 182; C prologue 196). Cautious mouse who warns against belling the cat in the Rat Parliament fable.

Nede [Need] (B11.430; C13.240). Allegorized figure said by Imaginatif to motivate a drunk man to pull himself out of a ditch. He reappears elaborately in a mysterious episode (B20.4; C22.4) before the poem's final dream, reminding Will of basic human weakness and frailties.

Omnia-probate [Test-everything] (A12.50). Unique to A12, a Pauline concept (1 Thess. 5:21) depicted as a little schoolboy whom Scripture sends to guide Will to her cousin Kind Wit.

Outlawe (B17.103; not in C). The Devil depicted in the imagery of the parable of the Good Samaritan as an outlaw hiding in the woods, vying with the Samaritan for control of the soul of the wounded man.

Pees [Peace] (B18.167; C20.170). One of the Four Daughters of God locked in debating the fate of mankind. Peace is also the victim of violence at the hands of Wrong (A4.34; B4.47; C4.45).

Pernele Proud-herte (A5.45; B5.62; C6.3). Specific name for the sin of pride. She weeps when faced with coming to terms with her past sins, promising to practice humility and asking the Lord for forgiveness.

Pilatus (B18.36; C20.35). The biblical and historical figure Pontius Pilate, appearing as a character in Will's vision of the trial of Jesus.

þe poore (B14.208; C16.49). Not "the poor" to whom the poem refers frequently but, in this episode where the "it" becomes a "he," an actual personification. However, in this extended conceit in praise of Poverty's invulnerability to the Seven Deadly Sins, the text does not make clear which instances refer to an allegorical entity.

Post mortem [After death] (B13.44; C15.50). In the Dinner Party scene, a mortar in which is ground the bitter sauce of pain for those who do not repent.

Preesthod [Priesthood] (B19.335; C21.334). Appointed by Grace, Piers's haywards (fence wardens) who keep cattle away from crops as the Plowman tills the field of Truth.

Pride of Parfit Lyuynge [Pride of Perfect Living] (B11.15; C11.176). A manifestation of human vanity serving as a companion of Concupiscencia Carnis and Coueitise of Eiȝes. His influence makes Will think lightly of Clergy.

Priour Prouincial [Provincial Prior] (B11.57; C12.9). The head of an area (province) of friars. Coueitise of Ei3es tells Will not to worry about following Fortune, suggesting he can always go to a "Priour Prouincial" who can provide cheap absolution.

Pro hac orabit omnis sanctus in tempore oportuno [For this shall every one that is holy pray (unto thee) in a seasonable time] (B13.56–56α; C15.61–61α). Food made metaphorically from Psalm 31:6, served at the Dinner Party.

Pruyde [Pride] (C6.14). One of the Seven Deadly Sins. In all versions, the sin of Pride is given the woman's name Pernele, but in C alone, after Pernele speaks, a new character, Pruyde, appears to begin his own confession, integrating at C6.14–60α material from Haukin's B13 confession. Pruyde is thus either an independent voice, new to C, or simply how Pernele names herself, making the personification explicit. See **Pernele Proud-herte**.

Quod-bonum-est-tenete [Hold fast that which is good] (A12.57). A borough where, in Scripture's directions, Will should stop while on the way to see Kind Wit, accompanied by Omnia-probate (see 1 Thess. 5:21).

raton of renoun (B prologue 158; C prologue 176). A reasonable rat who speaks in favor of belling the cat in the Rat Parliament fable in B and C. Editors usually associate him with Sir Peter de la Mare, Speaker of the House of Commons.

Rechelesnesse [Recklessness] (B11.34; C11.195). Character who spontaneously helps Fortune and his erotic companions convince Will to have fun while still young. In a confusing and controversial revision in the C text, he becomes the speaker of a long and varied discourse on salvation, spoken in B by Will and Trajan.

Religioun [Religion] (A11.211; B10.305; C5.150). As described by Clergy in A and B, a "rider," a man about town in search of profit, status, and the trappings of the gentry. In C's shifted version of this exposition, spoken by Reason, "religion" may no longer be a character per se.

Repentaunce [Repentance] (A5.43; B5.60; C6.1). A force of personal spiritual growth and specifically a priest, the formal confessor of the Seven Deadly Sins.

Resoun [Reason] (A4.14; B4.16; C4.14). A critical and combative force that appears throughout the text, including as Will's interrogator in the "apologia" in C5. He reacts with hostility to Lady Mede, inciting an ongoing discourse with the King on topics of morality, spirituality, and the proper governance of the realm.

Reuel [Revel] (B20.181; C22.181). A rich and merry place, sometimes called "the company of comfort," where Life, despairing of surgery and medicine, retreats. Essentially the doctrine "Eat, drink, and be merry."

Ricchesse [riches] (A11.116; B10.161; C11.108). In Study's directions, a place Will ought not to linger on the road to Clergy.

Rightwisnesse [Righteousness] (B18.164; C 20.167). Here one of the Four Daughters of God locked in debating the fate of humankind. She and her sister Truth lose the debate to Peace and Mercy.

Robertis [Robert] (A prologue 44; B prologue 44; C prologue 45). Generic name for scoundrels and perhaps associated with "robber," as later manifested in "Robert þe robbour," who joins the cast of sins confessing (A5.235; B5.462; C6.315).

Samaritan (B17.49; C19.49). The Samaritan from Jesus's parable (Luke 10:29–37), appearing here as Charity, completing Will's education in the Theological Virtues begun by Faith and Hope (Abraham and Moses).

Sathan [Satan] (B18.265; C20.274). Presumably the Devil. One of several diabolic figures in a pandemonium, in Will's vision of the Harrowing of Hell.

Scripture (1) (A11.107; B10.152; C11.96). Wife of Clergy and personification of the holy writings of Scripture, to which the "clergy" ought to be wedded. This couple constitutes Will's logical next step of inquiry after "study."

Scripture (2) (B13.37; C15.43). Serving food in the Dinner Party scene, Scripture has evidently become a male version of the female character formerly described as Clergy's wife.

Sey-soþ-so-it-be-to-done-in-no-manere-ellis-nouȝt-for-no-manis-biddyng [Tell-truth-so-it-will-be-done-in-no-manner-else-despite-any-man's-bidding] (A6.70–71; B5.583–84; C7.229–30). An allegorized but unidentifiable landmark or topographical feature on the road to Truth. It may obliquely relate to the Second Commandment.

Shame (B11.435; C13.244). A force that, Will agrees, can motivate personal reform more powerfully than any other. Where Imaginatif compares Will to a drunk in a ditch, stuck there until Need shames him into picking himself up, Schmidt takes the reference to Shame as allegorical.

Simplite-of-speche [Simplicity-of-speech] (A11.122; B10.167; not in C). Along with Sobriety, the last stop on the road to Clergy in Study's directions to Will.

Sire Geffrey (B15.123; not in C). Satiric name for a dandy, mocked by Anima.

Sire Inwit [Sir Inner Awareness] (A10.17; B9.18; C10.144). Knight who protects the soul, Anima, in Wit's chivalric conceit. In this he is aided by his sons the five senses (A10.19–21; B9.20–22; C10.146–48): **Sire Godefrey Go-wel** [Godfrey Go-well] (in C named Sire Goedfayth Go-wel), **Sire Here-wel** [Hear-well], **Sire Se-wel** [See-well], **Sire Sey-wel** [Say-well], and **Sire Werche-wel-wiþ-þin-hond** [Work-well-with-your-hand].

Sire Iohan (B15.123; not in C). Satiric name for a dandy, mocked by Anima.

Sire Lif-to-lyue-in-lecherie [Sir Life-to-live-in-lechery] (B20.312; C22.312). Ailing character, suffering from mild fasting and in need of easy penance and confession during the siege of Unity.

Sire Penetrans-domos [Sir Penetrate-the-houses] (B20.341; C22.341). Another name of Frere Flaterere, based on a phrase from 2 Timothy 3:6, in which Paul warns against the prideful, self-loving charmers who insinuate themselves into homes, presumably of the unsuspecting virtuous.

Sleuþe (1) (A5.215; B5.386; C7.1). One of the Seven Deadly Sins and the antithesis of hard work—an opposition that animates many of the conflicts in the poem. Sloth lists his follies and asks the Lord for forgiveness, though he relishes his sins and does not seem genuine in seeking forgiveness. In the A text, the wedding charter of Mede and False specifies "Sloupe" as the "signiure" or domain in which the couple will live and presumably hold sway (A2.66).

Sleuþe (2) (B20.158; C22.158). Son of Life and Fortune who marries a prostitute called Wanhope [Despair]. A skilled warrior, he makes a slingshot and spreads "drede of dispair" twelve miles around in the epic siege of the Church, Unity, indicating the people's descent into the vice of carelessness even in the face of Death.

Sobirte [Sobriety] (A11.122; B10.167; not in C). Along with Simplicity of Speech, the last stop on the road to Clergy, in Study's directions to Will.

Spek-yuel-bihynde [Backbiting] (B19.343; C21.342). One of Pride's spies in the army of sin that, with Antichrist, besieges the Church, Unity.

Spes [Hope] (B17.1; C19.1). The biblical Moses, impressionistically depicted as "a spy," who advances Faith's (Abraham's) instruction to Will in the Theological Virtues.

Spille-Loue [Destroy-Love] (B19.343; C21.342). One of Pride's spies in the army of sin besieging the Church, Unity.

Spiritus Fortitudinis [Spirit of Fortitude] (B19.291; C21.290). One of the four Cardinal Virtues depicted as "seeds" that Grace gives Piers to sow in the human soul as he tills the field of Truth.

Spiritus Iusticie [Spirit of Justice] (B19.300; C21.299). One of the four Cardinal Virtues depicted as "seeds" that Grace gives Piers to sow in the human soul as he tills the field of Truth.

Spiritus Paraclitus (B19.202; C21.202). The Holy Spirit, referenced widely in the poem, here appearing in Will's vision of the Pentecost.

Spiritus Prudencie [Spirit of Prudence] (B19.278; C21.277). One of the four Cardinal Virtues depicted as "seeds" that Grace gives Piers to sow in the human soul as he tills the field of Truth.

Spiritus Sanctus [Holy Spirit] (B16.90; C18.121). Invoked throughout the poem as part of the Holy Trinity, here a character in a vision recreating the moment of the Annunciation by speaking to Mary through Gabriel's mouth.

Spiritus Temperancie [Spirit of Temperance] (B19.283; C21.282). One of the four Cardinal Virtues depicted as "seeds" that Grace gives Piers to sow in the human soul as he tills the field of Truth.

Stele-nouȝt-ne-sle-nouȝt [Steal-not-and-slay-not] (A6.64; B5.577; C7.223). The Eighth and Sixth Commandments allegorized as a pair of "stokkis [stumps]" that the folk must encounter on the road to Truth as instructed by Piers Plowman. Piers advises the folk to keep these markers to the left, indicating that "stokkis" may here mean wooden idols—profane manifestations of the sins that the commandments forbid.

Study. See **Dame Study.**

Suffre-boþe-wele-and-wo [Suffer-both-weal-and-woe] (A11.114–15; B10.159–60; C11.106–7). A stop along the way to Clergy, in Study's directions to Will.

Suffre-þi-souereynes-to-hauen-here-wille-deme-hem-nouȝt-for-ȝif-þou-dost-þou-shalt-it-dere-abiggen-let-God-worþe-wiþal-for-so-His-woord-techiþ [Permit-your-rulers-to-have-their-will-judge-them-not-for-if-you-do-you-will-sorely-pay-for-it-let-God-rule-completely-for-so-his-word-teaches] (A7.72–74; B6.80–82; C8.82–83). Piers's son's name. The longest among the epithetic allegories, though shortened in C, it depicts comprehensive order and obedience to authority.

Suffre-til-I-se-my-tyme [Suffer-until-I-see-my-time] (A4.18; B4.20; C4.20). Reason's horse.

Surquidous [Presumption] (B19.342; C21.341). The sergeant of arms of Pride as he marshals an army against the Church, Unity.

Swere-noȝt-but-if-be-for-nede-and-nameliche-an-ydel-þe-name-of-God-almiȝty [Swear-not-unless-necessary-and-especially-do-not-take-in-vain-the-name-of-God-almighty] (A6.57–58; B5.570–71; C7.216–17). The Third Commandment allegorized as an unspecified landmark or topographical feature on the way to Truth as instructed by Piers Plowman.

Symonye [Simony] (A2.35; B2.63; C2.63). Named for Simon Magus in the New Testament (Acts 8:9–24), the corrupt practice of buying or selling ecclesiastical office or the crime of profiting from one's clerical work, such as the distribution of the sacraments. Personified as the conniving companion of Cyvuyle, he seeks to guarantee Mede's marriage to False in order to ensure continued clerical corruption.

Tercian [Tertian, (of the) Third] (A12.85). Incarnation of an intermittent fever, and one of the companions of the character Fever in the unique final passus of the A text.

Theologie [Theology] (A2.79; B2.115; C2.116). A figure both of divine knowledge and of practical reason, Theology believes Lady Mede should be wedded with Truth to ensure that humanity can become worthy of God's reward. Thus he opposes Mede's marriage to False, which he sees as antithetical to charity and dangerous to Holy Church.

Þou3t [Thought] (A9.65; B8.74; C10.72). Will's faculty of thought allegorized as his companion and interlocutor in the search for Dowel. After a few days of inconclusive debate, he introduces Will to Wit.

Tomme Trewe-tonge-tel-me-no-tales-Ne-lesynge-to-lau3en-of-for-I-loued-hem-neuere [Tom True-tongue-tell-me-no-tales-nor-lies-to-laugh-at-for-I-loved-them-never] (B4.18–19; C4.18–19). Loyal, honest knave of the character Reason.

Tomme Two-tonge (B20.162; C22.162). A false assizer (jurist) and father of Wanhope.

Tree of Charity (B16.1–9; C18.1–15). Allegorical tree tended by Piers Plowman, called specifically in B "Patience and pure simplicity of heart." The C text calls it Trewe-loue, planted by the Trinity, and names it also Ymago-Dei, the image of God, planted in Cor-hominis, the human heart. Variously in B and C, mercy is its root, its middle trunk compassion, and its leaves the true words of Holy Church's law. It blossoms forth in obedient speech and kind looks, bearing the fruit of Charity, the works of holiness, generosity, and care for those in need. Three props, or supports, depicting the members of the Trinity, hold up the tree and are used to beat down the Devil: Potencia Dei Patris [Power of God the Father] (B16.30; C18.34), Sapiencia Dei Patris [Wisdom of God the Father] (B16.36); C18:40), and a third prop unnamed at B16.50 but associated with the "Holy Goost" at B16.52 and explicitly named Spiritus Sanctus at C18.51.

Treuþe (1) [Truth] (A1.12; B1.12; C prologue 15). The virtue of loyalty and honesty. Truth also directly represents God. He holds the tower in the allegorical landscape in Will's first dream vision, signifying the core values of the poem and also the heavenly goal of Will's journey. The C text introduces Truth before A and B do, when first describing the tower, and then again at C1.12.

Troianus (B11.141; C12.77). The pagan Roman emperor Trajan, who bursts on the scene, interrupting Scripture and telling the story of his unlikely salvation, achieved by his fidelity to virtue and truth.

Truþe (2) [Truth] (B18.119; C20.122). Here one of the Four Daughters of

God locked in debating the fate of mankind. She and her sister Righteousness lose the debate to Peace and Mercy.

turpiloquio [vile speech] (B13.457; C7.116). A Latin word used to indicate a devilish song, a "lay of sorwe." As Will mocks the wealthy who patronize worthless minstrels instead of caring for the needy, he warns that such frivolous entertainers will be playing this song, joined by the Devil himself on fiddle, while they lead the rich into the feast of Lucifer—that is, hell.

Vnkyndenesse [Unkindness] (B19.225; C21.225). An uncharitable attitude appearing throughout the poem, here one of the mock cardinals who serve the Antichrist when Pride becomes pope.

Vetus Testamentum et Nouum (B19.275a; C21.274a). The Old and New Testaments manifested as two harrows that Grace provides Piers Plowman to till the field of Truth.

vix [barely] (C15.23). In C alone, a humble Latin adverb that in Langland's artful syntax becomes a personified heroic character in Will's formulation that "the just man is 'barely' saved"—but therefore *is* saved.

Wanhope [Despair] (B20.160; C22.160). A prostitute, wife of Sloth and daughter of Tomme Two-tonge.

Waryn Wisdom (A4.24; B4.27; C4.27). Not wisdom as a virtue but rather a corrupt force, along with Witty, who joins with Lady Mede to support her case to the King. In C he is called Wareyn Wisman.

Wastour [Waster] (A5.24; B5.24; C5.126). Sometimes a specific boisterous churl and in other instances a reference to a group of idle loafers. Wasters make nothing and consume what the labor of others produces.

Wil (A5.44; B5.61; C6.2). The name of the protagonist of the dream vision, a figure for the desirous human "will," and likely the poet William Langland. See **Longe Wille**.

Wyt [Wit] (A9.105; B8.112; C.10.111). An aspect of mind associated with understanding. Wit takes over from Thought in instructing Will about Dowel, Dobet, and Dobest. Following a chivalric conceit about how to care for the human soul, he offers a major discourse on proper marriage as a manifestation of Dowel. Wit is married to Dame Study, who then takes over Will's instruction, scorning both him and her husband for their foolish errors.

Witty [Wit, Cleverness] (A4.24; B4.27; C4.27). Companion of Waryn Wisdom who joins with Lady Mede to support her case to the King. In C he is called Wily-man.

the World (B16.27; C18.31). Essentially "worldliness," metaphorized as the "wicked wind" that attacks the Tree of Charity and brings along Covetousness, who wants to steal its fruit.

Wraþe [Wrath] (B5.133; C6.103). Omitted from the confession of the Seven Deadlies in A, but in B and C a figure of belligerence stirring up hostility in human social and economic relations, with a showcase appearance at convents, rousing hatred among nuns. This troublemaker avoids monasteries because of their stern discipline.

Wrong (A1.61; B1.63; C1.59). The antithesis of Truth: the Devil who lives in the Castle of Care. Holy Church identifies him in hopes of warning Will to stay away from the temptation that Adam and Eve, Lucifer, and many others fell prey to. The A text uniquely depicts him also as Mede's father (A2.19). Additionally, Wrong is the criminal who assaults Peace and his household (A4.35; B4.48; C4.46).

3euan-3elde-a3eyn-yf-Y-so-moche-haue-Al-þat-Y-wikkedly-wan-sithen-Y-witte-hadde [Evan-give-again-if-I-so-much-have-all-that-I-wickedly-won-since-I-had-wit] (C6.309–10). A unique addition to the C-text confession scenes, the contrite Welshman Evan who regrets his ill-gotten gains and longs to return them.

Ymaginatif [Imagination] (B12.1; C14.1). One of the highest and most complex faculties. As an expert on Will's mental history, Imaginatif offers a sprawling meditation on the dangers of wealth and on both the benefits and the dangers of academic learning in the quest for salvation. His coming is foretold at B10.117.

3oure-fadris-honouriþ [Honor-your-fathers] (A6.54; B5.567; C7.213). Adaptation of the Fifth Commandment allegorized as a ford on the road to Truth that the folk must wade and wash in, as instructed by Piers Plowman.

Ypocrisie [Hypocrisy] (B20.301; C22.301). Part of the army of Pride, leading an assault of tale-tellers and gossips on the gates of the Church, Unity, guarded by Peace.

Appendix 2

PRONUNCIATION GUIDE: READING *PIERS PLOWMAN* ALOUD

Reading *Piers Plowman* aloud dramatically helps readers to comprehend and appreciate the poem's complex rhythms and endless musical play. Reading Langland means "hearing" Langland, which means "vocalizing" Langland, which means "feeling" the reverberations in the mouth and through the entire body. The rough-and-ready alliterative long line must be received viscerally, though perhaps not at once cognitively understood. In his *Introduction to Geoffrey Chaucer* in the New Perspectives series, Tison Pugh, encouraging such reading aloud, refers to Chaucer's "daring acoustics" (199). Readers can compare Langland's artistry to Chaucer's in this regard, enhancing an appreciation of both poets.

The basic overview of sounds and metrics below is designed to permit a reader access to the magical sonic world of *Piers Plowman*. To hear a complete version of the B text, one can listen to the recording performed by the Chaucer Studio, which will profoundly assist in familiarizing new readers with the sounds and rhythms of Langland's Middle English. Hearing any such dramatic rendering, in fact, provokes the question of how *Piers* ought to be performed, for like Shakespeare's plays, *Piers* can be interpreted and acted out dramatically and in character. Any set of readers will interpret the text differently and produce an infinite variety of portrayals of such characters as Patience, Conscience, Lady Mede, and the indomitable Piers himself.

Linguistically, Middle English (ME) is a pre-vowel-shift language in which long vowels are pronounced not as in Modern English but as in medieval and modern Romance languages. Without instruction, native speakers of Romance languages read Middle English more accurately, including proper rolling of the *r*, than native English speakers do. For this reason and because of the poem's bilingualism, manifested in its frequent use of Latin, one hears an "authentic" experience of Middle English literature when the poem is read by a bilingual speaker of Romance and Germanic tongues. In the twenty-first-century multicultural classroom, such Romance speakers are most often Spanish speakers, and a central component of classroom instruction in phonology involves hearing such native Romance speakers recite from the poem. As one scholar has put it, in a slightly broader context that applies as well to Langland, "you have not really experienced Chaucer until you have heard him in the original Chicano." Every classroom is different: in addition to Romance languages, speakers of Greek, Armenian, Hebrew, and Arabic also have certain equivalent Middle English sounds in their sonic repertoire. Regardless of what community one reads in, teachers and students can create a sort of Silk Road setting of shared and compared linguistic experience. Reading *Piers Plowman* aloud becomes one of the most rewarding, festive, and memorable aesthetic experiences one can enjoy in the study of medieval literature.

Several literary anthologies, linguistic introductions, and editions of medieval texts include pronunciation guides, and using multiple sources can help establish and reinforce a sense of confidence, building on the basics outlined here.[1] Though historical linguistics is a science, different scholars explain sounds differently, and the various resources can complement one another. For convenience of reference, to illustrate certain sounds in the survey below I have drawn ME examples directly from Schmidt's parallel-text edition of *Piers Plowman*, while listing as well common words found frequently throughout the *Piers* corpus and in many different ME texts. International Phonetic Alphabet (IPA) symbols are presented where applicable, to help readers who have studied formal linguistics to identify critical sound differences, as are modern English words that illustrate the ME sound in question.

Phonology

I. Consonants

In general, Middle English consonants are pronounced like their Modern English equivalents, but many letters now silent were fully sounded in

Middle English, so all consonants in a word must be pronounced. Thus clusters such as *gn*, *kn*, and *wr* should be pronounced as two letters. Examples: B prologue 44, *knaues*; 56, *knowen*; 73, *knelynge*; 112, *Kniʒthod*; B10.57, *gnawen* (to gnaw); C16.66, *wrastle* (to wrestle).

The letter *h*, linguistically an aspirated consonant, poses some difficulties in recitation of Middle English verse. Initial *h* in unstressed words such as *him*, *his*, and *hem* may be elided with a preceding vowel. And though *h* is pronounced in native English words such as *holy* and *hous* (house), it is silent in French loan words, as at B prologue 211, *howues* (headdress, cap), and C6.40, *honoured* (honored). When silent *h* is preceded by a vowel, it too creates elision, as in B prologue 97, *hire houres* (their hours). In Langland's verse, *h* can alliterate with any vowel, making it a powerful sonic and melodic tool.

Note also the following specifics concerning consonants:

- *ch* is sounded like the *ch* [tʃ] in "church," not like the French *ch* [ʃ] of *champagne*.
- *f* should be unvoiced [f], like the *f* in "if" and "off," not like the voiced *f* [v] in "of" in Modern English (hereafter abbreviated ModE). Note that some common words in both ME and ModE that end in *f*, such as "shelf" and "wolf," are pluralized with a voiced *v* sound ("shelves," "wolves"). An example of such a plural is *wolues* at C9.226.
- *gh* represents the voiceless velar fricative [x] after back vowels (*a*, *o*, *ou*, *u*) and the voiceless palatal fricative [ç] after front vowels (most often *i*, *ei*).² These sounds are not identical to any in Modern English but rather to the *ch* sound in the Scottish word *loch* and in the German pronoun *ich* respectively; they also can be heard in Spanish in the medial consonants in such words as *baja* and *tejano* for the [x] and *mojito* and *México* for the [ç]. In *Piers* manuscripts and editions the sound can be represented by the ME letter yogh (ʒ) or by *gh* in such common ME words as *plough* and *thought* where the sound is [x], and *knight* and *right*, where the sound is [ç]. Examples: [x] at B prologue 6, *poʒte*; 20, *plouʒ*; 107, *kauʒte*; and [ç] at B prologue 32, *siʒt*; 127, *riʒtful*; 161, *briʒte*. Schmidt preserves the orthography of the manuscripts, so to use his edition one must be able to recognize ʒ; however, in many other editions, and in

most Chaucer editions as well, this letter is "regularized" to *gh*, *y*, or *z*, depending on its function.
- 3 can represent not only *gh* but also the sound of initial *y*, as in ModE "yell" and "yet"—examples: C prologue 101, 3ow, 3e; 103, 3oure; 132, 3ates (gates)—and the *z* sound [z], as in B prologue 63, *marchaundi3e*; B1.6, *ma3e* (maze).
- *r* is trilled as in Spanish. The sound is ubiquitous, but see for example the erupting sounds coming from Glutton, B5.343: *rounde, ruwet, ruggebones*.
- *s* [s] should be hissed like the *s* of ModE "snake" and "its." It should not be voiced like the *s* [z] of ModE "his." A good frequent word to practice on is the verb *was*, distinguishing it from ModE "was" [wʌz].

Note: In Middle English manuscripts, the letter sounded [v] is indistinguishable from the letter *u*, and Schmidt's *Parallel-Text Edition* preserves the manuscript orthography, so be prepared to read *u* as the sound [v] and *v* as the sound [u] in words such as *loue* (love), *proue* (prove), *coueite* (covet), *vnholy* (unholy), and *vp* (up).

II. Vowels and Diphthongs

A. *The Difference between Short and Long Vowels*

It will be important in reading Middle English to distinguish short from long vowels, something inherent in Modern English as well. For example, in ModE we distinguish the sounds of "fat" from "fate," "met" from "meet," "sit" from "site," "tot" from "tote," "cut" from "cute," where the first word contains the short vowel and the second the long. In both Middle and Modern English, long vowels are either doubled (see "meet" in this list) or a single vowel followed by a consonant and a final *e* (as in the other examples). Monosyllabic words in ME and ModE also end in long vowels (*to, do, go, he, she*). Most other vowels are short. With this clue in mind, one is better equipped to distinguish quickly the thousands of vowels read in any selection from *Piers*. Consider for example all the words in A prologue 4, "Wente wyde in þis world wondris to here": *wente* has short *e*; *wyde* has long *i* (*y* is simply another written form of the vowel *i*); the *i* in *in* and also in *this* are short; *world* and *wondris* both have short *o* before consonant clusters; while the *o* of *to* and the *e* of *here* are long (vowel +

consonant + *e*). It becomes a bit like reading music, a form of notation that takes practice to master.

B. Pronunciation of Middle English Short Vowels

Middle English short vowels are pronounced similarly to Modern English short vowels.

1. Short *a* (ME *man*) sounds like the *o* in ModE "hot" or the *a* in Jamaican English "man."
2. Short *e* (ME *bed*) sounds like ModE short *e*.
   Important: Unstressed final *e* is pronounced as a schwa, like the final *a* in ModE "china" or "sofa." If the following word begins with a vowel, the final *e* elides with it, but otherwise the final *e* is pronounced individually, especially at the end of the line: see the opening of the poem, A prologue lines 1, 2, 4, ending in *sonne, were, here*. Elision is widespread: see line 3 for example: "abite as" and "ermyte vnholy." In elision do not pronounce the first vowel but sound only the second, running the words together.
3. Short *i* or *y* (ME *þis, wiþ, wikkede*) sounds like ModE short *i*.
4. Short *o* (ME *softe, shop*) sounds like ModE short *o*.
5. Short *u* (ME *sunne, ful, dungeoun*) sounds like the *oo* in ModE "foot."

Important: Often words like *sunne* are spelled with *o* instead of *u* with no change of pronunciation (that is, the sound is still *u*), so look out for such common words as *comen* and *somer*, which are written with *o* but pronounced with *u*. This occurs before nasals (*n* and *m*) because in ME handwriting *u* is written with strokes called minims, and so are the letters *m* and *n*, so scribes avoided writing too many consecutive downstrokes that would be difficult to read; substituting an *o* for the two downstrokes of a *u* helped medieval readers to avoid this confusion.

C. Pronunciation of Middle English Long Vowels

1. Long *a* [a:] sounds like the *a* in ModE "father." See A prologue 15, *dale*; C prologue 49, *tales*.
2. Long close *e* [e:] sounds like the *a* in ModE "fame." See A prologue 16, *depe*, and the common words *he, me, we, be* passim.

3. Long open *e* [ɛ:] sounds like the *e* in ModE "there." See C prologue 36, *swete, grete*.
   Hint: If the modern spelling is *ee*, in for example the word "deep," then the ME word is likely to have the long close *e*. If the modern spelling is *ea*, in for example the word "sweat," then the ME word is likely to have the long open *e*, as in its ME version, spelled *swete*.
4. Long *i* or *y* [i:] sounds like the *ee* in ModE "feet." See A prologue 2, *I* (personal pronoun); 4, *wyde*.
5. Long close *o* [o:] sounds like the *o* in ModE "boat." This is the sound in the ME verb *do* and preposition *to*. See A prologue 38, *proue*; 42 *foode*.
6. Long open *o* [ɔ:] sounds like the *oa* in ModE "broad." We hear this sound in many very common ME words, such as *go, no, so,* and *holy*. If the modern sound is [o:], as in the Modern English versions of all these words, the ME sound is [ɔ:].
7. Long *u* [u:] sounds like the *oo* sound in ModE "rube." The sound is often written *ou*, to be distinguished from the diphthong *ou* (see below). Examples: A prologue 1, *sesoun*; 2, *shroudes*; and see the common ME words *out, plough, ploughman*.

D. Diphthongs

A diphthong is a combination of two vowels within a single syllable where one vowel sound glides into the other, as in the ModE examples "coin" (*oi*) and "sound" (*ou*).

1. *au/aw*: Pronounced like the vowel sound of ModE "shout."
2. *ai/ei* or *ay/ey*: Pronounced like the vowel sound of ModE "day" or "sleigh."
3. *eu/ew*: Pronounced like the final vowel sound of ModE "nephew" [iu]. Common ME examples: *new, knew*. Note that certain common words such as *lewed* (ignorant) and *fewe* have different linguistic origins and do not rhyme with *new*. The sound of this diphthong begins rather with more of an *e* sound and is represented [ɛu].
4. *oi/oy*: Pronounced like the vowel sound of ModE "toy."
5. *ou/ow*: Pronounced [ɔu] similarly to its ModE versions in words such as "ought" and "thought." Common examples: *growen, soule*.

The sound often precedes *gh*/3 and is sometimes reduced simply to the spelling *o: thought* or *thoght*. This diphthong must be distinguished from the long *u* [u:] (see above), a vowel that is also spelled *ou* in ME. A convenient way to distinguish them is to consider the modern pronunciation: if the modern sound rhymes with the words in the playful phrase "How now, brown cow?" it would be pronounced in ME as "Hu: nu:, bru:n cu:?"

Langland's Meter

The subject of Langland's meter, or "prosody," the formal rules of poetic structure, remains exciting and controversial.[3] The field can be quite scientific, based on the exact number of sounds in a given line. But for scholars to count syllables and decide which words get major and minor stress depends on agreement concerning which words the poet wrote, as opposed to words added (or deleted) by scribes in the transmission of the text. One has to establish the text, a major task, in order to guarantee, insofar as one can, that a theory of metrics reflects the poet's practice and not the accidental or erroneous clutter generated by scribes, who may or may not know anything of prosody. The reader needs to be aware of this before encountering the poem in multiple, divergent editions and before seeing manuscript images. If scholars do not agree about the text of any given line, they cannot agree on its meter. One must be prepared for diversity and conflict, and in *Piers Plowman* studies the fields of editing and of prosody are particularly dynamic and engaging—if not also sometimes enraging as well. Encountering the poem for the first time, readers need to know the basics of alliterative prosody, and then, with the help of the specialized works cited, they can wade into the complex and often feisty world of medieval metrics.

Langland writes in the "alliterative long line," the same form used in *Sir Gawain and the Green Knight, Cleanness, Patience,* the *Siege of Jerusalem,* and the *Wars of Alexander,* among others. Old English poetry such as *Beowulf* also follows alliterative patterning, though not in "long lines" because of the distinctly different syntax of Old English. The long line does not require a specific number of syllables, but it is divided into two halves, the a-verse and the b-verse, separated by a pause, called the caesura. When practicing aloud, readers may find themselves naturally delaying a bit at the caesura, providing dramatic effect and tempo to the verses. In transcription, scholars mark a stressed syllable with a large X and an alliterating stressed syllable with a large A; thus the most common, basic verse pattern is written AA/AX, with the virgule (/) here indicating the caesura (see the examples below). In another system of notation, often written directly over the top of the line for the sake of illustration, a small x indicates all the unstressed syllables and a virgule indicates stressed ones, both alliterating and not. Readers will quickly catch on to the various notations employed in the explanations of alliterative verse found in the anthologies and editions they encounter in their studies.

The a- and the b-verses must each have two stressed syllables (sometimes called lifts), for a total of four stresses in the line. Some, though not all, of these stressed syllables must receive alliteration to provide the core structure of the verse. Note that in alliterative verse, not only consonants alliterate but vowels as well, and all vowels alliterate with each other. An alliterating stressed syllable is called a stave. Rules define no express limit to the number of unstressed syllables (often called dips) that fill out the line around this frame, but in the b-verse, poets studiously avoid "double dipping," that is, a pattern of two unstressed syllables preceding each of the stressed ones. Outside of the frame, once the basic requirements of structure have been met, additional syllables might receive stress or alliteration or both, displaying the poet's art and creativity in shaping the sonic universe. But distinguishing the core structure—the frame that underpins the line—from what is decoratively added as creative adornment constitutes one of the complex aspects of studying medieval English alliterative poetry.

The opening of the poem in the B version illustrates the basics in practice. The transcription below the verses marks the basic pattern of staves (A) and lifts (X) and identifies the four words that contain the syllables for the alliterative pattern and thus provide this structure.

> In a somer seson, whan softe [mild] was þe sonne,
> I shoop me [clothed myself] into shroudes as I a sheep were,
> In habite as an heremite [hermit] vnholy of werkes,
> Wente wide in þis world wondres to here [to hear wondrous things].
> Ac [and] on a May morwenynge on Maluerne Hilles

Me bifel a ferly [a dream came to me], of fairye [the fairy realm] me
þoȝte.
I was wery [of]wandred [tired from wandering] and wente me to reste
Vnder a brood bank by a bournes [stream's] syde;
And as I lay and lenede [reclined] and loked on þe watres,
I slombred into a slepyng, it sweyed so murye [swayed so merrily].
 (B prologue 1–10)

1. AA/AA: somer, seson / softe, sonne
2. AA/AX: shoop, shroudes / sheep, were
3. AA/AX: habite, heremite / vnholy, werkes
4. AA/AX: wide, world / wondres, here
5. AA/AX: May, morwenynge / Maluerne Hilles
6. AA/AX: bifel, ferly / fairye, þoȝte
7. AA AX: wery, [of]wandred / wente, reste
8. AA/AX: brood, bank / bournes, syde
9. AA/AX: lay, lenede / loked, watres
10. AA/AX: slombred, slepyng / sweyed, murye

From this list one can observe the AA/AX pattern as the most common by far. Readers should look over these lines (and all others, of course) to seek other instances of stress and alliteration outside of the core structure, examining as well the role of the unstressed syllables, placed variously throughout the line, in differing numbers. Both the composition and the reception of alliterative verse are arts and not sciences, and thus enunciating and listening are key to detecting all kinds of alternate stresses and sound effects. Consider, for example, two lines from the A-text prologue, describing the range of human activity in the field of folk:

20. Summe putte hem to þe plouȝ, pleiȝede ful selde.
23. And summe putte hem to pride, aparailide hem þereaftir.

In neither line does the word "summe" receive stress or alliteration, and yet the dramatic contrast between the humble workers at the plough and the prideful, elegantly appareled slackers is conveyed by the scornful repetition of "summe." This powerful word, with its rumbling double nasals, might therefore receive more emphasis in performance than "putte," which technically receives stress and alliteration in both instances. So much depends on what readers hear and feel and on where they believe dramatic emphasis should be placed to express the meaning of Langland's long musical lines, which resound and echo in ever surprising ways throughout his sonorous poetry.

Notes

Preface

1. Some scholars consider the so-called Z text an early draft and thus a distinct version as well. See Rigg and Brewer, *Piers Plowman: The Z Version*.
2. On the fascinating history of the reception of *Piers Plowman* from the sixteenth to the nineteenth century in England, including its publication and embrace during the Reformation, see Kelen, *Langland's Early Modern Identities*. On the poem's relations to the European Reformation more broadly, see Robert Adams's essays "Langland as a Proto-Protestant" and "Langland and the *Devotio Moderna*."
3. The volumes by Stephen Barney and Andrew Galloway in the Penn Commentary Series target an advanced readership and provide detailed explanatory notes.
4. Malcolm Godden's *The Making of Piers Plowman* first explores the A text as an adaptation of Z (chapters 2–4), then B's adaptation of A (chapters 5–9), and then, in chapter 10, the C version.
5. Considering the demands of space needed to study three texts in parallel, it was not practical to consider the so-called Z text as a separate version. Readers can profit by studying that text and debating whether it is an early version of *Piers Plowman*, as Schmidt presents it in his *Parallel-Text Edition*, or is rather another, though eccentric, manuscript of the A text.
6. Derek Pearsall in "The Poetic Character of the C-text" mounts a strong defense of that text as "equally worthy of attention with the B-text," contending also that it "may well be thought a better poem." "Broadly speaking," writes Pearsall, "the C-text is substantially successful in achieving its overall purpose of reshaping and clarifying the general outline of the poem," while often displaying "the work of a poet at the height of his mature powers," with "no waning of . . . passion or purpose" (165).
7. Within the last decade alone, Míċeál Vaughan brought out *Piers Plowman:*

The A Version, Elizabeth Robertson and Stephen Shepherd's Norton Critical Edition of *Piers Plowman* went into its second printing, A.V.C. Schmidt completed his majestic *Piers Plowman: A Parallel-Text Edition of the A, B, C, and Z Versions*, Derek Pearsall released *Piers Plowman: A New Annotated Edition of the C-text*, and *The Cambridge Companion to "Piers Plowman,"* edited by Andrew Cole and Andrew Galloway, was published in 2014. The *Piers Plowman* Electronic Archive continues to publish hypertext editions of *Piers* manuscripts with facsimiles, and the Chaucer Studio has produced a performance of the B text based on the Norton edition. *The Yearbook of Langland Studies* annually chronicles *Piers* scholarship in its essays, book reviews, and bibliographies.

8. On the revolt, see the chronology and "Life of the Poet" in this book.

Note on the Texts

1. In part 2 of his edition, Schmidt provides detailed textual notes and an extensive literary and historical commentary on the poem, in addition to a thorough explanation of its textual history and of his editorial method. See also *Earthly Honest Things: Collected Essays on "Piers Plowman,"* a retrospective collection of Schmidt's scholarship on the poem.

2. Such glosses bring to mind the question of using translations of *Piers Plowman*. Though any medieval poem inevitably suffers from rendering into a modern language, translations can be useful and exciting tools and are sometimes works of art in themselves. Among the most available are Schmidt, *Piers Plowman: A New Translation of the B-Text*; E. Talbot Donaldson's translation of the B text in the Norton Critical Edition; Peter Sutton, *Piers Plowman: A Modern Verse Translation* (also the B text but with some passages from C patched in creatively); and George Economou, *William Langland's "Piers Plowman": The C Version*.

3. I accessed the Vulgate and the Douay-Rheims Bible at the Bible Hub website, which contains the Online Bible Study Suite. This site provides editions of the Holy Scriptures in all the original biblical languages and in the major historical versions and translations, offering an excellent academic resource for students of *Piers Plowman* and of medieval religious literature. (Readers should note that the Douay-Rheims Bible sequences the Psalms according to the Latin Vulgate, which differs in its numbering from the King James and other later versions—that is, Vulgate Psalm 22 corresponds to 23 in the King James. Further, the online edition of the Douay-Rheims Bible at biblehub.com aligns the Psalms with later versions of the Bible and not with the Vulgate, resulting in occasional differences of chapter and verse numbering between the online DRB and the print version. I have therefore used the Psalm numbering in the print edition of *The Holy Bible, Douay Rheims Version*, which corresponds exactly to the *Biblia Sacra Iuxta Vulgatam Versionem*, noting the difference between

these and the online version where applicable.) Two further websites will prove useful to students of *Piers Plowman*: the text of the Latin Vulgate (including the DRB translation) at www.latinvulgate.com and the Douay-Rheims Bible (including the Vulgate text) at www.drbo.org.

Life of the Poet

1. The situation of biography per se is therefore distinctly different than for Chaucer; see Donald Howard's *Chaucer: His Life, His Works, His World*.

2. In addition to Kane's important "Langland, William" entry in the *Oxford Dictionary of National Biography* (referred to as *ODNB* in citations), see also his book on the poet, *Piers Plowman: The Evidence for Authorship*.

3. "Claylands" is an old English agricultural term for mostly flat land of minimal fertility and bad drainage (because of the pervasive presence of clay in the soil). Transcription of the Latin annotations from Hm 128 are mine.

4. See "Narrative Reading Guide," section 7, for discussion of that self-portrait.

5. Adams also composed a short survey of his research in his essay "The Rokeles," to which he appends a historical index of "hitherto neglected references to Langland's extended family and their prominent public role in his own time as well as in the generations that preceded his birth" (88, and see 89–96).

6. Adams, *Rokele Family*, 14–15, nn8–10, identifies a tendency among critics to appropriate anachronistically the apparent details of the poet's life, as expressed in the poem's fictions, for ideological reasons.

7. In addition to Kane's overview, Pearsall's introduction to his new edition of the C text is one of the best introductions to the poet and his work. Schmidt's chapter "The Poem in Time" in *Parallel-Text*, 2.269–304, is a full and detailed introduction of particular utility to readers of this book. C. David Benson offers a comprehensive look at what he calls "the Langland myth" in his essay of the same title, conveniently bringing together—for the purpose of questioning—the stories told about the poem and poet. Ralph Hanna's *William Langland* is absolutely essential, as it compiles references to the known historical documents surrounding the poem, the poet, and his presumed family. All the raw data is here, including the 1388 Statute of Laborers and the documents and letters associated with the Peasant's Revolt of 1381. In a subsequent essay in *YLS*, "Emendations to a 1993 Vita de Ne'erdowel," Hanna offers systematic updates on issues and features of the 1993 work, collating it with newly revealed documents, historical research, and critical study on such topics as John But. As for the C text's autobiographical "apologia," see the entire collection of essays dedicated to this topic in the volume edited by Steven Justice and Kathryn Kerby-Fulton, *Written Work: Langland, Labor, and Authorship*, especially

Middleton's essay "Acts of Vagrancy," on the Statute of Laborers and the poet's depiction of his vagrancy. E. Talbot Donaldson's *Piers Plowman: The C-Text and Its Poet* is a classic study of the mind and art of the poet that created the final version of the poem.

8. In this overview of the Peasants' Revolt, I draw widely from Justice's book, which sets the uprising into religious, political, and literary-historical context. Also on the rebels' writings, see Ann Astell, "'Full of Enigmas': John Ball's Letters and *Piers Plowman*." Astell examines the literary ingenuity and the complex reading of *Piers Plowman* displayed in the documents circulated in the uprising, arguing that rebel leader and letter author John Ball "read Langland's poem as a political allegory," that "he did so with considerable sophistication," and that "Langland himself provided Ball with cues to encourage such an interpretation" (71).

9. Readers should see the section "Wycliffite Writings" in "Langland and His Contemporaries" in this book.

Narrative Reading Guide

Preface to the Narrative Reading Guide: Overview of A, B, and C

1. See John Bowers's essay "*Piers Plowman*'s William Langland: Editing the Text, Writing the Author's Life" and Jill Mann's "The Power of the Alphabet: A Reassessment of the Relation between the A and B Versions of *Piers Plowman*."

1. Working and Wandering as the World Asks: The Prologues of A, B, and C

1. This book's occasional use of the personal pronoun "us" and its related forms means to convey the immediacy and direct engagement that Langland creates with his audience. This is a rhetorical conceit and not an assumption about the religious standpoints of any reader. Whoever experiences the poem, for any reason or at any time, becomes part of this perpetual "we" that Langland addresses through Will.

2. Within the drama of the poem, certain figures use Latin to flaunt a haughty superiority. See for example B1.140–41a, where Holy Church humiliates Will and calls him a "doted daffe [stupid idiot]!" for not having studied enough Latin and thus for misspending his youth.

3. See the chapter "Langland and His Contemporaries" in this volume.

4. See appendix 2, "Reading *Piers Plowman* Aloud," for discussion of Langland's meter.

5. The B text was written in the early years of the reign of the young king

Richard II, when John of Gaunt was the most powerful man in the country, and this episode responds to concerns about his aggressive assertions of royal authority. His palace, the Savoy, would ultimately be burned in the Peasants' Revolt of 1381, so the danger of the rats and mice prophesied here was real.

6. See *Middle English Dictionary*, s.v. "communes," def. 4, which the *MED* offers with a question mark because of the particularity of Langland's usage: "Sustenance (?as contributed by or to a community or group of people)," citing just four examples, three of them from *Piers*. See def. 1a(a) for the usual meaning in the poem, "The common people (of a realm, county, city, etc.); the third estate of a body politic, consisting of the freemen (as distinct from the nobility and the clergy)."

2. Becoming a God by the Gospel: Passus 1 of A, B, and C

1. There is some variation in the manuscripts and among editors concerning this passage. Vaughan's rendering of the line refers not to Luke but to James: "by Seynt Jamys wordys" (passus 1.89). See his note on the potential scriptural sources of that allusion (*The A Version*, 151). Schmidt's edition prints all versions as referring to Luke and cites in his notes John 10:34 (which quotes Psalms 81:6) and also Luke 6:40 (*Parallel-Text*, 2.483). See Pearsall, *C-text*, 60, for other sources of the concept, including Luke 6:35, 8:21, 16:10, and 1 John 4:16.

2. See *Pearl*, passim, but esp. sections 9–11, where the Pearl Maiden tells the parable of the vineyard (Matt. 20:1–16).

3. Lady Mede Gets Ready for Her Close-Up: Passus 2 of A, B, and C

1. On Alice Perrers, see Stephanie Trigg's essay "The Traffic in Medieval Women."

2. Galloway continues helpfully: "As related entities—the first is the sin, the second the technical training that helped make the sin possible—Simony and Civil function throughout the passus as nearly inseparable though not indistinguishable twins" (*Penn Commentary*, 253).

3. "Assize" indicates "A session of a court charged with the deliberation and disposition of civil actions (esp. actions concerning land tenure and imprisonment)" or "the deliberations of such a court (the gathering of evidence, the hearing of the plaintiff, the defendant and the witnesses before a jury, the rendering of decisions)" (*MED*, s.v. "assise").

4. Schmidt, *Parallel-Text*, 2.493, indicates that "brede" in this context means to "spread out, distend," as pigs would from eating urban garbage, but he does not rule out the sexual meaning as well.

5. Since only the C text identifies Favel as Mede's father (one of two), this

moment of gratitude in C (2.162–63) actually depicts her betrothed and her sire as her strongest advocates, laboring to ensure the wedding. The chaotic shifting of similar names across versions, with the double attribution of fatherhood in C, notoriously confuses readers. Perhaps Langland attempted in this confusion to convey a sense of promiscuity and even incest.

4. Lady Mede Tries Everything: Passus 3 of A, B, and C

1. On this issue in the poem, see Calabrese, "Prostitutes."

2. Edward III abandoned his claim to France's throne in 1360 in the Treaty of Brétigny, which also included a French promise to pay three million crowns to ransom King John, who was held prisoner in England for three years.

3. In the A text, Conscience quotes the Psalm's answer from verse 5 but does not quote its opening question, which the B text adds (B3.234a).

4. See the description of the trinity at *Paradiso* 14.28–30: "Quell' uno e due e tre che sempre vive / e regna sempre in tre e'n due e'n uno, / non circunscritto, e tutto circunscrive" [That One and Two and Three who ever lives / and ever reigns in Three and Two and One, / not circumscribed and circumscribing all] (trans. Mandelbaum). And see the entirety of *Paradiso* 33.

5. An Illegal Interlude between Peace and Wrong: Passus 4 of A, B, and C

1. I am here paraphrasing the lines as all manuscripts render them, though editors tend to reject the reference to oats and chickens as unmetrical padding (see Schmidt, *Parallel-Text*, 2.335).

2. See "Narrative Reading Guide," section 7.

7. And I Confess as Well: Passus 5 of the B Text and C Text Passūs 5–7

1. See "Narrative Reading Guide," section 12, for a discussion of that episode in A and in B, including the controversy over attribution of the speaker in the A text.

2. This section, commenting on the apologia, is best read in conjunction with "Life of the Poet," which provides relevant bibliography.

3. In this context, the word must mean "A lazy vagabond, an idler, a fraudulent beggar" (*MED*, s.v. "loller(e)," def. 1).

4. See Middleton, "Acts of Vagrancy."

5. We can also, as Pearsall suggests, see Reason as the "waking dreamer's own rational self-analysis" (*C-text*, 110), so perhaps the scene is one of both external, social interrogation and also personal introspection.

6. These are the opening words of two antiphons—sung prayers based on the Psalms—that begin the Office of the Dead that Will sings; see Psalms 114:9

(116:9 in online *DRB*) for *placebo* [I will please the Lord] and 5:9 (5:8 in online *DRB*) for *dirige* [direct my way in thy sight]. From the latter word comes the modern musical term "dirge."

7. The first comes from Matt. 13:44, and the second is what Pearsall (*C-text*, 115) calls a "cue-reference" to the episode at Luke 15:8–9, where a woman with ten groats loses one, recovers it, and then tells her friends, "Rejoice with me, because I have found the groat which I had lost."

8. A Pilgrim and a Ploughman: Passus 6 of the A Text with the Conclusions of B5 and C7

1. The negative "nou3t" is dropped in the B and C versions for clarity. The meaning in A is "be aware that you do not rouse yourself in anger," and in B and C, "be aware of angering yourself."

9. The Hunger Artists: Passus 7 of the A Text with B6 and C8

1. See *Canterbury Tales*, general prologue (I), in Benson, *Riverside Chaucer*, 173–88.

2. As Vaughan explains, the Black Death "had marked effect on the availability and stability of laborers, in rural agriculture particularly." Accordingly, says Vaughan, "the king's council issued a Statute of Laborers to control the wages and movement of workers" (*The A Version*, 177). The poem here likely refers to that statute.

3. See the wider Gospel context: "But when thou art invited, go, sit down in the lowest place; that when he who invited thee cometh, he may say to thee: Friend, go up higher. Then shalt thou have glory before them that sit at table with thee" (Luke 14:10).

4. Pearsall notes how important the word is for Langland, as it reflects his need to criticize wandering beggars who refuse to work, but he also explains that the term does not yet explicitly refer to the "Lollards," which means that Langland's use of this word does not reflect any particular treatment of Wycliffism. See Pearsall, *C-text*, 25–29; and see *MED*, s.v. "loller(e)," def. 1, "A lazy vagabond, an idler, a fraudulent beggar," and 2(a), "An English Lollard." The *MED* says this word comes from "lollen v. [meaning "rest, lounge, loll"] & Lollard n." See also *MED*, s.v. "losel," meaning "rogue, rascal."

5. See my discussion "Langland and History" in the chapter "Life of the Poet."

10. Dreams of a Pardon: Passus 8 of the A Text with B7 and C9

1. Some editors print a form of "fowls" here, indicating the carefree birds of scripture that God feeds. See Matt. 6:26 and Luke 12:24. Schmidt, *Parallel-Text*,

2.376, notes that Langland was likely making a pun with fowls and the careless "fools" of scripture.

2. On the exclusion of this scene from the C text, see Hanna's essay "The 'Absent' Pardon-Tearing of *Piers Plowman* C," which argues that the perceived excision of this scene relates to the minimized role of Piers and the increased role of Will as a figure of ideology and authority. I am grateful to Professor Hanna for an Advanced Access version of his essay.

3. Pearsall, *C-text*, 176, explains how great lords would "retain minstrels in permanent employment." The wealthy evidently sought to curry favor with power by rewarding such minstrels, including the king's "high-class professional musicians," when, as Pearsall says, they "did the rounds" (144, in a note on a similar passage in C7).

11. On the Road in Search of Dowel: Passūs 9 and 10 of the A Text with B8–9 and C10

1. On the role of marriage in the poem, see Tavormina, *Kindly Similitude*.

2. I follow Schmidt's version of the passage, which various editors present differently. In Schmidt's text the pen is a metaphor for God's creative word, writing the words of Genesis that follow. See his explanation of his rendering in *Parallel-Text*, 2.381–82.

12. Dame Study Teaches a Lesson: Passus 11 of the A Text with B10 and 11 (opening) and C11

1. On this strange and violent conceit, see Lawton, *Blasphemy*, 100.

2. Romans 12:3. Since Langland attributes the idea to Augustine, he must be thinking of *City of God* 12.16, where Augustine quotes Paul's warning: "In virtue of the authority given to me by God's grace I say this to all in your company: do not be wiser than you ought to be: but be wise in moderation, in proportion to the faith which God has allotted to each of you."

3. See "Wife of Bath's Prologue" in Benson, *Riverside Chaucer*, 732–38; luckily Wit is spared Socrates's fate—to have a chamber pot dumped on his head because "after thunder must come rain."

4. For a recent study of Langland's visionary mysticism, see Jessica Barr, *Willing to Know God*.

5. Like most editors, Vaughan (*The A Version*, 186) attributes the speech that follows not to Clergy but to his wife Scripture, on the basis of a feminine pronoun in most A-text manuscripts at A11.182 introducing the speaker. Schmidt prints "he" and argues (*Parallel-Text*, 2.391) that scribal misreading of the masculine pronoun "he" as "heo" (another form of "she") caused the confusion and

that in fact Clergy is speaking, just as in the B and C texts, which identify him explicitly as answering Will. See Schmidt, *Earthly Honest Things*, 150–52, for a detailed discussion of the issue, arguing against his own prior adoption of the feminine pronoun in the 1995 version of his parallel-text edition.

6. The B text retains that passage about Gregory the Great, expanding it fully, and C, as we saw above, transfers that expanded B material to C5, after Will's apologia.

7. Matt. 23:2. See the next verse, 23:3, translated: "All things therefore whatsoever they shall say to you, observe and do: but according to their works do ye not; for they say, and do not." I assume Will speaks these lines in A, because he clearly offers them in question form in the B text (B10.330).

8. On the prayers in Latin required of lay people, see Duffy, "How the Plowman Learned his Paternoster."

9. As Pearsall explains, discussing the same image in the C version, "the world is a mirror because it is, as God's creation, an image of the mind of its creator, in its order and beauty, . . . here the mirror of the world merely reflects the dreamer's vanity and cupidity" (*C-text*, 208).

13. John But Puts an End to the A Version

1. I render passages quoted from A12.99ff. without italics in order to display the modern glosses more clearly, but Schmidt prints these verses in italics to emphasize their spurious nature.

2. The *MED* lists this line under "sclaundre," def. 4(c): "the ill effects of scandal, spiritual injury." It also cites this line under "scathe," def. 1(f): "reproach."

3. See *MED*, s.v. "trepeget," (b) "a device for catching birds or animals, . . . a snare or trap; also, a pitfall; (c) an instrument of punishment designed to dunk an offender under water; a cucking stool"; and *MED*, s.v. "trace (n.(1))," where several definitions may apply: 1(a), "A course, path, way"; 2(a), "A human track or trail"; 3(a), "A footstep . . . ; a step in a dance," in this case the dance of Death.

4. See *MED*, s.v. "light," def. 2(b): "the radiance or glory of Jesus, the Virgin, God or his countenance, angels; light of heaven or paradise."

5. On But's intervention, see Prendergast, "John But and the Problem of Langlandian Authority."

14. Farewell My Recklessness: Passus 11 of the B Text with C12–13

1. Schmidt, *Parallel-Text*, 2.604. Schmidt attributes B11.153–69 to Trajan, in addition to the longer discourse that seems to begin but really "resumes," he says, at line 170 and extends to 318.

2. Lines 179ff. support this idea, as Recklessness asserts the need for death,

loss, and failure as the "meschiefes" that must be endured as one awaits the grace of God. To support this doctrine he cites the Gospel verses "Nisi granum frumenti cadens in terram mortuum fuerit [unless the grain of wheat falling into the ground die]" (C12.180α; John 12:24).

3. But compare the compassionate tone and poignancy of Conscience's homage to the treasure of a "trewe wille" (B13.190–94).

4. Of the fifty-plus distinct meanings in the *MED* for "taken," perhaps 11a(f), "to have sexual relations with (sb., an animal); also, ravish (a woman, someone else's wife), take by force; of a bull: mount (a cow), mate with," applies best, though Langland's line is not cited there.

15. Just Will's Imagination: Passus 12 of the B Text and C14

1. See the book-length study of the history of the "imagination" by Michelle Karnes, with a chapter on its role in *Piers* (179–206). "Imagination participates centrally in the process by which anything is understood in its fullness," Karnes argues, and so "what most concerns Langland" at this point in the narrative "is how to make the transition from natural knowledge, the knowledge that the individual attains through the natural faculties of sense and reason, to what we might call spiritual understanding, that is, understanding created things as they pertain to God" (180).

2. "Bedes," besides meaning prayers or supplications (*MED*, s.v. "bēd(e)") can mean rosary beads, but that construction demands a preposition, as in A5.8: "so I babelide on my bedis."

3. Schmidt identifies Felice as the haughty and then abandoned heroine of the romance *Guy of Warwick* and Rosamounde as the mistress of Henry II, "allegedly poisoned by Henry's Queen Eleanor in 1177" and buried in Oxford (*Parallel-Text*, 2.615).

4. See *MED*, s.v. "catel," def. 1(a), "Property of any kind; goods, treasure, money, land, income, etc.," and the provisionally explained 1(c), "?the condition of being rich, wealth." Langland's use seems to support the latter, and also 1(b), which simply says the term can be used figuratively.

5. Robertson and Shepherd in the Norton edition, 193, explain Langland's logic: Luke 2:7 says that "there was no room for them in the inn," and since the poor do not even try to get rooms at inns, the holy family was not poor.

6. Paul adapts Psalms 31:1: "beatus cui dimissa est iniquitas et absconditum est peccatum [blessed are they whose iniquities are forgiven, and whose sins are covered]."

7. On the history of confession, see Little, *Confession and Resistance*. Glossing this line, Pearsall says that it was orthodox doctrine that contrition alone was sufficient "to deliver a man from sin" but that by the 1380s the argument

that confession was unnecessary had come to be associated with Lollardy (*C-text*, 243).

8. The C text ends the passus differently, saying that such fidelity as Trajan displayed is a form of love and a large reward from a loyal lord. C cites Matthew 25:21: "Quia super pauca fuisti fidelis," a phrase from the parable of the talents where the master congratulates his servant for putting his money to productive use: "His lord said to him: Well done, good and faithful servant, because thou hast been faithful over a few things, I will place thee over many things: enter thou into the joy of thy lord." Then Imaginatif comments:

> "And þat is loue and large huyre [generous payment], yf þe lord be trewe,
> And a cortesye more þen couenant [than contract] was, what so clerkes carpe [say]!
> For al worth as God wol [all goes as God wills]"—and þerwith he vanschede. (C14.215-17)

16. The Dinner Party: Passus 13 of the B Text and C15.1–233

1. An echo of Matt. 10:22: "he that shall persevere unto the end, he shall be saved." See Schmidt 2.627 on Langland's punning on "dia," a medicinal drug or potion, and "diu," meaning "for a long time."

2. See *MED*, s.v. "infinite (n.)," def. b: "something unlimited; infinite time." On this subject, see Middleton, "Two Infinites."

3. The context in Paul: "Revenge not yourselves, my dearly beloved; but give place unto wrath, for it is written: Revenge is mine, I will repay, saith the Lord. But if thy enemy be hungry, give him to eat; if he thirst, give him to drink. For, doing this, thou shalt heap coals of fire upon his head. Be not overcome by evil, but overcome evil by good" (Romans 12:19–21).

4. As Pearsall notes (*C-text*, 259), such cake-men would also tend to put on a show for amusement and thus were minstrels of sorts, permitting Langland to exploit the bawdy scatological humor associated with cheap entertainment.

5. What follows concerning Haukin should be read in conjunction with section 7 above, which also addresses this major shift of material from B to C.

For the rest, there is no perfect way to divide up and study in parallel the next few passūs, since the versions do not end together until B15 and C17. So I will divide the action as it unfolds into mini sections, marking the line and passus divisions to facilitate comparison.

6. C transfers this detail to Pride's confession (C6.43). For the large passages discussed in this section that C redistributes into his passūs 6 and 7, see Schmidt, *Parallel-Text*, 1.531ff. Then flip back to see them working in their new environments, 1.185ff.

7. In section 7 I noted, among other transferences, that Langland imports Will's meditation on the branches of Sloth from the Haukin episode (B13.410–21) to expand the portrait of that sin in C (C7.69–80).

8. Along with the discussion of the branches of Sloth, Langland transfers this extended meditation on replacing minstrels with the poor and needy into the C text (C7.81–118α).

17. The After Party: Passus 14 of the B Text and C15.234–C16.155

1. The actual biblical context from Solomon: "Many have been brought to fall for gold, and the beauty thereof hath been their ruin. Gold is a stumbling block to them that sacrifice to it: woe to them that eagerly follow after it, and every fool shall perish by it. Blessed is the rich man that is found without blemish: and that hath not gone after gold, nor put his trust in money nor in treasures. Who is he, and we will praise him? for he hath done wonderful things in his life" (Ecclesiasticus 31:6–9).

2. The context in B differs, as Patience there explains that true confession functions like a document of acquittal that defies the claims of the Devil for the human soul. The document serves mainly the "poore of herte. / Ellis is al on ydel, al þat euere we wr[o3]ten [made, did]" (B14.195–96).

18. Free Spirits: Passus B15.1–257 and C16.156–End

1. See section 10 above for discussion of the similar social alienation practiced by the wandering beggars in C9, whom Will praises as minstrels of heaven and God's messengers.

2. Spearing in "The Art of Preaching and *Piers Plowman*" associates Langland's "theory of composition" with musical practice. Like a sermon, *Piers* displays "an interweaving of sub-themes, involving frequent reappearances of the same set of words and ideas," an art akin to music's use of "recurrence, variation [and] transposition" (115).

3. On this critical moment in the text, see Davlin's essay "Petrus, Id Est, Christus: Piers the Plowman as 'The Whole Christ,'" which contextualizes in Christian doctrine the various but ultimately coherent identities of Piers in the poem. On the complexity of the character Piers across the versions, see Burrow, "The New Lives of Piers Plowman." Burrow wonders what if anything "guarantees the integrity of the figure of Piers in B and C," and studies the "failure of articulation" that results in most readers identifying Piers not as he is manifested late in the poem, spiritually in the *Vita Christi*, but rather as "the ploughman who so memorably puts forth his head in the half acre" episode (52). And see Knowles, "Langland's Empty Verbs," which studies Langland's

adaptation of Paul's concept of how Christ "emptied himself" (Phil. 2:7) to become human, an act of dutiful submission represented in the poem by Piers Plowman in his service to Truth.

19. Anima and Free Will Try to Unite the World: Passus B15.258–End and C17

1. The controversy over this passage lies in the word "foweles," which appears in all B manuscripts but is rejected by many editors, while accepted by Schmidt. Readers must be prepared to see such variation and disagreement among editions. Schmidt explains his choices and the apparent meaning of these verses in his textual notes and commentary in *Parallel-Text*, 2.428, 2.651.

2. As Pearsall points out in his note to Langland's first use of this quotation (*C-text*, 63), the phrase is proverbial but echoes Tobit 3:6: "enim mihi mori magis quam vivere," to which Langland adds the word "male," meaning "evilly, sinfully."

3. See Pearsall's notes to this passage (*C-text*, 287) and also his discussion of Lollardy (25–29). Pearsall argues that Langland's assertion of the sufficiency of faith refutes the Wycliffite position that "the priestly office is invalid if administered by a sinful priest" (287); it also asserts the role of faith in apprehending the mystery of transubstantiation, again combating a Wycliffite position.

4. Instead of the verb "to love" here, Pearsall prints "leve" (to believe); we would translate that line as "God would not instruct anyone to believe any doctrine that was not true."

5. For this paraphrase, I draw from Schmidt's helpful notes on this passage, explaining that pope and bishop endanger their souls "for not fulfilling their apostolic vocation" (*Parallel-Text*, 2.657). Glossing prior lines C17.188–93 (B15.492–99), where the text lists various Middle Eastern apostolic sees, Schmidt explains: "Bishops appointed to such sees . . . rarely went near them, as the prospect of death was assured" (*Parallel-Text*, 2.655). Nonetheless, their failure to enact Jesus's command to his disciples to preach, "Ite in vniuersum mundum [Go out into all the world]" (C17.191; Mark 16:15), leaves them blameworthy.

6. As Pearsall notes, the most recent instance was the "crusade launched by Urban VI in 1379, with mercenary soldiers, against the antipope, Clement VII, after the papal schism of 1378" (*C-text*, 292).

7. See, for example, Genesis 8:8–12, Luke 3:22.

20. Fighting for the Fruit of Charity: B16 and C18

1. I borrow this phrase from James Dean; see his study of age and time in medieval literature, *The World Grown Old*.

2. See Pearsall's helpful gloss on this difficult passage: "God in his Incarnation must live and suffer as a man . . . and must learn his job as a healer in terms of the capacities of the human Free Will" (*C-text*, 302).

3. On the changing role of the Jews in the C text, see the essay by Narin van Court, "The Hermeneutics of Suppression."

4. Pearsall identifies the verse as coming from the "gospels of the nativity of Mary, such as the *Pseudo-Matthaei Evangeliam*" (*C-text*, 305).

5. Line 245, explaining that God anticipates the couple's thought, does not seem to be based on any particular detail in Genesis but implies that Abraham and Sarah were naturally curious about God's purpose for the visit, revealed in his promise of a son.

21. A Spy, a Samaritan, and the Spirit's Flame: B17 and C19

1. On the centrality of the Samaritan to Langland's Christology, see David Aers, "Remembering the Samaritan, Remembering Semyuief." "This encounter with divine charity," argues Aers, "supersedes any claims that assumed the ability of humans to do well enough from putatively autonomous resources to make eternal beatitude theirs" (99).

2. The conceit is comic in Chaucer's poem, of course, but rather stern in Langland's. The biblical sources do not appear to be funny, but rather axiomatic. See Proverbs 27:15, "Roofs dropping through in a cold day, and a contentious woman are alike," and 21:9, "Better to live on a corner of the roof than share a house with a quarrelsome wife."

22. Christ Was on Rode: B18 and C20

1. As Pearsall notes (*C-text*, 326), a name and identity invented for the Roman centurion who spears Jesus at John 19:34.

2. On the topic of justice, see Myra Stokes, *Justice and Mercy in "Piers Plowman."*

3. For example, "kalketrappes" are "device[s] with sharp iron spikes set on the ground to cripple the feet of an advancing enemy," and a "mangonel" is "a machine used for hurling stones or other matter in the siege or defense of castles or cities" (*MED*, s.vv. "calketrappe," "mangonel").

4. Pearsall, *C-text*, 337, associates this unique digression with the free-flowing style of preaching, a topic studied in detail by Spearing, who mentions this passage as illustrating the poet's "awareness of his own tendency to let narrative slide across into homily" ("Art of Preaching," 112). See Calabrese, "Langland's Last Words," for further discussion of this scene.

5. Pearsall, *C-text*, 338–39, explains the complex biblical references behind

this imagery of drink. He cites, among other texts, Isaiah 51:17, 22, referring to the cup of suffering that Jesus wishes he could refuse at Matthew 26:39; and Matthew 27:48, where Christ is given bitter gall on the cross.

23. Last Man Plowing: B19 and C21

1. I will use the C-text version for quotation in these last two passūs simply because we have to choose one for citation and *perhaps* its text is more authoritative because of its better lineage.

2. Questions of revision relate to the larger understanding of the composition of the *Piers* corpus, which has prompted various critical understandings. Lawrence Warner, *The Lost History of "Piers Plowman,"* argues that B, as we know it, never really circulated as a "published" poem, asserting that C21–22 were written for C only and then used to create a more complete version of an already "finished" B text. Ralph Hanna, *Pursuing History*, traces the processes of the poet's revision on loose-leaf sheets and strips of paper upon which he wrote passages to be added in rolling revision. Bowers in *"Piers Plowman's* William Langland" and Mann in "The Power of the Alphabet" argue, however, that perhaps C was written first and that A is a condensed version, written last for a more popular audience.

3. See Pearsall's note on the schismatic papal wars, *C-text*, 360.

24. Anarchists and Antichrist: B20 and C22

1. Pearsall, *C-text*, 363. The character Need has generated much debate and confusion for readers, as the reasons for his appearance at this moment of the poem are never made clear. See Pearsall's notes, 363–64, for critical bibliography. See Jill Mann's essay "The Nature of Need Revisited," which surveys critical opinions. Mann argues that "need" functions throughout the poem as a force of "natural law," central to the poet's engagement with the "economic problems of his society" (28), however unsuccessful Langland may be in integrating his conception of need into any economic solutions—a problem, Mann says, that society still faces today. Robert Adams, in his essay "The Nature of Need," reads the character more darkly as a precursor of the Antichrist, a reading that Mann directly opposes.

2. The *MED* reads "byde" here as "to go begging" (s.v. "bidden," def. 3(a)), but Schmidt's glossary sees it as a form of "bīden," which *MED* defines as "to wait expectantly or patiently" (def. 5(a)) or "to suffer or bear (hardship, etc.)" (def. 8(b)). The ambiguity indicates the slipperiness of Need's arguments; he may be urging Will toward patient acceptance of his vulnerability or exhorting him to beg in order to fulfill his needs immediately.

3. See Stahl, *Commentary on the Dream of Scipio*, 88, concerning nightmares from hunger.

4. Pearsall, *C-text*, 366, glosses "foles," based on St. Paul, as "ordinary faithful Christians" (see 1 Cor. 4:10).

5. Langland draws the term not directly from Paul but from existing polemic. For historical background see Penn R. Szittya, *The Antifraternal Tradition in Medieval Literature*, which includes a chapter on *Piers* (247–87); see Szittya's index for a series of references to "penetrantes domos."

6. Schmidt takes all of lines 365–68 as the extended allegorical name of the plaster. Acknowledging that possibility, Pearsall, however, punctuates the verses differently (*C-text*, 377). In the manuscripts it is difficult to distinguish dialogue from Langlandian extended epithet.

Langland and His Contemporaries

1. See the comprehensive overview of this critical work in Mooney and Stubbs, *Scribes and the City*. For the identification of Pinkhurst, see Mooney, "Chaucer's Scribe."

2. See Burrow, *Ricardian Poetry*; Mehl, "Old Age in Middle English Literature"; Middleton, "Public Poetry."

3. See the classic study of the genre by Spearing, *Medieval Dream-Poetry*, esp. 138–62 on *Piers*, and Calabrese, "Interior Visions: *Piers Plowman* and the Dream Vision Genre."

4. See the excellent modern translation by Charles Dahlberg; for an introductory guide see Sarah Kay, *The Romance of the Rose*.

5. Dante's *Divine Comedy*, usually published in three separate volumes, is widely available in scores of translations, of which I recommend the parallel texts of Durling and of the Hollanders, as well as the Allen Mandelbaum versions offered at digitaldante.columbia.edu.

6. Because of its length and assumed lack of literary artistry, the *Pricke of Conscience* has not been translated and is seldom included, even in excerpt, in medieval anthologies. But it can be easily read in the recent EETS edition by Ralph Hanna and Sarah Wood, whose notes serve as an introduction to its critical study as well.

7. For Chaucer's works, see Larry Benson, *The Riverside Chaucer*; for the *Canterbury Tales* alone, see the excellent editions by John H. Fisher and Mark Allen and by Robert Boenig and Andrew Taylor. See also V. A. Kolve and Glending Olsen's Norton Critical Edition and the lively recent translation by Sheila Fisher. On Chaucer and Langland, see Kane, *Chaucer and Langland: Historical and Textual Approaches*, and Bowers, *Chaucer and Langland: The*

Antagonistic Tradition. See also W. A. Davenport's *Chaucer and His English Contemporaries* and, in this Florida series, Tison Pugh's *Introduction to Geoffrey Chaucer*.

8. The best edition for Gower's major English work, the *Confessio Amantis*, is the TEAMS edition edited by Russell A. Peck with Latin translations by Andrew Galloway. The *Vox Clamantis* is translated by Eric Stockton in *The Major Latin Works of John Gower*. A. G. Rigg in *Poems on Contemporary Events* has translated two important Latin texts that Gower added to the *Vox Clamantis*, the *Visio Anglie* (1381) and the *Cronica tripertita* (1400), focusing upon the revolt and then the deposition of Richard II. Gower scholars consider these the most crucial parts of the *Vox* for modern readers, and certainly Gower's perspective on society, order, and kingship invites comparison with Langland's exploration of these themes in *Piers*. On Gower's life and works, see the volume edited by Echard.

9. Some scholars also attribute a religious historical poem, *St. Erkenwald*, to the poet, though this text is not found in the same manuscript as the other four poems. Marie Borroff includes it in her translation *The Gawain Poet: Complete Works*.

10. The best complete edition of the poems is Malcolm Andrew and Ronald Waldron, *The Poems of the Pearl Manuscript*, and there are many good translations of the various poems, including those by the great Professor Tolkien in *Sir Gawain and the Green Knight, Pearl, and Sir Orfeo*. For an introductory critical study see, in this Florida series, John Bowers, *An Introduction to the "Gawain" Poet*.

11. The best way to read Julian today is not in translation but in the accessible yet magnificently complex original Middle English, in the edition by Nicholas Watson and Jacqueline Jenkins, *The Writings of Julian of Norwich*.

12. See Anne Hudson's *Premature Reformation* and *Selections from English Wycliffite Writings*. See also Cole, *Literature and Heresy in the Age of Chaucer*; Somerset, *Feeling Like Saints: Lollard Writings after Wyclif*; and Pearsall, "Langland and Lollardy: From B to C," which is included in a special section in the *Yearbook of Langland Studies* 17 (2003) titled "Langland and Lollardy." See as well the evolving bibliography at the Lollard Society site: http://lollardsociety.org/?page_id=10.

13. See Helen Barr, *The "Piers Plowman" Tradition*; James M. Dean, *Medieval English Political Writings*.

14. See Lynn Staley's *The Book of Margery Kempe* (Norton Critical Edition), and John Arnold and Katherine Lewis's *Companion to the Book of Margery Kempe*; see also the important article on her mental health by Mary Hardiman Farley, "Her Own Creature."

Appendix 1. Persons, Personifications, and Allegorizings in *Piers Plowman*

1. In presenting such names that extend over two or more verses, I have adapted the punctuation in Schmidt's edition in order to render them as continuous hyphenated entities.

2. Concerning Langland's art of creating characters, see Lavinia Griffiths, *Personification in "Piers Plowman,"* which helpfully designates personification as "the grammatical transformation of a noun or other part of speech into a proper name" (5). For a comprehensive reference guide to all the words in the poem in English, Latin, and French, see Joseph S. Wittig, *"Piers Plowman": Concordance.*

Appendix 2. Pronunciation Guide: Reading *Piers Plowman* Aloud

1. See "Reading Middle English," in Robertson and Shepherd, *Piers Plowman*, xvii–xxi; "Pronouncing Middle English," in Burrow and Turville-Petre, *A Book of Middle English*, 9–13. Garbáty, *Medieval English Literature*, 41–45, provides a delightful and extremely useful overview. For classic, complete resources, see Moore, *Historical Outlines of English Sounds and Inflections*; Mossé, *A Handbook of Middle English*; Kökeritz, *A Guide to Chaucer's Pronunciation*; Horobin and Smith, *An Introduction to Middle English*.

2. These sounds are notoriously difficult for Modern English speakers at first. A fricative is a consonant produced by expelling air through a space in the mouth formed by the placement of the tongue, teeth, or lips. Velar and palatal simply refer to the tongue's placement on either the hard palate or the soft palate (the velum). Readers will benefit from listening to recorded examples, hearing native German or Spanish speakers making the sounds as explained in the examples, and listening to a teacher performing the sounds. Once one notices the position of the tongue in the mouth after many attempts at making the sound, the linguistics will make sense, and the appreciation of the poetry will be immensely enhanced.

3. For some overviews of alliterative meter, see Lawton, "Alliterative Style"; Burrow and Turville-Petre, *A Book of Middle English*, 56–61; Barney, "Langland's Prosody"; Duggan, "Notes on the Metre of *Piers Plowman*" and "The End of the Line."

Bibliography

Editions and Translations of *Piers Plowman*

Donaldson, E. Talbot, trans. *See* Robertson and Shepherd.

Economou, George, trans. *William Langland's Piers Plowman: The C Version; A Verse Translation*. Philadelphia: University of Pennsylvania Press, 1996.

Kane, George, ed. *Piers Plowman: The A Version*. London: Athlone Press; Berkeley: University of California Press, 1960.

Kane, George, and E. Talbot Donaldson, eds. *Piers Plowman: The B Version*. 2nd ed. London: Athlone Press; Berkeley: University of California Press, 1988.

Pearsall, Derek, ed. *Piers Plowman: A New Annotated Edition of the C-text*. Exeter: University of Exeter Press, 2008.

Rigg, A. G., and Charlotte Brewer, eds. *Piers Plowman: The Z Version*. Toronto: Pontifical Institute of Medieval Studies, 1983.

Robertson, Elizabeth, and Stephen H. A. Shepherd, eds. *Piers Plowman: The Donaldson Translation, Select Authoritative Middle English Text, Sources and Backgrounds, Criticism*. New York: Norton, 2006.

Russell, George, and George Kane, eds. *Piers Plowman: The C Version*. London: Athlone Press; Berkeley: University of California Press, 1997.

Schmidt, A.V.C., ed. *Piers Plowman: A New Translation of the B-Text*. Oxford: Oxford University Press, 1992.

———. *Piers Plowman: A Parallel-Text Edition of the A, B, C, and Z Versions in Two Volumes*. 2nd ed. Kalamazoo, Mich.: Medieval Institute Publications, 2011.

Skeat, Walter W., ed. *The Vision of William concerning Piers the Plowman in Three Parallel Texts; Together with Richard the Redeless*. Oxford: Clarendon Press, 1886.

Sutton, Peter, trans. *Piers Plowman: A Modern Verse Translation*. Jefferson, N.C.: McFarland, 2014.

Vaughan, Míċeál F., ed. *Piers Plowman: The A Version*. Baltimore: Johns Hopkins University Press, 2011.

Handbooks, Guidebooks, and Companions

Alford, John A., ed. *A Companion to "Piers Plowman."* Berkeley: University of California Press, 1988.

The still classic introduction to the poem examines *Piers* in its historical, poetic, critical, textual, and literary contexts, with chapters composed by various experts on the poem's features, themes, techniques, and histories. Cole and Galloway's *Cambridge Companion* updates and pairs with it.

———, ed. *"Piers Plowman": A Glossary of Legal Diction*. Cambridge: D. S. Brewer, 1988.

A comprehensive alphabetical listing of legal words and phrases used in *Piers Plowman*, defining the terms, charting their instances in the three versions, providing primary references to medieval legal texts that witness them, and offering secondary references to modern scholarship on legal matters. Many entries also contain cross-references to other definitions. Alford seeks to "identify the words in *Piers Plowman*, both common and technical, that have reference to the law, and thus to indicate the nature and extent of the poet's legal frame of thought," and also to provide a reference guide for "students of other Middle English authors, such as Chaucer, Gower, and the Pearl poet, whose diction reflects a similar preoccupation with the law" (vii).

———. *Piers Plowman: A Guide to the Quotations*. Binghamton, N.Y.: Medieval & Renaissance Texts & Studies, 1992.

Alford's comprehensive guide identifies the sources of the biblical, patristic, grammatical, legal, literary, and liturgical quotations, in Latin and in French, that appear in *Piers Plowman*, divided by passus, for the A, B, and C versions, keyed to the text of the Athlone editions. Index 2 lists the scriptural quotations in the order of biblical books, and index 3 lists all quotations alphabetically. Alford begins with a critical introduction about Langland's multilingualism, his use of sources, their complex functions in the poem and manuscripts, and the difficulties of presenting quotations in modern editions.

Baldwin, Anna. *A Guidebook to "Piers Plowman."* New York: Palgrave Macmillan, 2007.

This excellent narrative guide focuses on the B text, summarizing and analyzing the poem, vision by vision, passus by passus, and event by event, in clearly divided sections. It offers "text boxes" that supply historical information and bibliography on aspects of English political and religious history mentioned in the poem, such as "Church Courts," "Secular Law Courts," "Minstrels and Poets," and "Monks and Friars."

Barney, Stephen A. *The Penn Commentary on "Piers Plowman."* Vol. 5. Philadelphia: University of Pennsylvania Press, 2006.

Part 5 but the first published of a proposed five-volume series of critical commentary on the poem. This volume covers the C version, passūs 20–22, and B 18–20. Using the line numbers of the Athlone editions as rubrics, the *Penn Commentary* offers detailed literary critical and historical commentary on each episode in the poem, often noting differences and revisions between the versions. A headnote on the main action of the passus prefaces each section, and the volumes include a helpful index of passages discussed in the book by passus and line. The commentary also functions as a guide to scholarship on the poem and includes an extensive list of works cited and an index of historical and modern works. See also Galloway's volume in this series listed below.

Cole, Andrew, and Andrew Galloway, eds. *The Cambridge Companion to "Piers Plowman."* Cambridge: Cambridge University Press, 2014.

Updating Alford's classic *Companion*, Cole and Galloway assemble a host of experts to reconsider major aspects in the field of *Piers* studies, in order to provide a twenty-first-century guide to reading and studying the poem in its various and evolving critical and theoretical contexts. After an overview of the poem's major episodes, the book offers chapters on textual history, literary history, allegory, Langland's family biography, religious institutions, political forms, Christian philosophy, non-Christians depicted in the poem, manuscript history, the Plowman tradition in later writings, and thoughts on *Piers Plowman* and contemporary theory.

Galloway, Andrew. *The Penn Commentary on "Piers Plowman."* Vol. 1. Philadelphia: University of Pennsylvania Press, 2006.

See the description of the *Penn Commentary* under Barney above. Galloway contributes volume 1 of the proposed five-volume series, here covering the A, B, and C versions from prologue to passus 4.

Godden, Malcolm. *The Making of "Piers Plowman."* New York: Longman, 1990.

Godden made the first attempt to integrate a study of the various versions of *Piers Plowman*, including the Z text. His first chapter offers an overview of the "poem and its poet" in biographical and historical context. Then in sequential study he divides the poem into its visions and traces the process of self-conscious revision, revealing frequently "Langland's own awareness that he is rewriting or reinterpreting the poem's past" (159). Inherent in Godden's understanding of the major B- and C-text expansions is what he calls Langland's "radical shifts of attitude" in approaching the problems of society, which were unresolved in the earlier versions, from social, monarchical, and then messianic perspectives.

Simpson, James. *Piers Plowman: An Introduction.* Exeter: University of Exeter Press, 1990; rev. ed., 2007.

This book inspired Anna Baldwin's *Guidebook*, and it too focuses on the B text. Simpson's *Introduction* seeks to inspire undergraduates to read *Piers* and understand its historical centrality as a document about reforming social and religious institutions, focused on issues of justice and mercy. In a vision-by-vision guide to each passus, Simpson traces the poem's movement from larger social reform to a "journey into the deepest aspects of the self" as Will negotiates the complex relations between the self and the social, political, and ecclesiastical institutions of medieval Christian England.

Steiner, Emily. *Reading "Piers Plowman."* New York: Cambridge University Press, 2013.

In an inventive approach to guiding readers, Steiner divides the poem into major themes, almost like musical movements: Value, Community, Learning, Practice, Belief, and Institutions. She studies how each set of episodes in the poem explores the larger historical, social, and religious issues associated with these concepts. In this way she enacts a running dialogue between the poem and the histories it reflects and chronicles. Though she keys her guide to B, as she explores Langland's meditations on these major themes, Steiner draws examples as well from the A and C texts.

Wittig, Joseph S. *William Langland Revisited.* New York: Twayne, 1997.

After providing an overview of the poet, his times, and his art, Wittig offers a step-by-step analysis of the poem, navigating its many plots twists and turns. Focusing almost exclusively on the B version, Wittig wants to avoid seeing the poem as an "artifact produced by a distant culture" (viii) and so approaches it "from the inside" and "in its own terms" (ix). Wittig argues that *Piers Plowman* emerges from an individual author's "particular concerns as well as his enormous poetic skill and imaginative energy," and he attends at once to the "poem's situation in its culture" (ix). Wittig's approach is opposite, yet complementary, to Steiner's method of thematic division.

Books and Essays on Langland's Life, Work, Language, and Contemporaries

Adams, Robert. "Langland and the *Devotio Moderna*: A Spiritual Kinship." In Burrow and Duggan, *Medieval Alliterative Poetry*, 23–40.

———. *Langland and the Rokele Family: The Gentry Background to "Piers Plowman."* Dublin: Four Courts Press, 2013.

———. "Langland as a Proto-Protestant: Was Thomas Fuller Right?" In Calabrese and Shepherd, *Yee? Baw for Bokes*, 245–66.

———. "The Nature of Need in *Piers Plowman* XX." *Traditio* 34 (1978): 273–301.

———. "The Rokeles: An Index for a 'Langland' Family History." In Cole and Galloway, *Cambridge Companion*, 85–96.

Aers, David. *Chaucer, Langland, and the Creative Imagination*. London: Routledge and Kegan Paul, 1980.

———. *Community, Gender, and Individual Identity: English Writing, 1360–1430*. New York: Routledge, 1988.

———. *Faith, Ethics, and Church: Writing in England, 1360–1409*. Cambridge: D. S. Brewer, 2000.

———. "Remembering the Samaritan, Remembering Semyuief." In *Salvation and Sin*, 83–131.

———. *Salvation and Sin: Augustine, Langland, and Fourteenth-Century Theology*. Notre Dame, Ind.: University of Notre Dame Press, 2009.

———. *Sanctifying Signs: Making Christian Tradition in Late Medieval England*. Notre Dame, Ind.: University of Notre Dame Press, 2004.

Aers, David, and Lynn Staley. *The Powers of the Holy: Religion, Politics, and Gender in Late Medieval English Culture*. University Park: Pennsylvania State University Press, 1996.

Andrew, Malcolm, and Ronald Waldron, eds. *The Poems of the Pearl Manuscript*. 1979. Exeter: University of Exeter Press, 1996.

Arnold, John H., and Katherine J. Lewis, eds. *A Companion to "The Book of Margery Kempe."* Woodbridge, Suffolk: D. S. Brewer, 2004.

Astell, Ann W. "'Full of Enigmas': John Ball's Letters and *Piers Plowman*." In *Political Allegory in Late Medieval England*, 44–72. Ithaca, N.Y.: Cornell University Press, 1999.

Augustine. *Concerning the City of God against the Pagans*. Translated by Henry Bettenson. London: Penguin, 1972.

Barney, Stephen. "Langland's Prosody." In *The Endless Knot: Essays on Old and Middle English in Honor of Marie Borroff*, edited by M. Teresa Tavormina and R. F. Yeager, 65–85. Cambridge: D. S. Brewer, 1996.

Barr, Helen, ed. *The "Piers Plowman" Tradition: A Critical Edition of "Pierce the Ploughman's Crede," "Richard the Redeless," "Mum and the Sothsegger," and "The Crowned King."* London: J. M. Dent, 1993.

Barr, Jessica. *Willing to Know God: Dreamers and Visionaries in the Later Middle Ages*. Columbus: Ohio State University Press, 2010.

Benson, C. David. "The Langland Myth." In *William Langland's "Piers Plowman": A Book of Essays*, edited by Kathleen M. Hewett-Smith, 83–99. New York: Routledge, 2001.

———. *Public "Piers Plowman": Modern Scholarship and Late Medieval English Culture*. University Park: Pennsylvania State University Press, 2004.

Benson, Larry D., ed. *The Riverside Chaucer*. 3rd ed. Boston: Houghton Mifflin, 1987.

Biblia Sacra Iuxta Vulgatam Versionem. Stuttgart: Deutsche Bibelgesellschaft, 1969.

Bloomfield, Morton W. *"Piers Plowman" as a Fourteenth-Century Apocalypse*. New Brunswick, N.J.: Rutgers University Press, 1962.

Boenig, Robert, and Andrew Taylor, eds. *The Canterbury Tales*. 2nd ed. Buffalo, N.Y.: Broadview, 2012.

Borroff, Marie, trans. *The Gawain Poet: Complete Works*. New York: Norton, 2011.

Bowers, John M. *Chaucer and Langland: The Antagonistic Tradition*. Notre Dame, Ind.: University of Notre Dame Press, 2007.

———. *An Introduction to the "Gawain" Poet*. Gainesville: University Press of Florida, 2012.

———. "*Piers Plowman*'s William Langland: Editing the Text, Writing the Author's Life." *Yearbook of Langland Studies* 9 (1995): 65–90.

Burrow, J. A. "The New Lives of Piers Plowman." In Burrow and Duggan, *Medieval Alliterative Poetry*, 41–52.

———. *Ricardian Poetry: Chaucer, Gower, Langland and the "Gawain" Poet*. London: Routledge and K. Paul, 1971.

Burrow, John A., and Hoyt N. Duggan, eds. *Medieval Alliterative Poetry: Essays in Honour of Thorlac Turville-Petre*. Dublin: Four Courts Press, 2010.

Burrow, J. A., and Thorlac Turville-Petre. *A Book of Middle English*. Oxford: Blackwell, 1992.

Calabrese, Michael. "Interior Visions: *Piers Plowman* and the Dream Vision Genre." In DeMaria, Chang, and Zacher, *Companion to British Literature*, 1:180–201.

———. "Langland's Last Words." In *Readings in Medieval Textuality: A Festschrift for A. C. Spearing*, edited by Cristina Maria Cervone and D. Vance Smith. Woodbridge, Suffolk: Boydell and Brewer, 2016.

———. "Prostitutes in the C-Text of *Piers Plowman*." *Journal of English and Germanic Philology* 105 (2006): 275–311.

Calabrese, Michael, and Stephen H. A. Shepherd, eds. *Yee? Baw for Bokes: Essays on Medieval Manuscripts and Poetics*. Los Angeles: Marymount Institute Press, 2013.

Cicero. *The Dream of Scipio*. In *On the Good Life*, translated by Michael Grant, 341–55. New York: Penguin, 1971.

Cole, Andrew. *Literature and Heresy in the Age of Chaucer*. Cambridge: Cambridge University Press, 2008.

Dahlberg, Charles, trans. *The Romance of the Rose*, by Guillaume de Lorris and Jean de Meun. Princeton, N.J.: Princeton University Press, 1971.

Davenport, W. A. *Chaucer and His English Contemporaries*. New York: St. Martin's Press, 1998.

Davlin, Mary Clemente. *A Journey into Love: Meditating with "Piers Plowman."* Los Angeles: Marymount Institute Press, 2008.

———. "Petrus, Id Est, Christus: Piers the Plowman as 'The Whole Christ.'" *Chaucer Review* 6.4 (1972): 280–92.

———. *The Place of God in "Piers Plowman" and Medieval Art*. Burlington, Vt.: Ashgate, 2001.

Dean, James M. *Medieval English Political Writings*. Kalamazoo, Mich.: Medieval Institute Publications, 1996.

———, ed. *Richard the Redeless; and, Mum and the Sothsegger*. Kalamazoo, Mich.: Medieval Institute Publications, 2000.

———, ed. *Six Ecclesiastical Satires*. Kalamazoo, Mich.: Medieval Institute Publications, 1991.

———. *The World Grown Old in Later Medieval Literature*. Cambridge, Mass.: Medieval Academy of America, 1997.

DeMaria, Robert, Jr., Heesok Chang, and Samantha Zacher, eds. *A Companion to British Literature*. 4 vols. Chichester, West Sussex: Wiley-Blackwell, 2014.

Donaldson, Talbot E. *Piers Plowman: The C-Text and Its Poet*. New Haven, Conn.: Yale University Press, 1949.

Duffy, Eamon. "How the Plowman Learned his Paternoster." In *The Stripping of the Altars: Traditional Religion in England, c. 1400–c. 1580*, 53–90. New Haven, Conn.: Yale University Press, 1992.

Duggan, Hoyt N. "The End of the Line." In Burrow and Duggan, *Medieval Alliterative Poetry*, 67–79.

———. "Notes on the Metre of *Piers Plowman*: Twenty Years On." In *Approaches to the Metres of Alliterative Verse*, edited by Judith Jefferson and Ad Putter, 159–86. Leeds Texts and Monographs, n.s. 17. Leeds: School of English, University of Leeds, 2009.

Durling, Robert, ed. *The Divine Comedy of Dante Alighieri*. Vol. 1, *Inferno*. Oxford: Oxford University Press, 1997.

Echard, Siân, ed. *A Companion to Gower*. Cambridge: D S. Brewer, 2004.

Farley, Mary Hardiman. "Her Own Creature: Religion, Feminist Criticism, and the Functional Eccentricity of Margery Kempe." *Exemplaria* 11 (1999): 1–22.

Fisher, John H., and Mark Allen, eds. *The Complete Canterbury Tales of Geoffrey Chaucer*. Boston: Thomson, 2006.

Fisher, Sheila. *The Selected Canterbury Tales: A New Verse Translation*. New York: Norton, 2011.

Froissart, Jean. *Chronicles*. Edited and translated by Geoffrey Brereton. Harmondsworth: Penguin, 1968.

Garbáty, Thomas J. *Medieval English Literature*. Lexington, Mass.: D. C. Heath, 1984.

Gower, John. *Confessio Amantis*. Edited by Russell A. Peck. Translations from Latin by Andrew Galloway. 2nd ed. Kalamazoo, Mich.: Medieval Institute Publications, 2006.

———. *The Major Latin Works of John Gower: The Voice of One Crying, and The Tripartite Chronicle*. Translated by Eric W. Stockton. Seattle: University of Washington Press, 1962.

———. *Poems on Contemporary Events*. Edited by David R. Carlson. Translated by A. G. Rigg. Toronto: Pontifical Institute of Mediaeval Studies, 2011.

Griffiths, Lavinia. *Personification in "Piers Plowman."* Cambridge: D. S. Brewer, 1985.

Hanna, Ralph. "The 'Absent' Pardon-Tearing of *Piers Plowman* C." *Review of English Studies* 66.275 (2015): 449–64.

———. "Emendations to a 1993 Vita de Ne'erdowel." *Yearbook of Langland Studies* 14 (2000): 185–98.

———. *Pursuing History: Middle English Manuscripts and Their Texts*. Stanford, Cal.: Stanford University Press, 1996.

———. *William Langland*. Aldershot, Hants.: Ashgate, 1993.

Hanna, Ralph, and Sarah Wood, eds. *Richard Morris's "Prick of Conscience": A*

Corrected and Amplified Reading Text. Early English Text Society o.s. 342. Oxford: Oxford University Press, 2013.

Hollander, Robert, and Jean Hollander, eds. *Dante: The Inferno*. New York: Random House, 2000.

The Holy Bible, Douay Rheims Version. Rockford, Ill.: TAN, 1971.

Horobin, Simon, and Jeremy Smith. *An Introduction to Middle English*. Oxford: Oxford University Press, 2002.

Howard, Donald R. *Chaucer: His Life, His Works, His World*. New York: E. P. Dutton, 1987.

Hudson, Anne. *The Premature Reformation: Wycliffite Texts and Lollard History*. Oxford: Oxford University Press, 1988.

———. *Selections from English Wycliffite Writings*. Cambridge: Cambridge University Press, 1978.

Hume, David. "Of the Standard of Taste." In *Four Dissertations*, 201–40. London: A. Millar, 1757.

Julian, of Norwich. *The Writings of Julian of Norwich*. Edited by Nicholas Watson and Jacqueline Jenkins. Turnhout: Brepols, 2006.

Justice, Steven. *Writing and Rebellion: England in 1381*. Berkeley: University of California Press, 1994.

Justice, Steven, and Kathryn Kerby-Fulton, eds. *Written Work: Langland, Labor, and Authorship*. Philadelphia: University of Pennsylvania Press, 1997.

Kane, George. *Chaucer and Langland: Historical and Textual Approaches*. London: Athlone Press; Berkeley: University of California Press, 1989.

———. *Piers Plowman: The Evidence for Authorship*. London: Athlone Press, 1965.

———. "Langland, William." *Oxford Dictionary of National Biography*, 32:488–93. Oxford: Oxford University Press, 2004.

Karnes, Michelle. *Imagination, Meditation, and Cognition in the Middle Ages*. Chicago: University of Chicago Press, 2011.

Kay, Sarah. *The Romance of the Rose*. London: Grant & Cutler, 1995.

Kelen, Sarah A. *Langland's Early Modern Identities*. New York: Palgrave Macmillan, 2007.

Kerby-Fulton, Kathryn. *Books Under Suspicion: Censorship and Tolerance of Revelatory Writing in Late Medieval England*. Notre Dame, Ind.: University of Notre Dame Press, 2006.

———. "Piers Plowman." In *The Cambridge History of Medieval English Literature*, edited by David Wallace, 518–38. Cambridge: Cambridge University Press, 1999.

Knowles, Jim. "Langland's Empty Verbs: Service, Kenosis, and Adventurous Christology in *Piers Plowman*." *Yearbook of Langland Studies* 28 (2014): 191–224.

Kökeritz, Helge. *A Guide to Chaucer's Pronunciation*. Toronto: University of Toronto Press, 1978.

Kolve, V. A., and Glending Olson, eds. *The Canterbury Tales: Fifteen Tales and the General Prologue*. 2nd ed. New York: Norton, 2005.

Kristensson, Gillis, ed. *Instructions for Parish Priests*, by John Mirk. Lund, Sweden: CWK Gleerup, 1974.

Lawton, David A. "Alliterative Style." In Alford, *A Companion to "Piers Plowman,"* 223–49.

———. *Blasphemy*. Philadelphia: University of Pennsylvania Press, 1993.

———. "Lollardy and the *Piers Plowman* Tradition." *Modern Language Review* 76 (1981): 780–93.

Little, Katherine C. *Confession and Resistance: Defining the Self in Late Medieval England*. Notre Dame, Ind.: University of Notre Dame Press, 2006.

Mandelbaum, Allen, trans. *Paradiso*, by Dante Alighieri. Berkeley: University of California Press, 1984.

Mann, Jill. "The Nature of Need Revisited." *Yearbook of Langland Studies* 18 (2004): 3–29.

———. "The Power of the Alphabet: A Reassessment of the Relation between the A and B Versions of *Piers Plowman*." *Yearbook of Langland Studies* 8 (1994): 21–49.

Mehl, Dieter. "Old Age in Middle English Literature: Chaucer, Gower, Langland and the Gawain-Poet." In *Old Age and Ageing in British and American Culture and Literature*, edited by Christa Jansohn, 29–38. Münster, Germany: LIT, 2004.

Middleton, Anne. "Acts of Vagrancy: The C Version Autobiography and the Statute of 1388." In Justice and Kerby-Fulton, *Written Work*, 208–317.

———. "The Idea of Public Poetry in the Reign of Richard II." *Speculum* 53.1 (1978): 94–114.

———. "Two Infinites: Grammatical Metaphor in *Piers Plowman*." *ELH* 39 (1972): 169–88.

Mooney, Linne R. "Chaucer's Scribe." *Speculum* 81.1 (2006): 97–138.

Mooney, Linne R., and Estelle Stubbs. *Scribes and the City: London Guildhall Clerks and the Dissemination of Middle English Literature, 1375–1425*. Woodbridge, Suffolk: York Medieval Press, 2013.

Moore, Samuel. *Historical Outlines of English Sounds and Inflections*. Revised by Albert H. Marckwardt. Ann Arbor, Mich.: George Wahr, 1951.

Mossé, Fernand. *A Handbook of Middle English*. Translated by James A. Walker. Baltimore: Johns Hopkins University Press, 1952.

Narin van Court, Elisa. "The Hermeneutics of Suppression: The Revision of the Jews from the B to the C text of *Piers Plowman*." *Yearbook of Langland Studies* 10 (1996): 43–87.

Neal, Derek G. *The Masculine Self in Late Medieval England*. Chicago: University of Chicago Press, 2008.

Pearsall, Derek. "Langland and Lollardy: From B to C." *Yearbook of Langland Studies* 17 (2003): 7–23.

———. "The Poetic Character of the C-Text of *Piers Plowman*." In Burrow and Duggan, *Medieval Alliterative Poetry*, 153–65.

Prendergast, Thomas. "John But and the Problem of Langlandian Authority." In Calabrese and Shepherd, *Yee? Baw For Bokes*, 67–85.

Pugh, Tison. *An Introduction to Geoffrey Chaucer*. Gainesville: University Press of Florida, 2013.

Rice, Nicole R. *Lay Piety and Religious Discipline in Middle English Literature*. Cambridge: Cambridge University Press, 2008.

Salter, Elizabeth. "*Piers Plowman*": *An Introduction*. Oxford: Basil Blackwell, 1962.

Schmidt, A.V.C. *Earthly Honest Things: Collected Essays on "Piers Plowman."* Newcastle: Cambridge Scholars, 2012.

———. "The Poem in Time." In *Piers Plowman: A Parallel-Text Edition*, 2:269–304.

Shelley, Percy Bysshe. "A Defense of Poetry." In *Essays, Letters from Abroad, Translations and Fragments*, 25–62. London: Edward Moxon, 1840.

Smith, Vance D. *The Book of the Incipit: Beginnings in the Fourteenth Century*. Minneapolis: University of Minnesota Press, 2001.

Somerset, Fiona. *Feeling Like Saints: Lollard Writings after Wyclif*. Ithaca, N.Y.: Cornell University Press, 2014.

Spearing, A. C. "The Art of Preaching and *Piers Plowman*." In *Criticism and Medieval Poetry*, 2nd ed., 107–34. New York: Barnes & Noble, 1972.

———. *Medieval Dream-Poetry*. Cambridge: Cambridge University Press, 1976.

Stahl, William Harris, ed. and trans. *Commentary on the Dream of Scipio*, by Macrobius. New York: Columbia University Press, 1990.

Staley, Lynn, ed. and trans. *The Book of Margery Kempe*. New York: Norton, 2001.

Stokes, Myra. *Justice and Mercy in "Piers Plowman": A Reading of the B-Text Visio*. London: Croon Helm, 1984.

Szittya, Penn R. *The Antifraternal Tradition in Medieval Literature*. Princeton, N.J.: Princeton University Press, 1986.

Tavormina, M. Teresa. *Kindly Similitude: Marriage and Family in "Piers Plowman."* Cambridge: D. S. Brewer, 1995.

Tolkien, J.R.R., ed. *Sir Gawain and the Green Knight, Pearl, and Sir Orfeo*. London: Allen & Unwin, 1975.

Trigg, Stephanie. "The Traffic in Medieval Women: Alice Perrers, Feminist Criticism, and *Piers Plowman*." *Yearbook of Langland Studies* 12 (1998): 5–29.

Vaughan, Míċeál F., ed. *Suche Werkis to Werche: Essays on "Piers Plowman" in Honor of David C. Fowler*. East Lansing, Mich.: Colleagues Press, 1993.

Warner, Lawrence. *The Lost History of "Piers Plowman": The Earliest Transmission of Langland's Work*. Philadelphia: University of Pennsylvania Press, 2011.

Wittig, Joseph S. *"Piers Plowman": Concordance*. London: Athlone Press, 2001.

Wood, Sarah. *Conscience and the Composition of "Piers Plowman."* Oxford: Oxford University Press, 2012.

Zeeman, Nicolette. *"Piers Plowman" and the Medieval Discourse of Desire*. Cambridge: Cambridge University Press, 2006.

Electronic Resources

The Chaucer Studio. creativeworks.byu.edu/chaucer.
A not-for-profit organization that produces recordings of medieval poetry, prose, and music for classroom use.

Gower Translation Project. gowertranslation.pbworks.com.
A Wiki translation project for Gower's Latin works.

Douay-Rheims Bible. Bible Hub: Online Bible Study Suite. 2014. biblehub.com/drb.
An English rendering dating to 1584–1610 of the Latin Vulgate, the book that Langland and his audience used.

Douay-Rheims Bible + Challoner Notes. 2001–2014. drbo.org.
An eighteenth-century reworking of the original version.

Piers Plowman Electronic Archive. piers.iath.virginia.edu.
An ongoing project, founded by Hoyt Duggan of the University of Virginia, that publishes electronic editions and provides textual study of the Medieval manuscripts of *Piers Plowman*.

Yearbook of Langland Studies. piersplowman.org/yearbook/editor.htm.
An annual journal dedicated to publishing essays, book reviews, and a bibliography in *Piers Plowman* studies. The leading journal in the field.

INDEX

To clarify which note is signaled when two notes of the same number appear in the endnotes, the author specifies the number of the narrative reading guide (nrg) in which the note appears.

Abraham. *See* Faith
Abstinence (character), 77, 95, 113
Active Life (Activa Vita). *See* Haukin the Active Man
Adams, Robert, 2–3, 6–9, 321nn5–6, 333n1
Aeneid (Virgil), 272. *See also* Virgil
Aers, David, 332n1nrg21
Agite penitenciam (do penance; a sour loaf of bread), 178
Alchemy, 135
Alice's Adventures in Wonderland, xii, 176–77
Ambrose (church Father served as food), 178
Amend-30w, 95–96
Amends (mother of Mede), 49
Anasthasian Creed, 110
Anima: as complex personification of the soul, 196–221 *passim*; as the human soul locked in the castle of Caro, 123–24, 279
Animal Farm (George Orwell), 29
Anthony, St. (friar fed by a bird), 207
Antichrist, 20, 22, 47, 254, 260–69
Aristotle, 134, 137, 170, 174
Ark, Noah's, 141
Astronomy, 135
Augustine of Hippo, 18, 133, 137–38, 143–44, 170, 172, 326n2nrg12; served as food, 178
Avarice: of the clergy, 42, 54, 204, 266; depicted as an Earl, 122; opposed by Conscience, 264

Bale, John (Tudor historian), 1
Ball, John (leader of the Peasants' Revolt), 10, 322n8

"Beati quorum" (psalm verse served as food), 178, 285
Bede, The Venerable: *History of the English Church and People*, 136
Begging (and beggars), 82–84, 91, 108, 130, 136, 160–61, 191–93, 199, 204–5, 209, 333n2nrg24; excluded from the Pardon, 110, 115–16; false, 28, 103, 325n4; by Friars, 266–67
Benson, C. David, 321n7
Beþ-buxum-of-speche (brook along road to Truth), 67
Betty the Brewer, 76
Bhagavad Gita, 258
Bible, 114, 122, 140, 156, 181, 204–5, 210. *See also* Holy Writ
—Biblical characters in *Piers Plowman*: Abraham, 160, 220–30 (as Faith), 240; Adam (and Eve), 11, 21, 37–38, 95–96, 102, 105, 112, 126, 133, 165, 174, 200, 210, 226, 241, 244; Agag (and the Amalec), 56; Cain, 37–38, 125–26, 233; Daniel, 114; David, King, 40, 57, 137, 148, 237, 245; Dismas, 77; Dives, 108, 191–92, 233; Elijah, 190; Jeremiah, 131–32; Job, 125, 131–32, 139, 147, 160, 284; Joseph, 114; Judas, 37–38, 128, 224; Lazarus, 108, 218, 227, 242; Lot, 36, 128; Magi, 172, 253; Mary Magdalene, 137, 143; Nebuchadnezzar, 114, 278; Nicodemus, 137; Noah, 128, 263; Pharaoh, 114; Samaritan, Parable of the Good, 121, 220, 225, 228–37; Samson, 170; Samuel, 56–57; Saul, 56–58; Seth, 126;

350 • Index

Biblical characters—*continued*
  Sodomites, 72, 183, 189, 278; Solomon, 62–63, 137, 143, 170, 190; Tobit, 208–9; Virgin Mary, 18, 26, 41, 76, 90, 92, 96; Whore of Babylon, 46, 50
  —Books of the Bible: Genesis, 11, 36, 39, 103, 105, 123, 125–27, 133, 210, 226, 233, 238–39, 244; Job, 125, 132, 139; Jonah, 279; Psalms, 11, 56, 65, 83, 92, 100, 113, 125, 139, 148, 156, 173, 178–79, 203–5, 234, 240, 245, 267, 285; Revelation, 22, 26, 46, 262
Black Death (Plague), 10, 98, 126, 130, 150, 325n2
Bloomfield, Morton, 26
Boethius. See *Consolation of Philosophy*
Book (character), 239, 242
Bowers, John, 278, 333n2nrg23
Brewers (and beer), 76–77, 104, 116, 207, 214, 257–58
Burns, Robbie, 124
Burrow, John, 330n3
But, John (Johan), 18–19, 145–52
Buxomness, 67–68, 94, 99, 184, 221

California State University, Los Angeles, xviii
Canterbury Tales. *See also* Chaucer, Geoffrey
  —*General Prologue*: Parson's portrait, 28; Monk's portrait, 100
  —Individual tales: *Merchant's Tale*, 126; *Pardoner's Tale*, 73, 111, 273; *Parson's Prologue and Tale*, 278; *Reeve's Tale*, 89, 185; *Wife of Bath's Prologue and Tale*, 45, 73, 134, 234, 273
Cardinals, 257
Cardinal Virtues, 255, 257–61, 264, 267
Caritas, 25, 38, 169
Carlson, John, 277
Castle of Perseverance (medieval drama), 240
Cato the Elder (Roman ethicist), 64, 114
Chaplin, Charlie, 194
Charity (as concept and variously personified), 19, 25, 27, 41–42, 49, 54, 74, 77, 86, 91, 95, 102–18 *passim*, 129, 139, 141, 157, 161, 170, 174, 179–80, 187, 197–219 *passim*, 220–27 *passim*, 256, 272; as Samaritan, 228–35. *See also* Tree of Charity

Chastity: as character, 95; as topic, 42, 222
Chaucer, Geoffrey: "Chaucer's Wordes unto Adam, His Owne Scriveyn," 270; compared to Langland, 7–8, 19, 24, 110, 241; dream vision poetry, author of, 271–72; *House of Fame*, 272; *Parliament of Fowles*, 272; *Troilus and Criseyde*, 270, 276–77. *See also Canterbury Tales*
Chaucer Studio, 309, 320n7
Chavez, Cesar, xvi
Christ. *See* Jesus Christ
Chrysostomos, John, 200
Cicero, *The Dream of Scipio*, 34–35, 271–72
Civil (character), 47, 50
Clergy: as character, 79–80, 131–49 *passim*, 165, 176–82, 197, 266; disendowment of, 80, 216; exploitative practices of, 10–11, 31, 47, 54, 71, 73, 83, 113, 198–201, 208–22 *passim*, 247, 258; ideal behavior of, 42, 80–81, 121–23; as synonym for academic learning, 170–74
Comfort (character), 263
Concupiscencia Carnis, 141–42
Confession: of the Seven Deadly Sins, 70–92, 98–99, 256–57; personified as a cart horse, 256; as topic, 20–21, 58, 173, 178, 183–85, 189, 193–94, 265–69
Confessions. *See* Augustine of Hippo
Conscience: as character, 21–22, 31, 44–73 *passim*, 78, 80, 84, 113, 149, 176–90 *passim*, 199, 210, 216, 250–69 *passim*; as topic, 64, 72–73, 78, 161, 180–81, 252, 268–69, 275, 283
Consolation of Philosophy (Boethius), 34, 271–72
Contemplation (character), 97
Contrition: as character, 210, 256, 265, 268–69; as topic, 77, 173, 189, 194, 197, 268, 328n7
Cotidian (fever), 150
Covetousness, 159, 205; as character, 74–76, 89, 185, 194–95, 264; as a dove, 217
Covetousness of the Eyes, 141–42, 144, 155
Crucifixion (Gospel episode), 236, 238, 250, 285
Crusades, 216, 218, 331n6
Cultural Revolution, Chinese, 99

Dame Study (character), 130–43
Dante: *Divine Comedy* (*Commedia*), compared to *Piers Plowman*, xiii, 20, 24, 27, 34, 46, 51, 62, 67, 73, 135, 174, 191, 213, 237, 242–43; and Langland, continental influence on, xii, 274
Davlin, Mary Clemente, 330n3
Dead Body (character), 239
Death (character), 18, 146, 150–51, 263–64; Christ's battle with, 236–40, 245, 250–58 *passim*, 279
Declaration of Independence, 35
"Defence of Poetry" (Shelley), 119, 252
Desert Fathers (exemplars of God's care), 206, 211–12
Devils (including the Devil in various guises), 33, 37–38, 65, 99, 124, 126, 193, 220–23, 227, 231, 236–56 *passim*, 263
Dharma Bums, 270
Dia perseuerans (drink served by Scripture), 178
Dickens, Charles, 32
Dinner Party scene, 176–87
Dominick, St., 266. *See also* Friars
"Donation of Constantine" (false endowment to Pope Sylvester), 216
Dostoyevsky, Fyodor, 116, 198
Dowel, 25, 114–15, 118–40 *passim*, 143, 146–50, 155, 165, 169, 179–82, 198, 200, 204, 224, 253–54; with Dobet and Dobest as virtuous triad, 19, 91, 194, 228, 253
Dreams, medieval theories of interpreting, 115, 262, 272
Dream vision genre, 3, 32, 114, 271–73, 276

Economou, George, 246
Edmund and Edward (sainted kings), 204
Edward III, 3, 46, 53, 55, 324n2nrg4; mistress of, 45
Egredius, St. (St. Giles; hermit saint fed with deer's milk), 206–7
Elde (Old Age): as character, 142, 155, 177, 222, 226; allied with Death, 263–64; assaults Will, 265
Elizabethan poets, 270
Envy: as character, 74–75, 86, 90, 184, 267, 284; as topic, 98, 185, 256
Everyman (medieval drama), 146

Faith (manifested as Abraham), 220–21, 225, 228–40 *passim*, 285
False (character), 44–45, 48–51, 55
False-Witness (character), 50
Favel (Flattery; character), 44, 50
Felix culpa, 92
Feuere-on-þe-ferþe-day (character), 150
Fever (character), 18–19, 145–46, 150–52
Field of folk, 17–19, 23, 29–32, 40, 103, 221, 254
Flatterer: personified, 210–11; manifested as Friar, 268
Flood (biblical story), 72, 126, 128, 278
Fortune (character), 5, 19, 142–43, 153–55, 176, 264, 285
Four Daughters of God, Debate of the, 43, 234, 240–42, 255
Francis, St., 204, 266. *See also* Friars
Friars, 28, 51, 54–55, 58, 86, 105, 118, 120–22, 136, 139, 155, 172–73, 177–78, 199–200, 207–8, 247, 262, 266–69. *See also* Flatterer
Froissart, Jean (*Chronicles*), 11

Galloway, Andrew, 47, 323n2nrg3
Gawain poet: xii–xiii, 270, 278–79; *Cleanness*, 278–79; *Patience*, 279; *Pearl*, 174, 205, 271, 275, 278; *Sir Gawain and the Green Knight*, 279; *St. Erkenwald*, 335n9
Geometry, 135
Gile/Guile (character), 50, 211
Giles. *See* Egredius, St.
Glinda the Good Witch, 46
Glutton (and Gluttony), 9, 74, 76–77, 89–90, 178, 185–86
Goblin, 245
God, xiv, 13, 25, 33; depicted as writer, 127–28, 170; His grace displayed in grammar, 61–63; manifested in nature, 72, 123; manifested in the person of Piers Plowman, 20, 250; manifested as Truth, 34–43, 95; as provider of law and justice, 55–57, 84, 94, 100, 157–58, 175, 205, 232–35; as provider of sustenance, 30, 129, 189–91, 206–8, 227, 265; as target of pseudointellectual babble, 132–33. *See also under* Holy Trinity; Jesus Christ; Truth
Godden, Malcolm, xiv, 20

352 • Index

Gospels: served as food, 178; as topic, 23, 84, 99, 161, 229, 238, 241
Gower, John, 270, 276–77; *Confessio Amantis*, xii, 277; *Cronica triperitta*, 277; *Visio Anglie*, 276; *Vox Clamantis*, 277
Grace (character), 95–96, 254–55, 262, 269
Gregory the Great: as exemplary pope, 79–80, 140; *The Pastoral Care*, 136; Trajan and, 156
Guillaume de Lorris. See *Roman de la Rose*

Half-acre episode. See under Piers Plowman (character)
Hanna, Ralph, 2, 321n7
Harrowing of Hell, 231, 246, 252, 255, 274
Haukin the Active Man, 20, 85–91, 176, 183–90, 195–97, 203
Henry of Lancaster, 277
Henry VIII, 216
Hippocrates, 170
Holy Church: as character, xii, 34–55 *passim*, 148, 235, 261, 272, 277–78; as topic, 61, 73, 80, 85, 124, 139, 141, 209–17 *passim*, 258. See also Unity
Holynesse (character), 155
Holy Spirit (*Spiritus Sanctus*), 139, 217, 219, 223, 232–33; gifts of, 258–61
Holy Trinity, 61–62, 132, 200, 222–35 *passim*
Holy Writ, 132; as roofing material, 255
Hope: personified, 92; as Moses (Spes), 220–35 *passim*
Hume, David, 21
Humility: as character, 95; of God, 62; as human virtue, 57, 74, 94, 99, 117, 122, 124–27, 130, 156, 172, 194, 237, 261, 264
Hundred Years War, 55
Hunger (character), 27, 98–108, 113, 150, 152, 183, 194, 264, 266

Il libro de Buen Amor, xii
Imaginatif (character), 167–77, 197
Incarnation, the, 62, 223–24, 230, 237, 255, 258
Interfaith dialogue, xviii, 39, 182, 214–15, 219, 256
Isidore of Seville (*Etymologies*), 200
"I sing of a maiden" (Middle English lyric), 41

Jean de Meun. See *Roman de la Rose*
Jerusalem, 230, 236–37, 278
Jesus Christ, xvii, 30, 36–37, 42, 56, 75, 96, 113, 136–37, 157, 160–61, 170, 195, 205, 229–30; jousting in Piers's arms (Passion scene and Harrowing of Hell), 92, 218–19, 224, 236–49, 251–55; as knight, king, and conqueror, 250, 253, 279; Marjorie Kempe and, 281; taught by Piers Plowman, 224
Jews, 39, 128–29, 137, 156, 174, 182, 206, 211–24 *passim*, 238–40; expulsion from England, 69, 129. See also Interfaith dialogue
John, St., 173, 262
John of Gaunt, 29, 323n5nrg1
Joyce, James, 147
Julian of Norwich, 279, 281; *A Revelation of Love* and *A Vision Showed to a Devout Woman*, 279
Justice, Steven, 10–11

Kane, George, 2–6, 8
Karnes, Michelle, 328n1
Kempe, Margery (*The Book of Margery Kempe*), 280–81
Kerouac, Jack, 6
Kind Wit (kynde wit), 30, 32, 37, 58, 149, 170–71, 216
King (character), 44, 50–57, 60, 64–73, 80, 149
Kingship (topic), 53, 122, 136, 140, 335n8
Knights Templar, 216
Knowles, Jim, 330n3
Kynde (nature; personified and as concept), 51, 58, 89, 123, 128, 142, 153, 163, 174, 186, 263–66, 269
Kynde knowing, 38, 40, 121
Kytte (wife of Will), 81, 248

Lady Mede, 21, 44–70 *passim*, 190, 264
Langland, William: compared to contemporary medieval authors, 270–81; education and family history, 3–9; evidence for authorship of *Piers Plowman*, 1–2; represented in *Piers Plowman* (see under Will)
Largess (character), 95
Lawrence, St., 49–50, 209
Lawton, David, 132, 280
Leautee, 46

Lechery (character), 74–75, 87–89, 185, 195, 264
Lennon, John, 7, 265
Liar (character), 51
Libera Voluntas Dei (free will of God), 223
Liberum Arbitrium, 196–225
Lollardy (and Lollards), 47, 105, 173, 216, 280
London Guildhall, 270
"Lord þat lyuede aftur lust," 263
Lucifer, 242–46, 248, 252; ambition and rebellion of, 13, 29, 31, 34, 38, 40, 78, 170, 200, 210
Lyf (also Life; variously personified), 149–50, 238, 264–65, 285

Macaronic verse: defined, 25; Langland's use of, 177, 218, 238
Macrobius (*Commentary on the Dream of Scipio*), 262, 272
Magus, Simon, 47. See also Simony
Mandeville, John, 214
Mann, Jill, 333n2nrg23
Marriage, xviii, 48–50, 76, 121, 125–34 *passim*, 195, 226
Marxism, 37, 74
Mary Magdalene, 137, 143, 284
McCartney, Sir Paul, 32
Mercede (alternate manifestation of Mede), 60, 62
Mercy: as character, 156; as daughter of God, 43, 240–41; as root of Tree of Charity, 221
Middle Earth, 141–42, 162–63
Milton, John, 242–43, 245, 248
Minstrelsy, 91, 117, 132, 186–87, 326n3nrg10, 329n4, 330n8. See also Haukin the Active Man
Miserere mei, Deus (as food served at the Dinner Party), 178
Mond the Milner, 48
Mooney, Linne, 270
Moses, 106, 136, 171, 190, 218. See also Hope
Muhammad, 214–15, 217
Muslims, xviii, 39, 136, 174, 182, 206, 211, 214–15, 218–19. See also Interfaith dialogue

Nature. See Kynde
Need (character), 166, 197, 260–62, 266, 333n1nrg24

Office of the Dead, 324n6
Omnia-probate, 62–63, 149, 152
Ophni and Phinees (sons of Heli as exempla of misbehaving clergy), 31, 140

Pacientes vincunt, 180, 189
Palm Sunday, 236–37
Parables, 108, 188, 205, 230, 233–34, 237, 278, 329n8. See also Samaritan
Pardon, 233, 267, 253; Truth's grant of a pardon to Piers, 18, 109–19, 169
Paternoster, 76, 138, 143, 205; served as food for pilgrimage, 190
Patience (character), 95, 176–83, 188–97, 279
Paul, St., 62, 122, 133, 136–37, 139, 148–49, 169–70, 173, 180, 199–202, 268, 284
Peace (male figure victimized by Wrong), 64–70. See also Four Daughters of God, Debate of the; Seven Sister Virtues
Pearsall, Derek, 12, 31, 177, 247, 260, 266
Peasants' Revolt of 1381, 10–13, 78, 106, 276, 321n7
Penance, 47, 54, 75, 77, 85–86, 95, 113, 136, 138, 173, 178–79, 189, 194, 256–57, 267. See also Agite penitenciam
Pentecost, 250, 254
Pernelle Proud-Heart (as a name for Pride) 74, 85–86
Perrers, Alice (mistress of Edward III), 45
Pharisees, 106, 136, 170
Piers Plowman (character): family of, 101; figure for Christ, 20, 99, 203, 223, 236–38, 251–52; guiding folk on pilgrimage to Truth, 94–108; plowing the half-acre, 98–108, 150; receiving and rejecting the Pardon, 18, 109–11, 116, 119; as Reeve of Unity, 254–55; tending the Tree of Charity, 33, 86, 169, 220–23
Piers Plowman: editions of, xx, 319–20n7; manuscripts of, 17; pronunciation and performance of, xix, 27, 309–18; rubrics of: *Visio* and *Vita*, xi, 19, 121; taught in the multicultural classroom, xvi–xviii, 9, 26, 309–10
Piers Plowman Tradition, 280
Pilate, 148
Pinkhurst, Adam, 270

Plato, 134, 174, 267
Polo, Marco: *Travels*, 214
Post mortem (sour sauce served at the Dinner Party), 178
Poverty: as character, 194–96; of Christ, 172; clerical, 12, 37, 161, 266; in medieval England, 115, 118; "patient poverty," 134, 153–63, 188
Pricke of Conscience, 26, 274–75
Pride (Pruyde; character), 74, 85–86, 94–95, 190, 200; leads siege against the Church, Unity, 20, 47, 255–57, 260–68 *passim*, 285
Pride of Perfect Living, 141–43
Princeps huius mundi (the Devil), 123–24
Prometheus, 244
Prostitutes (and Prostitution), 55, 70, 75–76, 87, 99, 105, 195, 256. *See also* Lady Mede
Purgatory, 99, 160, 192, 274; on earth, 118–19

Quod-bonum-est-tenete, 63, 149

Randolf the Reeve, 48
Reason (character), 9, 21, 37, 53, 57, 71, 78–80, 91, 142, 163–66, 172, 176–77, 180, 182, 197, 199; discourse on social hierarchies, 13; interrogates Will, 81–85; role in the trial of Lady Mede, 64–70; in the *Romance of the Rose*, 34
Recklessness (character), 5, 12, 142–44, 153–66, 172, 185, 221
Redde quod debes, 254, 257, 267
Reformation, English, xvi, 11, 216, 280
Repentance (character), 71, 73–75, 86, 89, 92
Revel (character), 265
"Ricardian poets," 270, 277
Richard II, 10, 29, 270, 277
Righteousness (character), 43, 241
Robertson, Elizabeth, 320n7, 328n5
Robert þe robbour, 77
Robin Hood, 90
Rokele, Stacy, 1, 9
Rokele, William, 2–5
Roman de la Rose (*Romance of the Rose*), xii, 19, 34, 271, 273–74
—Characters from: *Faux Semblant*, 273; Reason (*Raison*), 34; *La Vieille*, 273
Romantic poets, 252, 270

Salter, Elizabeth, 8
Samaritan, Parable of the Good. *See under* Bible, biblical characters in *Piers Plowman*; Charity
Sapiencia Dei Patris, 223
Schmidt, A.V.C., xiv, 2, 8, 13, 26, 145, 151, 154, 204, 208, 225, 261
Scripture (character), 18–19; as Clergy's wife, 134–43; 148–49, 153, 156, 167, 176; as male figure serving at the Dinner Party, 178, 181
Seneca, 267
Seven Deadly Sins, 58, 277; confessions of, 71, 73–79
Seven Sister Virtues, 95
Shakespeare, William: characters and works of, 8, 158, 222, 247, 309
Shepherd, Stephen, 320n7, 328n5
Simony (character and practice), 47, 50, 52, 54, 284
Sire Inwit and his five sons (as characters and concepts), 123–24, 128–29
Sire Penetrans-domos, 268
Sir Lyf-to-lyue-in-lecherye, 267
Sisour (character), 47
Sloth (character) 74, 77, 90–91, 185; as child of Life and Fortune, 264, 266, 268
Social justice, xvi–xvii, 8, 11, 29, 74, 257, 277, 279
Socrates, 134
Sothnesse, 51
Spearing, A. C., 330n2nrg18, 332n4nrg22
Speke-euele-bihynde, 256
Spes. *See* Moses
Spille-Loue, 256
Statutes of Laborers, 3, 10, 81, 98, 276
Study. *See* Dame Study
Suffre-boþe-wele-and-wo (highway to Clergy), 134
Suffre-til-I-se-my-tyime (Reason's horse), 64
Surquidours (character), 255–56
Sylvester, Pope, 216

Ten Commandments, 94, 137, 170, 200, 229
Tercian (fever), 150
Theology: as bewildering subject, 134–35; as character, 44, 49–50, 53, 66, 147–48
Thought (character), 120–23, 127, 141, 143, 167

Three Theological Virtues, 220. *See also under* Abraham; Moses; Samaritan
Tomme Two-tonge, 264
Trajan (Roman Emperor exemplifying pagan virtue), 153–57, 162–63, 173, 175, 329n8
Treaty of Brétigny, 324n2nrg4
Tree of Charity, 86, 169, 220, 222, 225
Truth: as giver of the Pardon, 109–10; as God (including the pilgrimage to Truth), 18, 34–35, 38–42, 44, 67, 73, 77, 93–104 *passim*, 204, 215, 262; as ideal human virtue, 49, 157, 175, 212–14, 221, 235, 259, 279; as one of Four Daughters of God, 43, 240–44; as proposed husband of Mede, 49

Unity, 22, 47, 151, 255–68 *passim*. *See also* Holy Church
Universalism. *See* Interfaith dialogue

Vaughan, Míçeál, 145, 323n1nrg2, 325n2
Virgil, 170; character in Dante's *Commedia*, xiii, 34, 46, 243
Virginity, 222, 226. *See also* Tree of Charity

"The Wanderer" (Old English elegy), 36
Wanhope (character): sibling of Recklessness, 142; wife of Sloth, 264
Wareyn Wisman (also Waryn Wisdom), 64–65, 67

Warner, Lawrence, 333n2nrg23
Wars of Alexander, 243
Waster (character and concept), 30, 72, 82–83, 100–104
Will (character): *apologia*, 9, 70, 79, 81–85, 105, 168–69; as an everyman, 19, 24, 28, 141, 277; family of, 81, 248–49, 251, 258; paradigm of youthful folly, xviii, 19, 155, 159–60, 168; representing William Langland, xi, 21, 147, 201–2, 248; victim of old age, 265–66
Wit (character), 66, 120, 123–34, 141, 143, 167
Witty (character), 64–65
The Wizard of Oz, 46
Wood, Sarah, xiv
Wordsworth, William, 172
Wrath (character), 71, 75, 86–87, 89
Wrong (character): as manifestation of the Devil, 37–38, 44, 48, 70; as Mede's father, 44; as violator of Peace, 64–70, 241
Wyclif, John, 11, 13, 47, 105, 280
Wycliffite writings (and Wycliffism), 11–13, 21, 276, 280, 331n3
Wynchestre fayre, 161

Yearbook of Langland Studies, 320n7

Z text of *Piers Plowman*, 319nn1,5

Michael Calabrese lives in Los Angeles, where he is professor of English at California State University, LA. His published works include *Yee? Baw for Bokes: Essays on Medieval Manuscripts and Poetics in Honor of Hoyt N. Duggan* and *Chaucer's Ovidian Arts of Love*.

New Perspectives on Medieval Literature: Authors and Traditions

EDITED BY R. BARTON PALMER AND TISON PUGH

An Introduction to Christine de Pizan, by Nadia Margolis (2011; first paperback edition, 2012)

An Introduction to the "Gawain" Poet, by John M. Bowers (2012; first paperback edition, 2013)

An Introduction to British Arthurian Narrative, by Susan Aronstein (2012; first paperback edition, 2014)

An Introduction to Geoffrey Chaucer, by Tison Pugh (2013; first paperback edition, 2014)

An Introduction to the Chansons de Geste, by Catherine M. Jones (2014)

An Introduction to Piers Plowman, by Michael Calabrese (2016; first paperback edition, 2017)

www.ingramcontent.com/pod-product-compliance
Lightning Source LLC
Chambersburg PA
CBHW020227150126
38294CB00018B/214